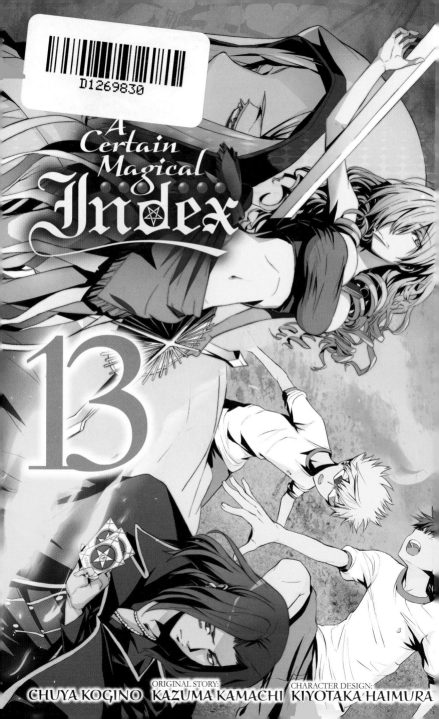

A
Certain
Magical
Index

13

ORIGINAL STORY:
CHUYA KOGINO   KAZUMA KAMACHI

CHARACTER DESIGN:
KIYOTAKA HAIMURA

A CERTAIN MAGICAL INDEX ⑬ TABLE OF CONTENTS

Index Librorum Prohibitorum

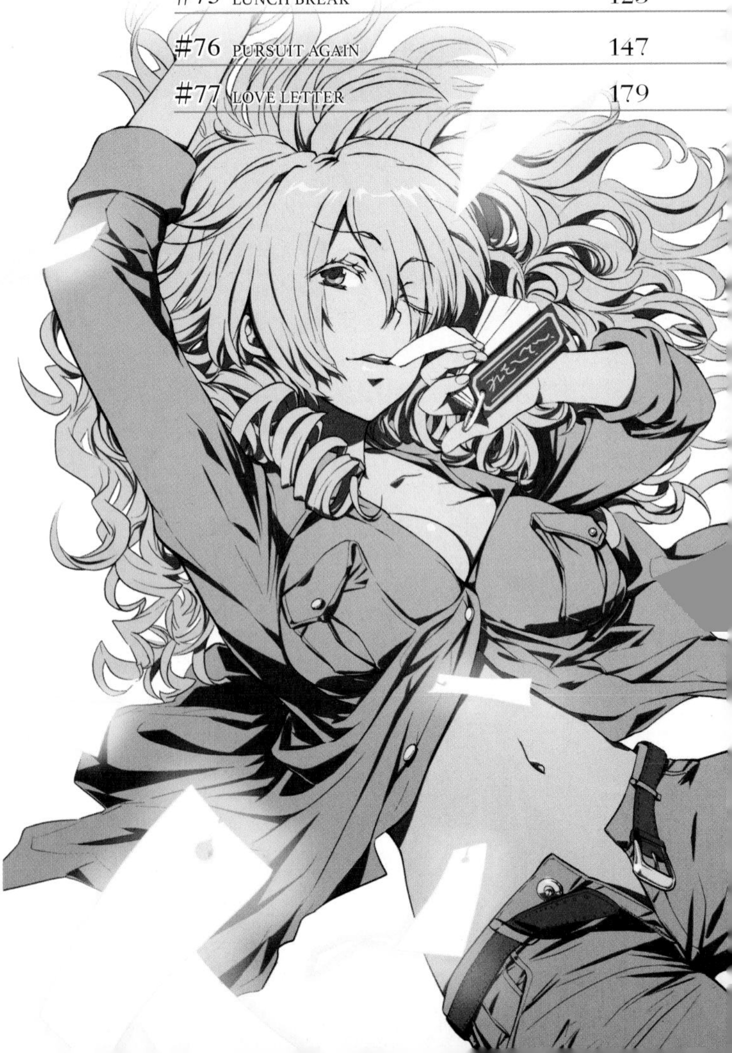

#71 SHORTHAND ②

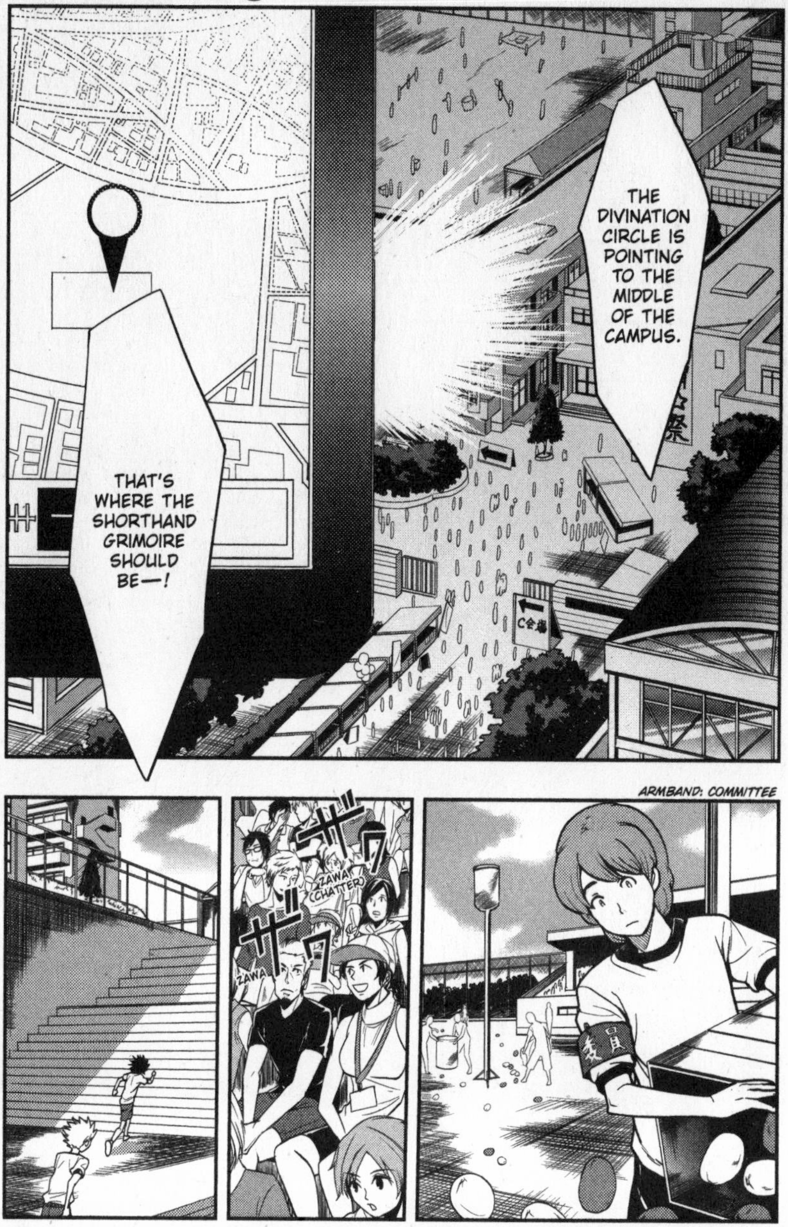
THE DIVINATION CIRCLE IS POINTING TO THE MIDDLE OF THE CAMPUS.
THAT'S WHERE THE SHORTHAND GRIMOIRE SHOULD BE—!
ARMBAND: COMMITTEE
ZAWA (CHATTER)
ZAWA

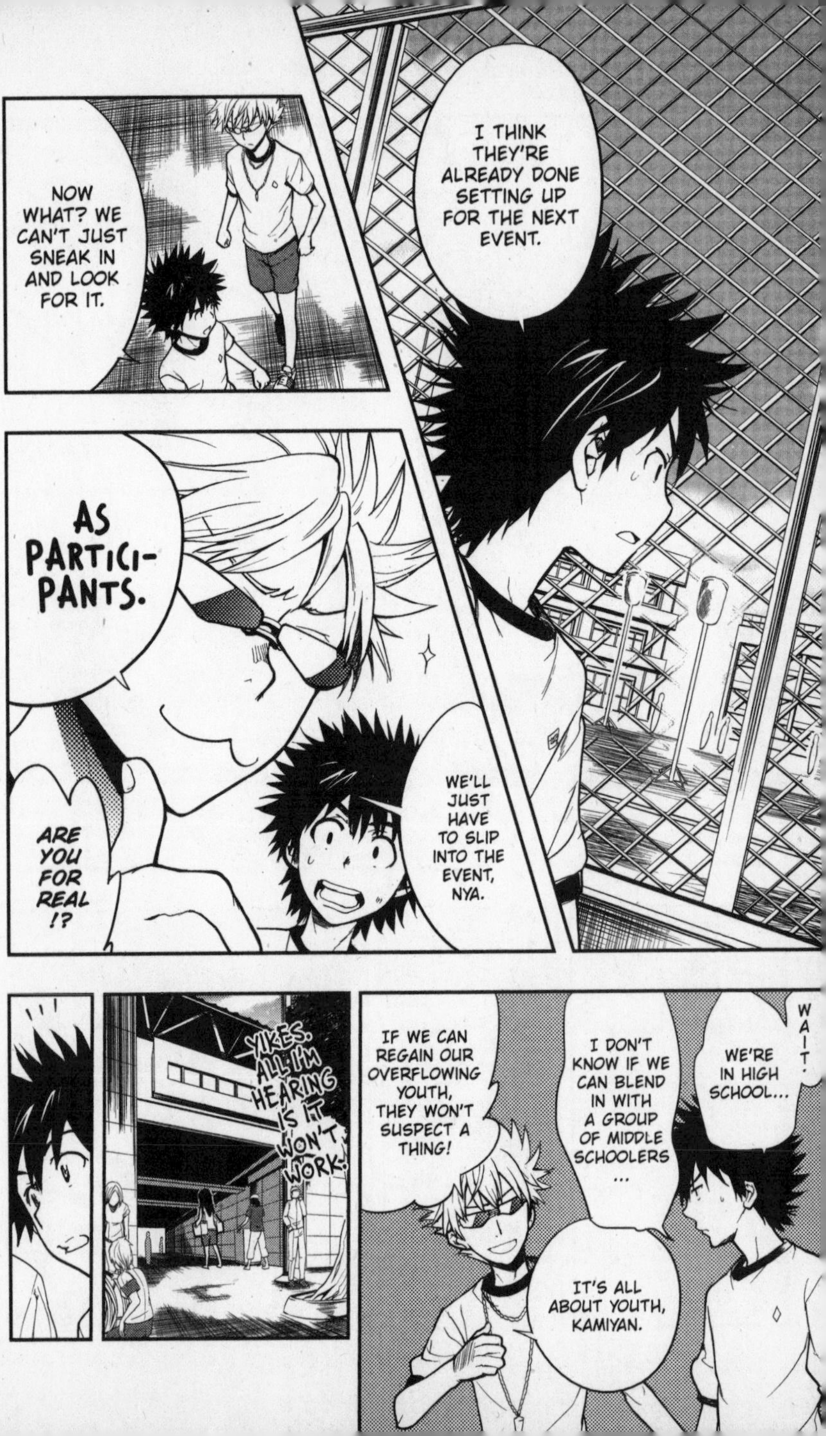
I THINK THEY'RE ALREADY DONE SETTING UP FOR THE NEXT EVENT.
NOW WHAT? WE CAN'T JUST SNEAK IN AND LOOK FOR IT.
WE'LL JUST HAVE TO SLIP INTO THE EVENT, NYA.
AS PARTICI-PANTS.
ARE YOU FOR REAL!?
WAIT.
WE'RE IN HIGH SCHOOL...
I DON'T KNOW IF WE CAN BLEND IN WITH A GROUP OF MIDDLE SCHOOLERS...
IF WE CAN REGAIN OUR OVERFLOWING YOUTH, THEY WON'T SUSPECT A THING!
IT'S ALL ABOUT YOUTH, KAMIYAN.
YIKES. ALL I'M HEARING IS IT WON'T WORK.

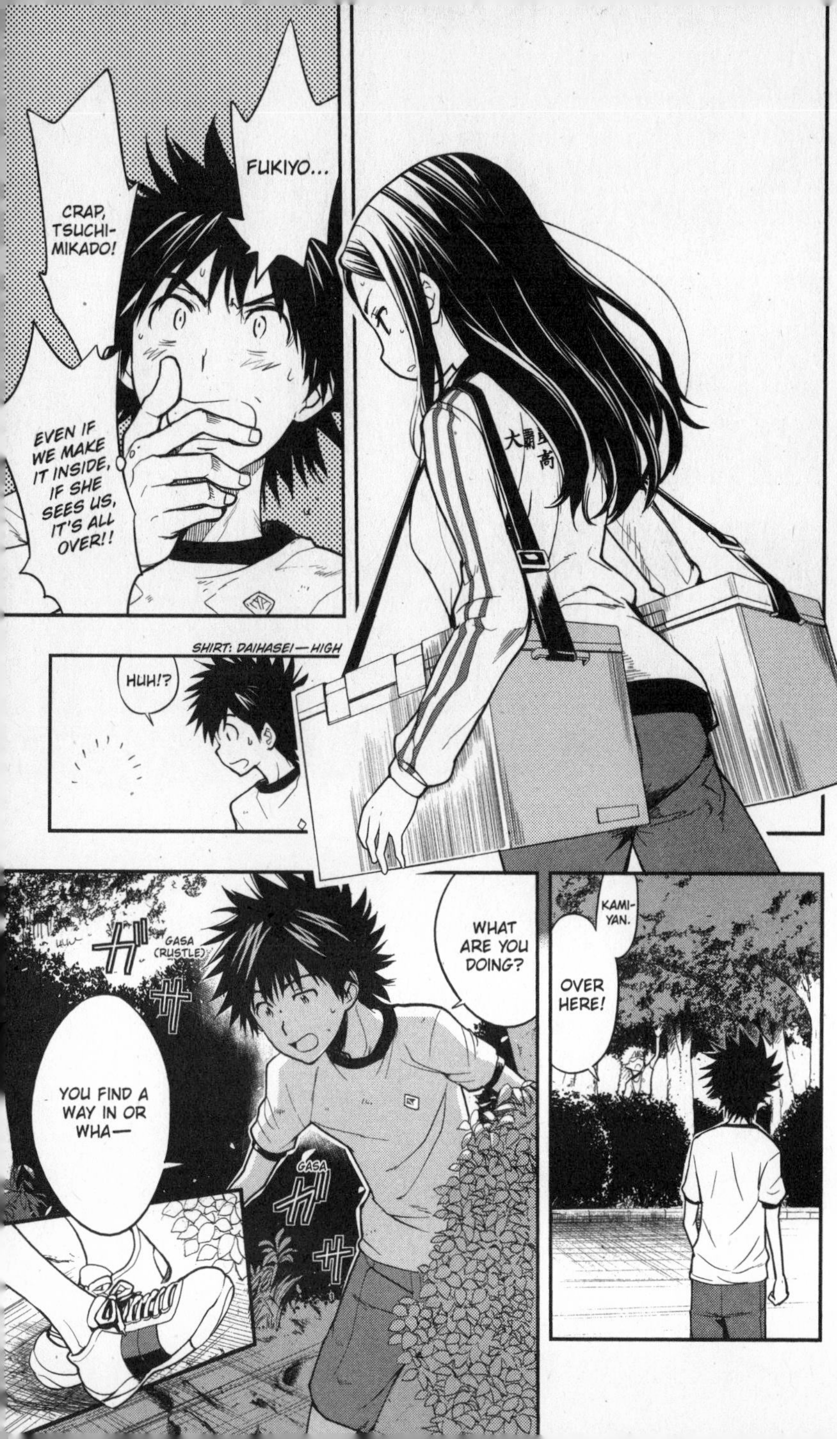
SHIRT: DAIHASEI—HIGH
FUKIYO...
CRAP, TSUCHIMIKADO!
EVEN IF WE MAKE IT INSIDE, IF SHE SEES US, IT'S ALL OVER!!
HUH!?
KAMI-YAN.
OVER HERE!
WHAT ARE YOU DOING?
GASA (RUSTLE)
YOU FIND A WAY IN OR WHA—
GASA

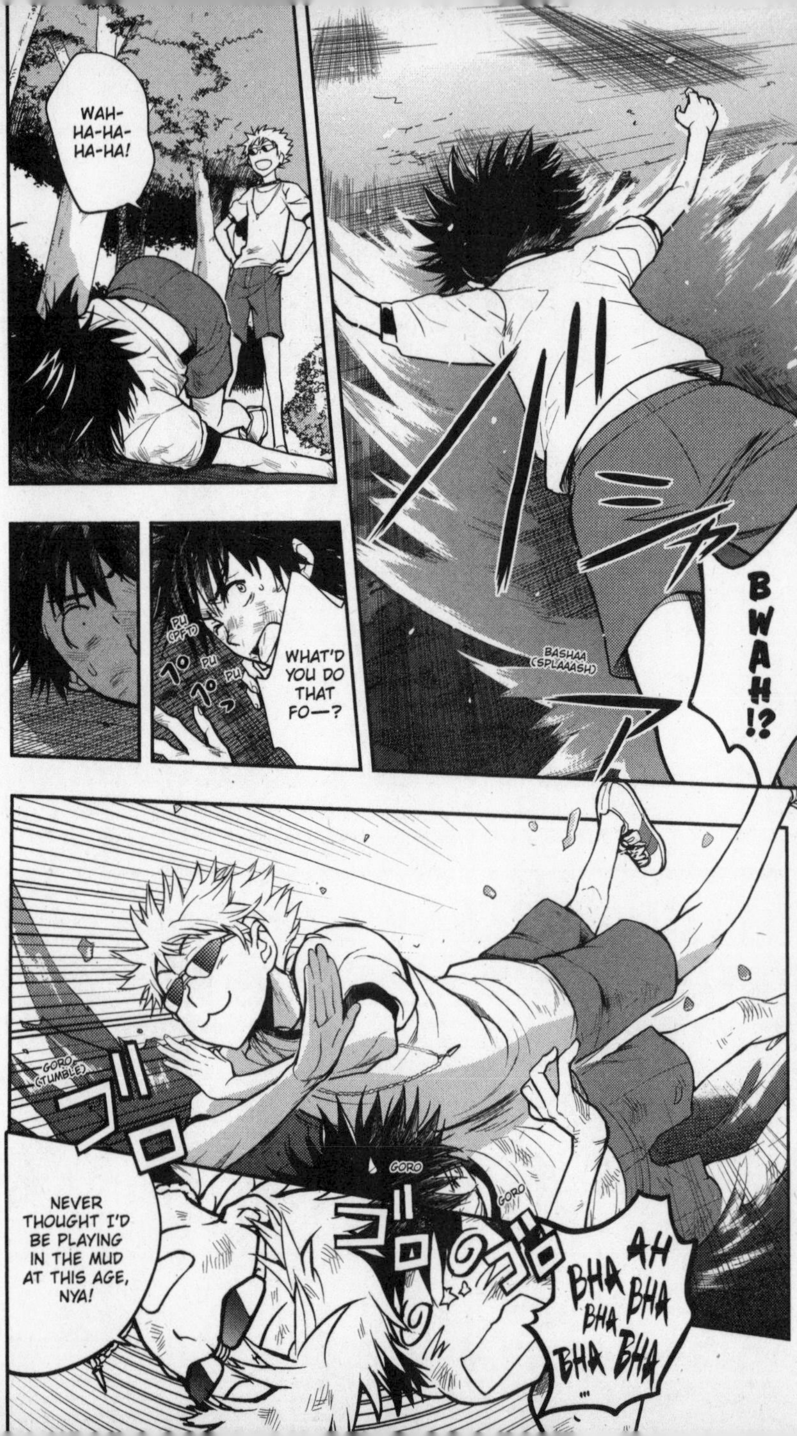
BWAH!?
BASHAA (SPLAAASH)
WAH-HA-HA-HA-HA!
PU (PFFT) PU PU
WHAT'D YOU DO THAT FO—?
AH BHA BHA BHA BHA BHA ...
GORO GORO
GORO (TUMBLE)
NEVER THOUGHT I'D BE PLAYING IN THE MUD AT THIS AGE, NYA!

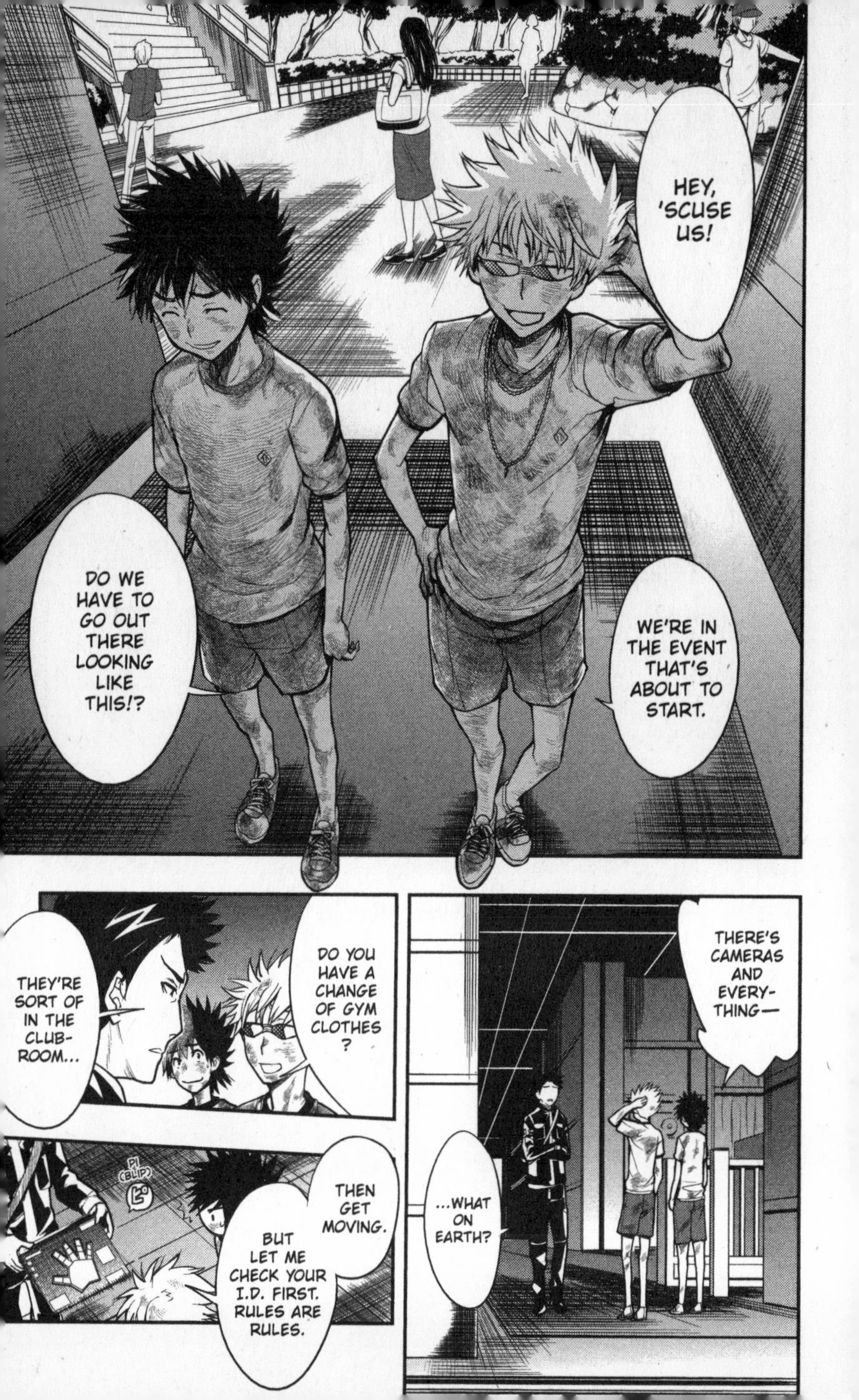
HEY, 'SCUSE US!
WE'RE IN THE EVENT THAT'S ABOUT TO START.
DO WE HAVE TO GO OUT THERE LOOKING LIKE THIS!?
THERE'S CAMERAS AND EVERY-THING—
...WHAT ON EARTH?
DO YOU HAVE A CHANGE OF GYM CLOTHES?
THEY'RE SORT OF IN THE CLUB-ROOM...
THEN GET MOVING.
BUT LET ME CHECK YOUR I.D. FIRST. RULES ARE RULES.
PI (BLIP)

WHY, YOU... COULDN'T YOU WIPE YOUR HANDS FIRST!?

SORRY, I WAS IN A HURRY...

AHH, WE'RE RUNNING OUT OF TIME...!

OKAY, THERE WE GO! ♪

ERROR

BUCHO (SPLOTCH)

THANK YOU SO MUCH!!!

THEY WON'T LET YOU IN MIDWAY THROUGH!

FINE, JUST GO.

IT'S COMMON KNOWLEDGE THAT THE NURSE'S OFFICE HAS SPARE GYM UNIFORMS!

...PHEW. WE FOOLED HIM.

WHAT, THAT?

BUT WE CAN'T BLEND IN WITH ALL THIS MUD, CAN WE!?

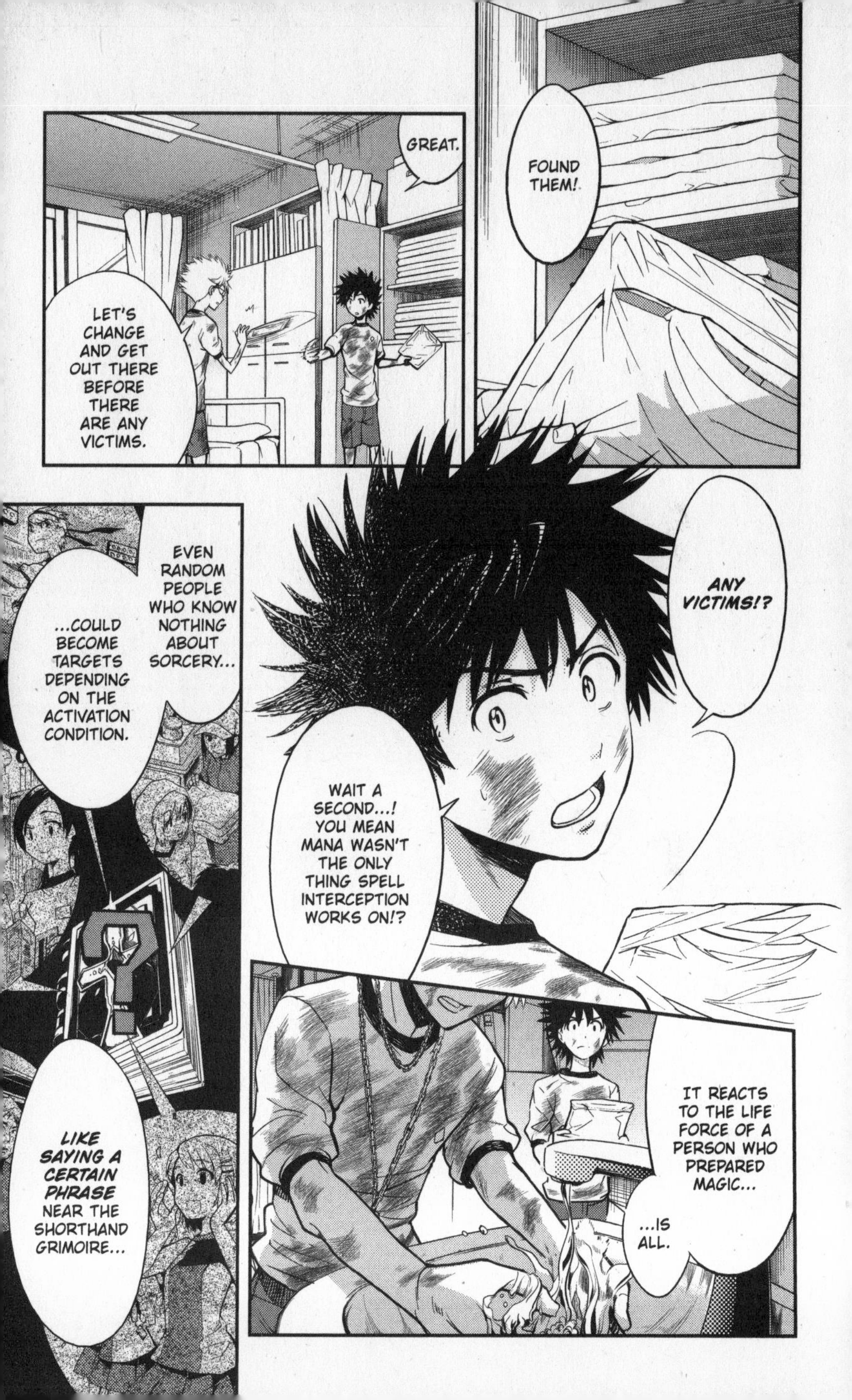
FOUND THEM!
GREAT.
LET'S CHANGE AND GET OUT THERE BEFORE THERE ARE ANY VICTIMS.
ANY VICTIMS!?
WAIT A SECOND...! YOU MEAN MANA WASN'T THE ONLY THING SPELL INTERCEPTION WORKS ON!?
IT REACTS TO THE LIFE FORCE OF A PERSON WHO PREPARED MAGIC...
...IS ALL.
EVEN RANDOM PEOPLE WHO KNOW NOTHING ABOUT SORCERY...
...COULD BECOME TARGETS DEPENDING ON THE ACTIVATION CONDITION.
LIKE SAYING A CERTAIN PHRASE NEAR THE SHORTHAND GRIMOIRE...

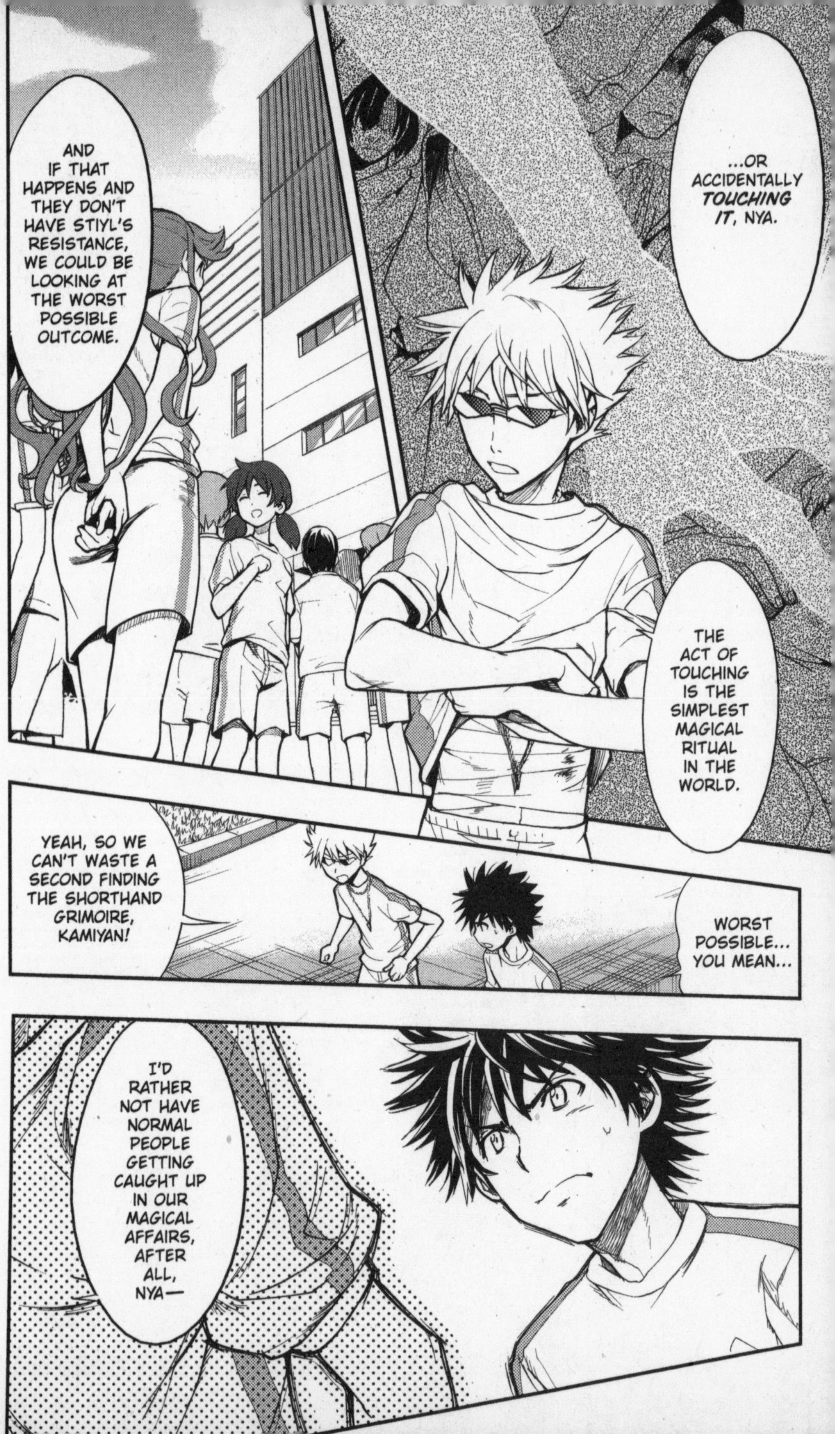

...OR ACCIDENTALLY TOUCHING IT, NYA.
THE ACT OF TOUCHING IS THE SIMPLEST MAGICAL RITUAL IN THE WORLD.
AND IF THAT HAPPENS AND THEY DON'T HAVE STIYL'S RESISTANCE, WE COULD BE LOOKING AT THE WORST POSSIBLE OUTCOME.
WORST POSSIBLE... YOU MEAN...
YEAH, SO WE CAN'T WASTE A SECOND FINDING THE SHORTHAND GRIMOIRE, KAMIYAN!
I'D RATHER NOT HAVE NORMAL PEOPLE GETTING CAUGHT UP IN OUR MAGICAL AFFAIRS, AFTER ALL, NYA—

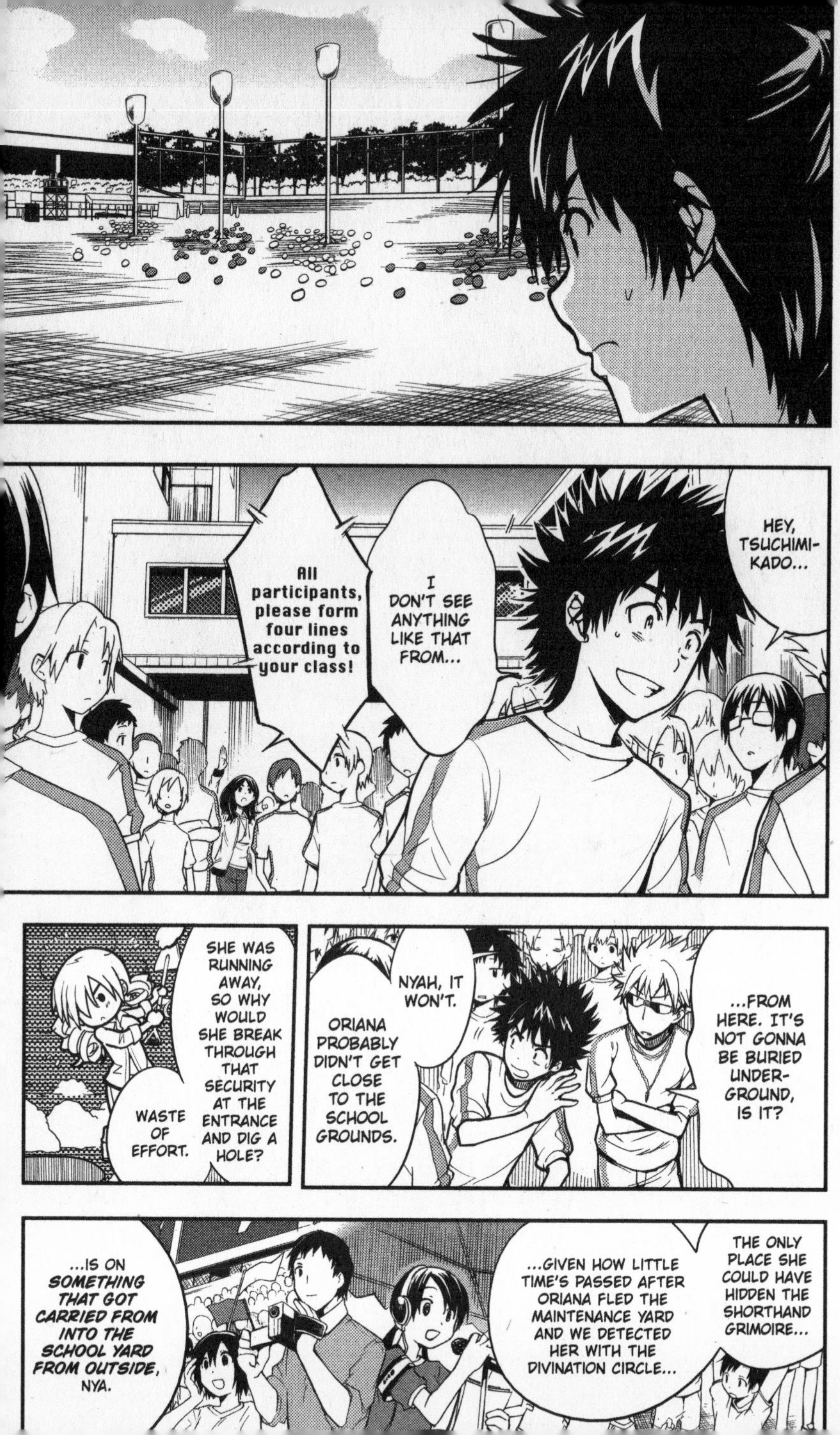

HEY, TSUCHIMIKADO...
I DON'T SEE ANYTHING LIKE THAT FROM...
All participants, please form four lines according to your class!
...FROM HERE. IT'S NOT GONNA BE BURIED UNDERGROUND, IS IT?
NYAH, IT WON'T.
ORIANA PROBABLY DIDN'T GET CLOSE TO THE SCHOOL GROUNDS.
SHE WAS RUNNING AWAY, SO WHY WOULD SHE BREAK THROUGH THAT SECURITY AT THE ENTRANCE AND DIG A HOLE?
WASTE OF EFFORT.
THE ONLY PLACE SHE COULD HAVE HIDDEN THE SHORTHAND GRIMOIRE...
...GIVEN HOW LITTLE TIME'S PASSED AFTER ORIANA FLED THE MAINTENANCE YARD AND WE DETECTED HER WITH THE DIVINATION CIRCLE...
...IS ON SOMETHING THAT GOT CARRIED FROM INTO THE SCHOOL YARD FROM OUTSIDE, NYA.

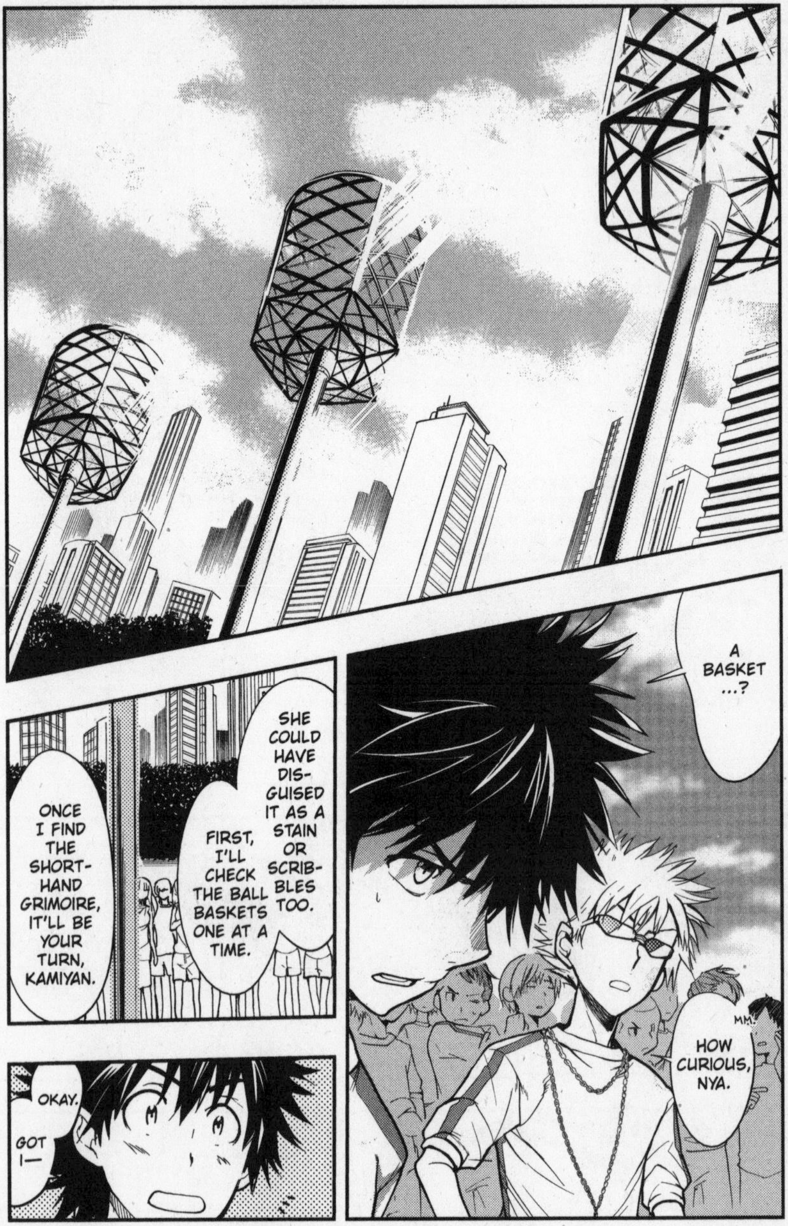
A BASKET ...?
MM. HOW CURIOUS, NYA.
SHE COULD HAVE DISGUISED IT AS A STAIN OR SCRIBBLES TOO.
FIRST, I'LL CHECK THE BALL BASKETS ONE AT A TIME.
ONCE I FIND THE SHORTHAND GRIMOIRE, IT'LL BE YOUR TURN, KAMIYAN.
OKAY.
GOT I—

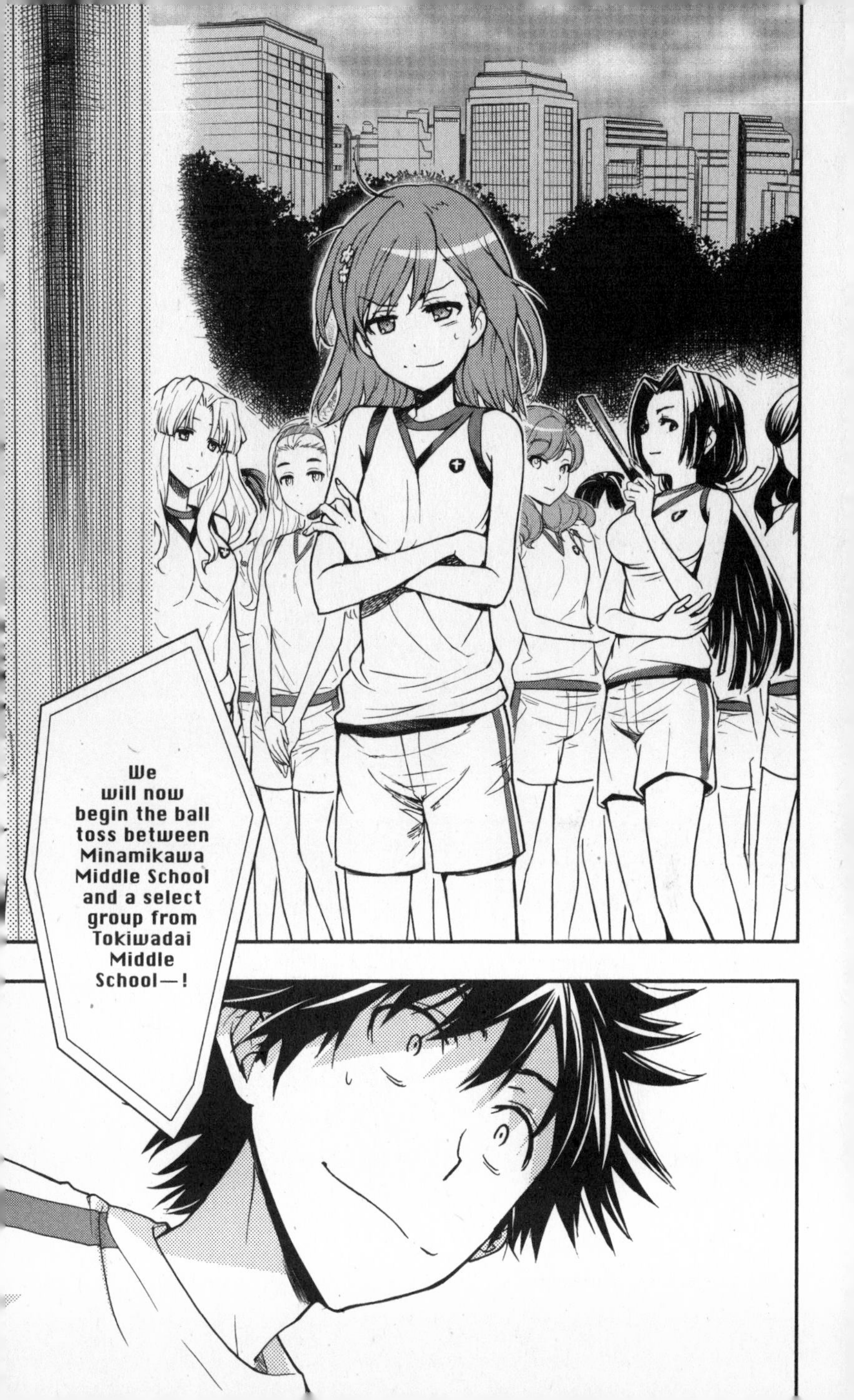
We will now begin the ball toss between Minamikawa Middle School and a select group from Tokiwadai Middle School—!

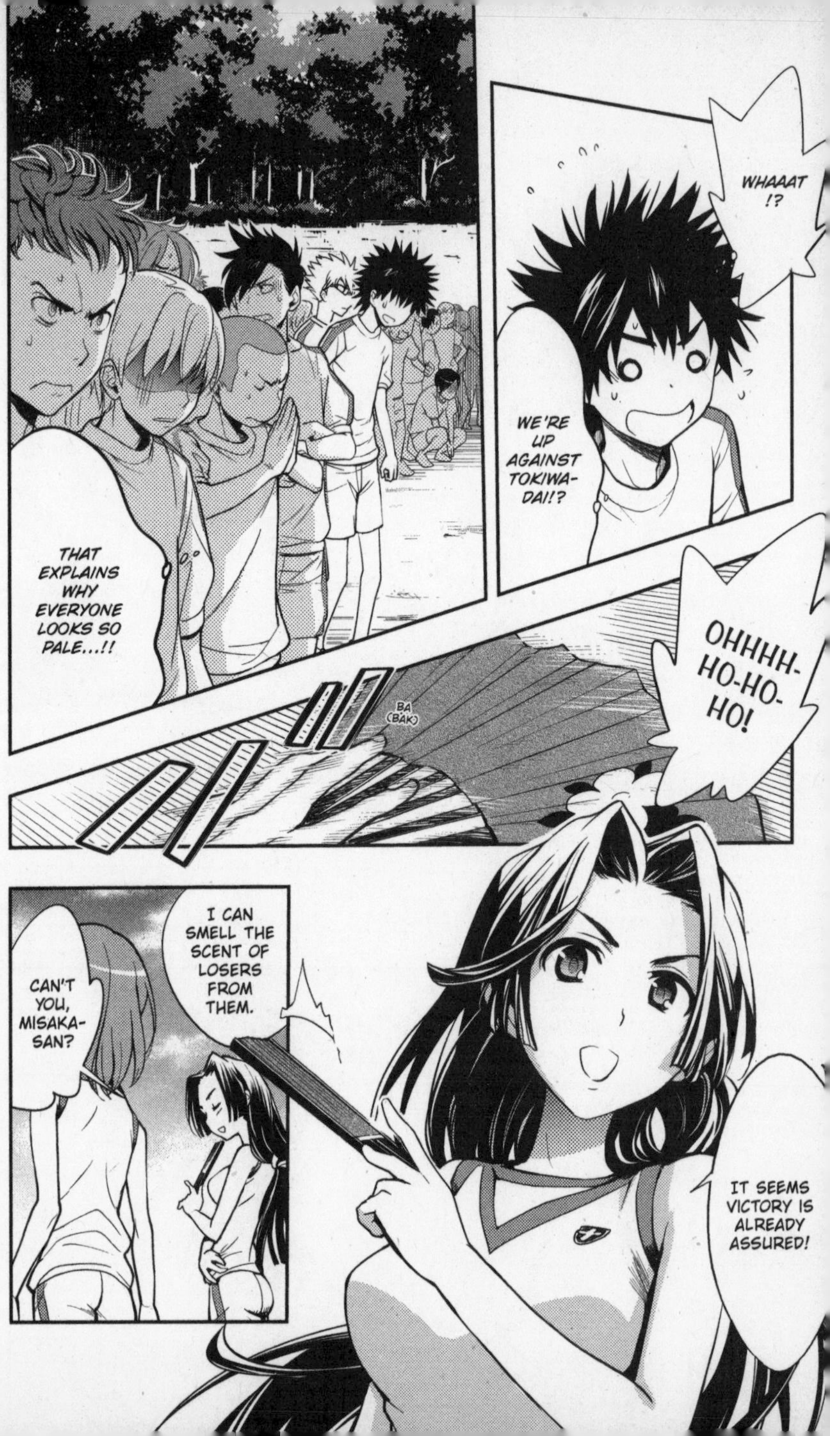
WHAAAT!?
WE'RE UP AGAINST TOKIWA-DAI!?
THAT EXPLAINS WHY EVERYONE LOOKS SO PALE...!!
OHHHH-HO-HO-HO!
BA (BAK)
IT SEEMS VICTORY IS ALREADY ASSURED!
I CAN SMELL THE SCENT OF LOSERS FROM THEM.
CAN'T YOU, MISAKA-SAN?

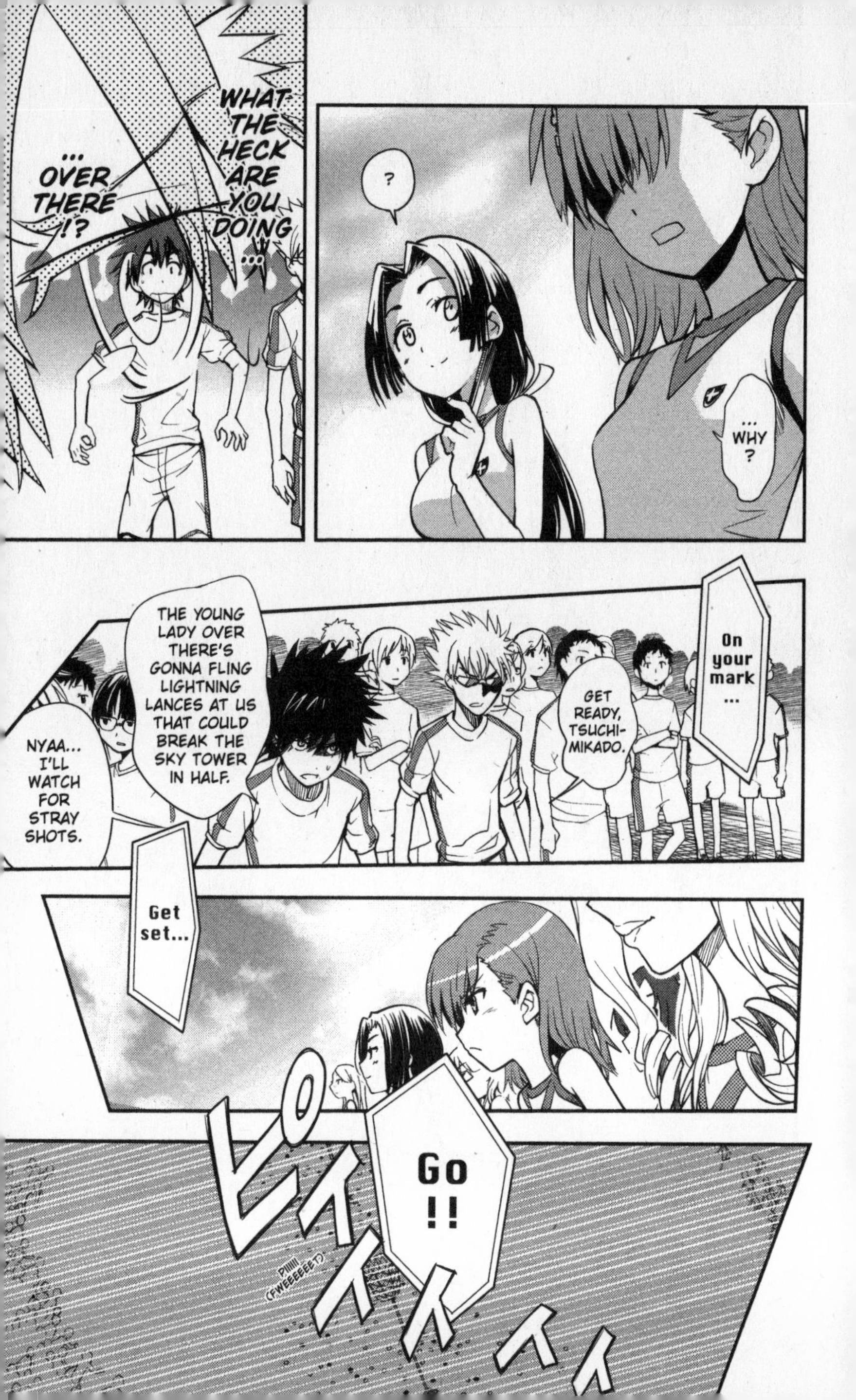

...WHY?
?
WHAT THE HECK ARE YOU DOING...
...OVER THERE!?
On your mark...
GET READY, TSUCHI-MIKADO.
THE YOUNG LADY OVER THERE'S GONNA FLING LIGHTNING LANCES AT US THAT COULD BREAK THE SKY TOWER IN HALF.
NYAA... I'LL WATCH FOR STRAY SHOTS.
Get set...
Go!!
ピィィィィ
PIIIII (FWEEEEEET)

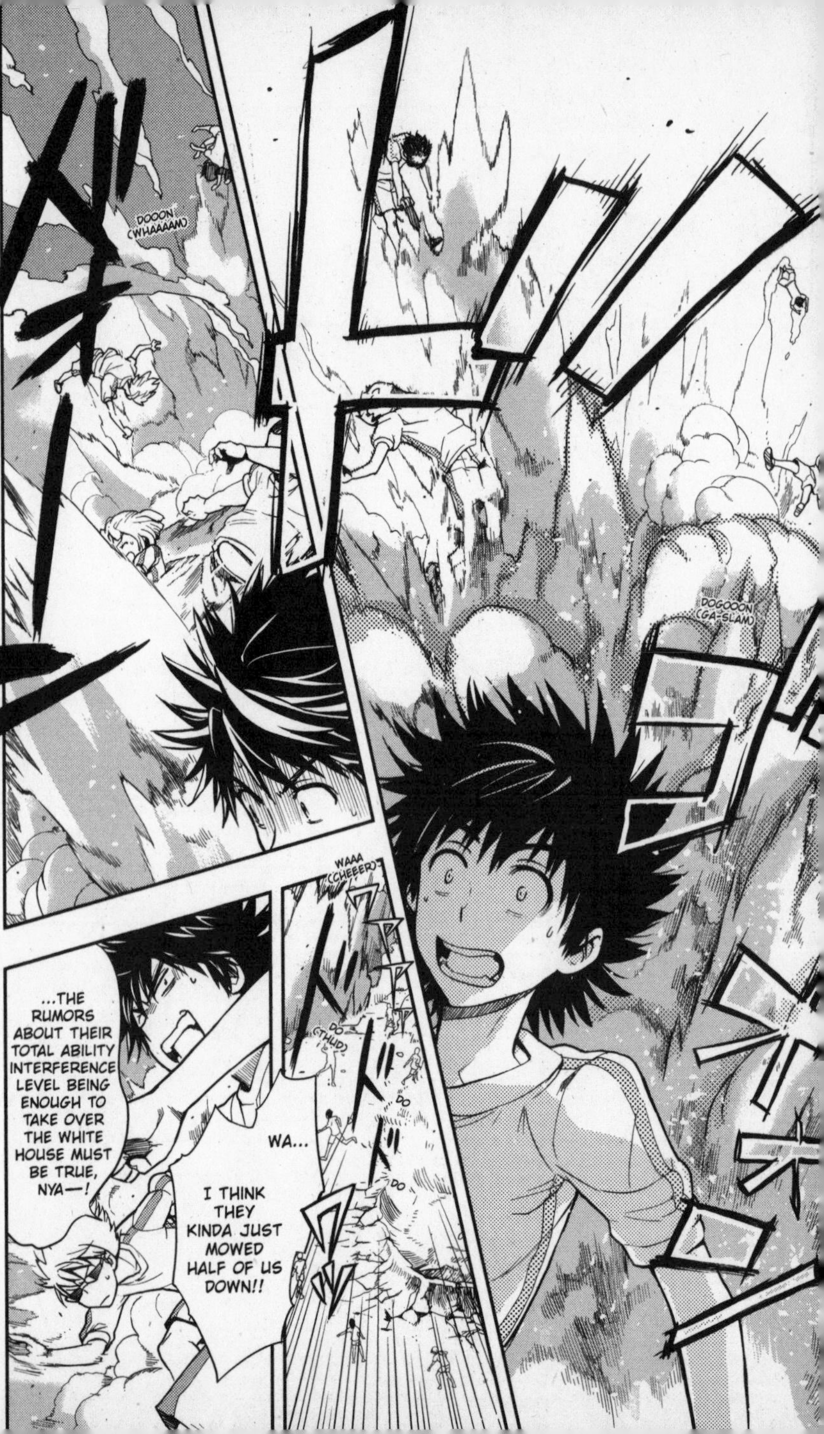
DOGOOON (GA-SLAM)
DOOON (WHAAAAM)
WAAA (CHEEER)
DO (THUD)
DO
DO
WA...
I THINK THEY KINDA JUST MOWED HALF OF US DOWN!!
...THE RUMORS ABOUT THEIR TOTAL ABILITY INTERFERENCE LEVEL BEING ENOUGH TO TAKE OVER THE WHITE HOUSE MUST BE TRUE, NYA—!

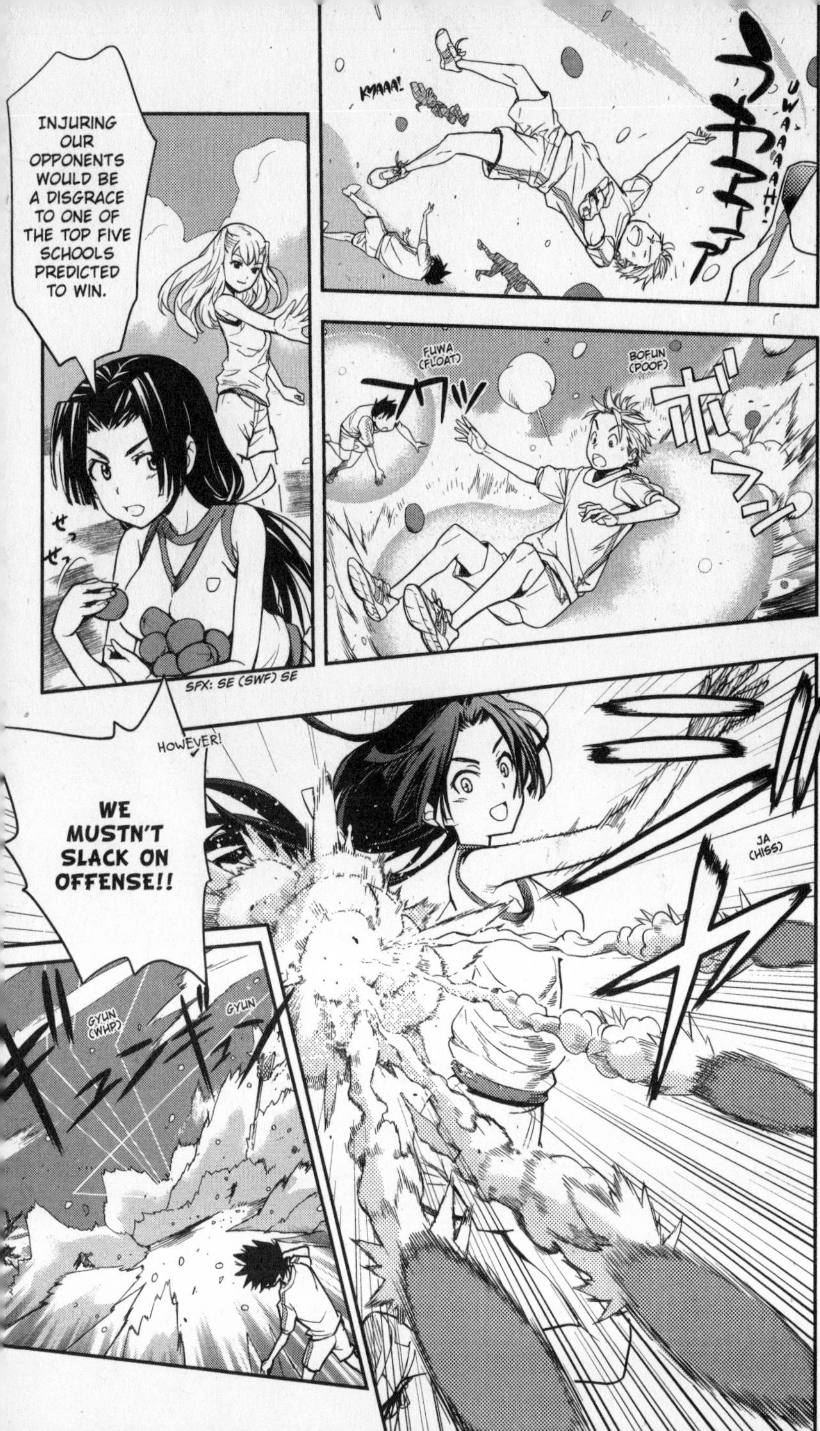
UWAAAAAH!
KYAAA!
BOFUN (POOF)
FUWA (FLOAT)
INJURING OUR OPPONENTS WOULD BE A DISGRACE TO ONE OF THE TOP FIVE SCHOOLS PREDICTED TO WIN.
SFX: SE (SWF) SE
HOWEVER!
WE MUSTN'T SLACK ON OFFENSE!!
JA (HISS)
GYUN
GYUN (WHP)

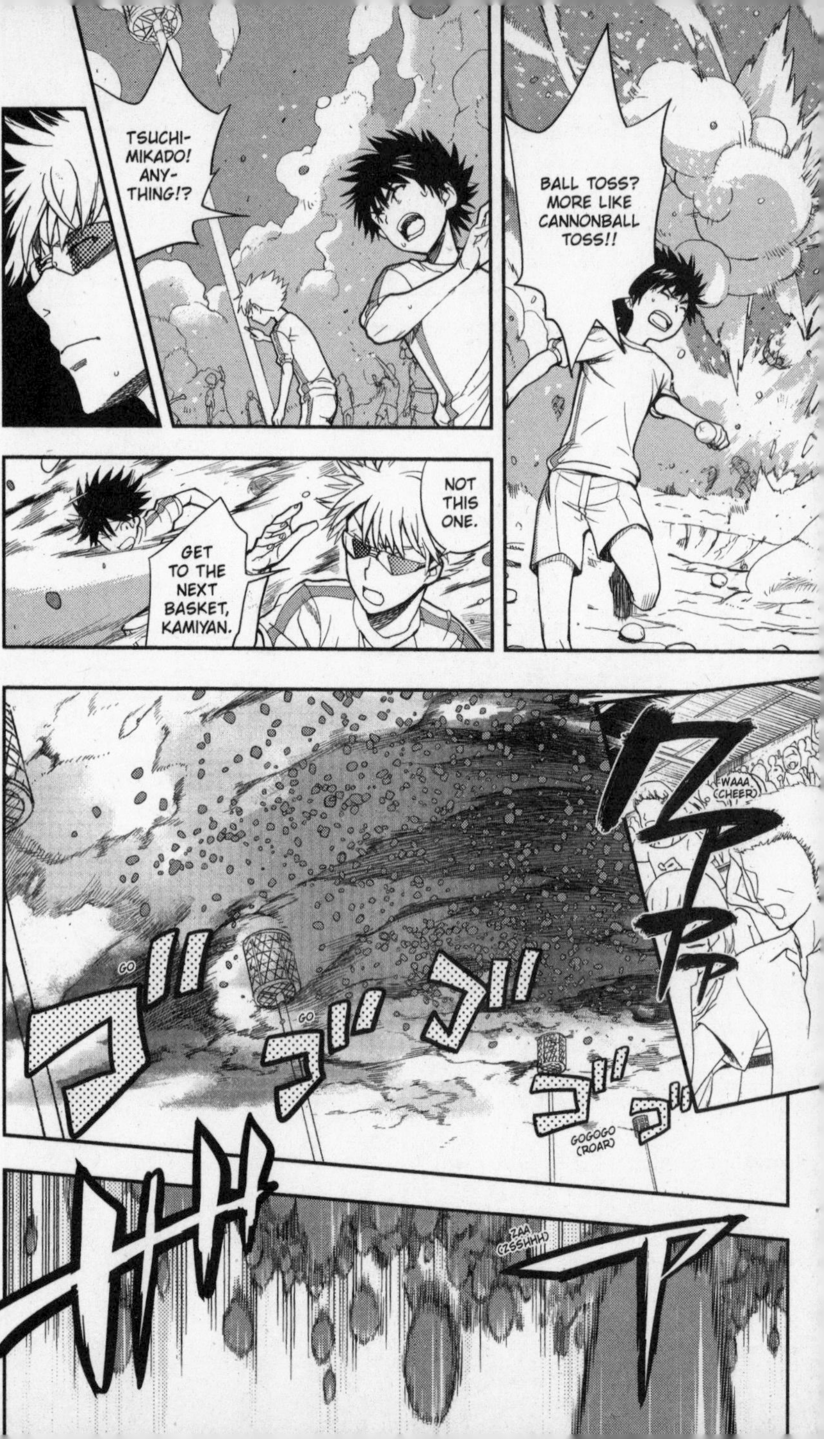
BALL TOSS? MORE LIKE CANNONBALL TOSS!!
TSUCHI-MIKADO! ANY-THING!?
NOT THIS ONE.
GET TO THE NEXT BASKET, KAMIYAN.
WAAA (CHEER)
GO
GO
GOGOGO (ROAR)
ZAA (ZSSHHH)

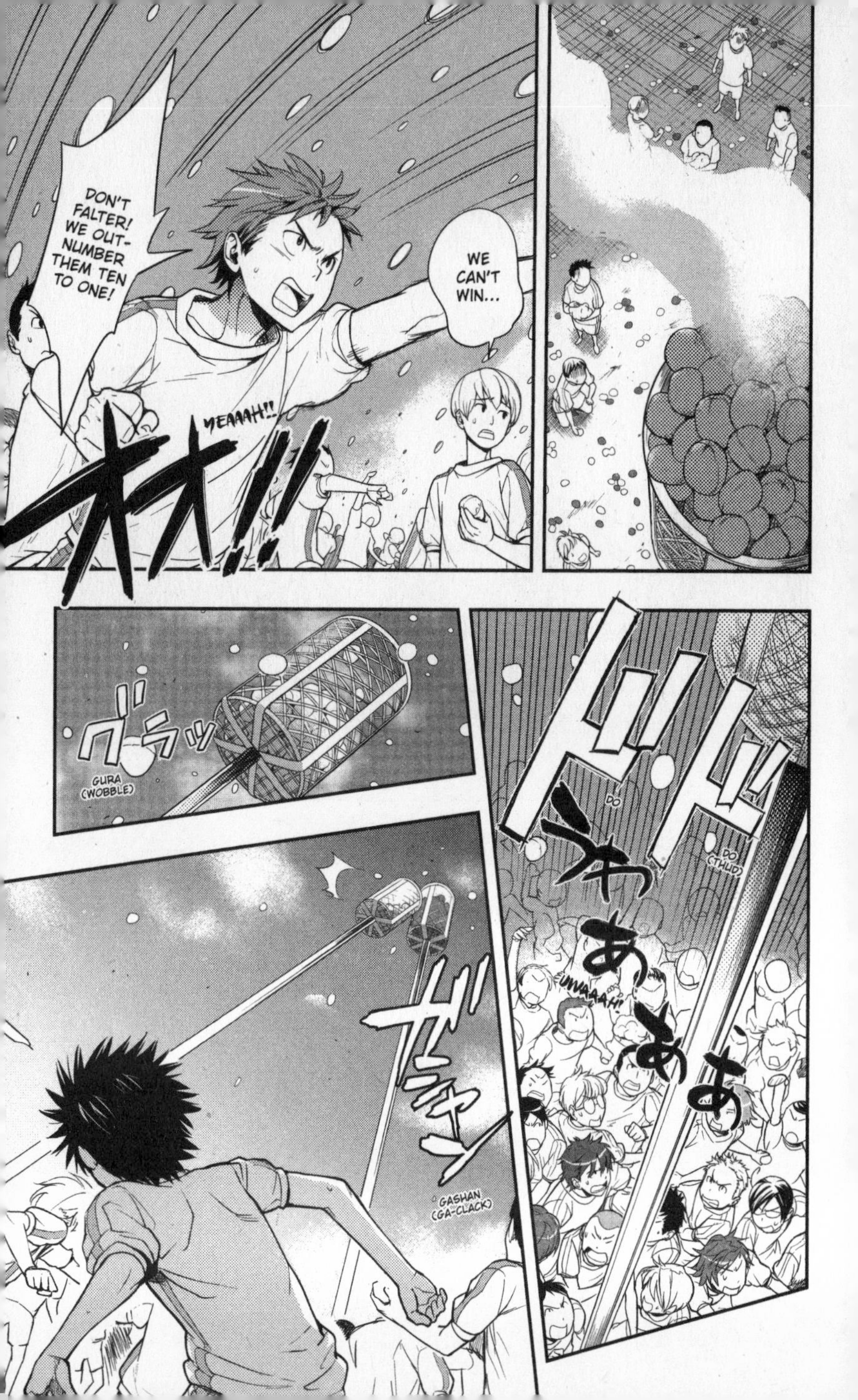
WE CAN'T WIN...
DON'T FALTER! WE OUT-NUMBER THEM TEN TO ONE!
YEAAAH!!
DO
DO (THUD)
UWAAAAH!
GURA (WOBBLE)
GASHAN (GA-CLACK)

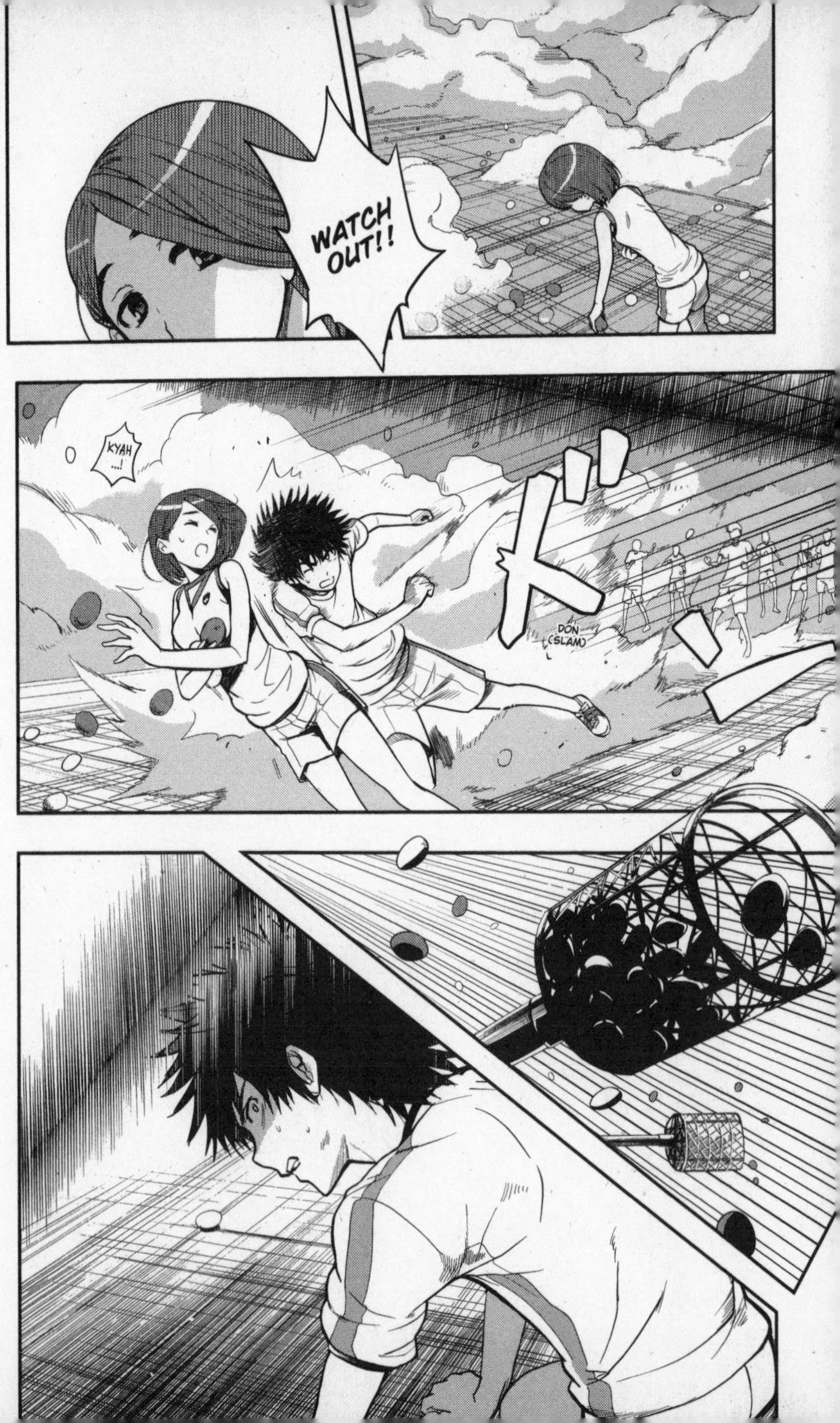
WATCH OUT!!
KYAH ...!
DON (SLAM)

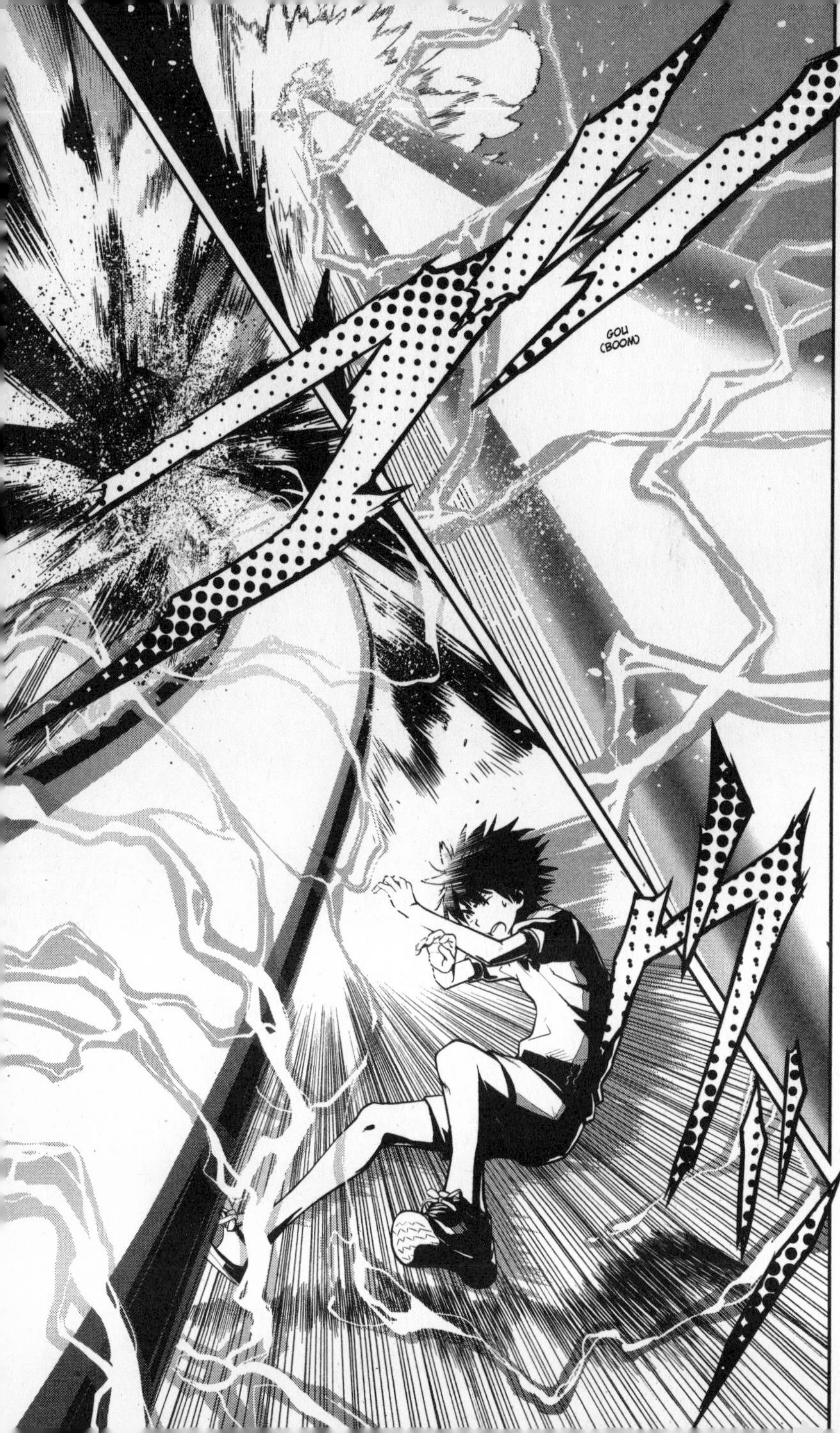
GOU
(BOOM)

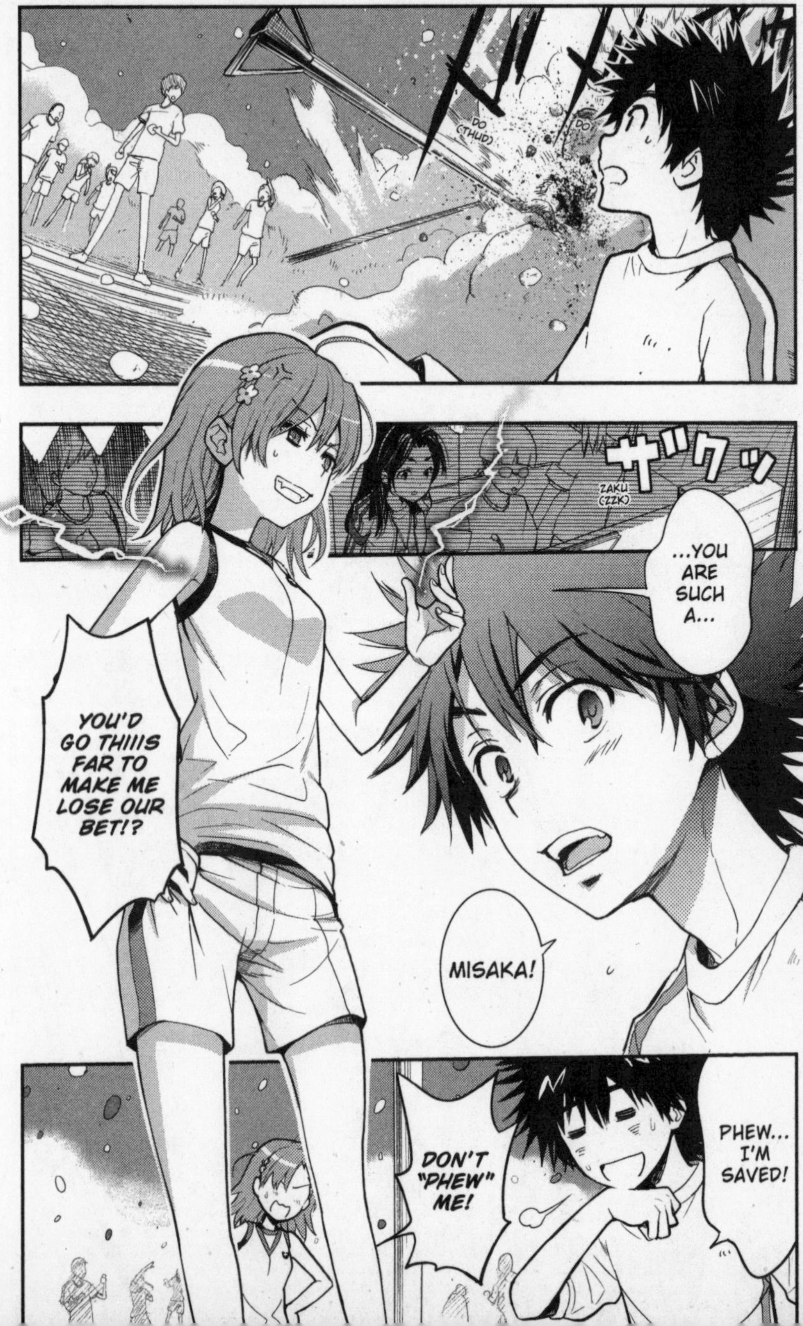
DO
DO (THUD)
ZAKU (ZZK)
...YOU ARE SUCH A...
MISAKA!
YOU'D GO THIIIS FAR TO MAKE ME LOSE OUR BET!?
PHEW... I'M SAVED!
DON'T "PHEW" ME!

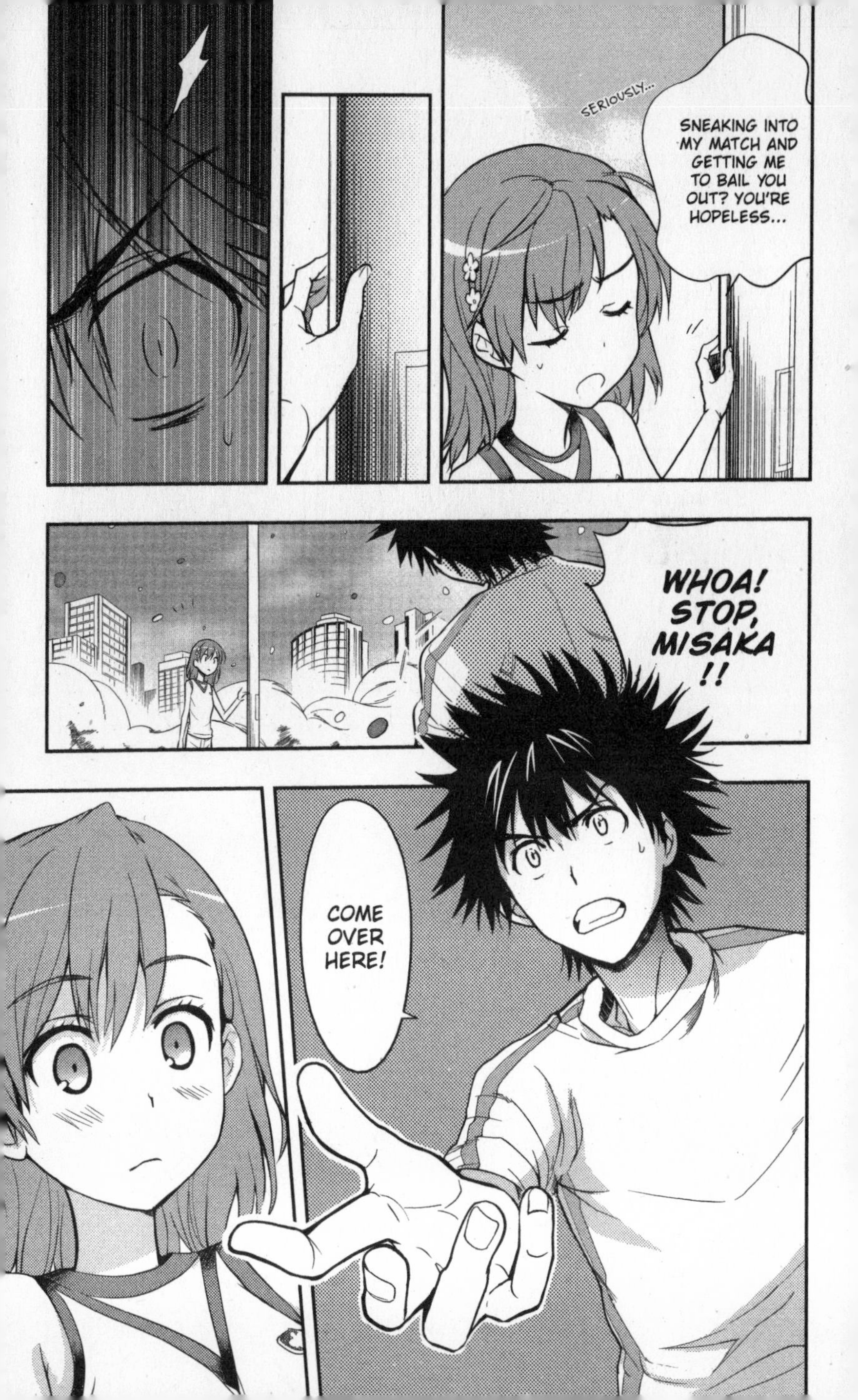
SERIOUSLY...
SNEAKING INTO MY MATCH AND GETTING ME TO BAIL YOU OUT? YOU'RE HOPELESS...
WHOA! STOP, MISAKA!!
COME OVER HERE!

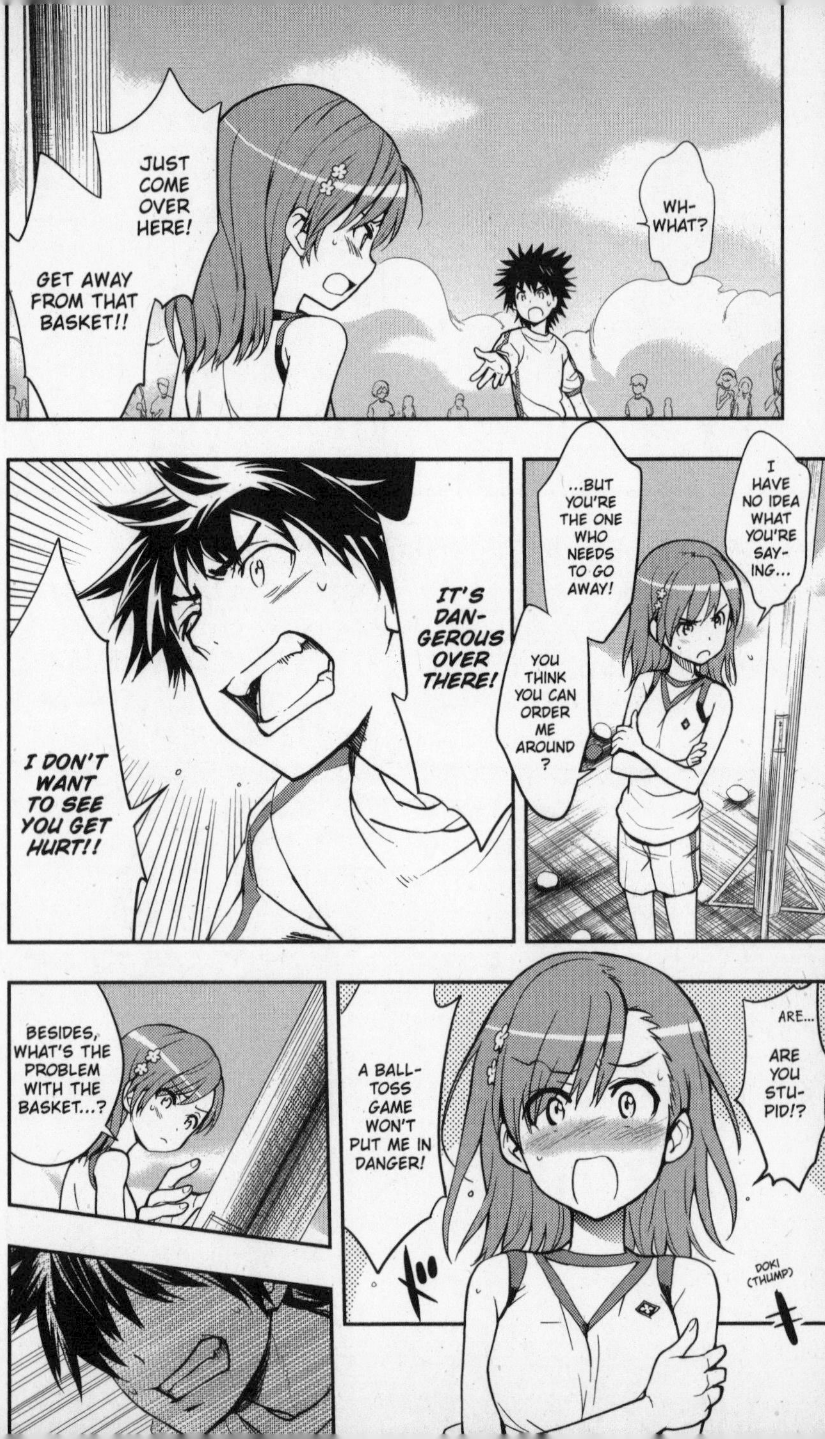
WH- WHAT?
JUST COME OVER HERE!
GET AWAY FROM THAT BASKET!!
I HAVE NO IDEA WHAT YOU'RE SAYING...
...BUT YOU'RE THE ONE WHO NEEDS TO GO AWAY!
YOU THINK YOU CAN ORDER ME AROUND?
IT'S DANGEROUS OVER THERE!
I DON'T WANT TO SEE YOU GET HURT!!
ARE...
ARE YOU STUPID!?
A BALL-TOSS GAME WON'T PUT ME IN DANGER!
DOKI (THUMP)
BESIDES, WHAT'S THE PROBLEM WITH THE BASKET...?

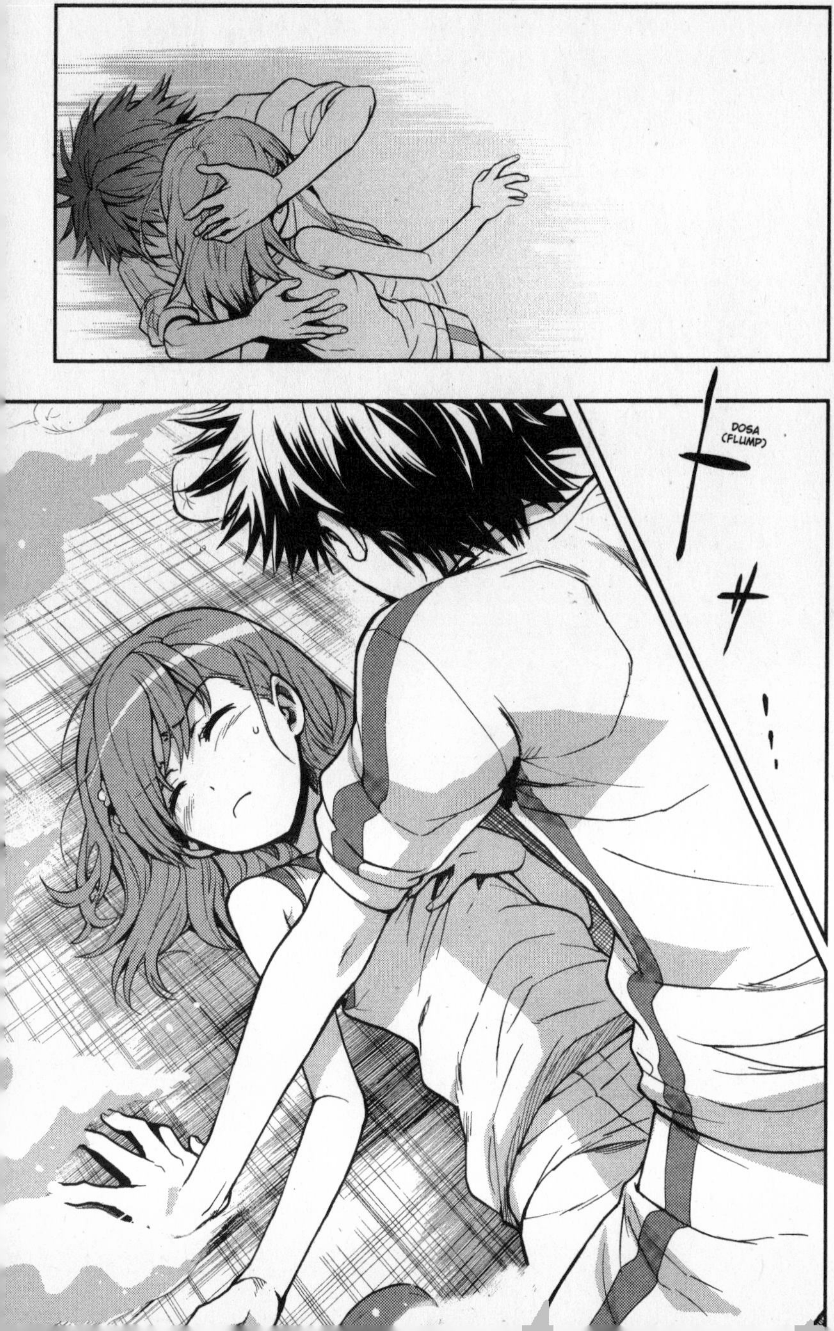
DOSA (FLUMP)
!!

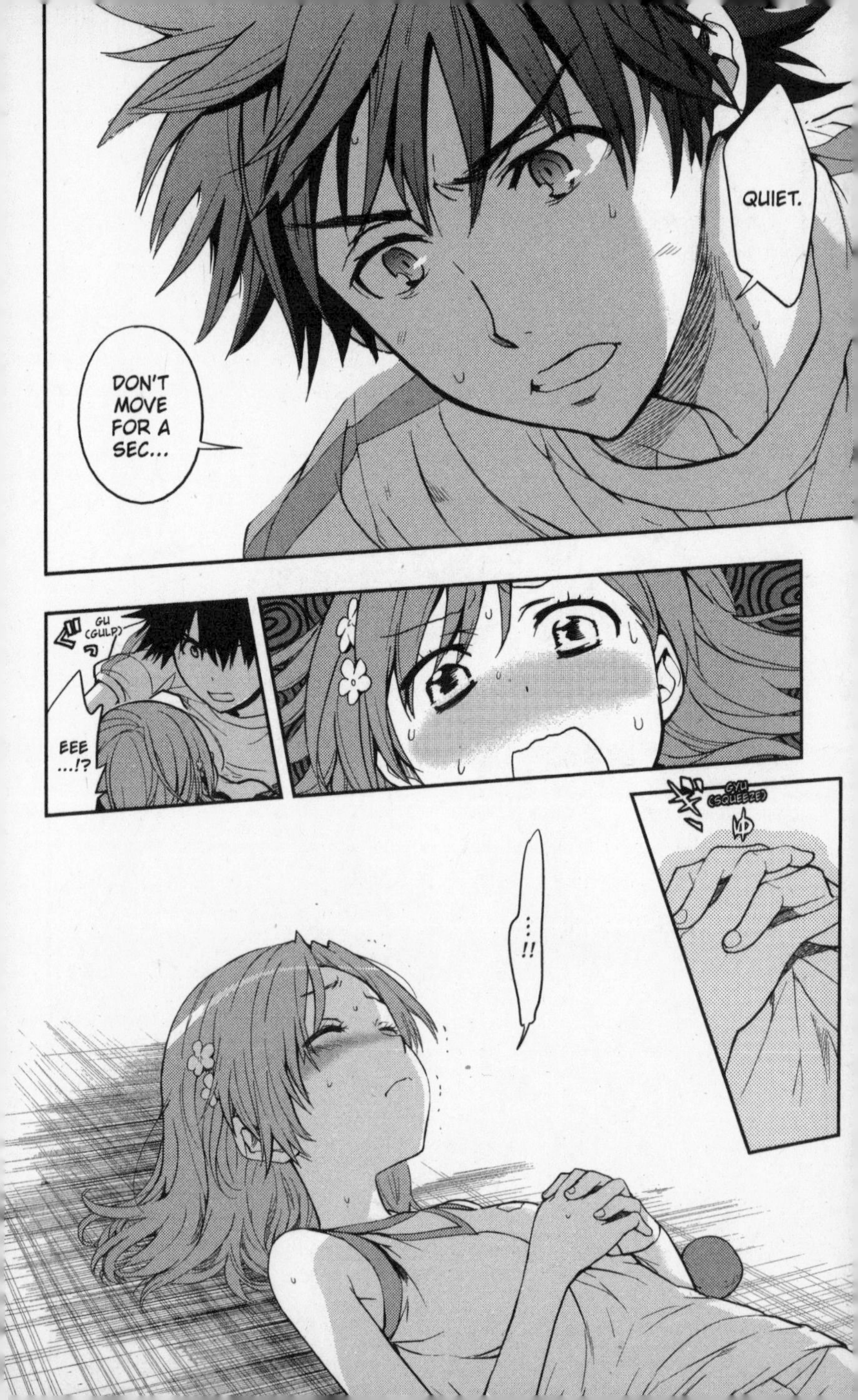
QUIET.
DON'T MOVE FOR A SEC...
GU (GULP)
EEE ...!?
GYU (SQUEEZE)
...!!

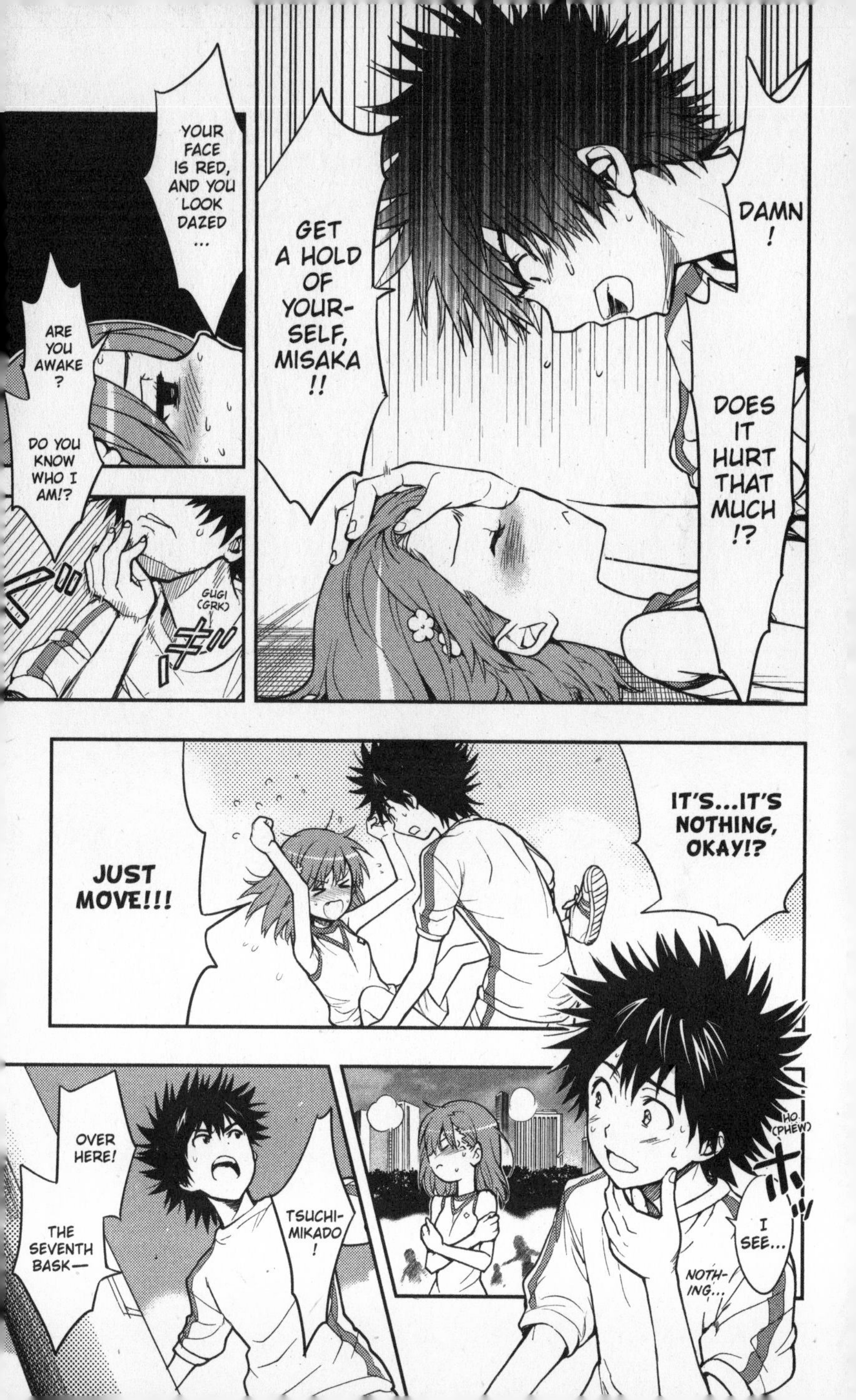
DAMN!
GET A HOLD OF YOURSELF, MISAKA!!
DOES IT HURT THAT MUCH!?
YOUR FACE IS RED, AND YOU LOOK DAZED...
ARE YOU AWAKE?
DO YOU KNOW WHO I AM!?
GUGI (GRK)
IT'S...IT'S NOTHING, OKAY!?
JUST MOVE!!!
HO (PHEW)
I SEE...
NOTHING...
OVER HERE!
TSUCHI-MIKADO!
THE SEVENTH BASK—

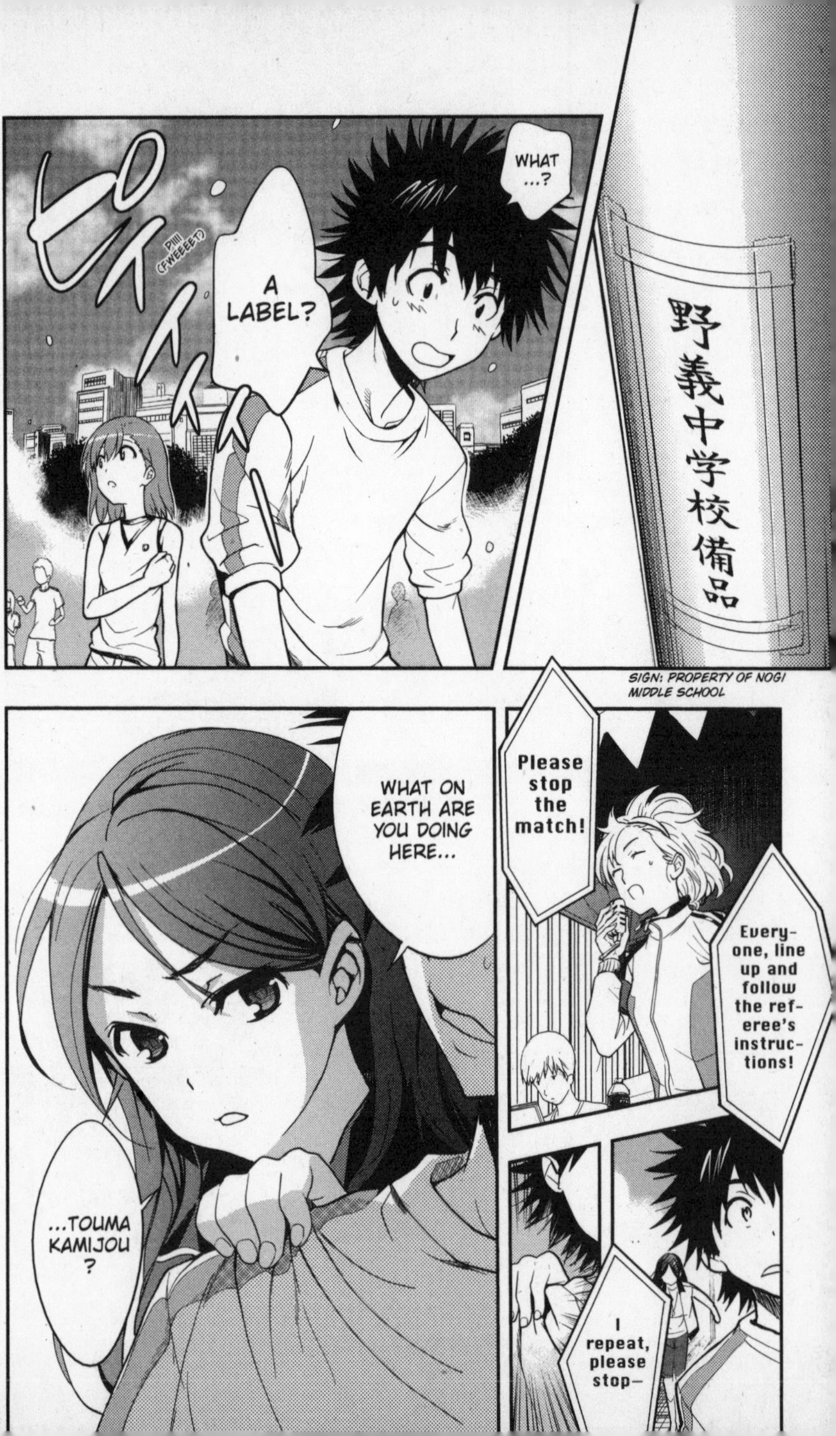

野義中学校備品
SIGN: PROPERTY OF NOGI MIDDLE SCHOOL
WHAT ...?
ピィィィィ
PIIII (FWEEEEET)
A LABEL?
Please stop the match!
Every-one, line up and follow the ref-eree's instruc-tions!
I repeat, please stop—
WHAT ON EARTH ARE YOU DOING HERE...
...TOUMA KAMIJOU ?

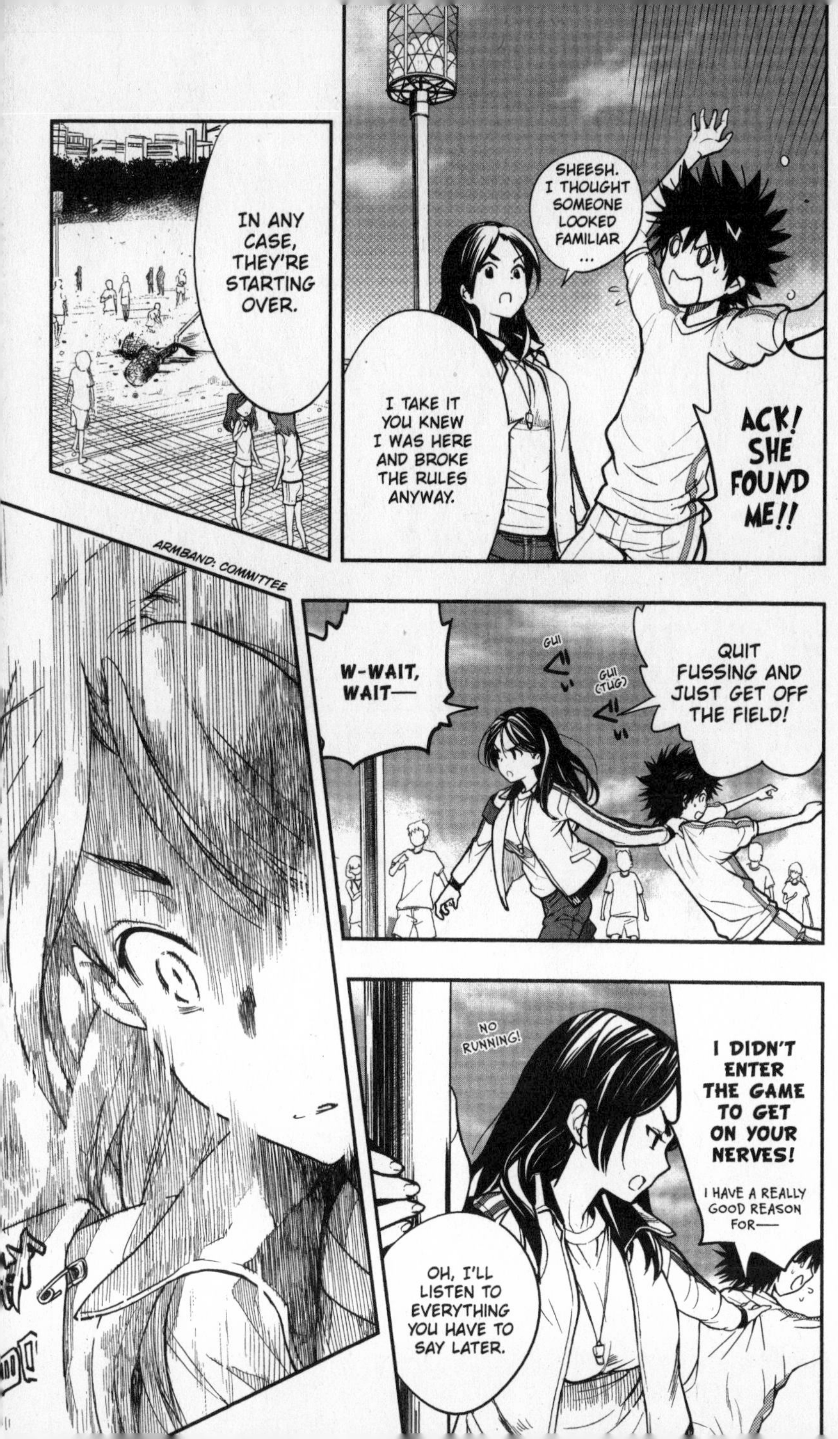
SHEESH. I THOUGHT SOMEONE LOOKED FAMILIAR ...
ACK! SHE FOUND ME!!
I TAKE IT YOU KNEW I WAS HERE AND BROKE THE RULES ANYWAY.
IN ANY CASE, THEY'RE STARTING OVER.
QUIT FUSSING AND JUST GET OFF THE FIELD!
GUI (TUG)
GUI
W-WAIT, WAIT—
I DIDN'T ENTER THE GAME TO GET ON YOUR NERVES!
I HAVE A REALLY GOOD REASON FOR—
NO RUNNING!
OH, I'LL LISTEN TO EVERYTHING YOU HAVE TO SAY LATER.
ARMBAND: COMMITTEE

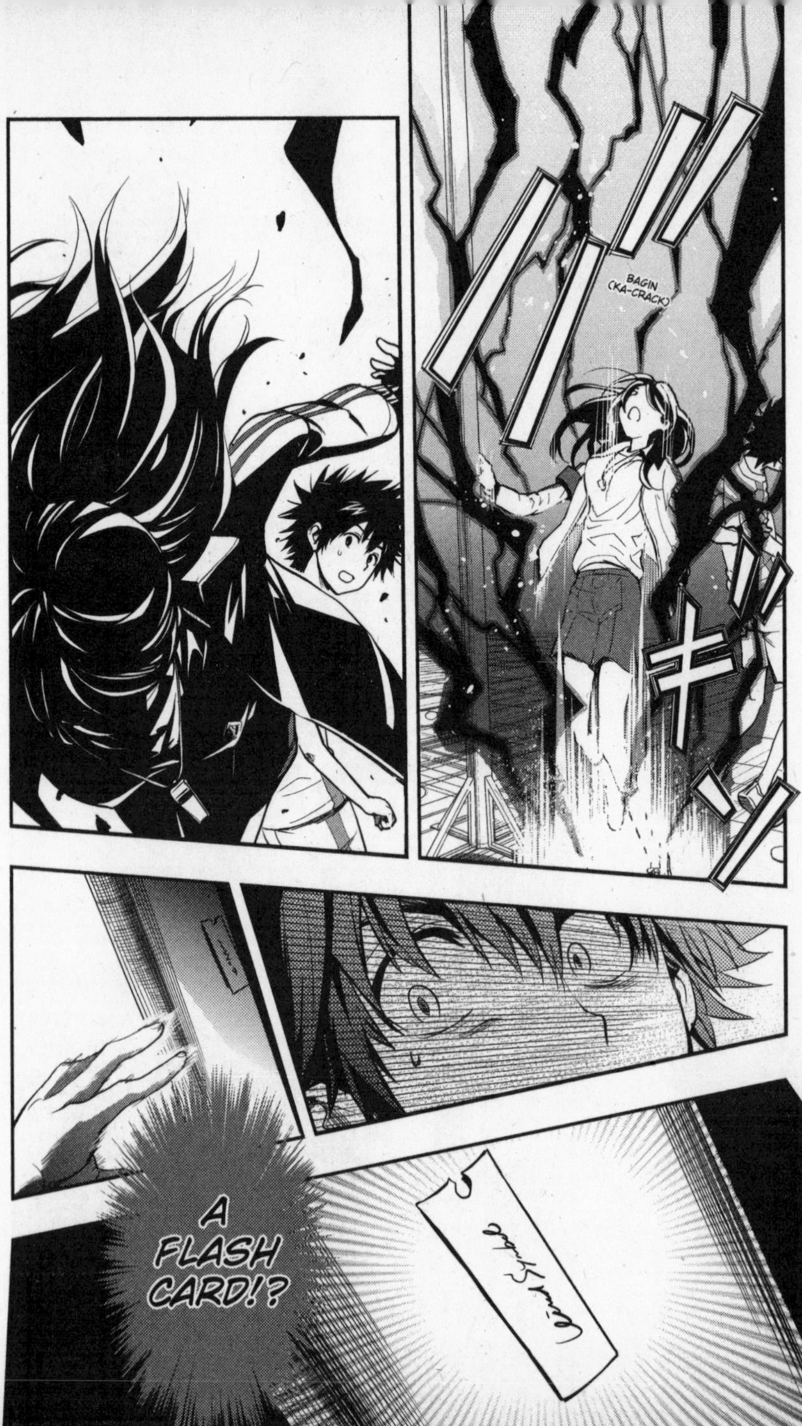
BAGIN
(KA-CRACK)
A FLASH CARD!?
Wind Symbol

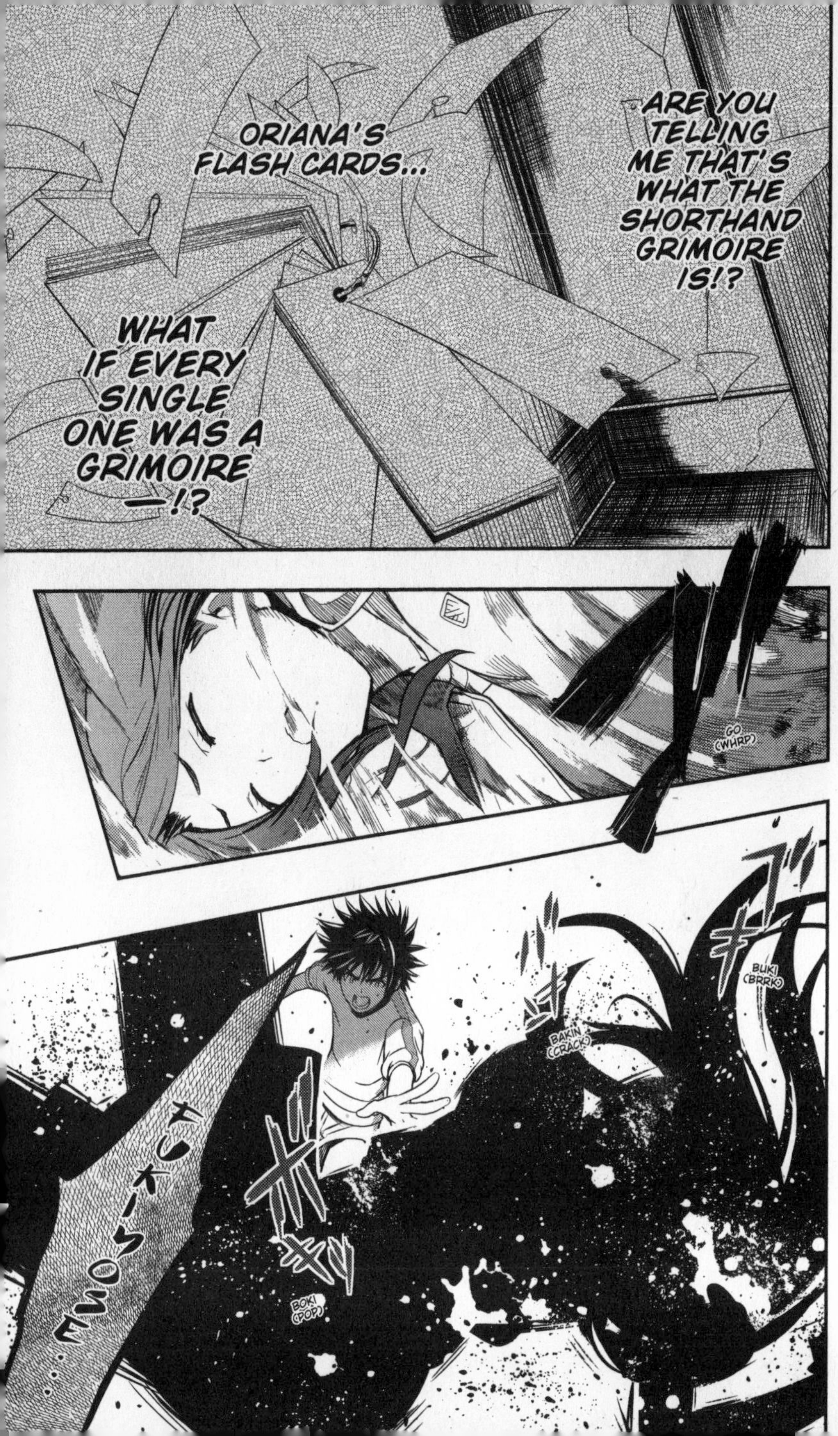
ARE YOU TELLING ME THAT'S WHAT THE SHORTHAND GRIMOIRE IS!?
ORIANA'S FLASH CARDS...
WHAT IF EVERY SINGLE ONE WAS A GRIMOIRE—!?
GO (WHRP)
BUKI (BRRK)
BAKIN (CRACK)
BOKI (POP)

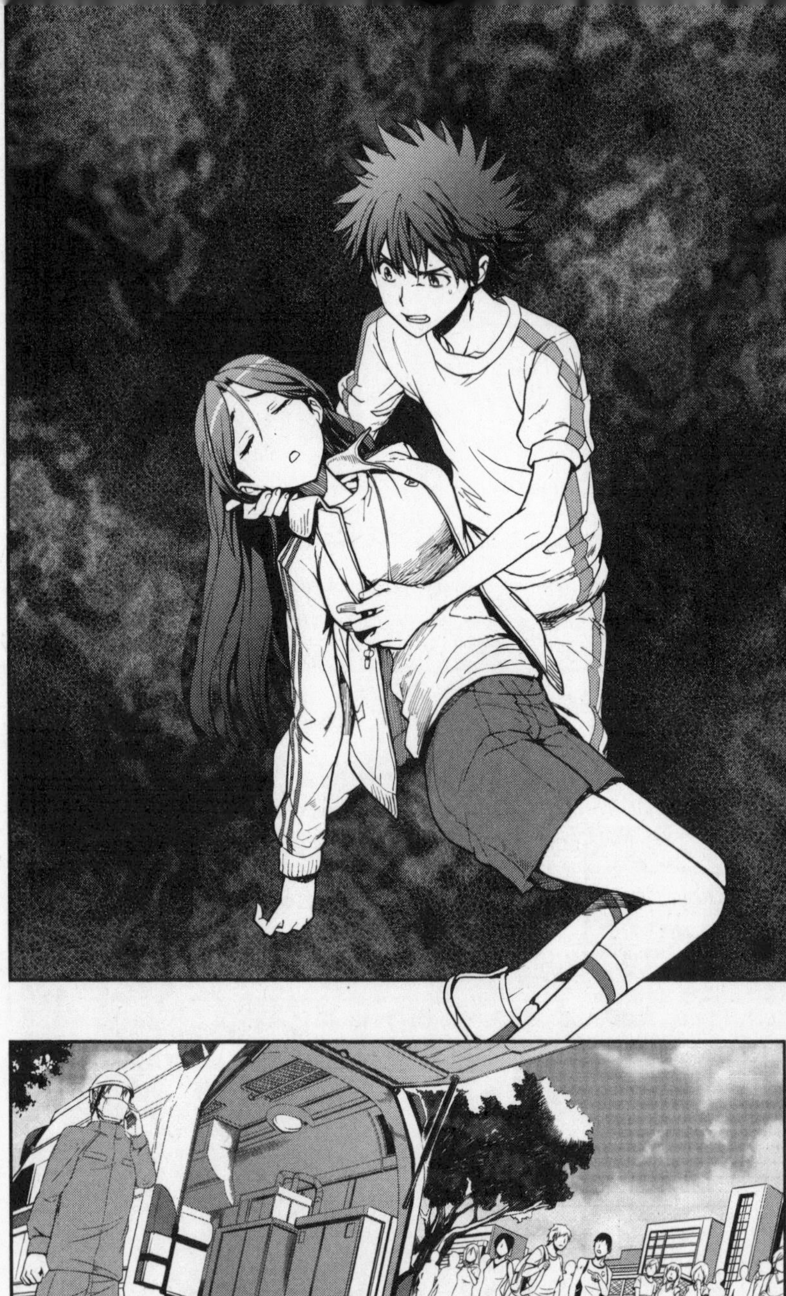

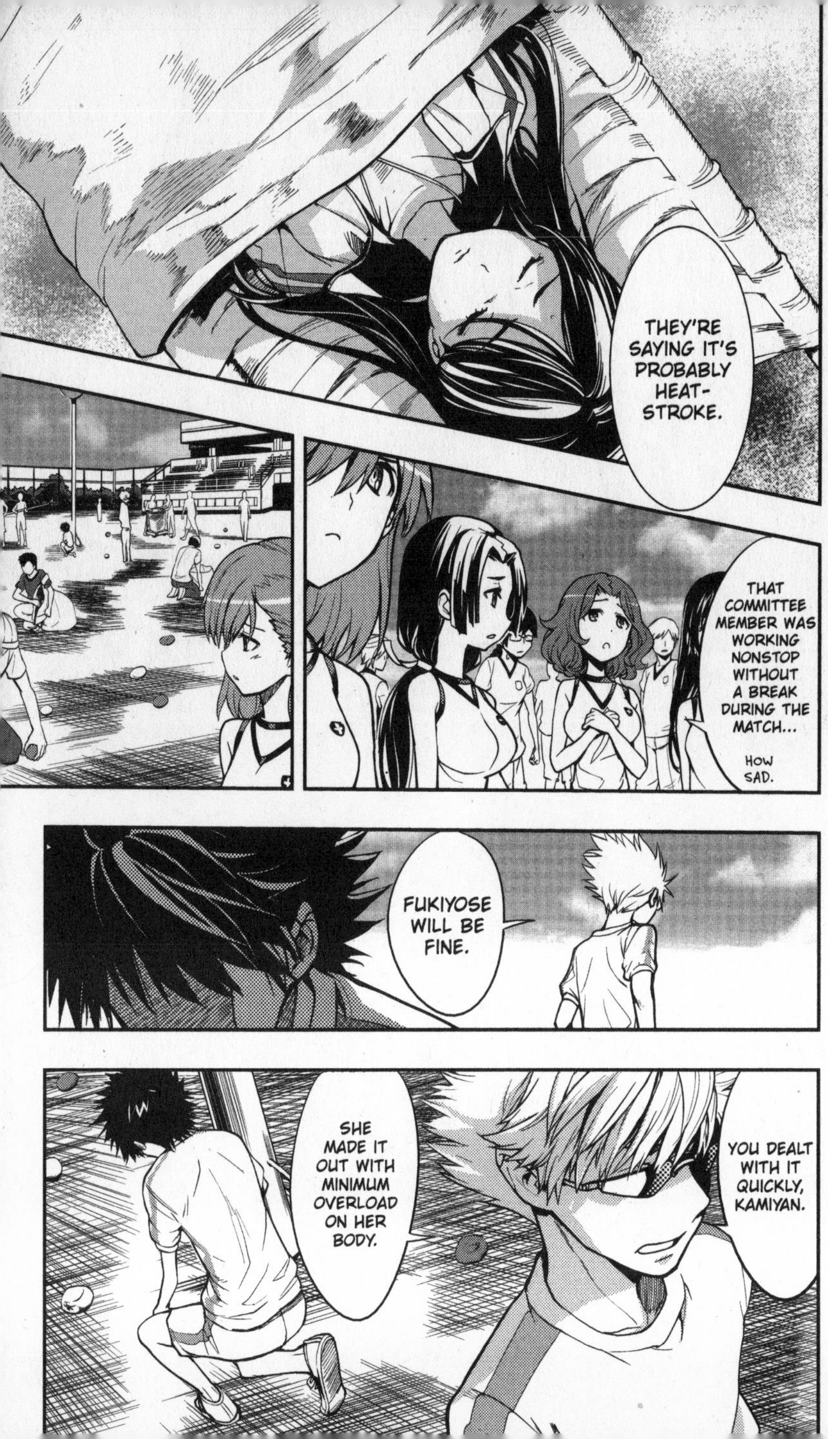
THEY'RE SAYING IT'S PROBABLY HEAT-STROKE.
THAT COMMITTEE MEMBER WAS WORKING NONSTOP WITHOUT A BREAK DURING THE MATCH...
HOW SAD.
FUKIYOSE WILL BE FINE.
YOU DEALT WITH IT QUICKLY, KAMIYAN.
SHE MADE IT OUT WITH MINIMUM OVERLOAD ON HER BODY.

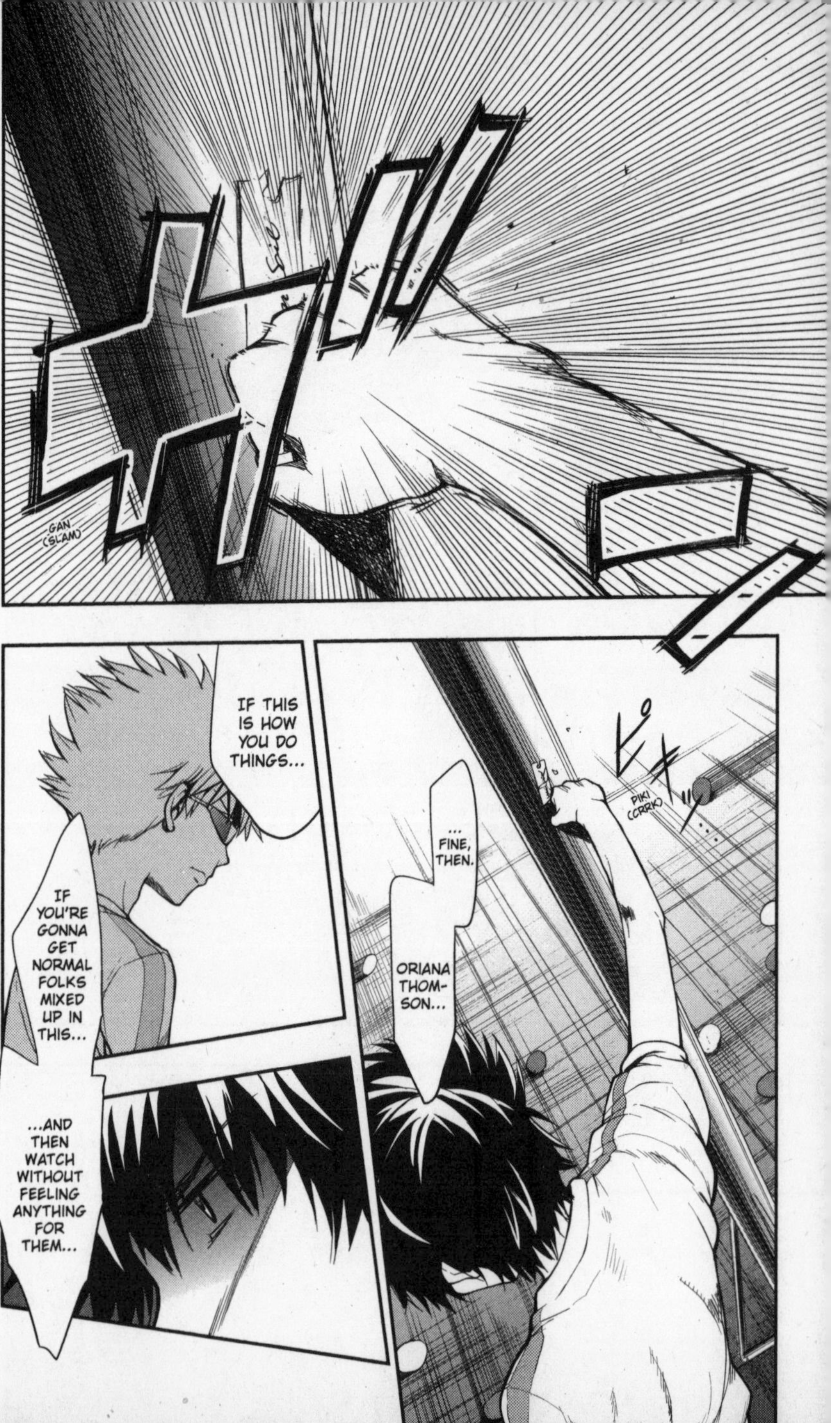
GAN (SLAM)
PIKI (CRRK)
... FINE, THEN.
ORIANA THOMSON...
IF THIS IS HOW YOU DO THINGS...
IF YOU'RE GONNA GET NORMAL FOLKS MIXED UP IN THIS...
...AND THEN WATCH WITHOUT FEELING ANYTHING FOR THEM...

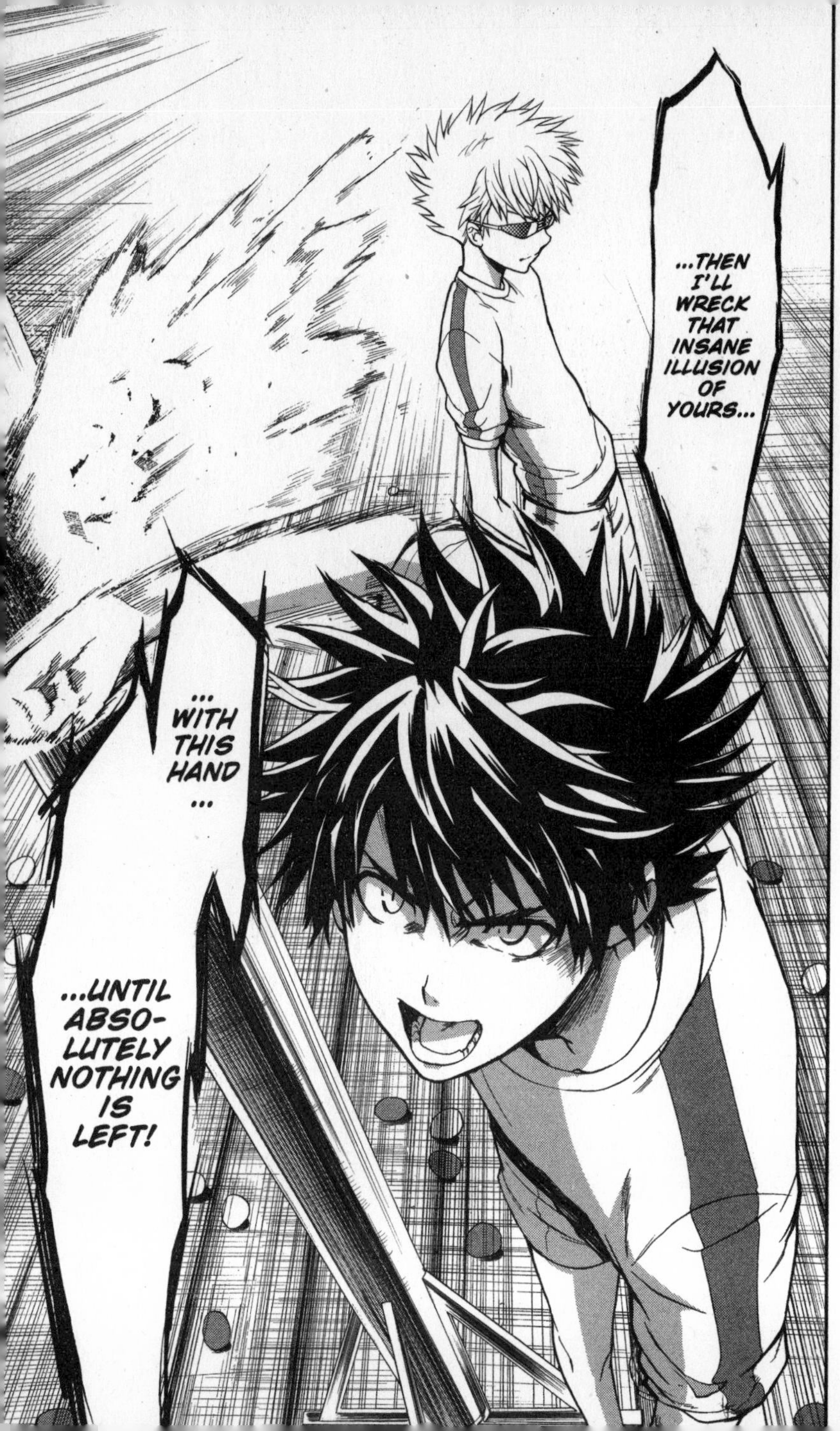
...THEN I'LL WRECK THAT INSANE ILLUSION OF YOURS...
...WITH THIS HAND...
...UNTIL ABSO-LUTELY NOTHING IS LEFT!

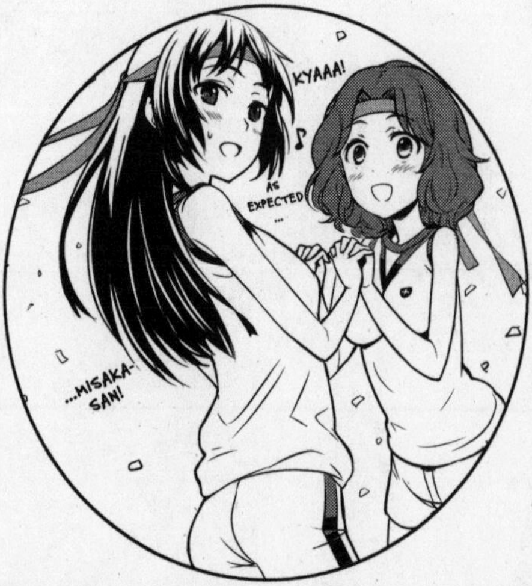
KYAAA!
AS EXPECTED ...
...MISAKA-SAN!

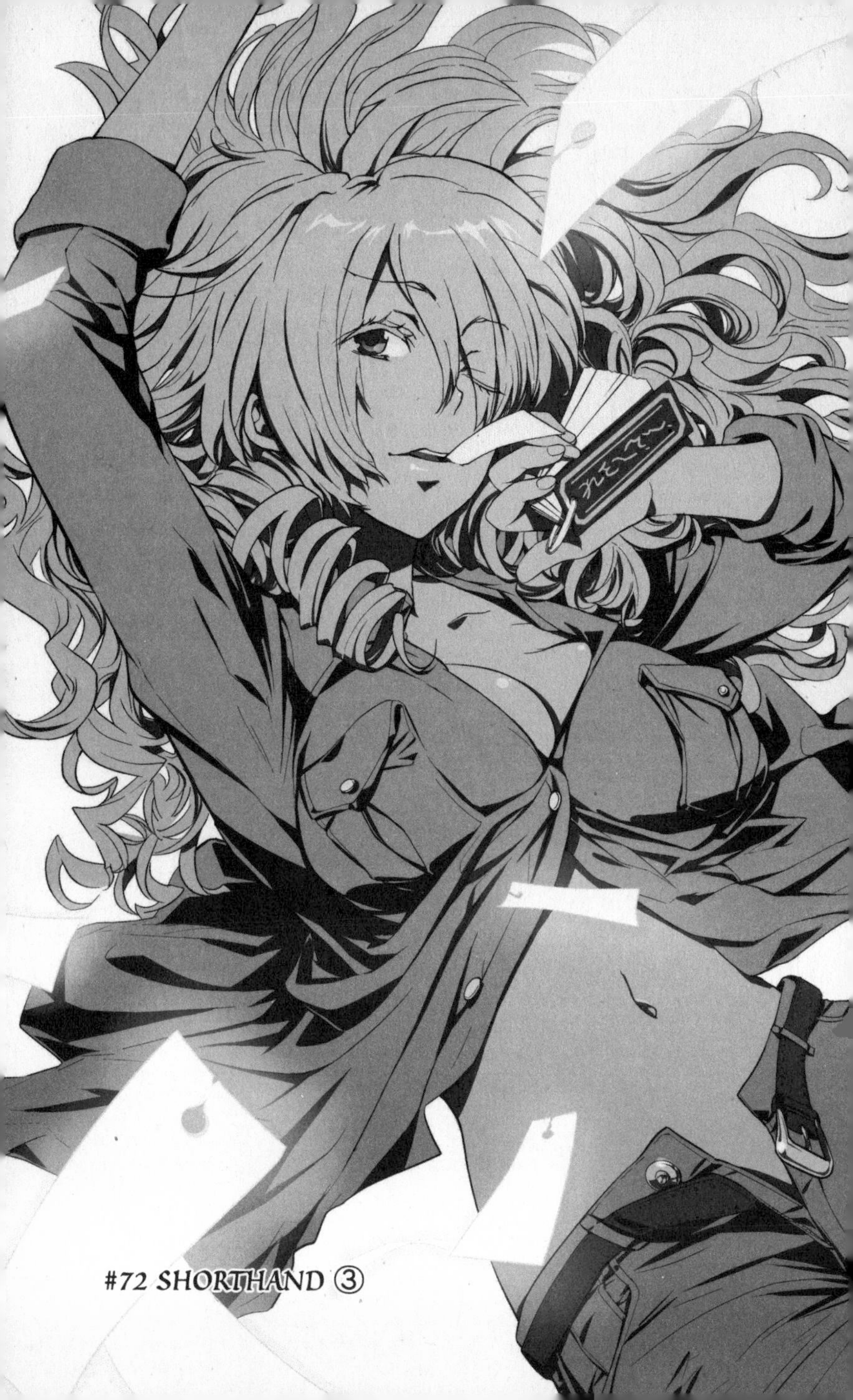

#72 SHORTHAND ③

A Certain Magical Index

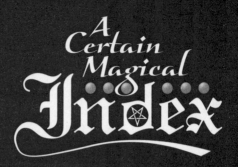

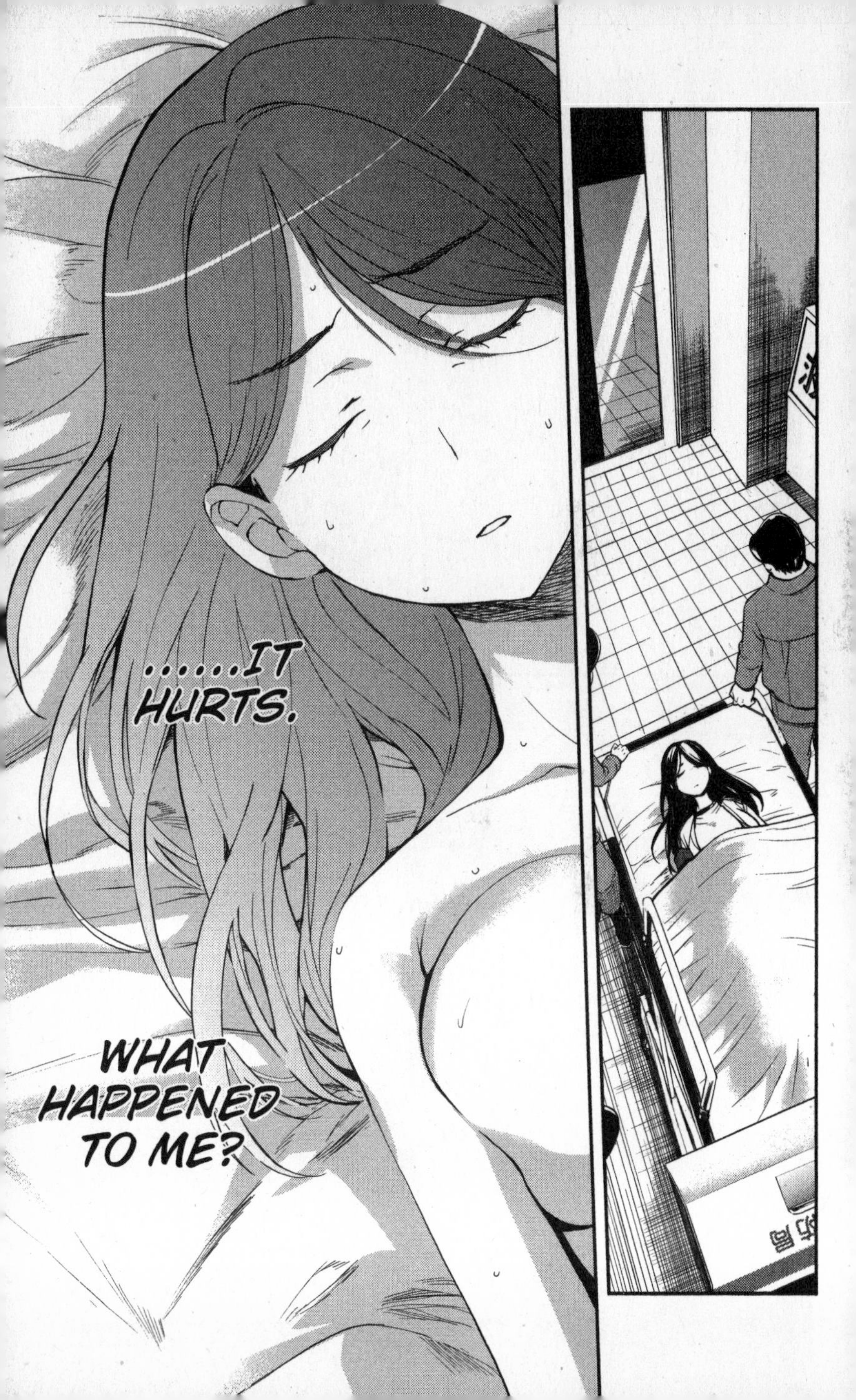
......IT HURTS.
WHAT HAPPENED TO ME?

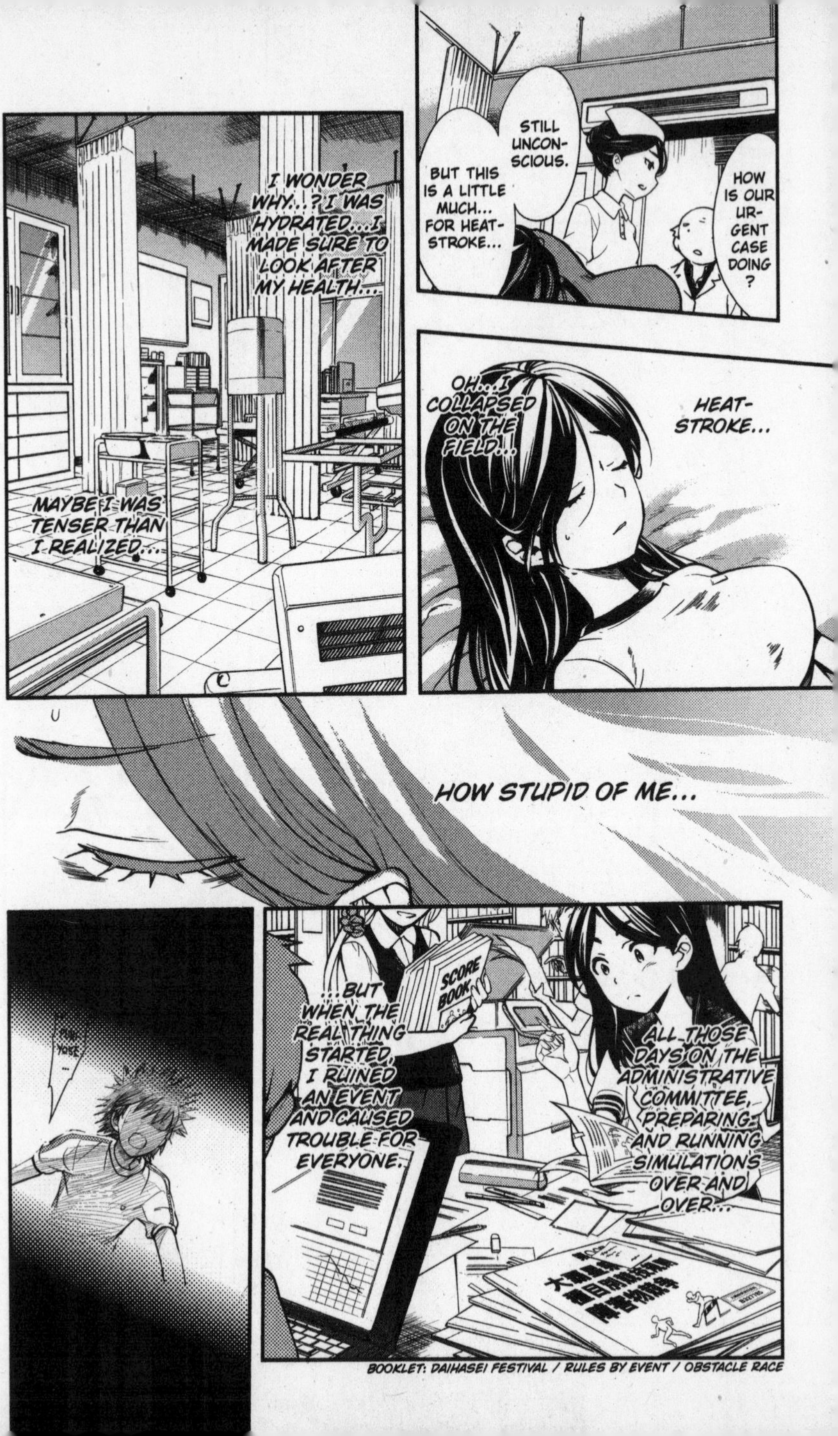
HOW IS OUR URGENT CASE DOING?
STILL UNCONSCIOUS.
BUT THIS IS A LITTLE MUCH... FOR HEATSTROKE...
HEATSTROKE...
OH... I COLLAPSED ON THE FIELD...
I WONDER WHY...? I WAS HYDRATED... I MADE SURE TO LOOK AFTER MY HEALTH...
MAYBE I WAS TENSER THAN I REALIZED...
HOW STUPID OF ME...
ALL THOSE DAYS ON THE ADMINISTRATIVE COMMITTEE, PREPARING AND RUNNING SIMULATIONS OVER AND OVER...
SCORE BOOK
...BUT WHEN THE REAL THING STARTED, I RUINED AN EVENT AND CAUSED TROUBLE FOR EVERYONE.
BOOKLET: DAIHASEI FESTIVAL / RULES BY EVENT / OBSTACLE RACE

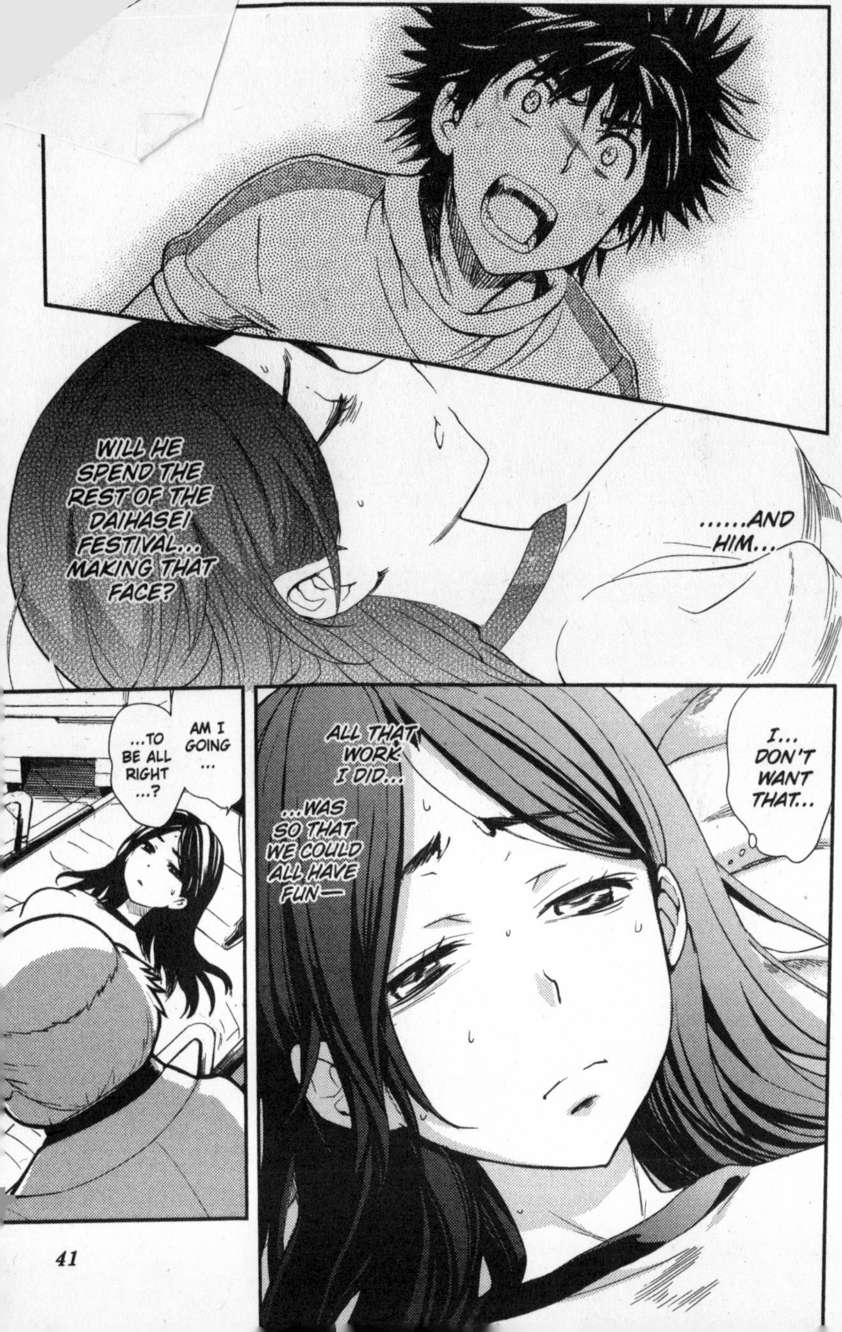

......AND HIM...
WILL HE SPEND THE REST OF THE DAIHASEI FESTIVAL... MAKING THAT FACE?
I... DON'T WANT THAT...
ALL THAT WORK I DID...
...WAS SO THAT WE COULD ALL HAVE FUN—
AM I GOING ...
...TO BE ALL RIGHT ...?

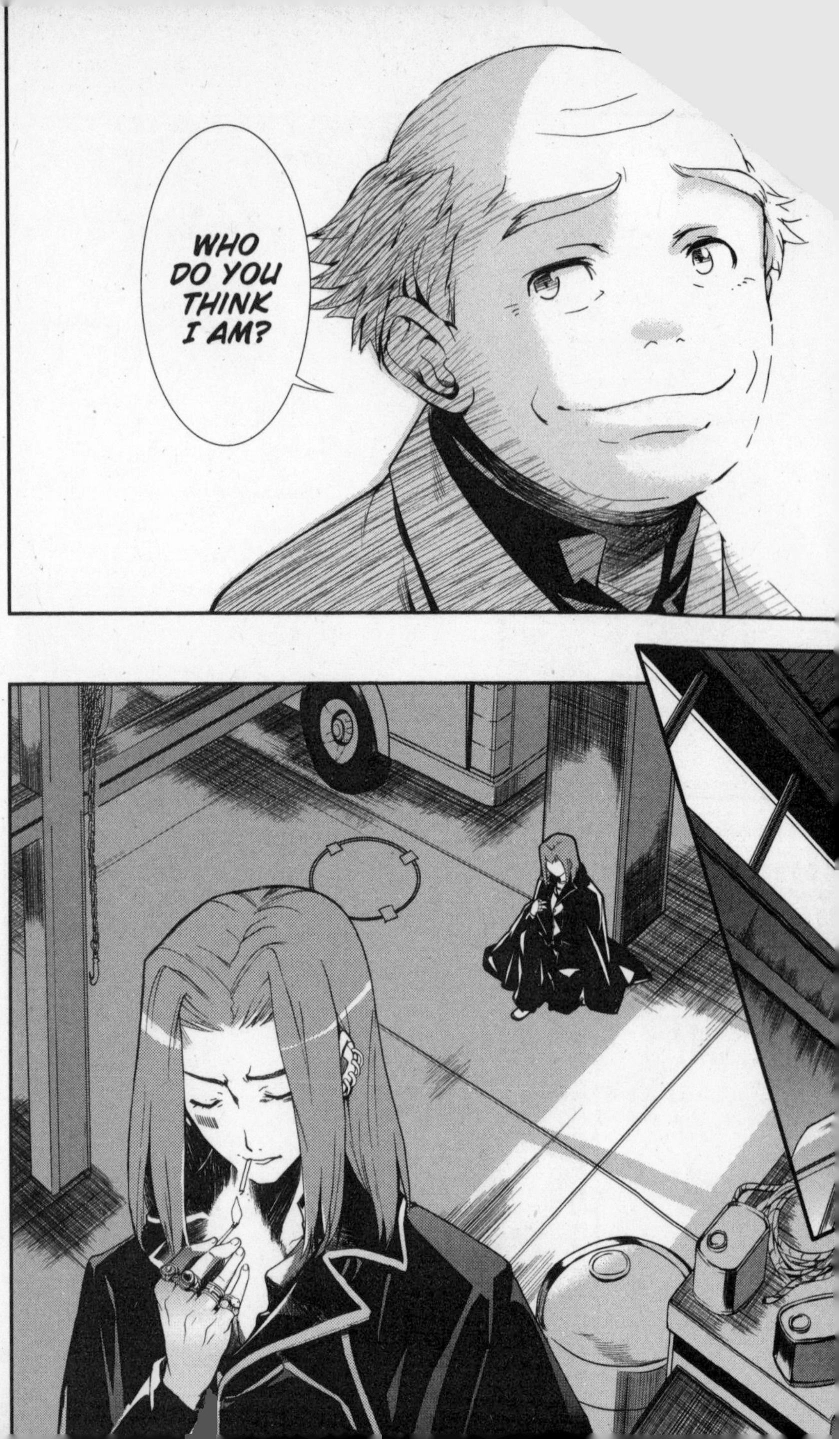
WHO DO YOU THINK I AM?

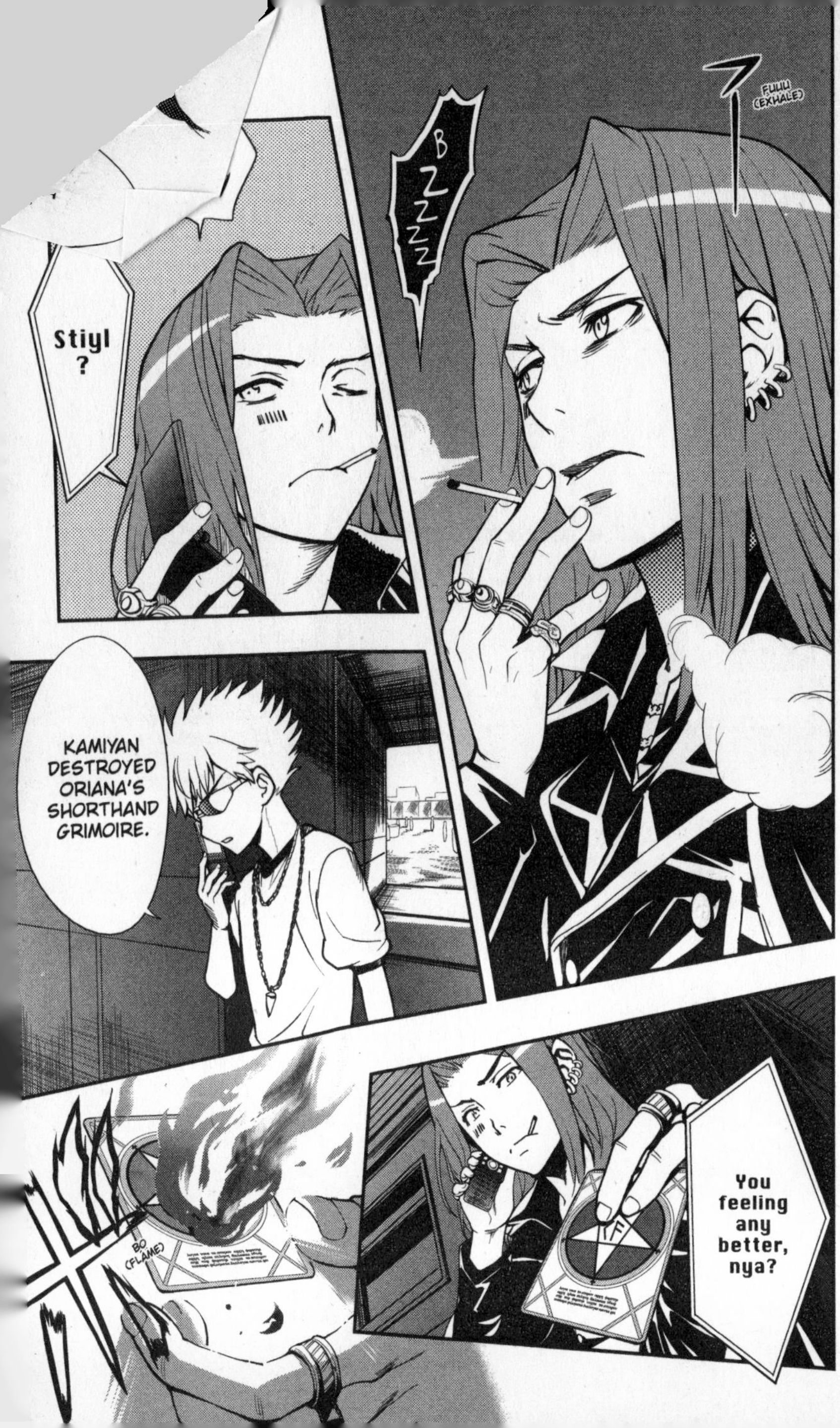
FUUU (EXHALE)
BZZZZ
Stiyl ?
KAMIYAN DESTROYED ORIANA'S SHORTHAND GRIMOIRE.
You feeling any better, nya?
BO (FLAME)

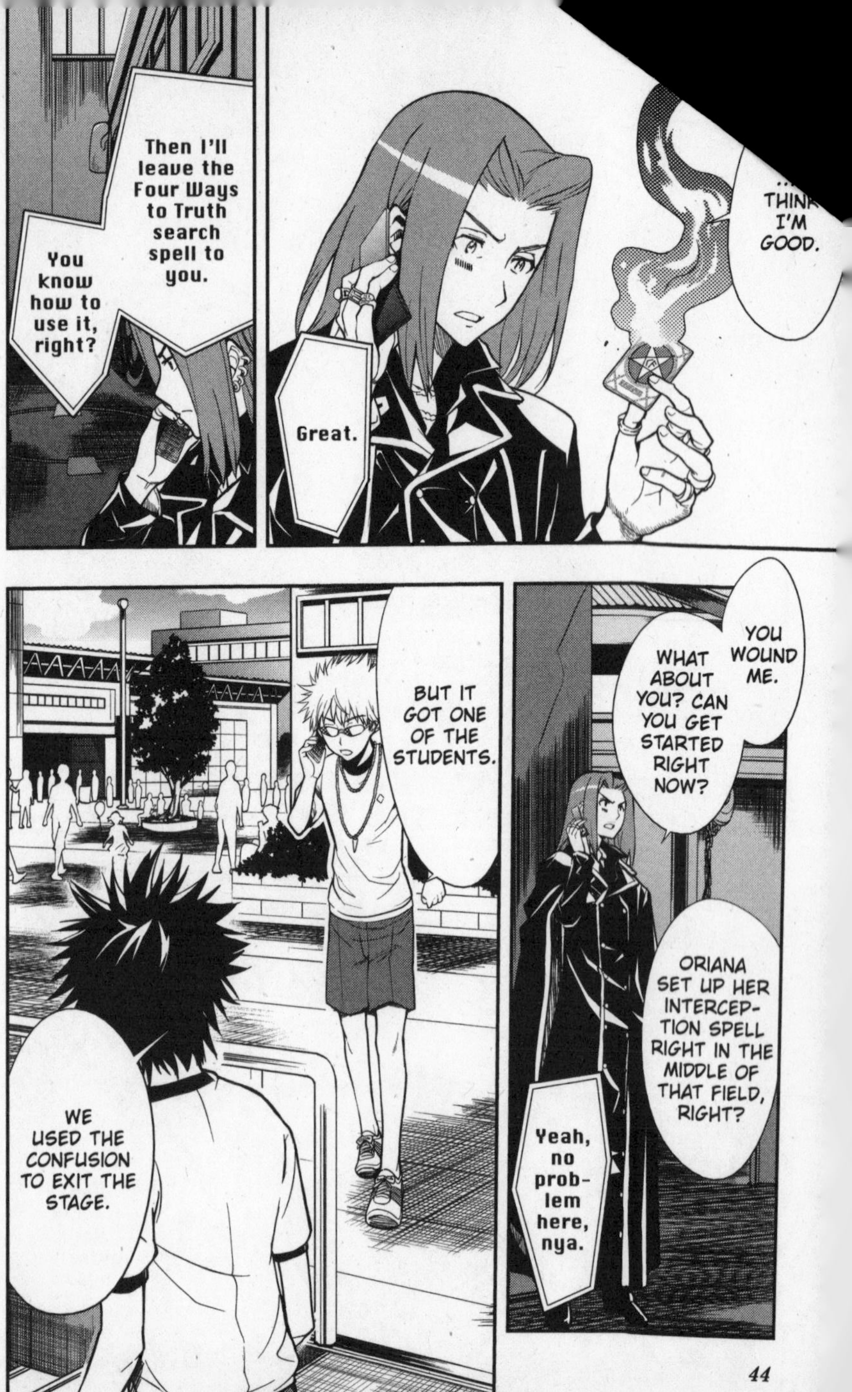

THIN I'M GOOD.
Great.
Then I'll leave the Four Ways to Truth search spell to you.
You know how to use it, right?
YOU WOUND ME.
WHAT ABOUT YOU? CAN YOU GET STARTED RIGHT NOW?
ORIANA SET UP HER INTERCEPTION SPELL RIGHT IN THE MIDDLE OF THAT FIELD, RIGHT?
Yeah, no problem here, nya.
BUT IT GOT ONE OF THE STUDENTS.
WE USED THE CONFUSION TO EXIT THE STAGE.

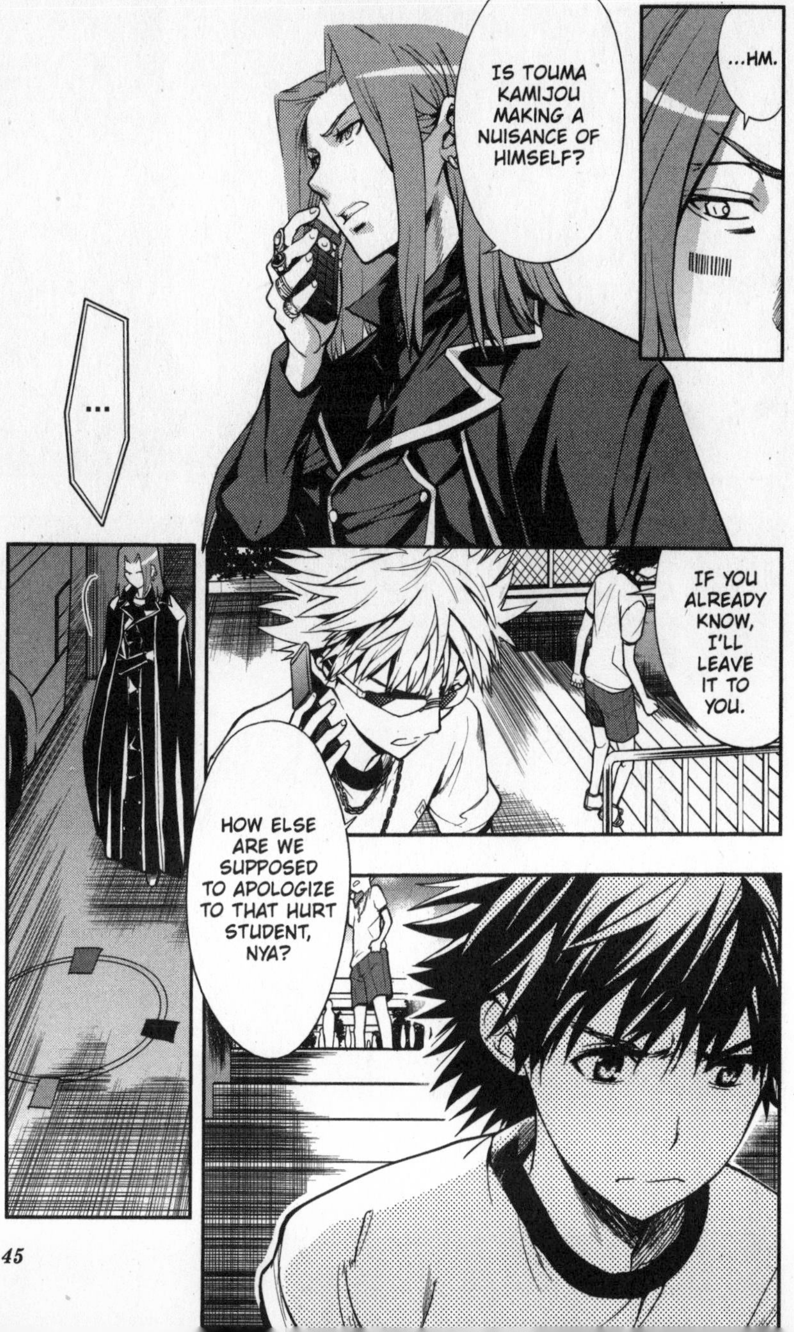
...HM.
IS TOUMA KAMIJOU MAKING A NUISANCE OF HIMSELF?
...
IF YOU ALREADY KNOW, I'LL LEAVE IT TO YOU.
HOW ELSE ARE WE SUPPOSED TO APOLOGIZE TO THAT HURT STUDENT, NYA?

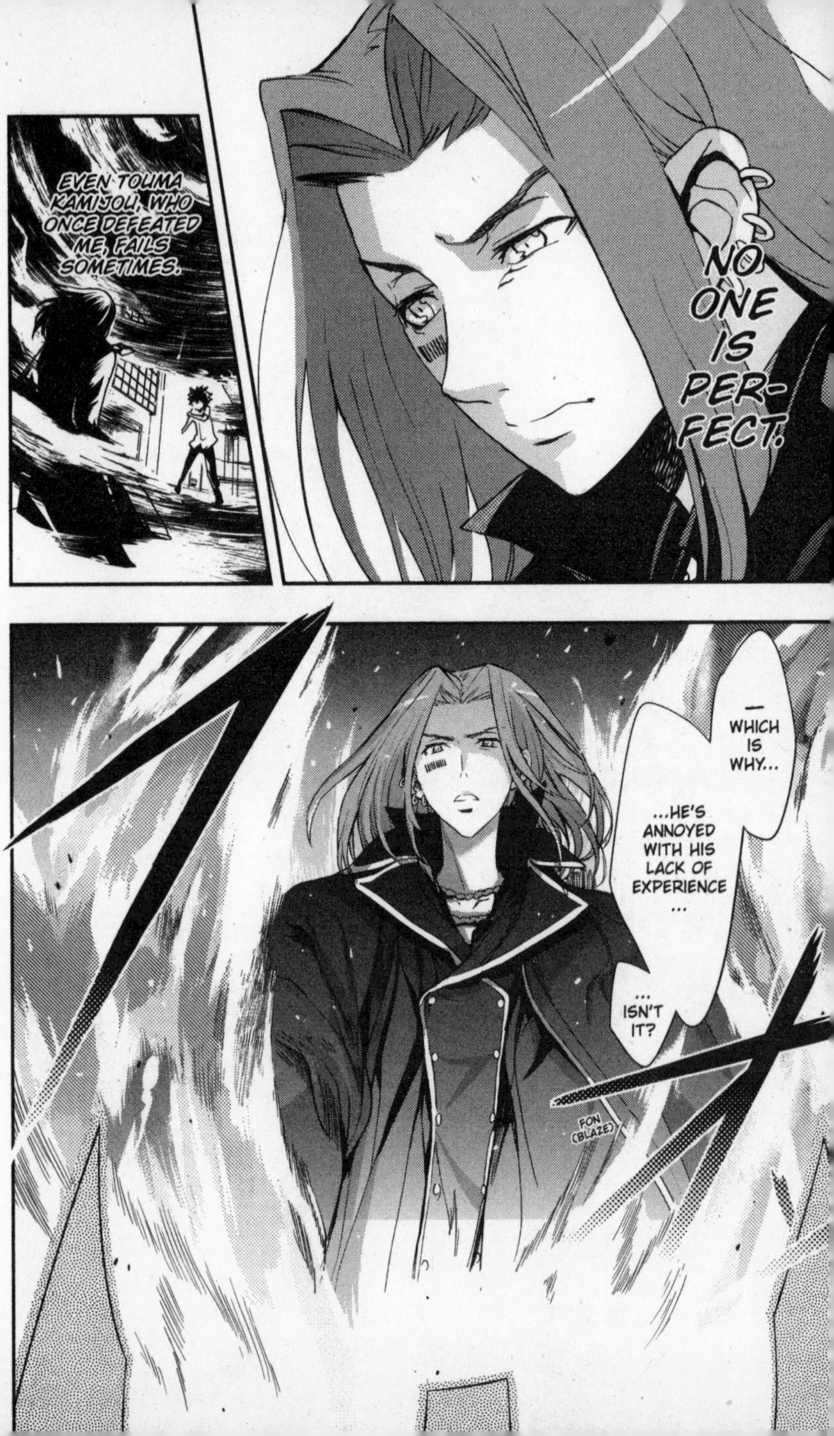
NO ONE IS PER-FECT.
EVEN TOUMA KAMIJOU, WHO ONCE DEFEATED ME, FAILS SOMETIMES.
—WHICH IS WHY...
...HE'S ANNOYED WITH HIS LACK OF EXPERIENCE...
...ISN'T IT?
FON (BLAZE)

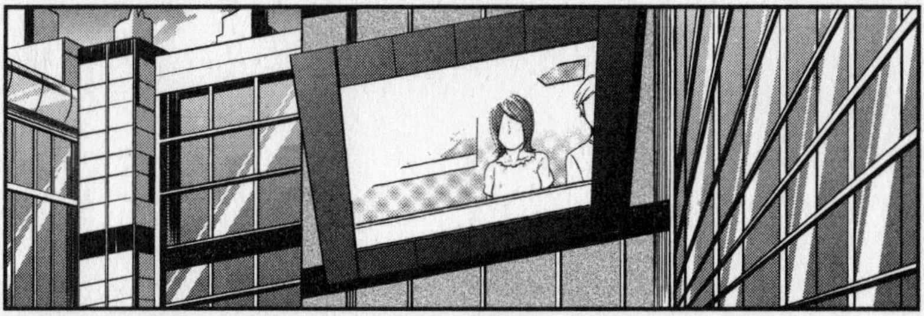

HEADLINES: STAR PLAYER EVENT DELAYED / ONE FEMALE STUDENT UNCONSCIOUS

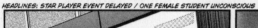

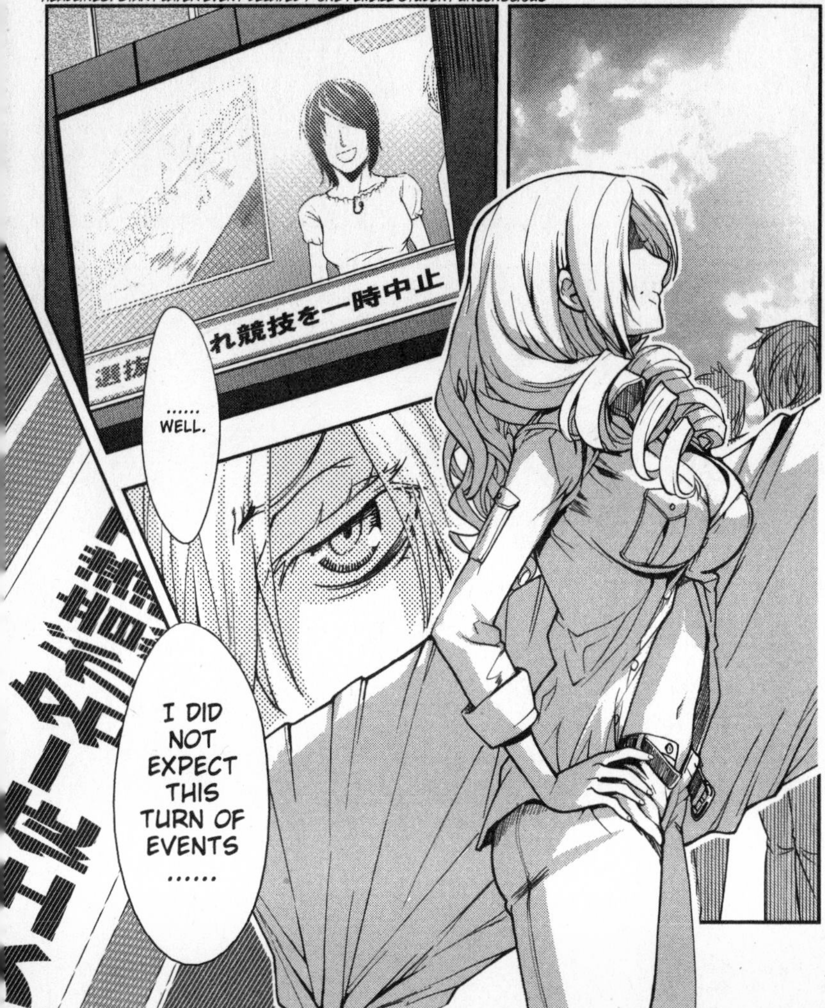
選抜
れ競技を一時中止
......WELL.
I DID NOT EXPECT THIS TURN OF EVENTS ......

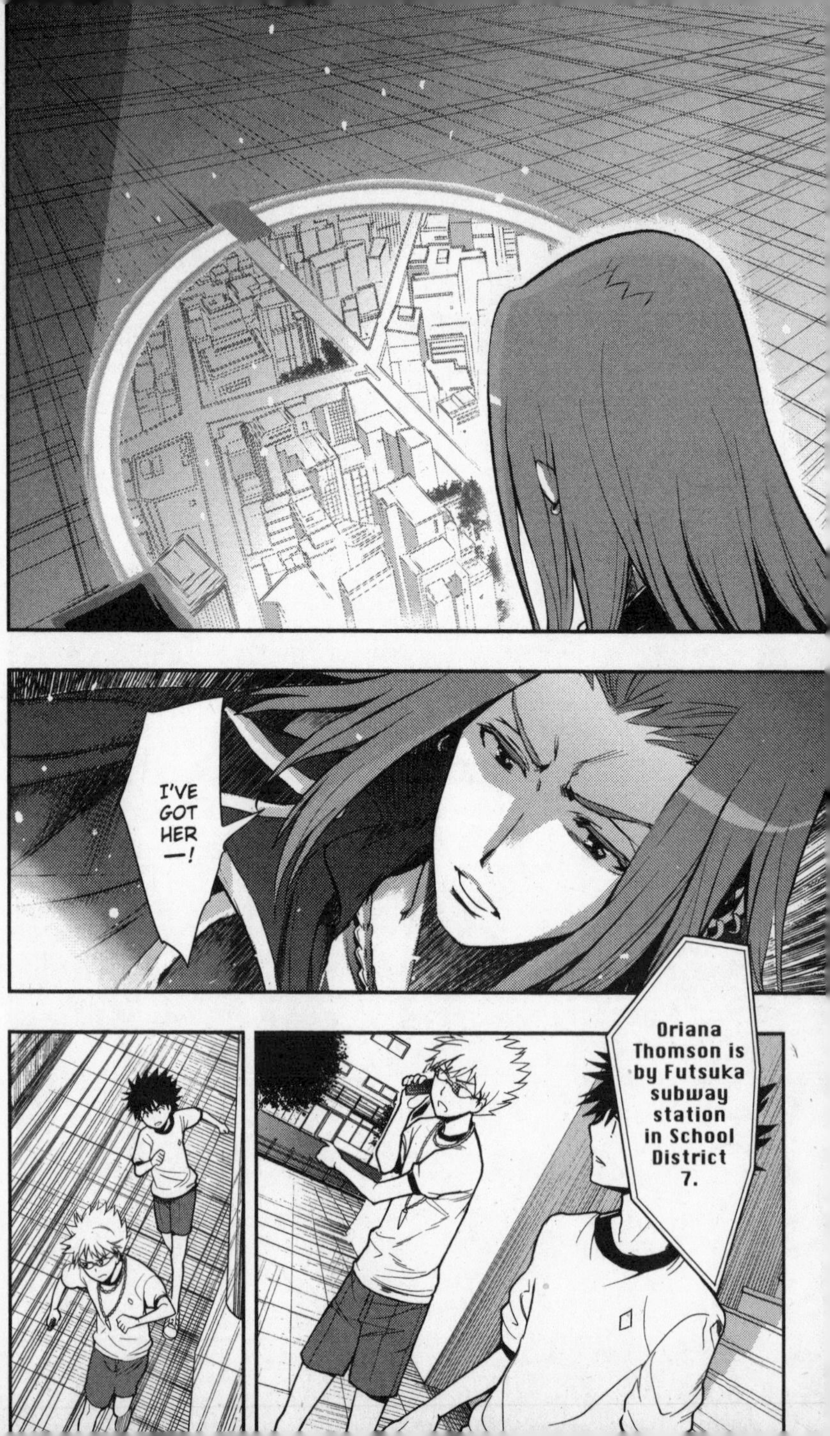
I'VE GOT HER —!
Oriana Thomson is by Futsuka subway station in School District 7.

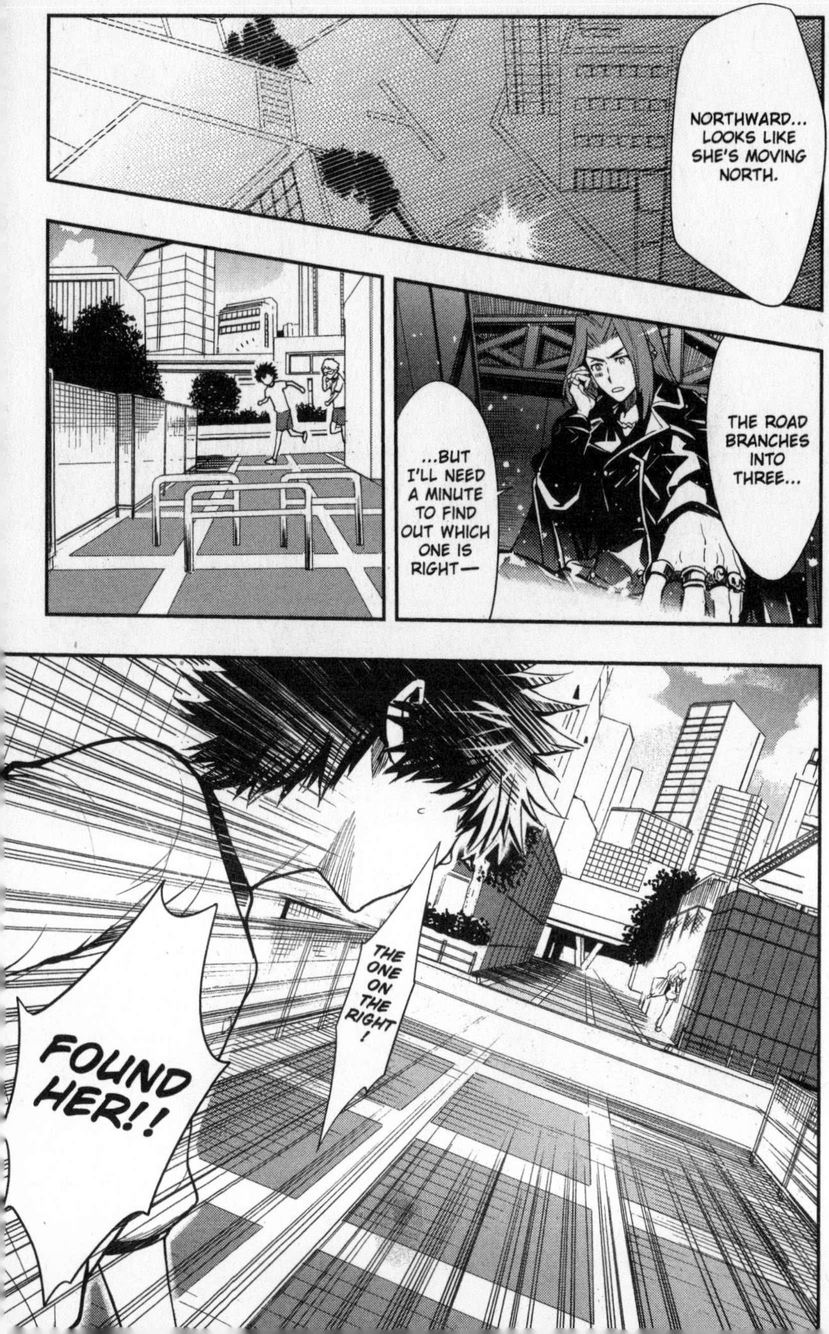
NORTHWARD... LOOKS LIKE SHE'S MOVING NORTH.
THE ROAD BRANCHES INTO THREE...
...BUT I'LL NEED A MINUTE TO FIND OUT WHICH ONE IS RIGHT—
THE ONE ON THE RIGHT!
FOUND HER!!

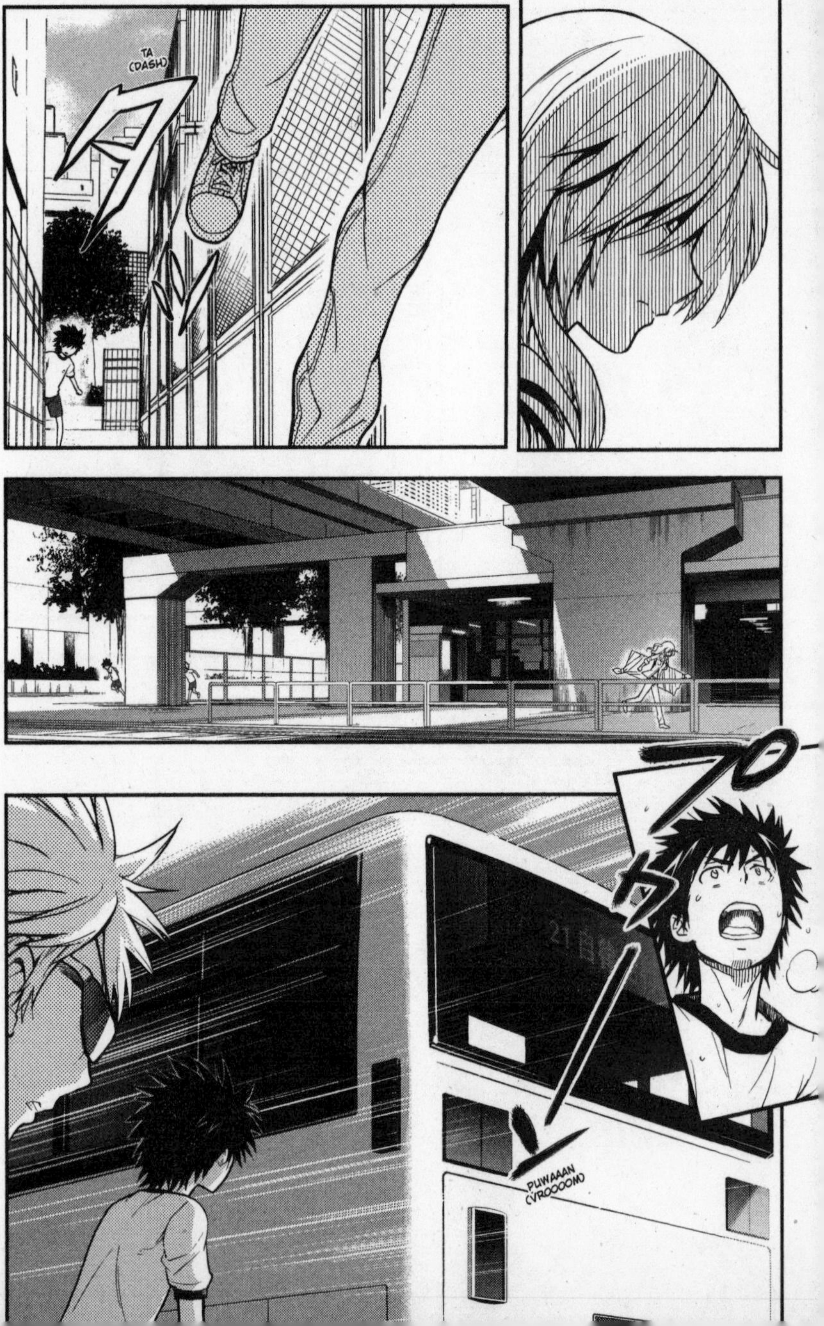
TA
(DASH)
PUWAAAN
(VROOOOM)

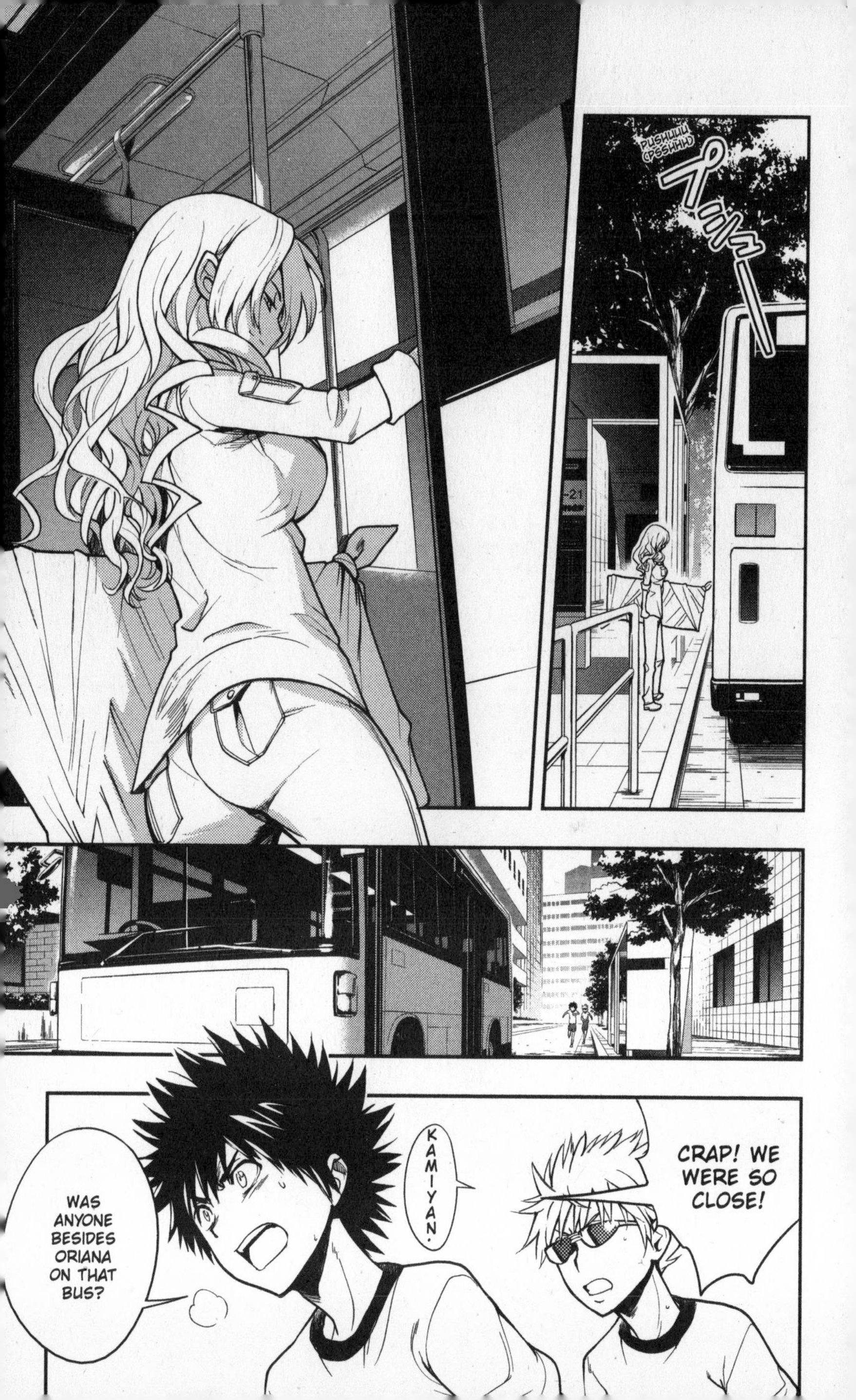
PUSHUUU (PSSHHH)
CRAP! WE WERE SO CLOSE!
KAMIYAN.
WAS ANYONE BESIDES ORIANA ON THAT BUS?

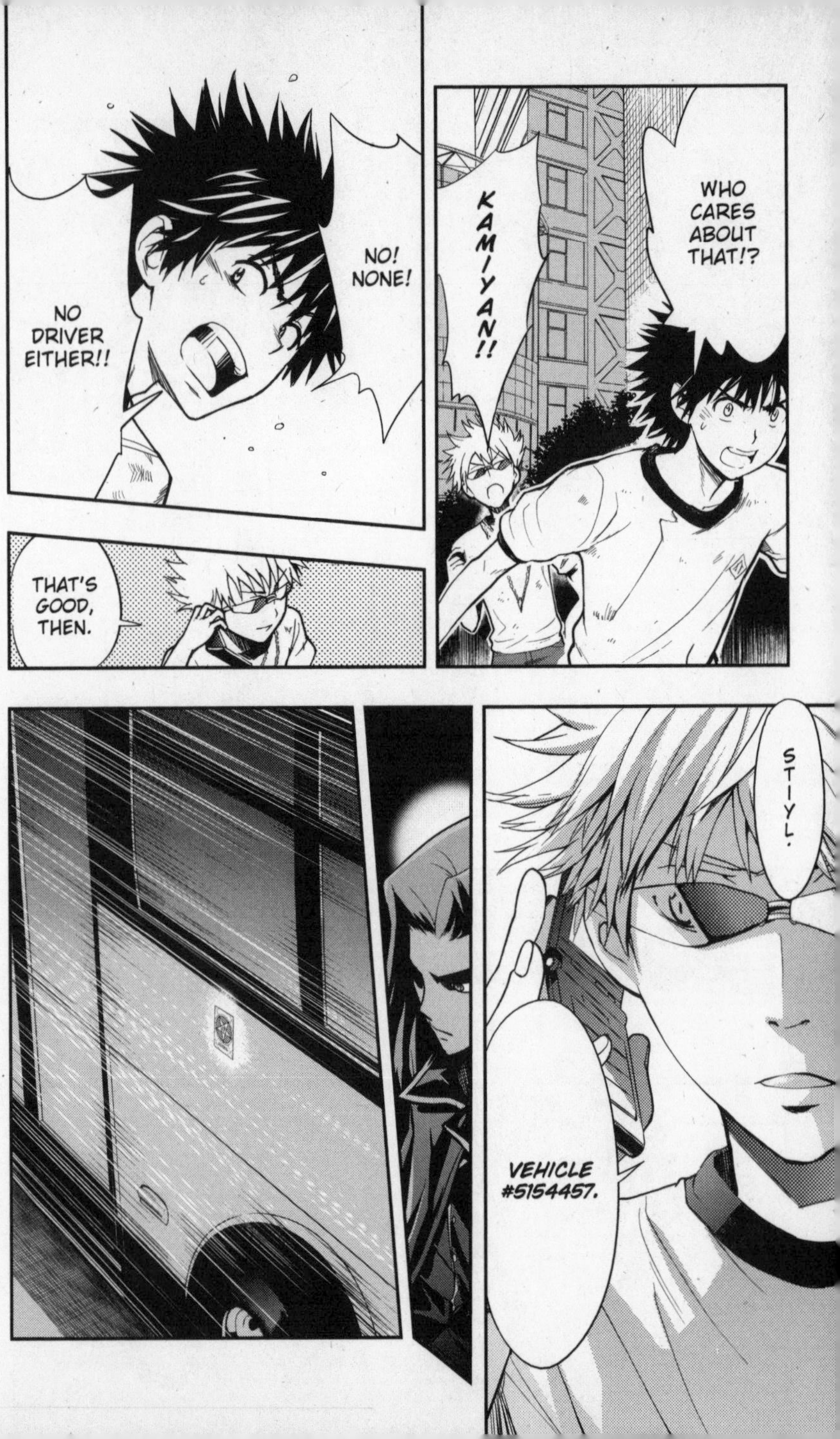
WHO CARES ABOUT THAT!?
KAMIYAN!!
NO! NONE!
NO DRIVER EITHER!!
THAT'S GOOD, THEN.
STIYL.
VEHICLE #5154457.

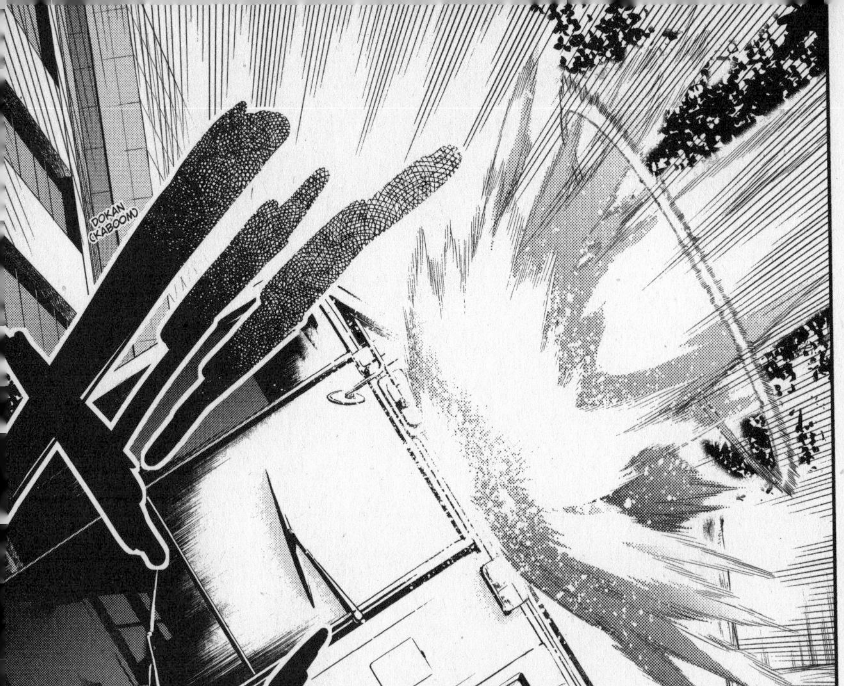
DOKAN
(KABOOM)
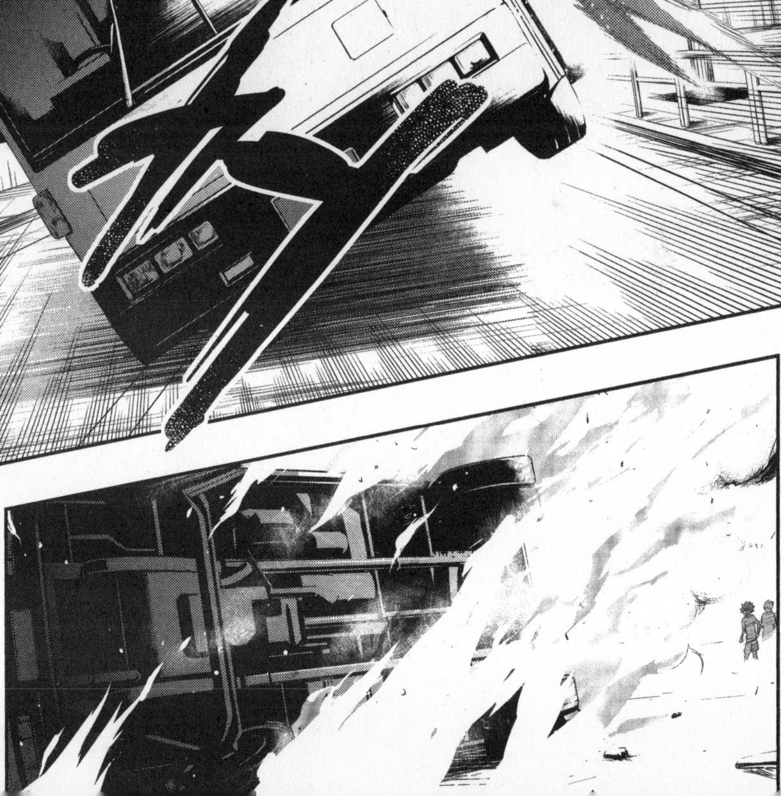

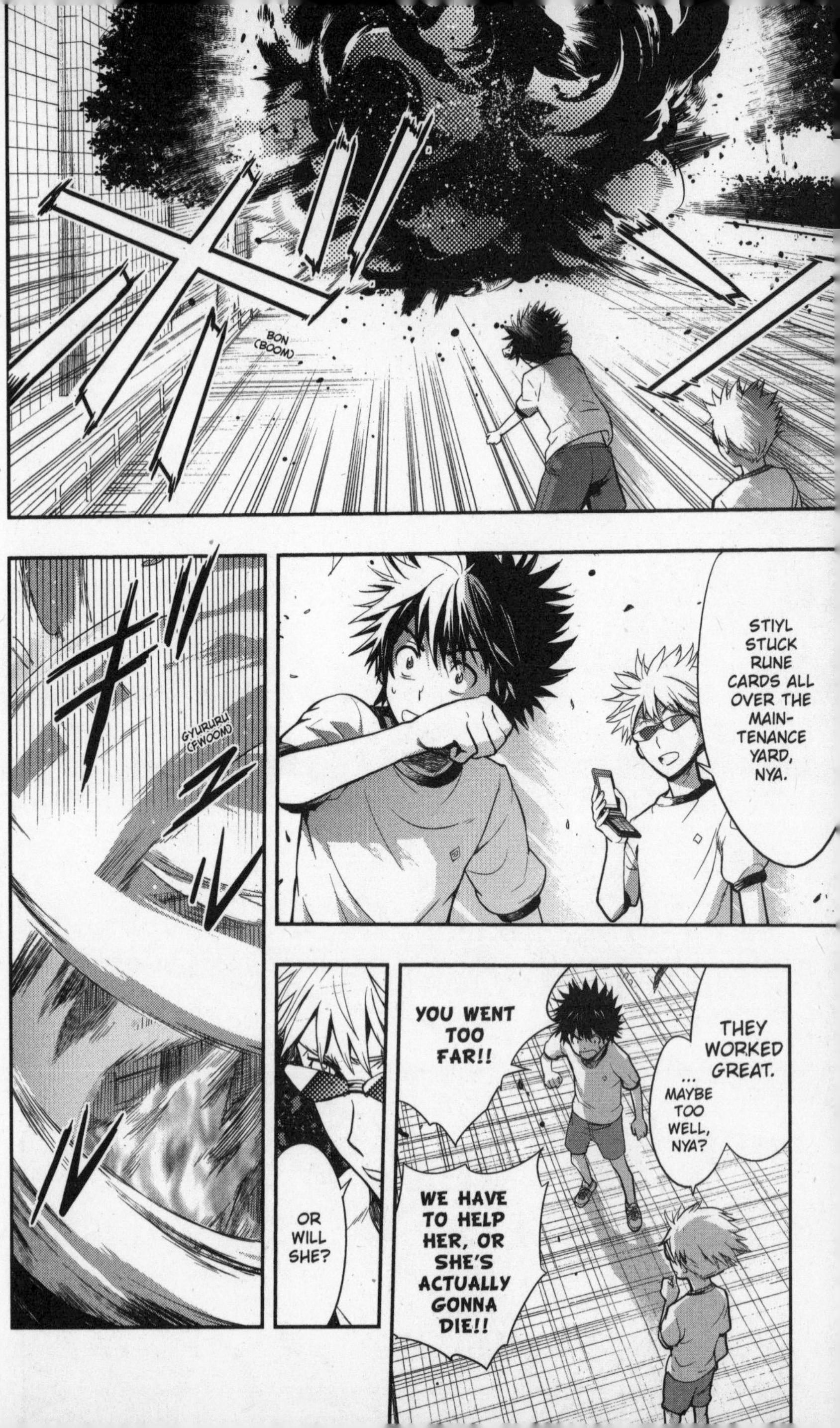
BON (BOOM)
STIYL STUCK RUNE CARDS ALL OVER THE MAINTENANCE YARD, NYA.
THEY WORKED GREAT.
... MAYBE TOO WELL, NYA?
YOU WENT TOO FAR!!
WE HAVE TO HELP HER, OR SHE'S ACTUALLY GONNA DIE!!
OR WILL SHE?
GYURURU (FWOOM)

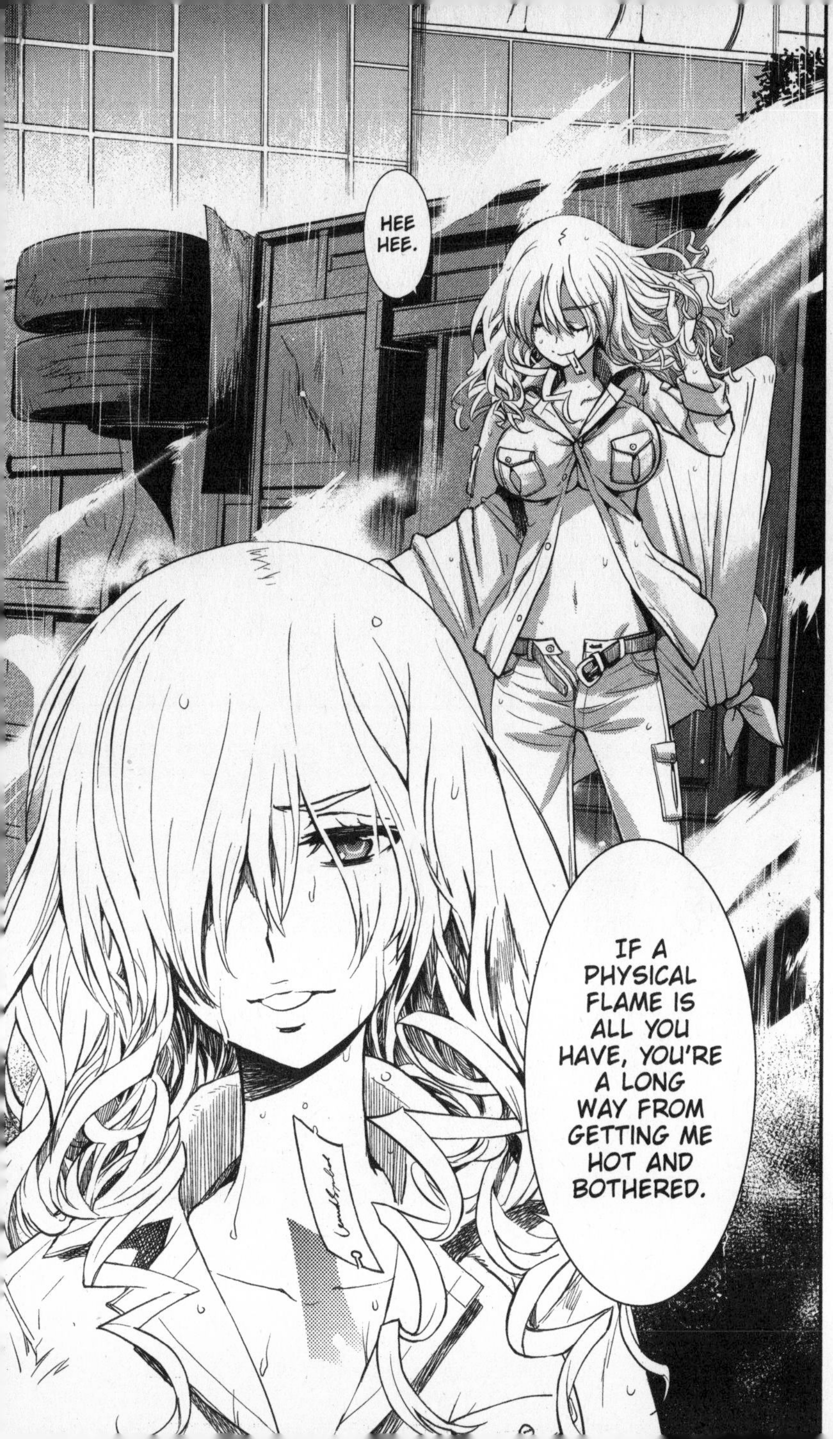
HEE HEE.
IF A PHYSICAL FLAME IS ALL YOU HAVE, YOU'RE A LONG WAY FROM GETTING ME HOT AND BOTHERED.

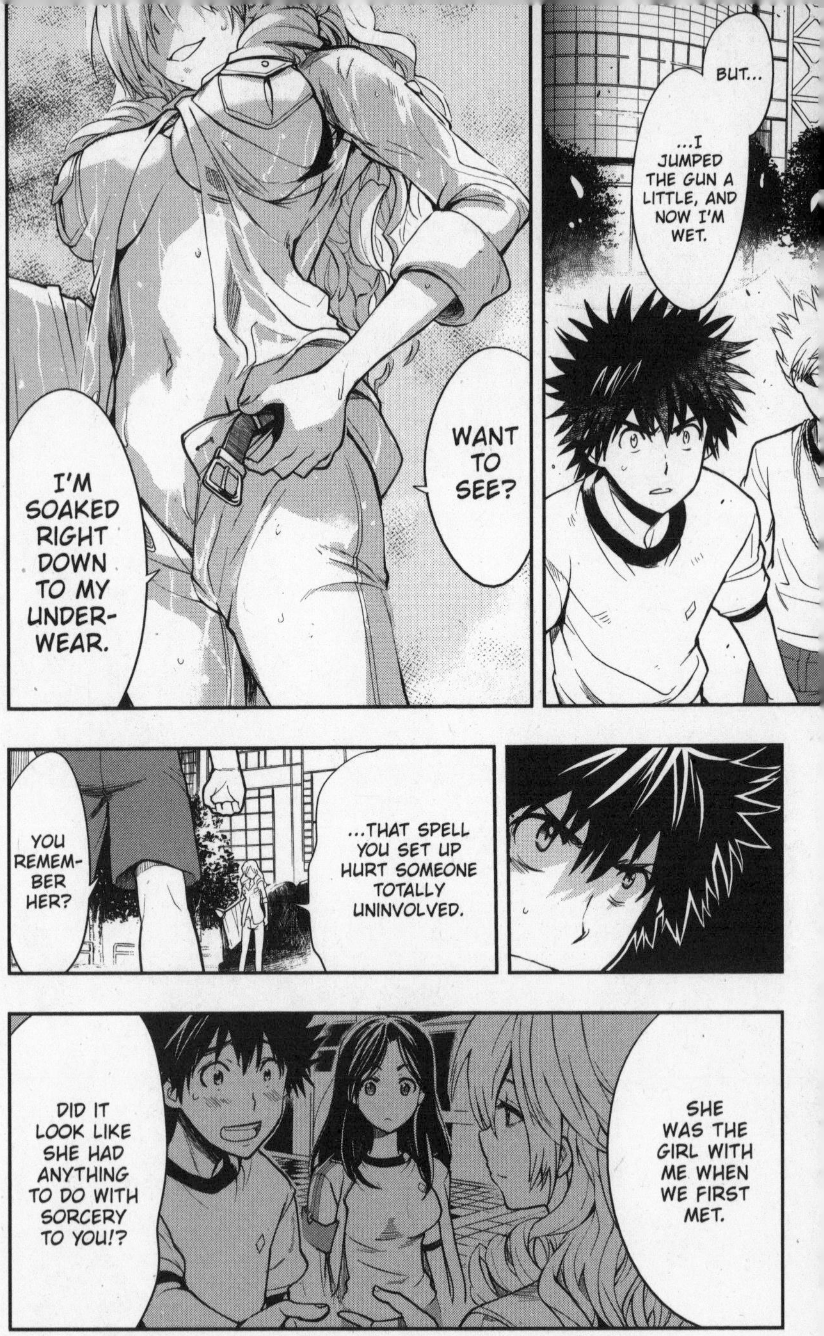
BUT...
...I JUMPED THE GUN A LITTLE, AND NOW I'M WET.
WANT TO SEE?
I'M SOAKED RIGHT DOWN TO MY UNDER-WEAR.
...THAT SPELL YOU SET UP HURT SOMEONE TOTALLY UNINVOLVED.
YOU REMEM-BER HER?
SHE WAS THE GIRL WITH ME WHEN WE FIRST MET.
DID IT LOOK LIKE SHE HAD ANYTHING TO DO WITH SORCERY TO YOU!?

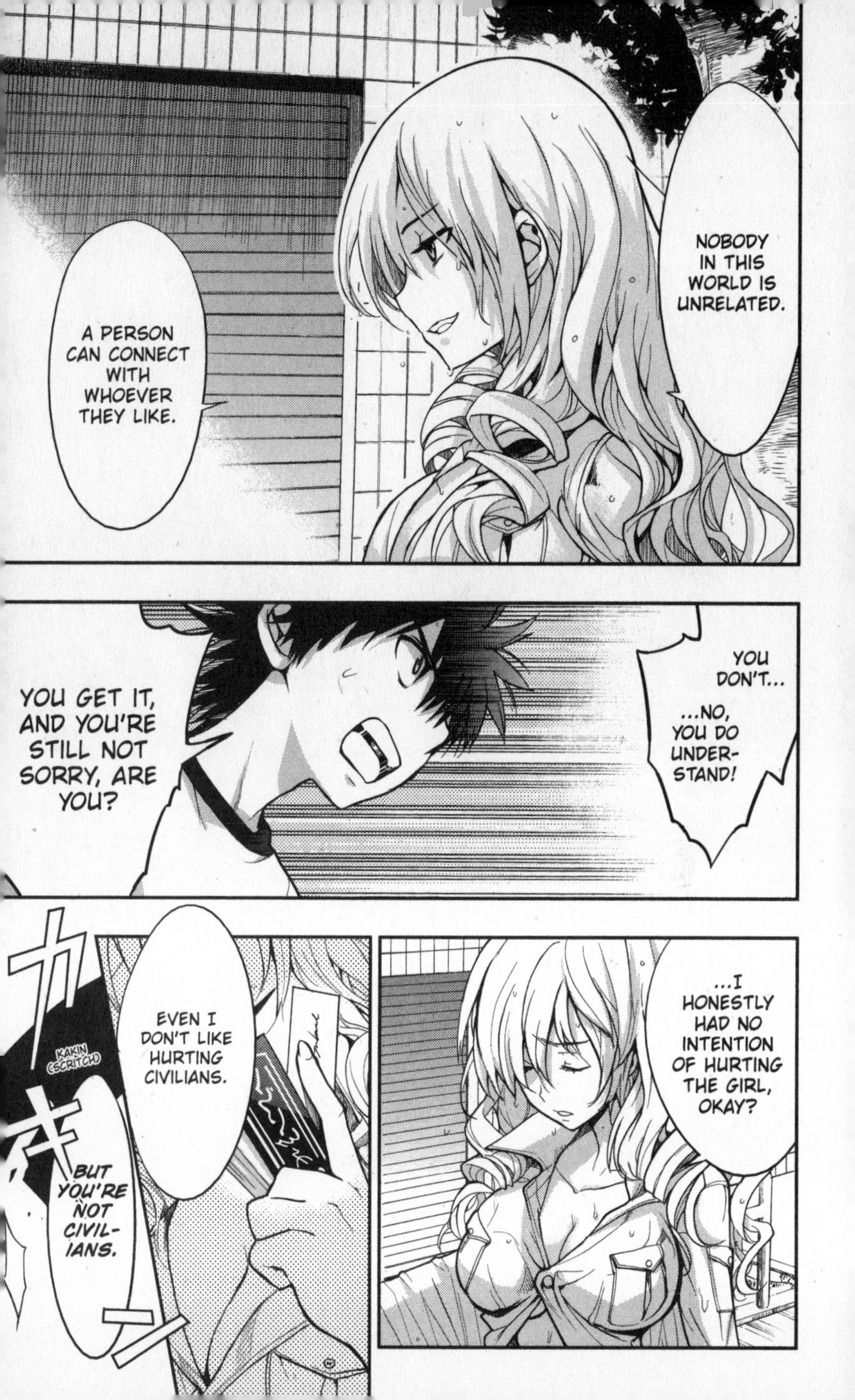
NOBODY IN THIS WORLD IS UNRELATED.
A PERSON CAN CONNECT WITH WHOEVER THEY LIKE.
YOU DON'T...
...NO, YOU DO UNDER-STAND!
YOU GET IT, AND YOU'RE STILL NOT SORRY, ARE YOU?
...I HONESTLY HAD NO INTENTION OF HURTING THE GIRL, OKAY?
EVEN I DON'T LIKE HURTING CIVILIANS.
KAKIN (SCRITCH)
BUT YOU'RE NOT CIVIL-IANS.

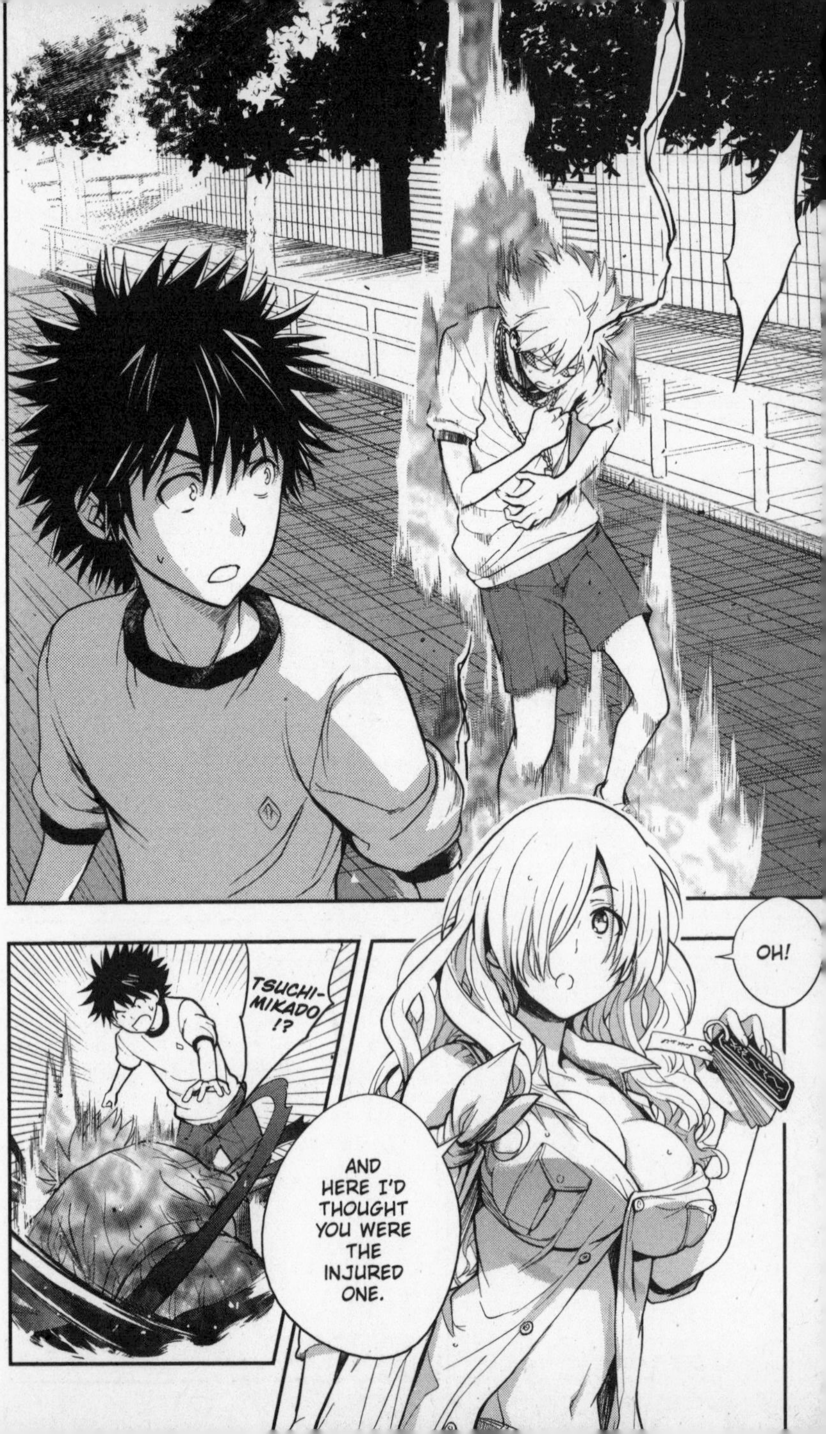
OH!
AND HERE I'D THOUGHT YOU WERE THE INJURED ONE.
TSUCHIMIKADO!?

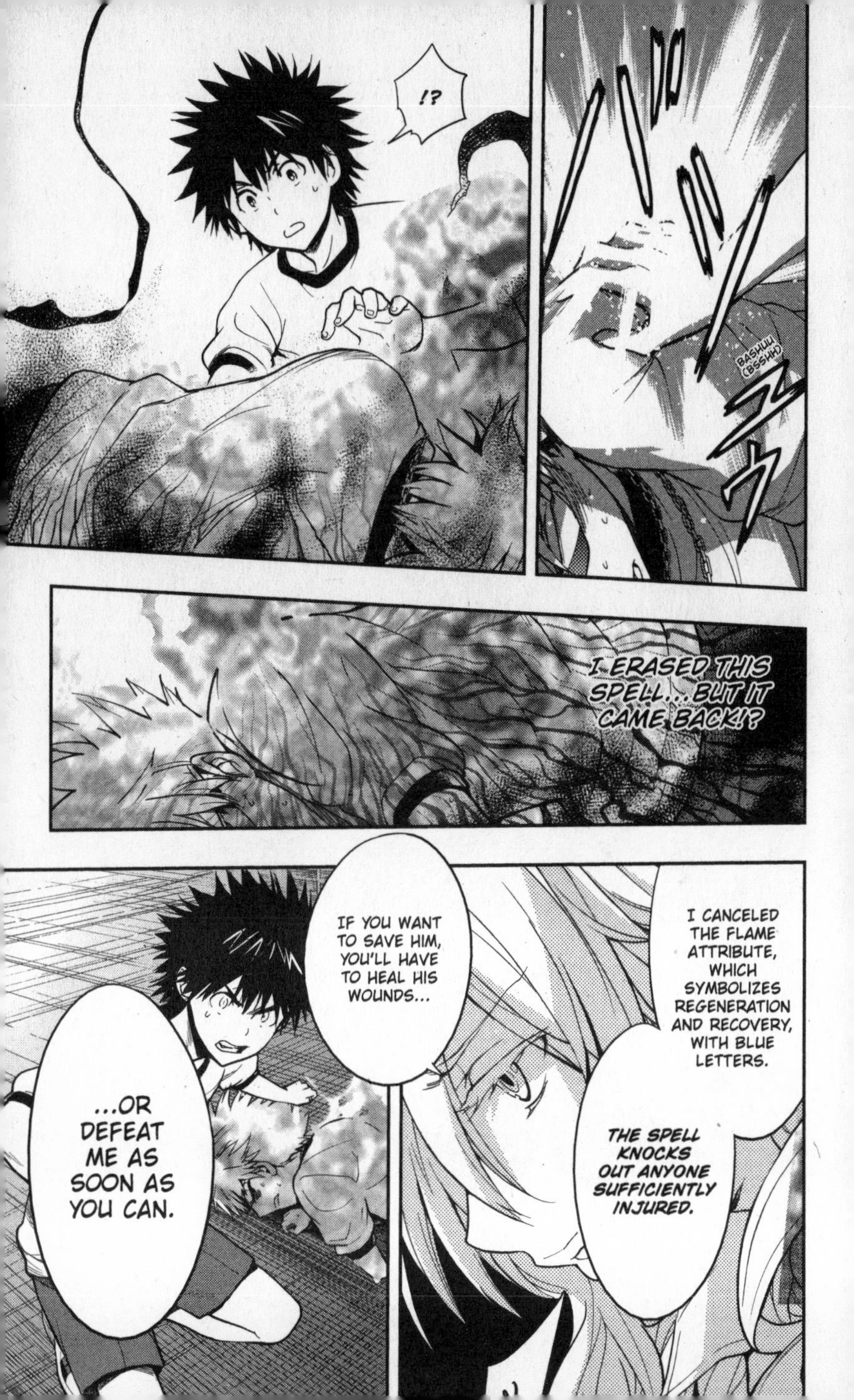
BASHUU (BSSHH)
!?
I ERASED THIS SPELL...BUT IT CAME BACK!?
I CANCELED THE FLAME ATTRIBUTE, WHICH SYMBOLIZES REGENERATION AND RECOVERY, WITH BLUE LETTERS.
THE SPELL KNOCKS OUT ANYONE SUFFICIENTLY INJURED.
IF YOU WANT TO SAVE HIM, YOU'LL HAVE TO HEAL HIS WOUNDS...
...OR DEFEAT ME AS SOON AS YOU CAN.

A Certain Magical Index

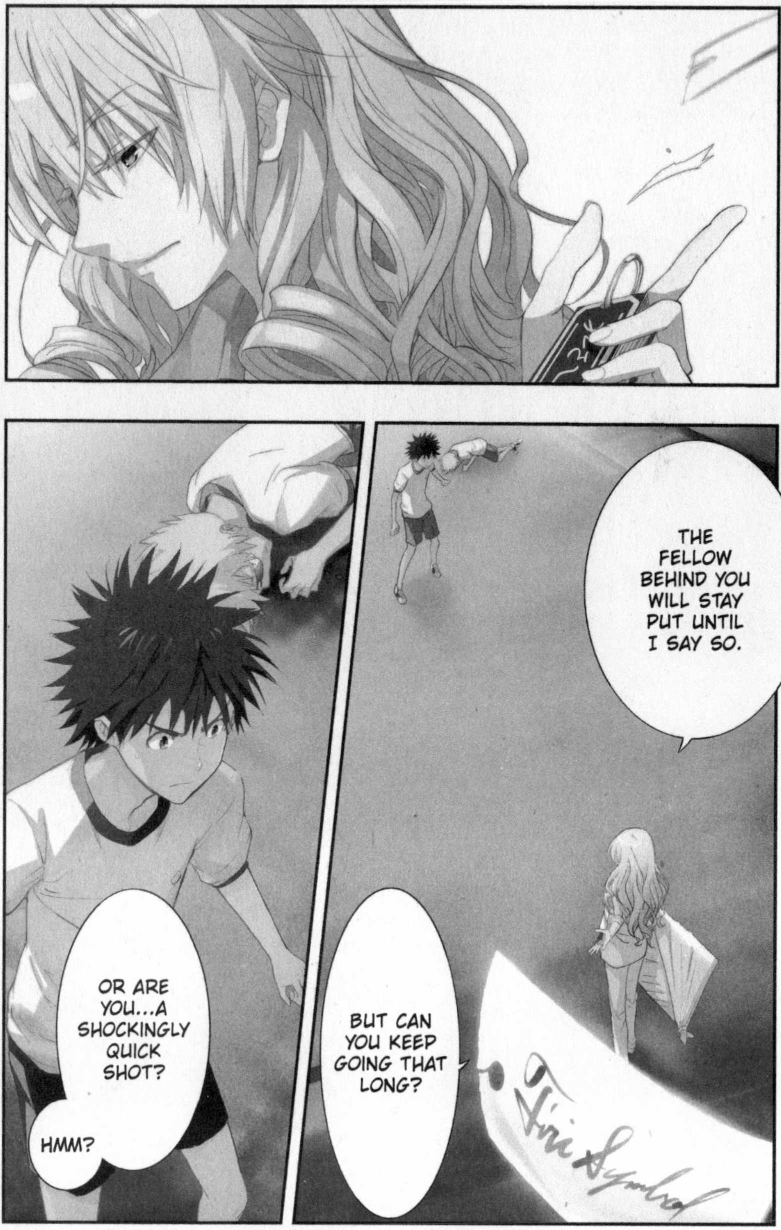
THE FELLOW BEHIND YOU WILL STAY PUT UNTIL I SAY SO.
BUT CAN YOU KEEP GOING THAT LONG?
OR ARE YOU...A SHOCKINGLY QUICK SHOT?
HMM?

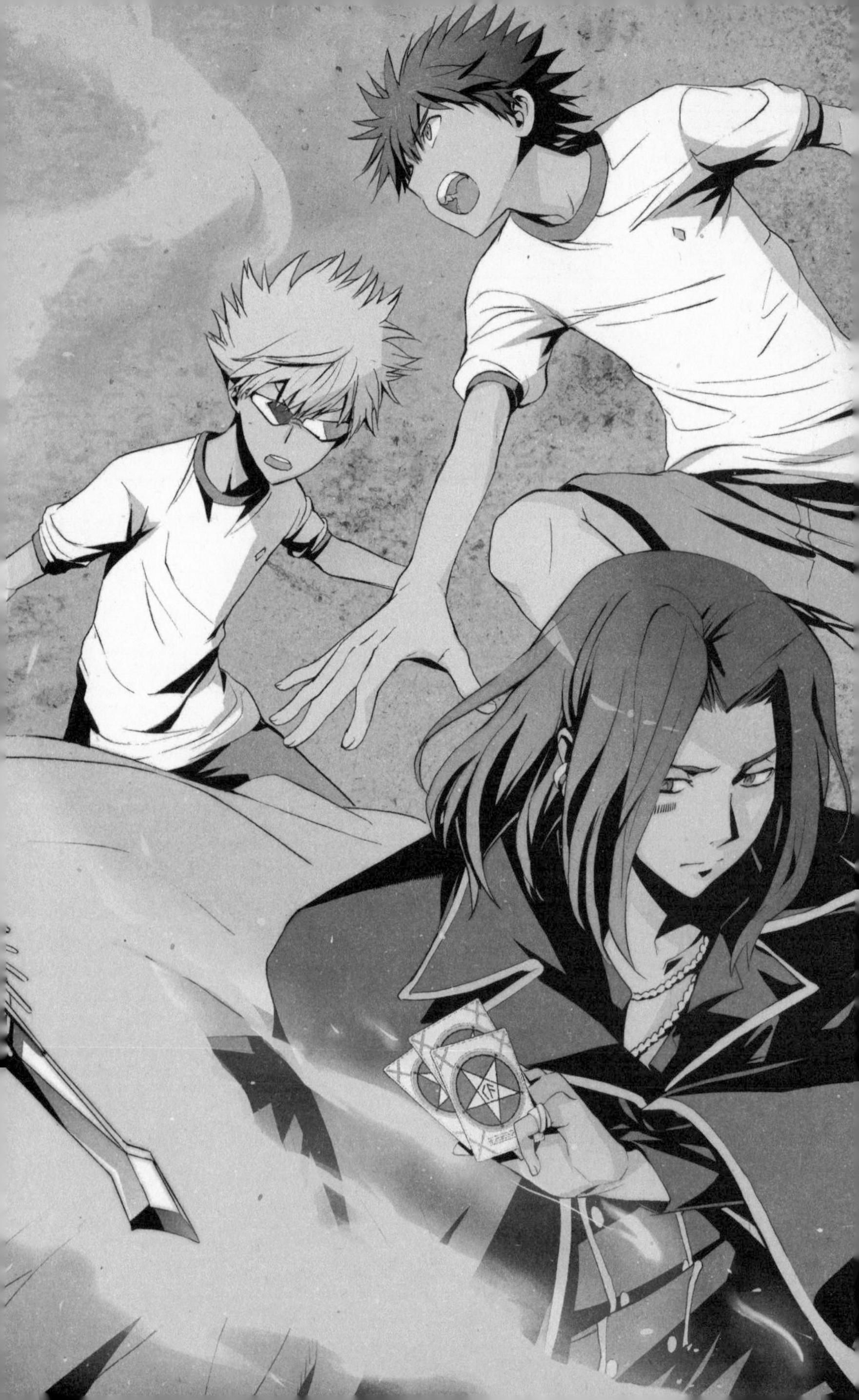

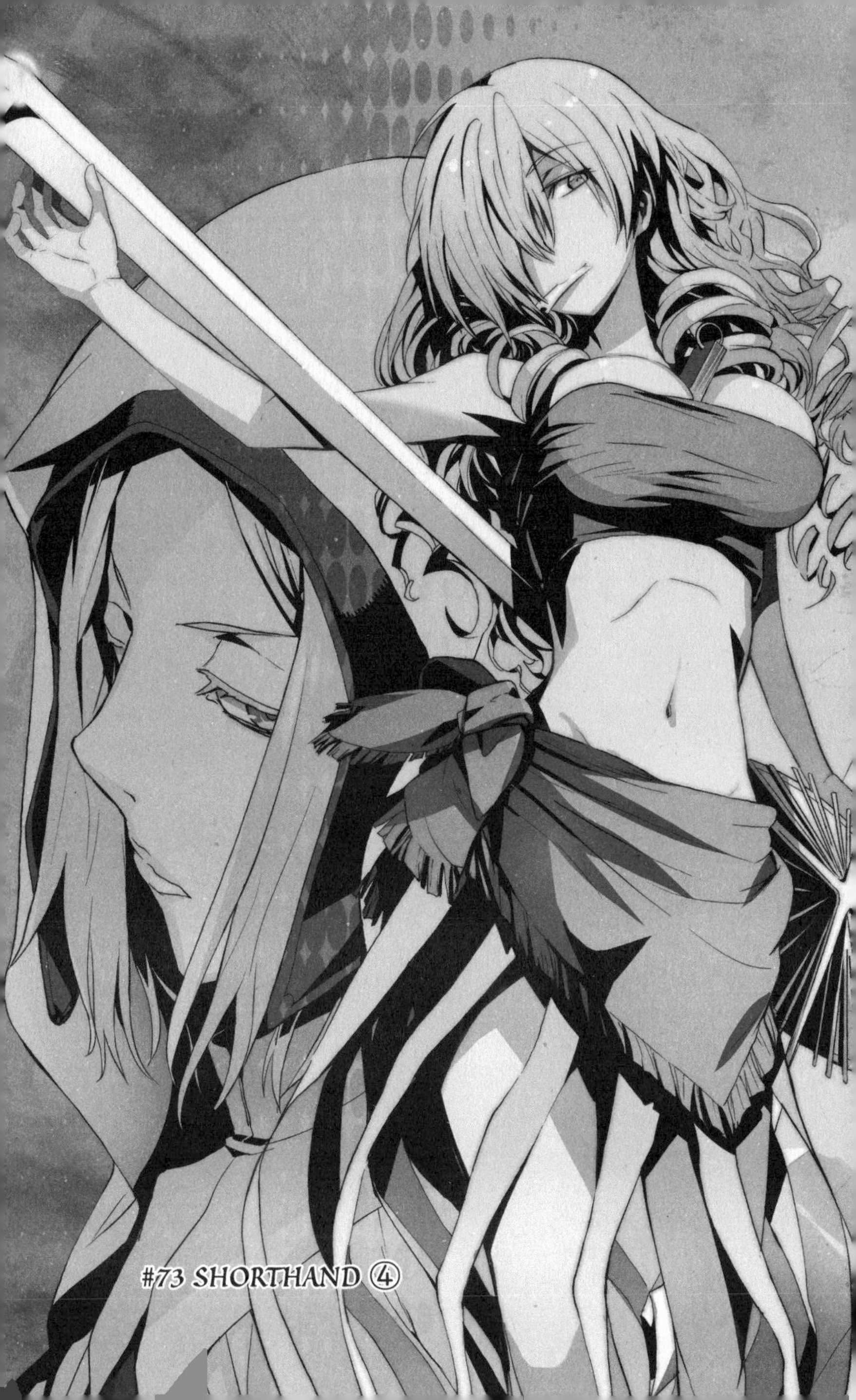
#73 SHORTHAND ④

A Certain Magical Index

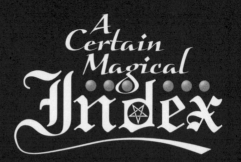

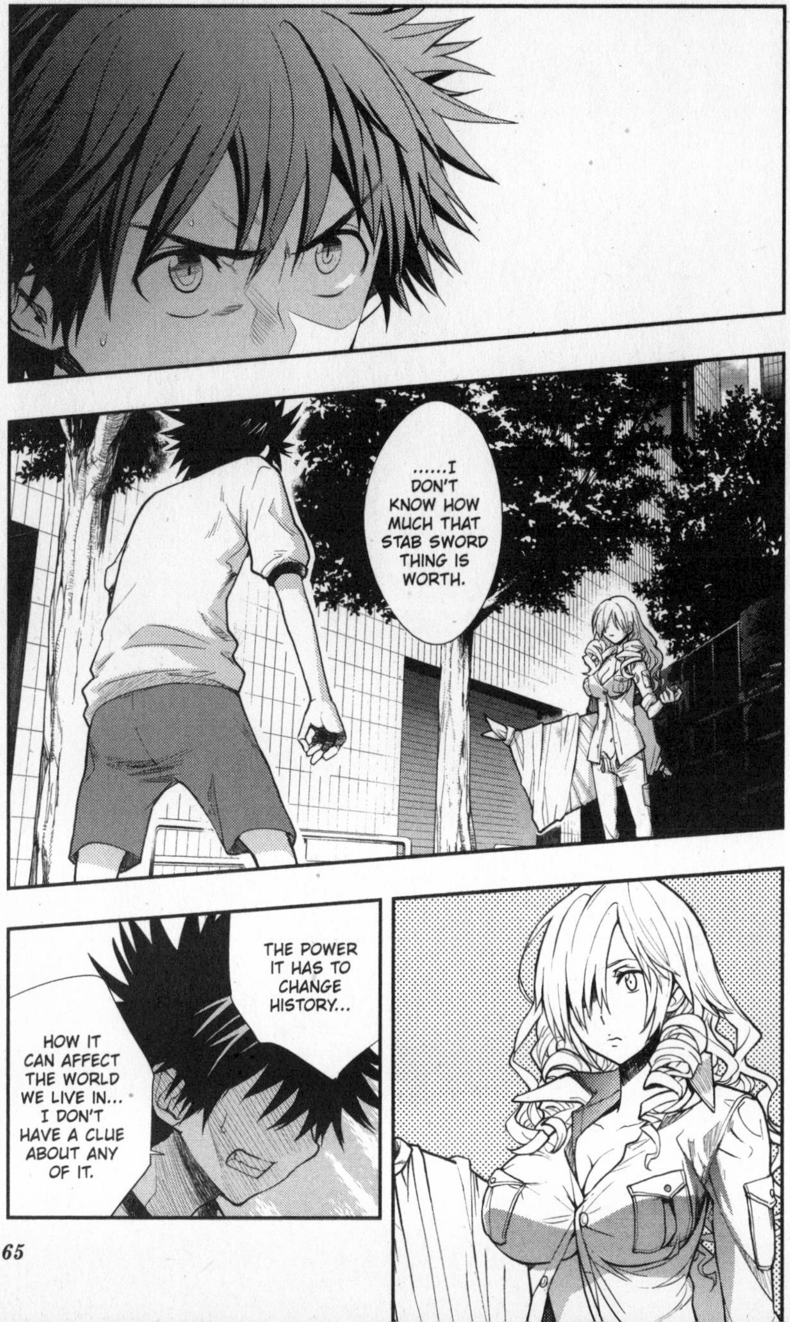

......I DON'T KNOW HOW MUCH THAT STAB SWORD THING IS WORTH.
THE POWER IT HAS TO CHANGE HISTORY...
HOW IT CAN AFFECT THE WORLD WE LIVE IN... I DON'T HAVE A CLUE ABOUT ANY OF IT.

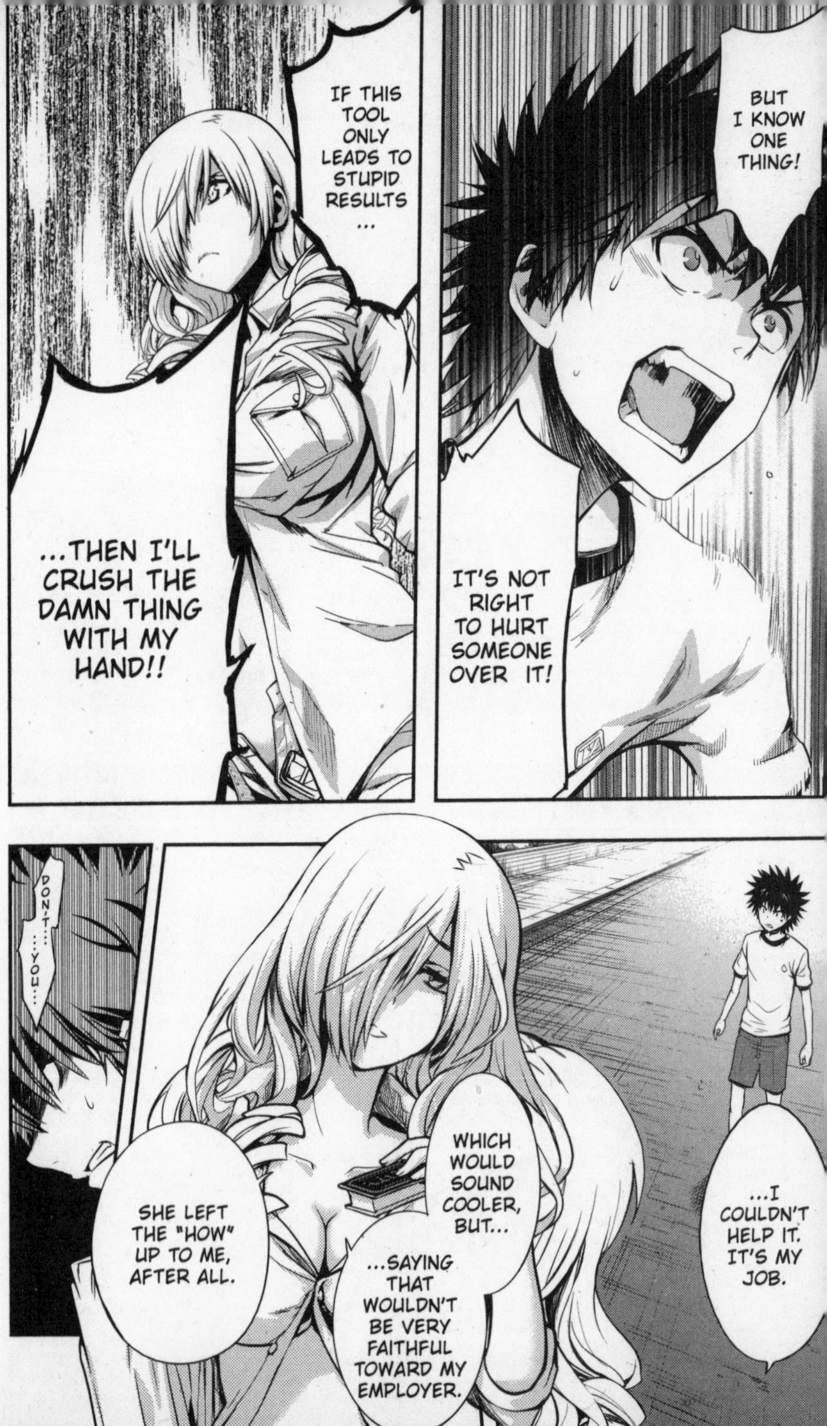
BUT I KNOW ONE THING!
IT'S NOT RIGHT TO HURT SOMEONE OVER IT!
IF THIS TOOL ONLY LEADS TO STUPID RESULTS ...
...THEN I'LL CRUSH THE DAMN THING WITH MY HAND!!
...I COULDN'T HELP IT. IT'S MY JOB.
WHICH WOULD SOUND COOLER, BUT...
...SAYING THAT WOULDN'T BE VERY FAITHFUL TOWARD MY EMPLOYER.
SHE LEFT THE "HOW" UP TO ME, AFTER ALL.
DON'T... ...YOU...

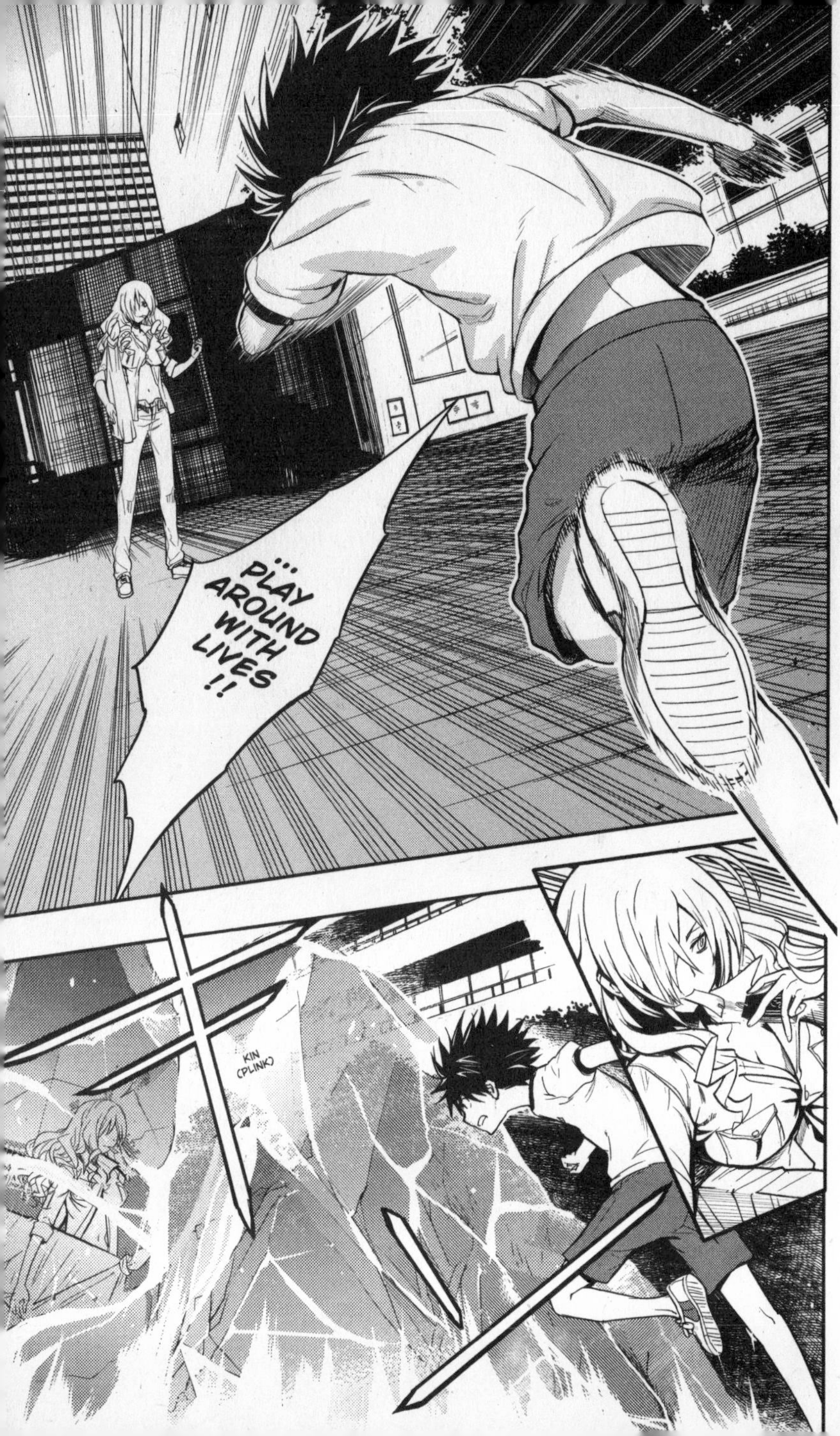
...PLAY AROUND WITH LIVES!!
KIN (PLINK)

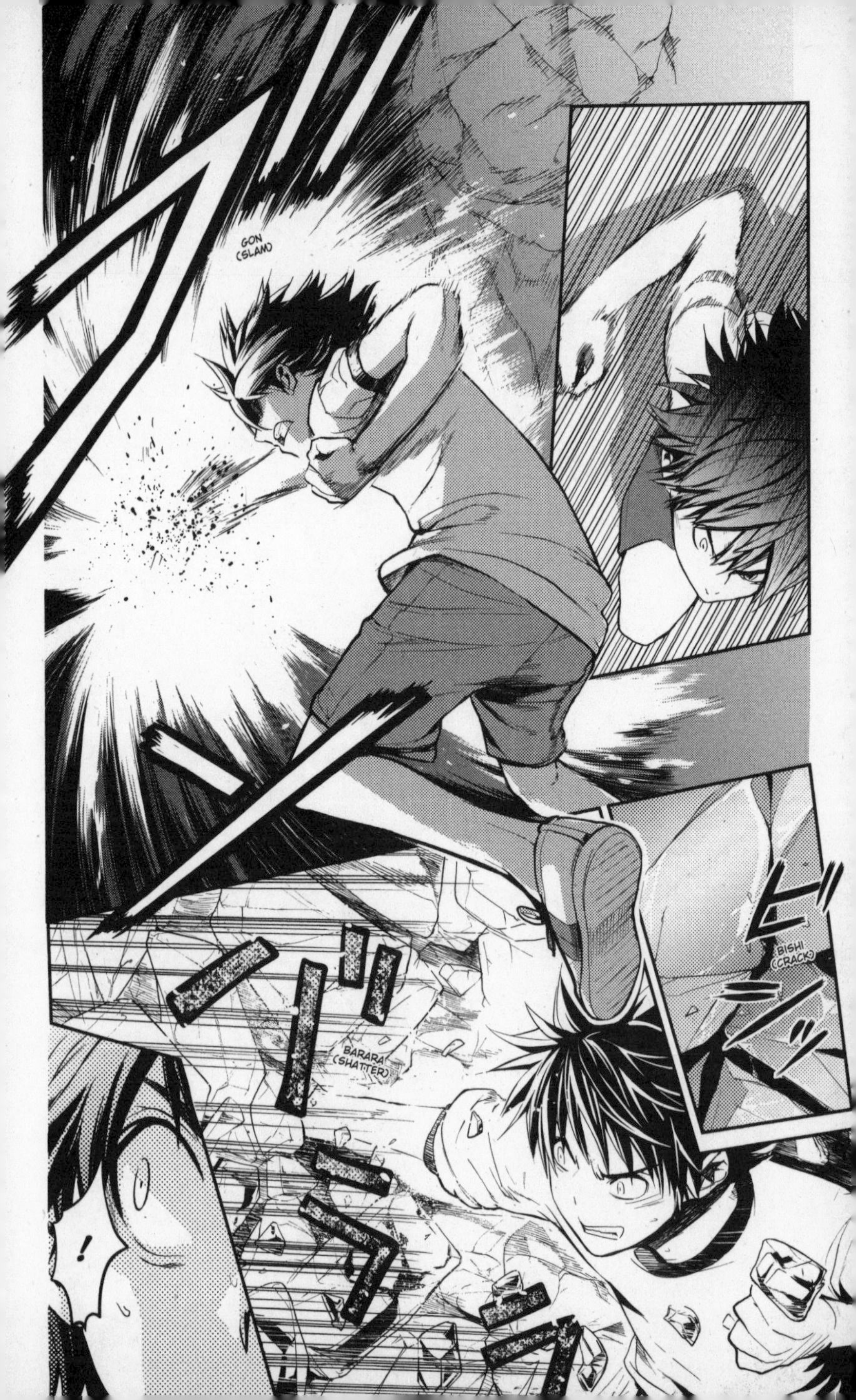
GON (SLAM)
BISHI (CRACK)
BARARA (SHATTER)
!

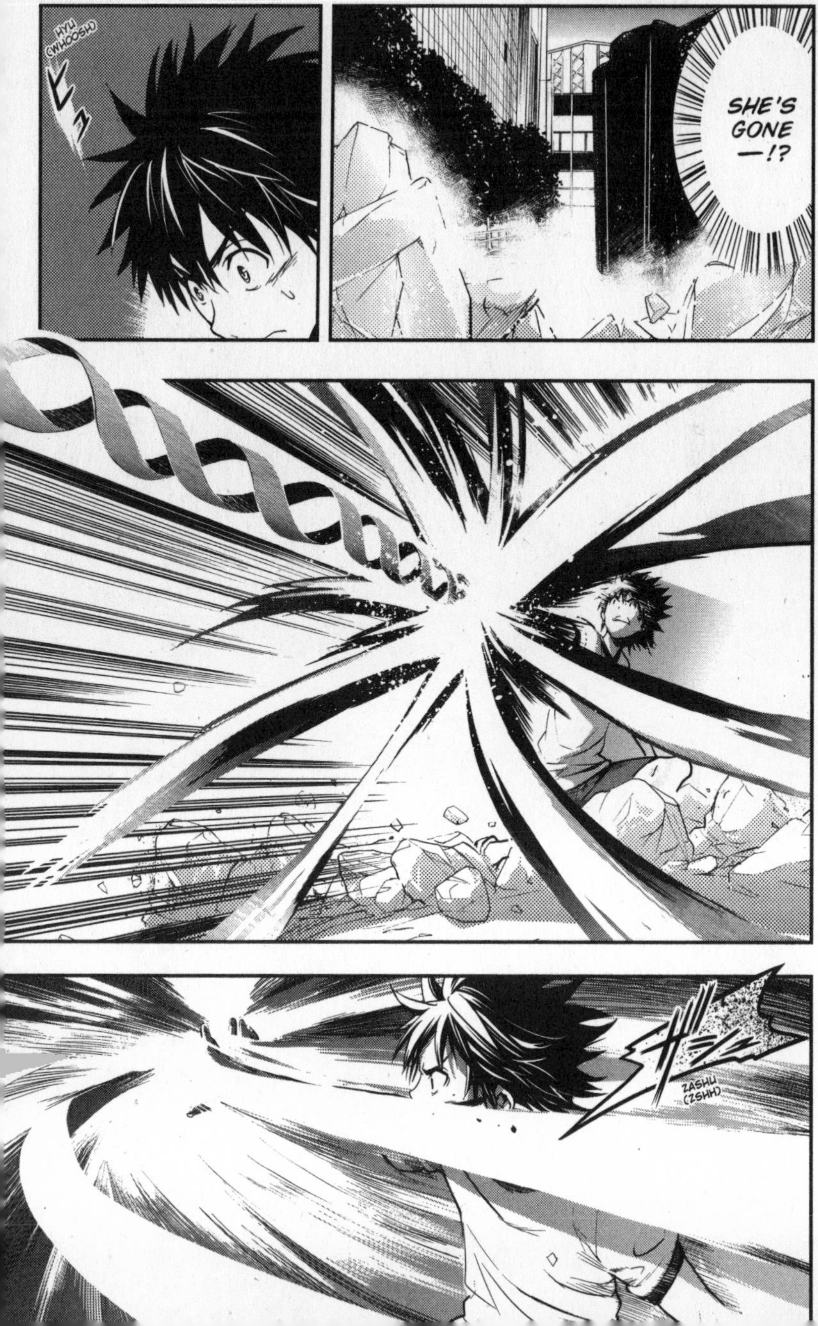
SHE'S GONE —!?
HYU (WHOOSH)
ZASHU (ZSHH)

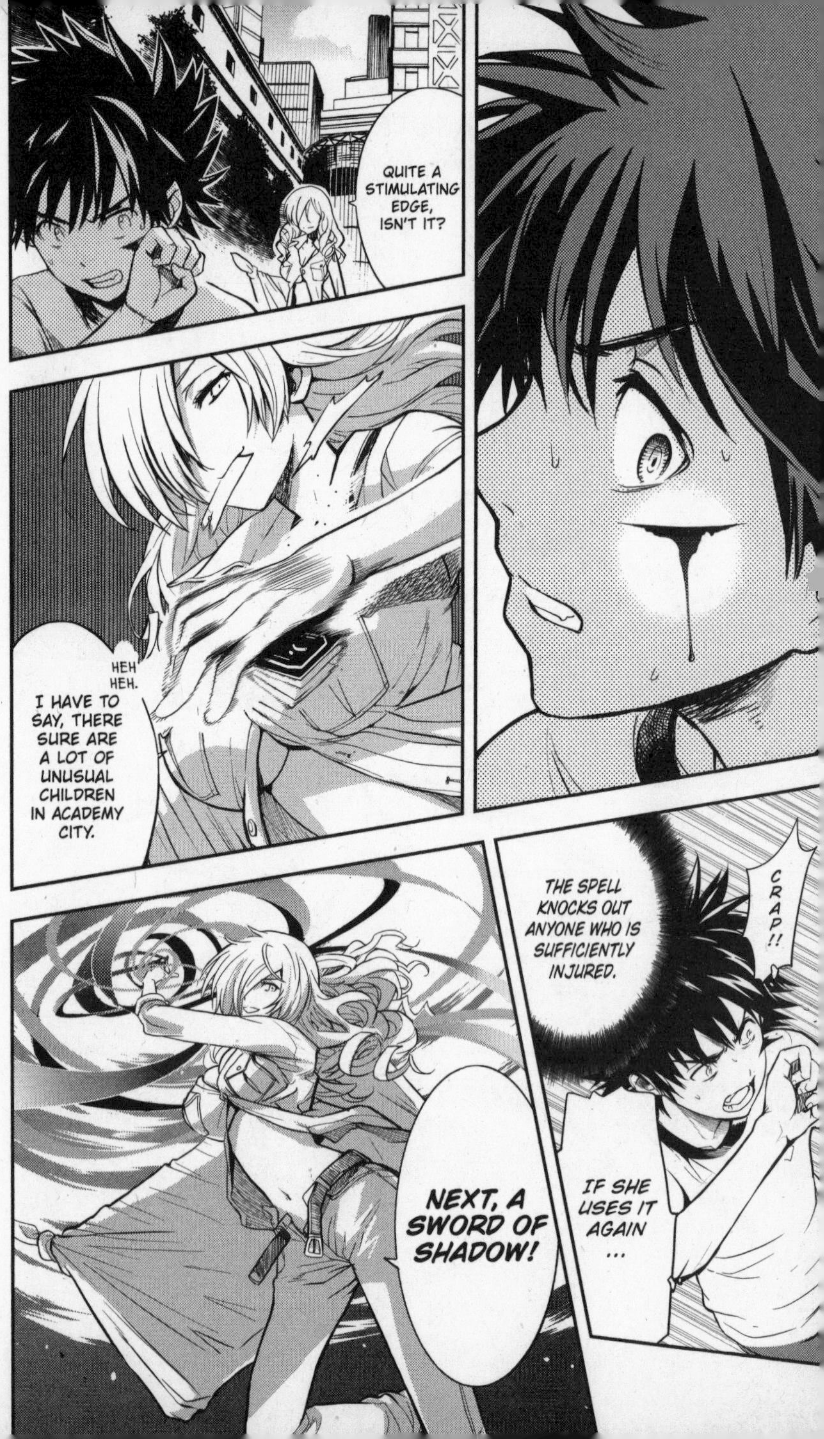
QUITE A STIMULATING EDGE, ISN'T IT?
HEH HEH.
I HAVE TO SAY, THERE SURE ARE A LOT OF UNUSUAL CHILDREN IN ACADEMY CITY.
CRAP!!
THE SPELL KNOCKS OUT ANYONE WHO IS SUFFICIENTLY INJURED.
IF SHE USES IT AGAIN ...
NEXT, A SWORD OF SHADOW!

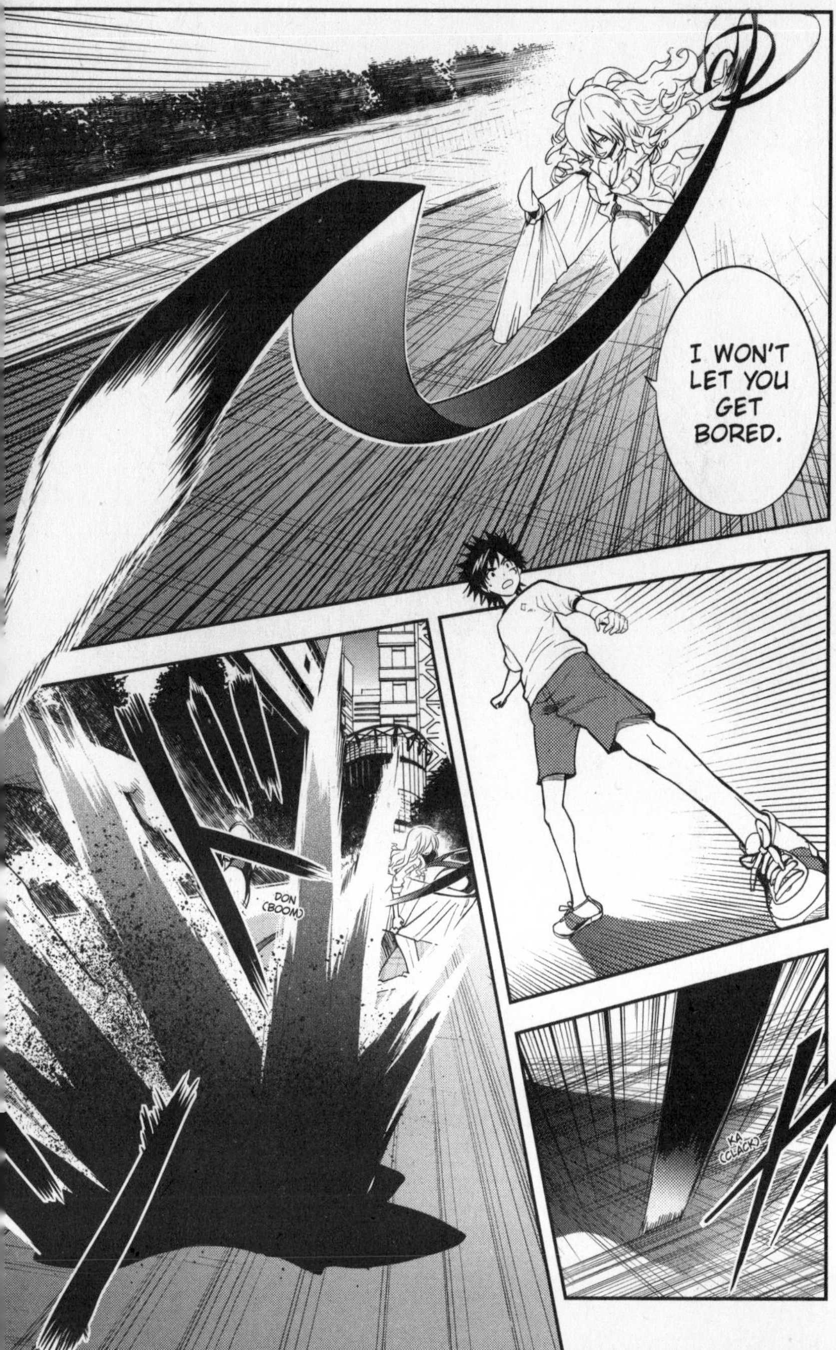
I WON'T LET YOU GET BORED.
DON (BOOM)
KA- (CLACK)

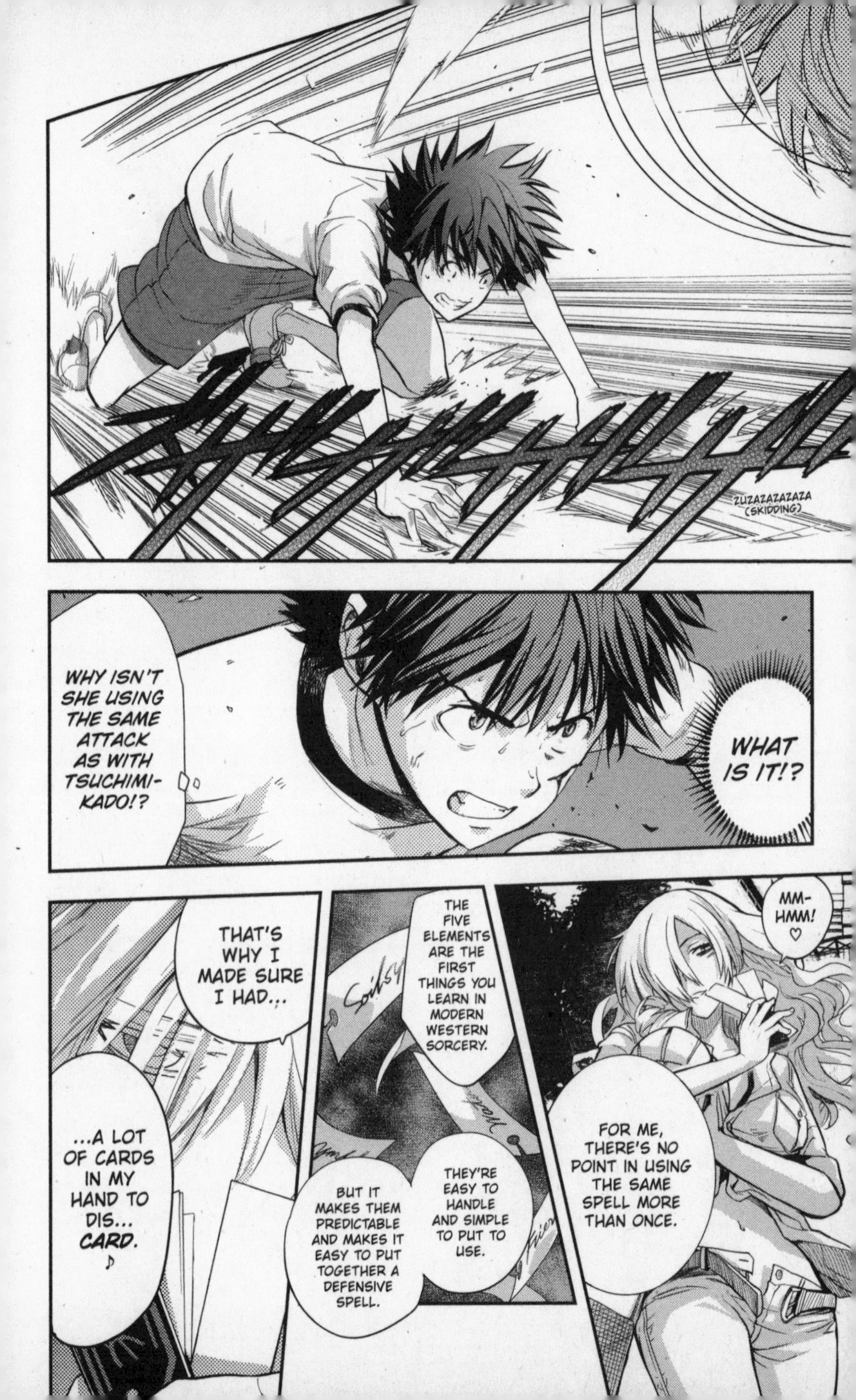
ZUZAZAZAZAZA (SKIDDING)
WHAT IS IT!?
WHY ISN'T SHE USING THE SAME ATTACK AS WITH TSUCHIMI-KADO!?
MM-HMM! ♡
FOR ME, THERE'S NO POINT IN USING THE SAME SPELL MORE THAN ONCE.
THE FIVE ELEMENTS ARE THE FIRST THINGS YOU LEARN IN MODERN WESTERN SORCERY.
THEY'RE EASY TO HANDLE AND SIMPLE TO PUT TO USE.
BUT IT MAKES THEM PREDICTABLE AND MAKES IT EASY TO PUT TOGETHER A DEFENSIVE SPELL.
THAT'S WHY I MADE SURE I HAD...
...A LOT OF CARDS IN MY HAND TO DIS... **CARD.** ♪

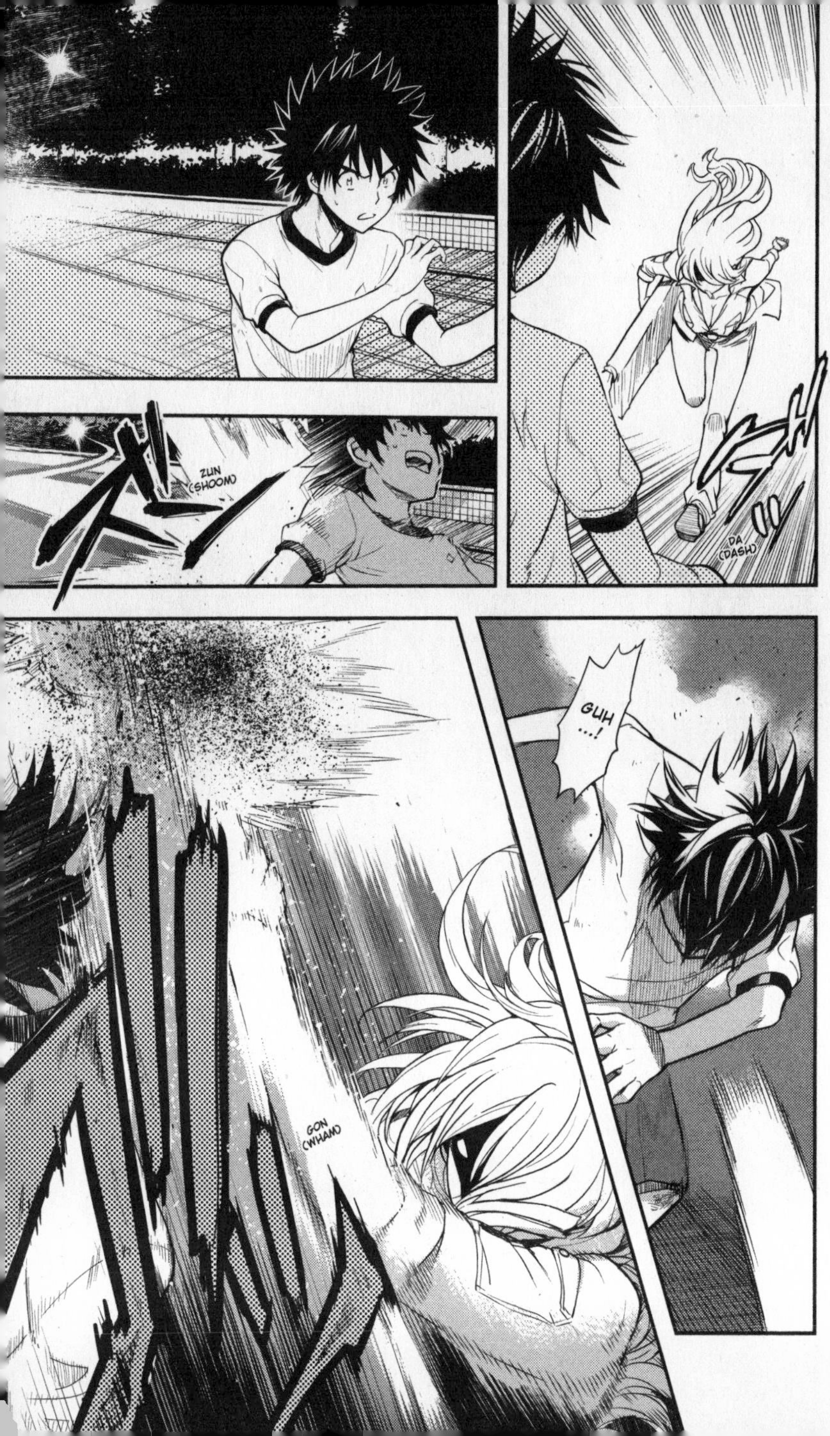
DA (DASH)
ZUN (SHOOM)
GUH ...!
GON (WHAM)

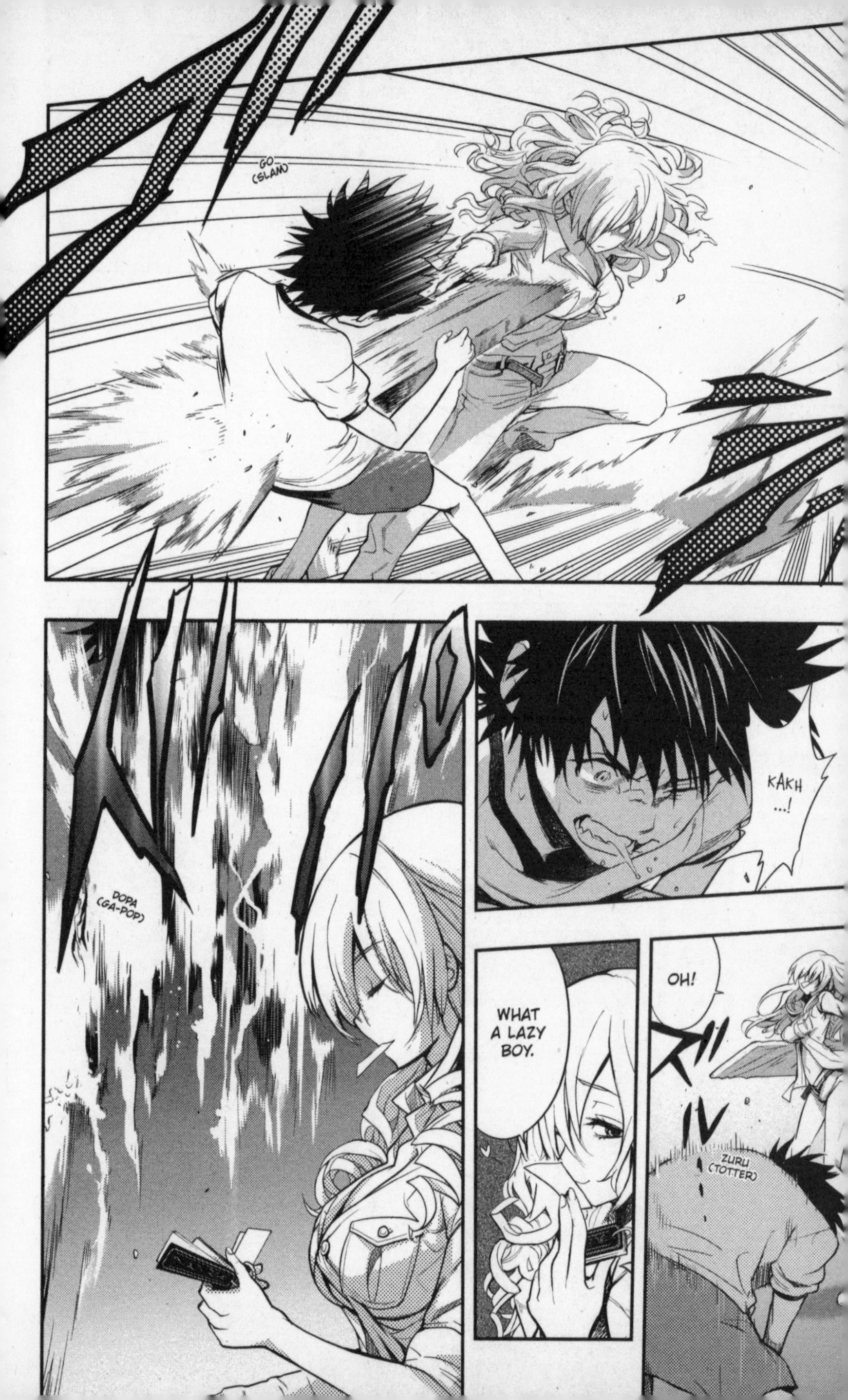

GO (SLAM)
KAKH ...!
OH!
ZURU (TOTTER)
WHAT A LAZY BOY.
DOPA (GA-POP)

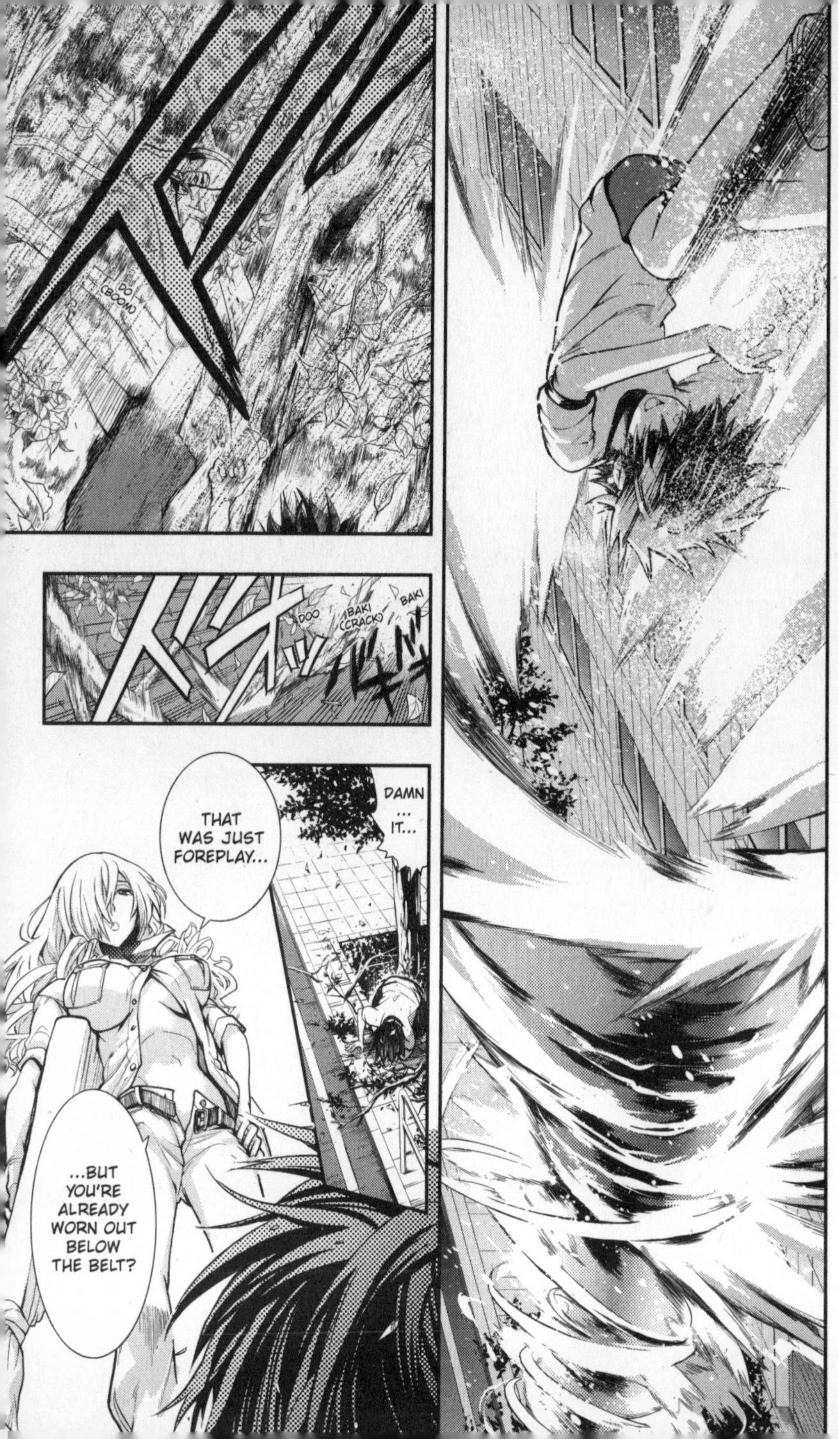
DO (BOOM)
BAKI
BAKI (CRACK)
DOO
DAMN ... IT...
THAT WAS JUST FOREPLAY...
...BUT YOU'RE ALREADY WORN OUT BELOW THE BELT?

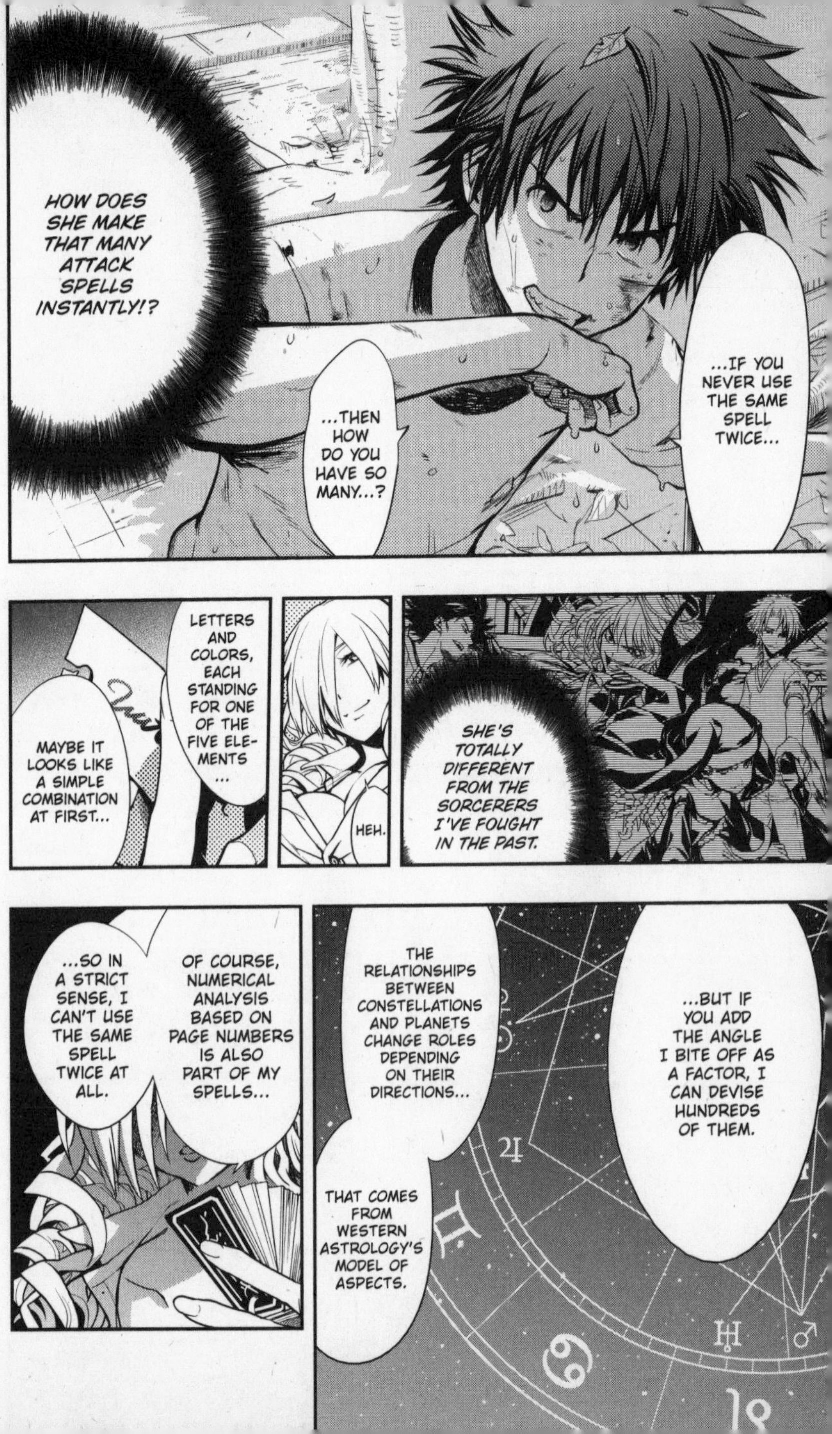
...IF YOU NEVER USE THE SAME SPELL TWICE...
...THEN HOW DO YOU HAVE SO MANY...?
HOW DOES SHE MAKE THAT MANY ATTACK SPELLS INSTANTLY!?
SHE'S TOTALLY DIFFERENT FROM THE SORCERERS I'VE FOUGHT IN THE PAST.
HEH.
LETTERS AND COLORS, EACH STANDING FOR ONE OF THE FIVE ELE-MENTS...
MAYBE IT LOOKS LIKE A SIMPLE COMBINATION AT FIRST...
...BUT IF YOU ADD THE ANGLE I BITE OFF AS A FACTOR, I CAN DEVISE HUNDREDS OF THEM.
THE RELATIONSHIPS BETWEEN CONSTELLATIONS AND PLANETS CHANGE ROLES DEPENDING ON THEIR DIRECTIONS...
THAT COMES FROM WESTERN ASTROLOGY'S MODEL OF ASPECTS.
OF COURSE, NUMERICAL ANALYSIS BASED ON PAGE NUMBERS IS ALSO PART OF MY SPELLS...
...SO IN A STRICT SENSE, I CAN'T USE THE SAME SPELL TWICE AT ALL.

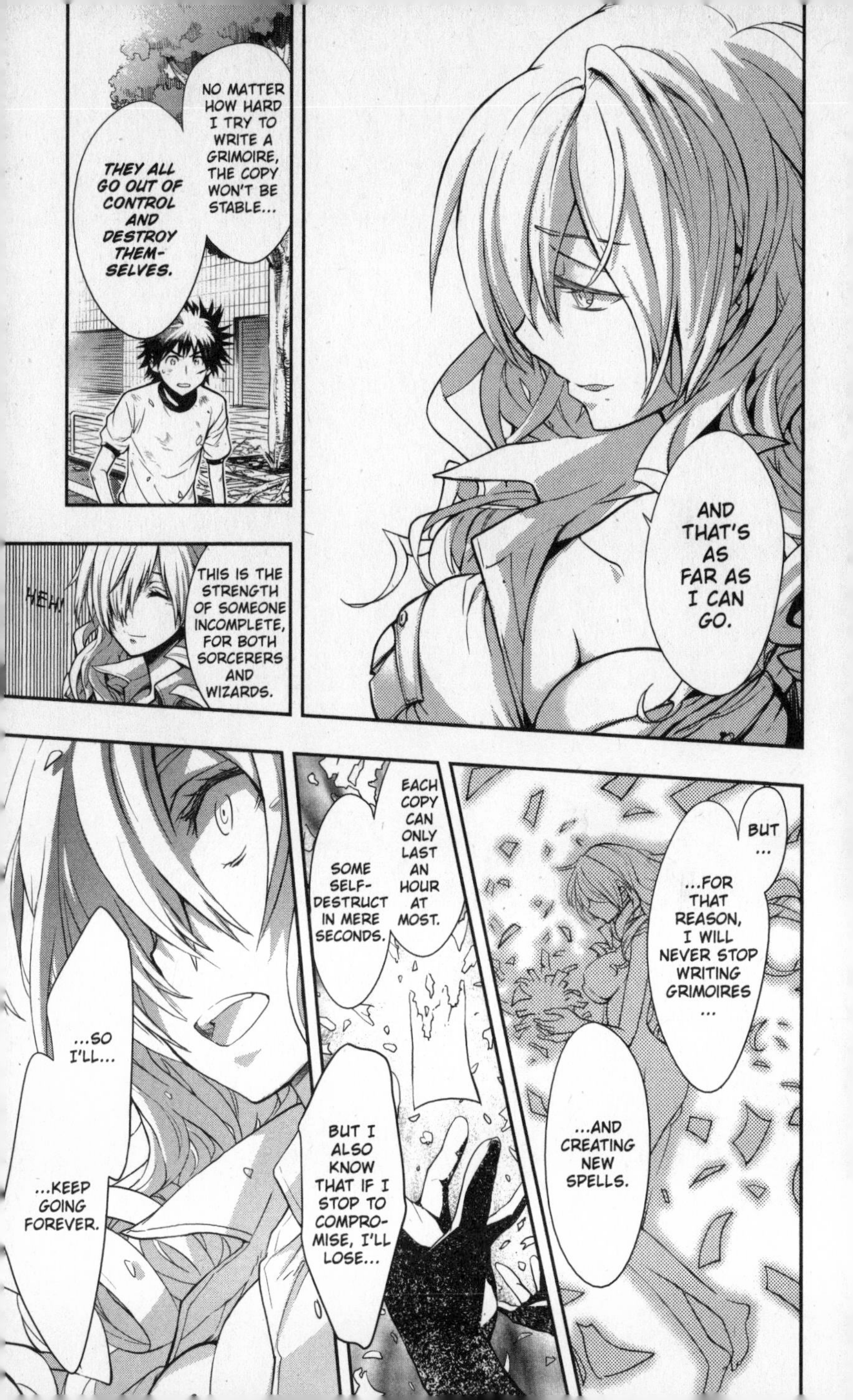
AND THAT'S AS FAR AS I CAN GO.
NO MATTER HOW HARD I TRY TO WRITE A GRIMOIRE, THE COPY WON'T BE STABLE...
THEY ALL GO OUT OF CONTROL AND DESTROY THEM-SELVES.
THIS IS THE STRENGTH OF SOMEONE INCOMPLETE, FOR BOTH SORCERERS AND WIZARDS.
HEH!
BUT...
...FOR THAT REASON, I WILL NEVER STOP WRITING GRIMOIRES...
...AND CREATING NEW SPELLS.
EACH COPY CAN ONLY LAST AN HOUR AT MOST.
SOME SELF-DESTRUCT IN MERE SECONDS.
BUT I ALSO KNOW THAT IF I STOP TO COMPRO-MISE, I'LL LOSE...
...SO I'LL...
...KEEP GOING FOREVER.

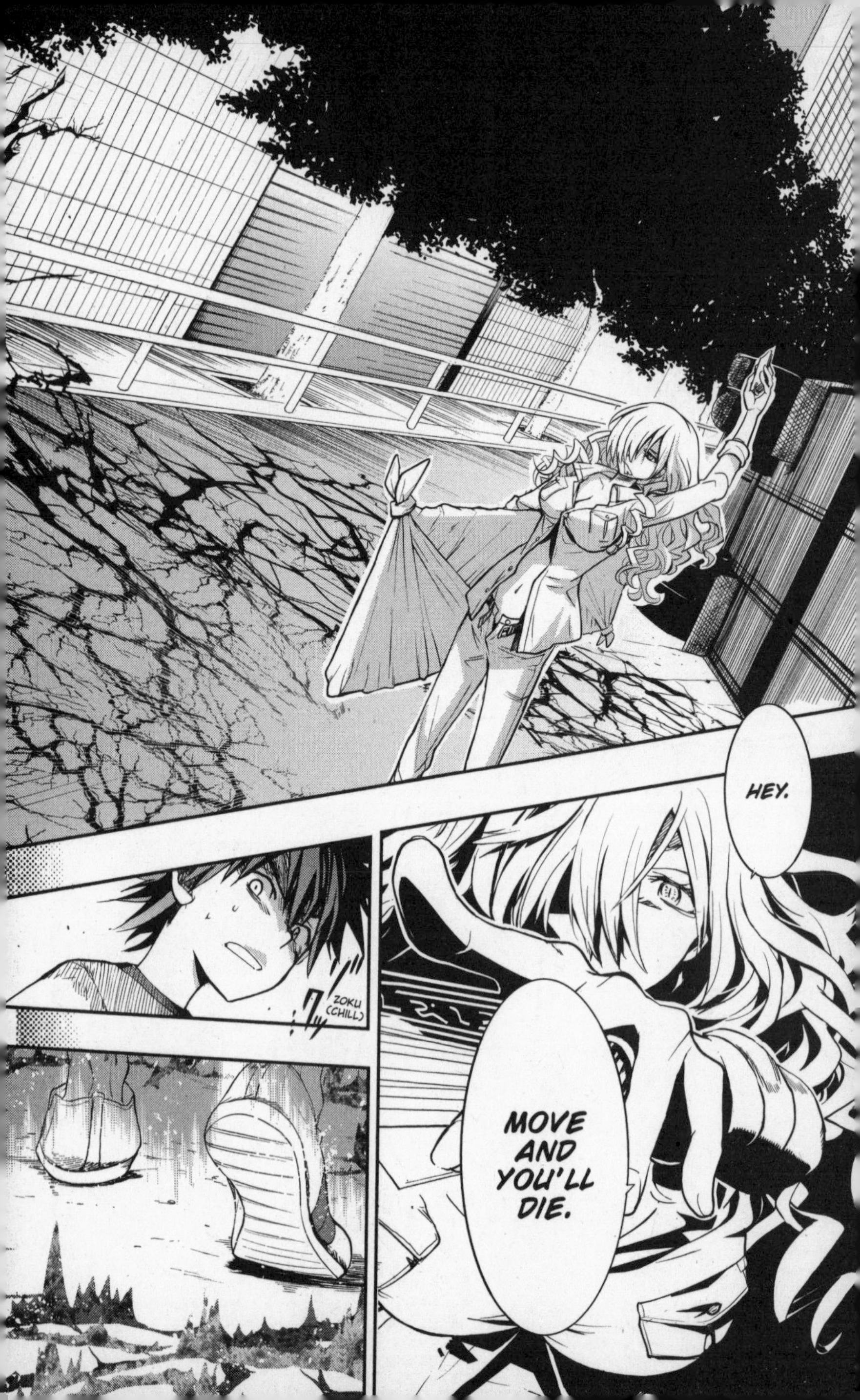
HEY.
ZOKU (CHILL)
MOVE AND YOU'LL DIE.

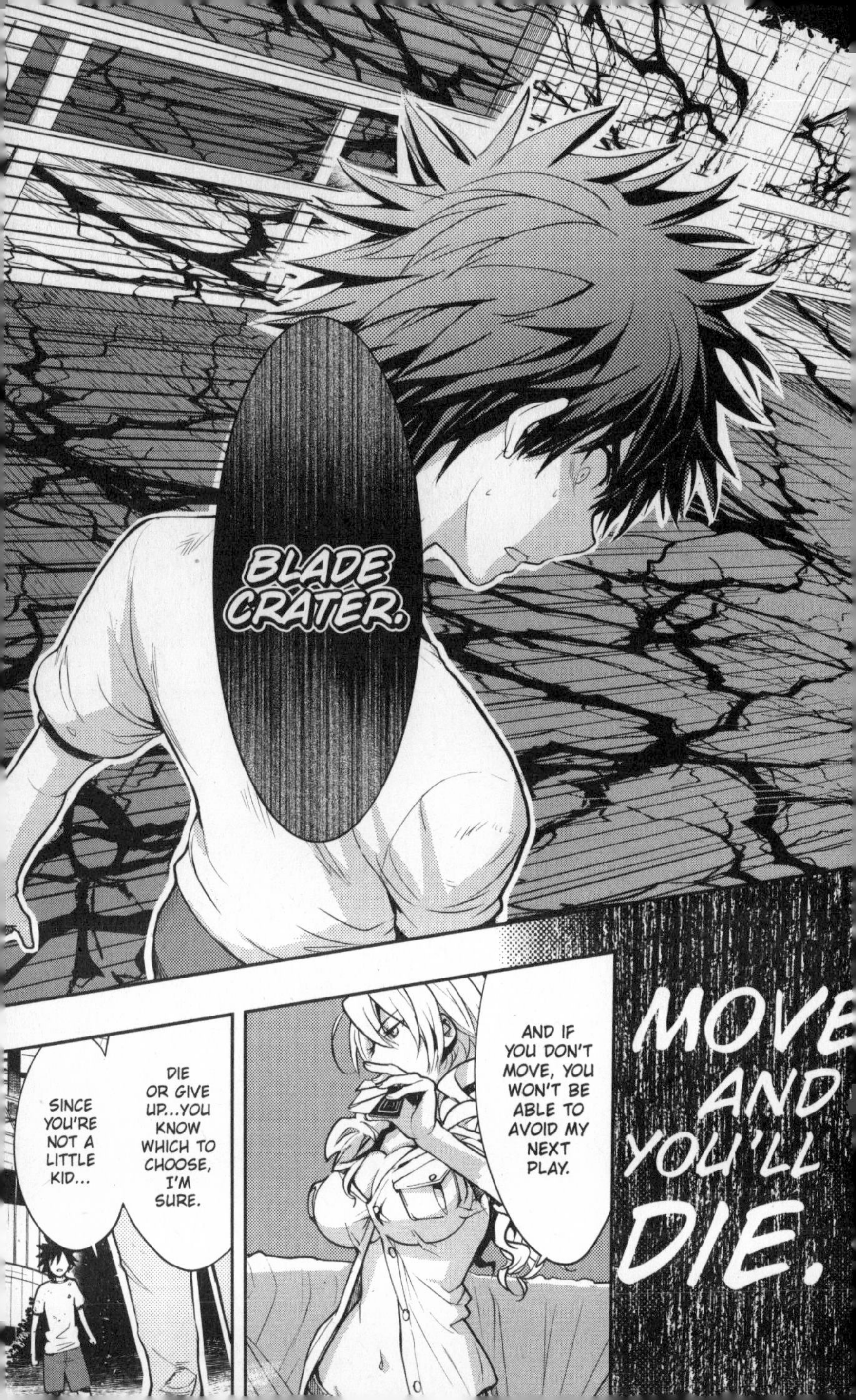
BLADE CRATER.
MOVE AND YOU'LL DIE.
AND IF YOU DON'T MOVE, YOU WON'T BE ABLE TO AVOID MY NEXT PLAY.
DIE OR GIVE UP...YOU KNOW WHICH TO CHOOSE, I'M SURE.
SINCE YOU'RE NOT A LITTLE KID...

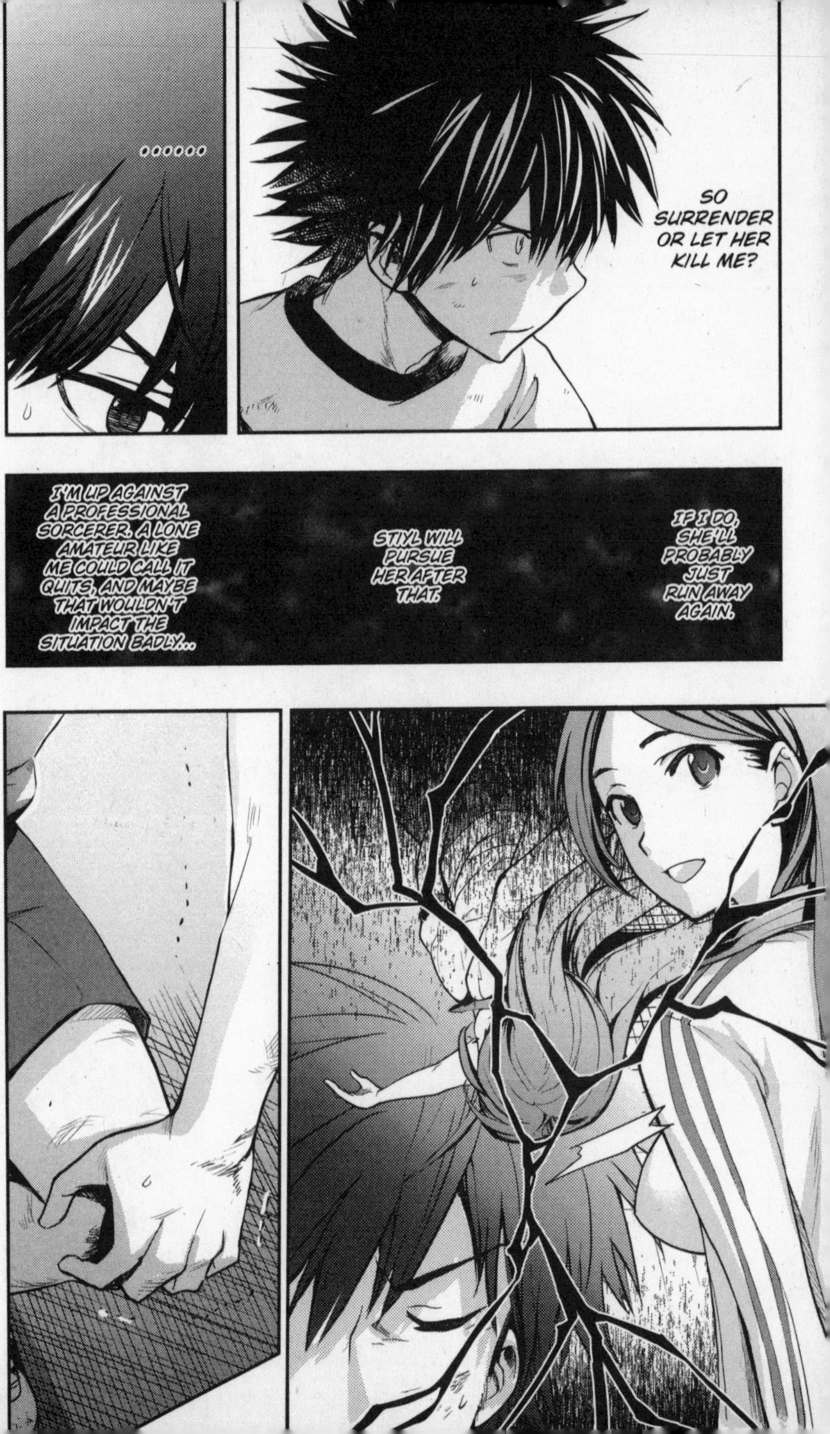
SO SURRENDER OR LET HER KILL ME?
......
IF I DO, SHE'LL PROBABLY JUST RUN AWAY AGAIN.
STIYL WILL PURSUE HER AFTER THAT.
I'M UP AGAINST A PROFESSIONAL SORCERER. A LONE AMATEUR LIKE ME COULD CALL IT QUITS, AND MAYBE THAT WOULDN'T IMPACT THE SITUATION BADLY...

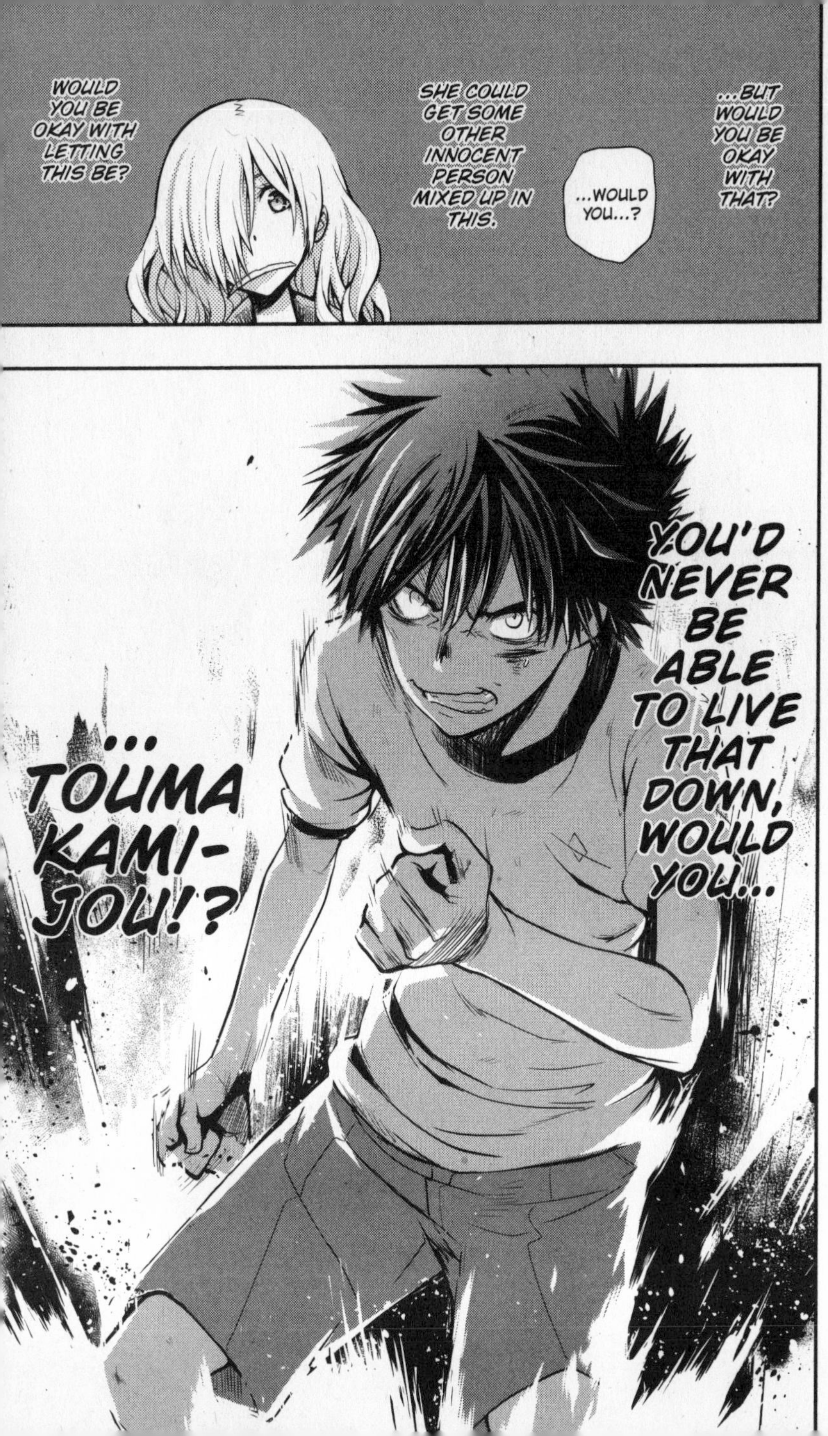
...BUT WOULD YOU BE OKAY WITH THAT?
...WOULD YOU...?
SHE COULD GET SOME OTHER INNOCENT PERSON MIXED UP IN THIS.
WOULD YOU BE OKAY WITH LETTING THIS BE?
YOU'D NEVER BE ABLE TO LIVE THAT DOWN, WOULD YOU...
...TOÜMA KAMI-JOU!?

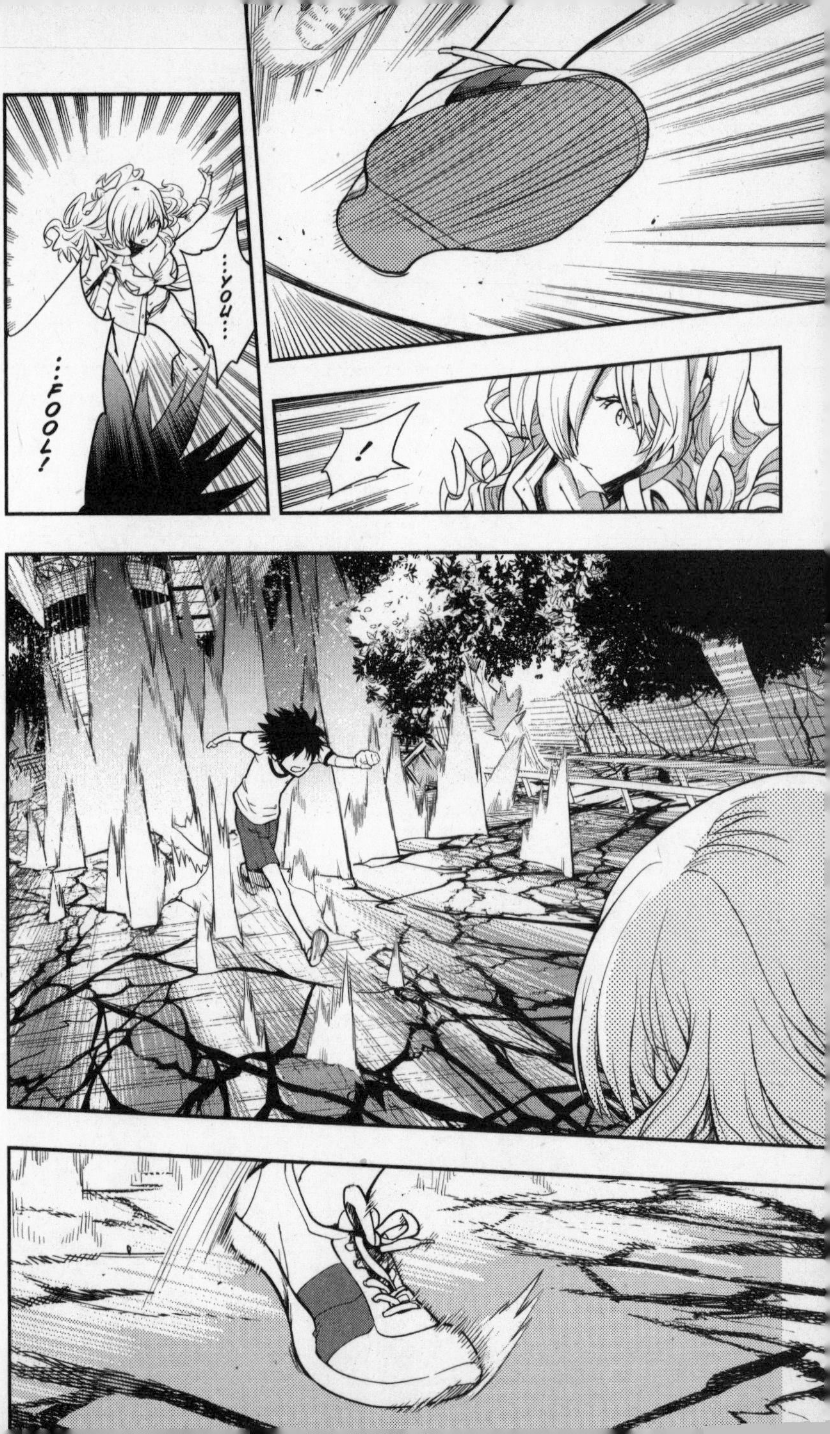
!
...YOU...
...FOOL!

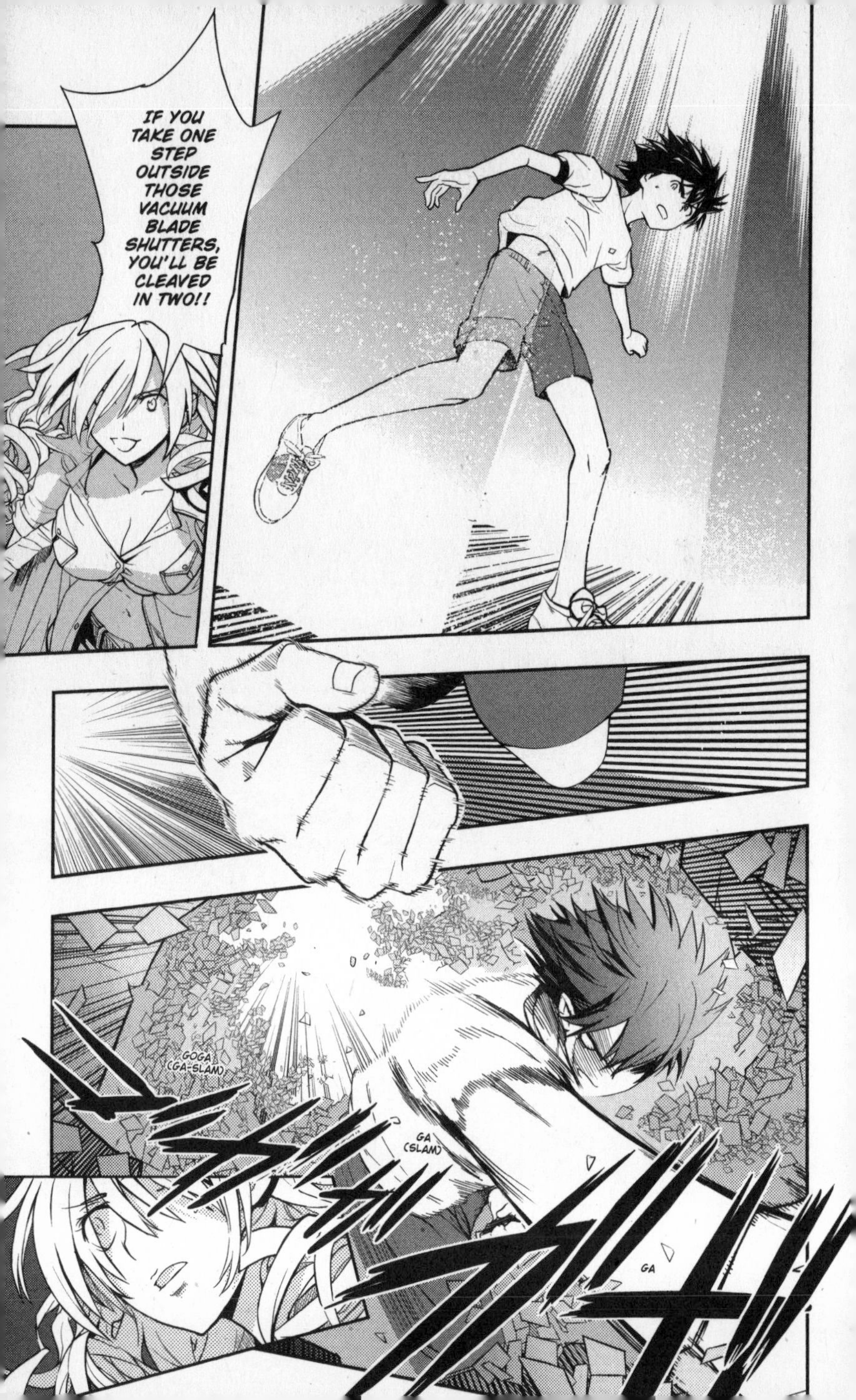
IF YOU TAKE ONE STEP OUTSIDE THOSE VACUUM BLADE SHUTTERS, YOU'LL BE CLEAVED IN TWO!!
GA (SLAM)
GOGA (GA-SLAM)
GA

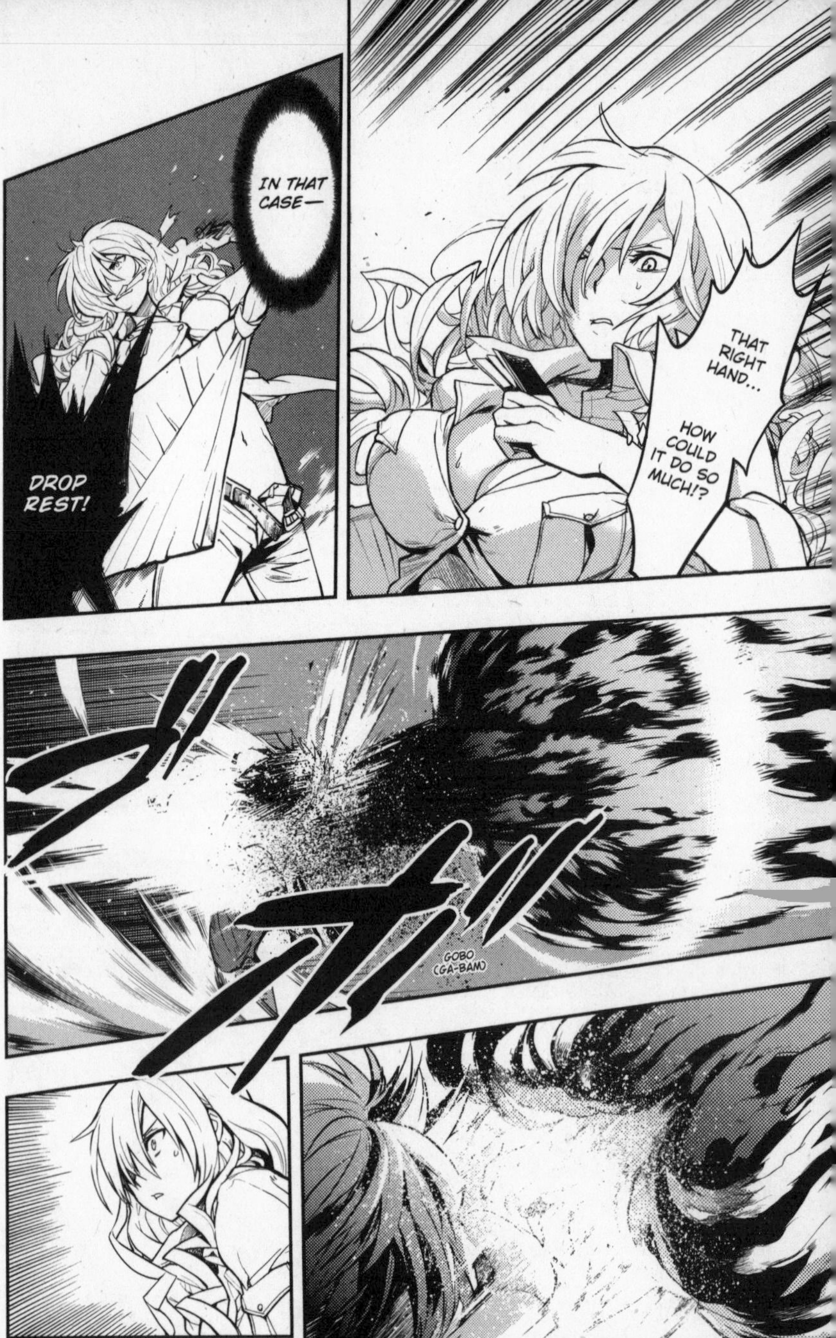
THAT RIGHT HAND...
HOW COULD IT DO SO MUCH!?
IN THAT CASE—
DROP REST!
GOBO (GA-BAM)

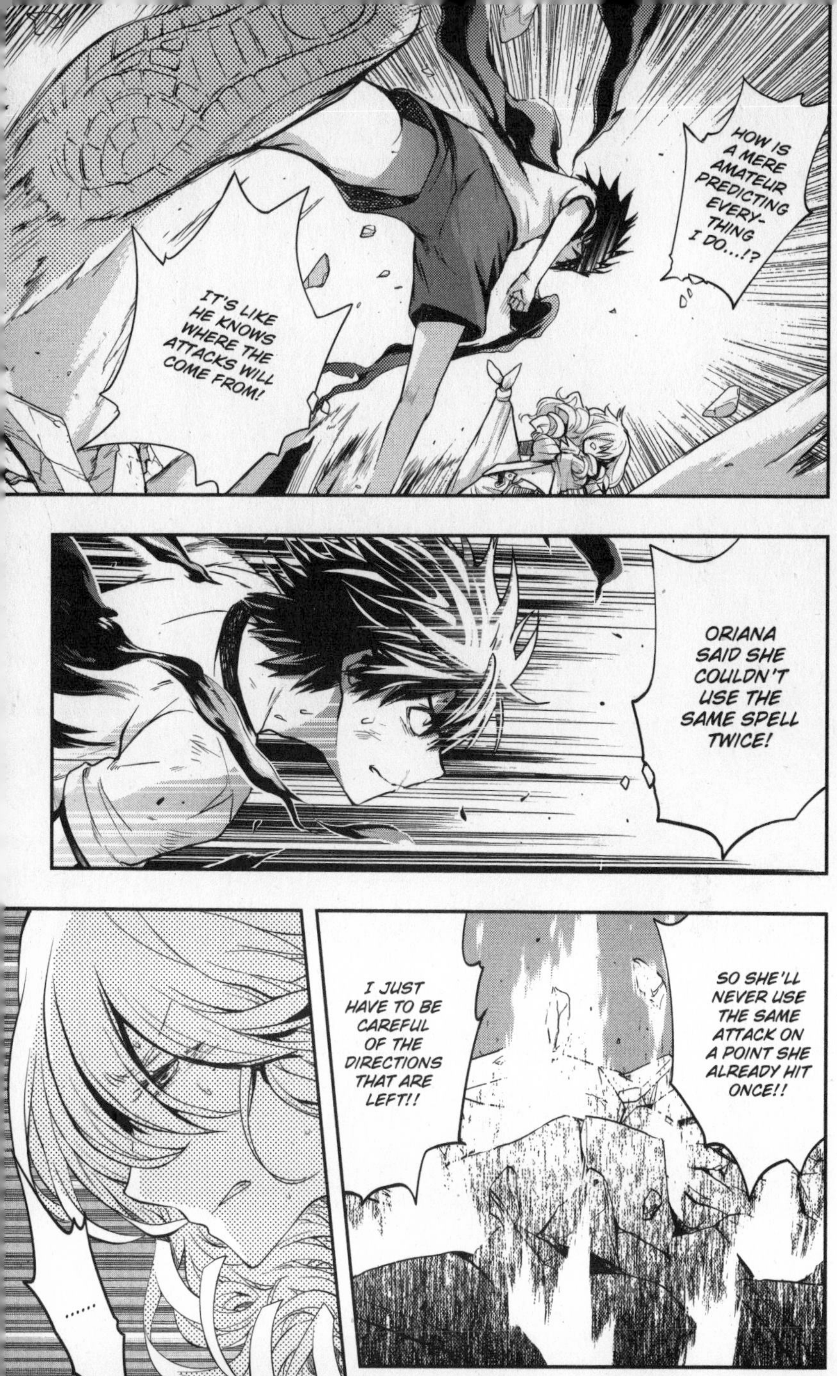
HOW IS A MERE AMATEUR PREDICTING EVERY-THING I DO...!?
IT'S LIKE HE KNOWS WHERE THE ATTACKS WILL COME FROM!
ORIANA SAID SHE COULDN'T USE THE SAME SPELL TWICE!
SO SHE'LL NEVER USE THE SAME ATTACK ON A POINT SHE ALREADY HIT ONCE!!
I JUST HAVE TO BE CAREFUL OF THE DIRECTIONS THAT ARE LEFT!!
......

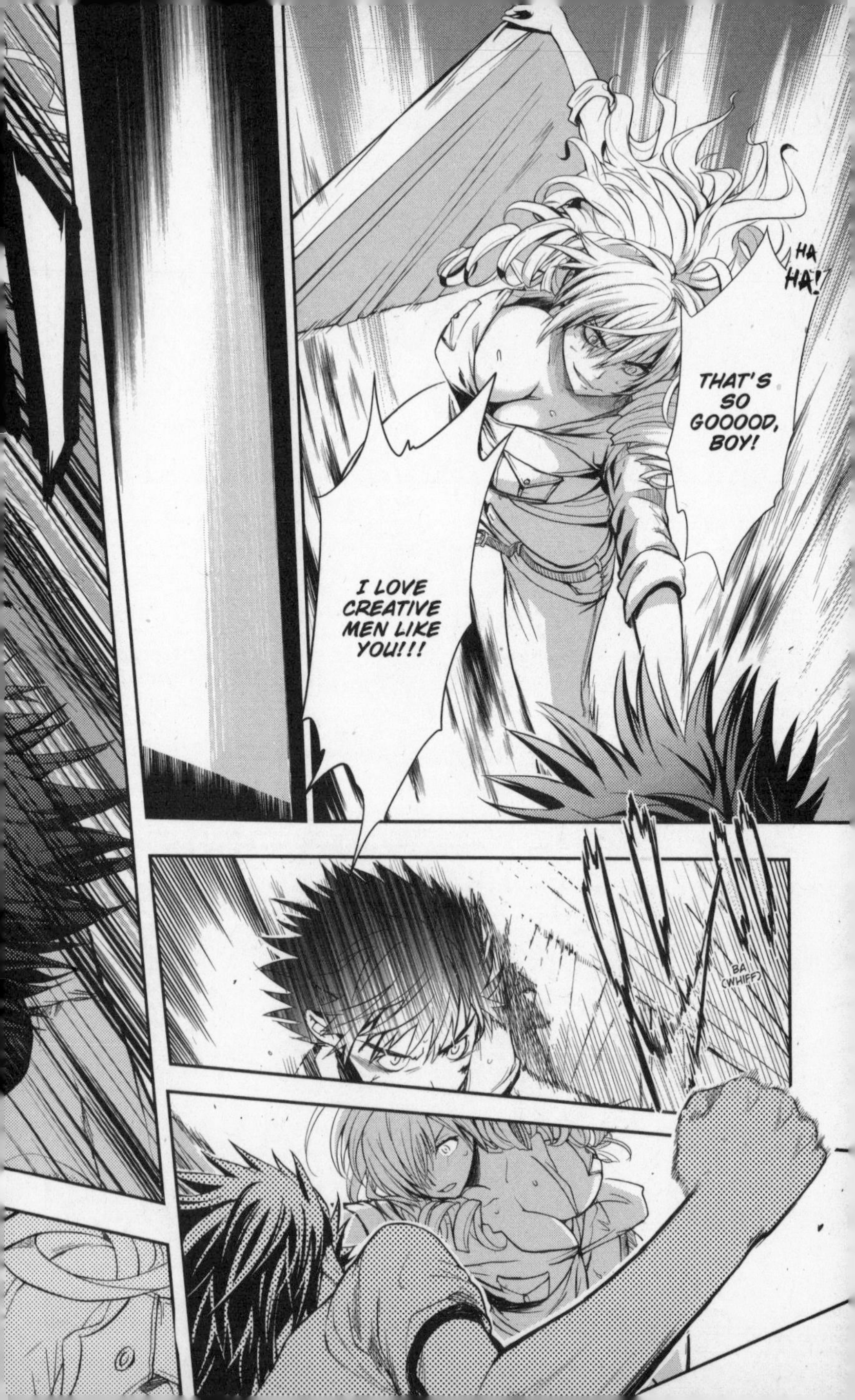
HA HA!
THAT'S SO GOOOOD, BOY!
I LOVE CREATIVE MEN LIKE YOU!!!
BA (WHIFF)

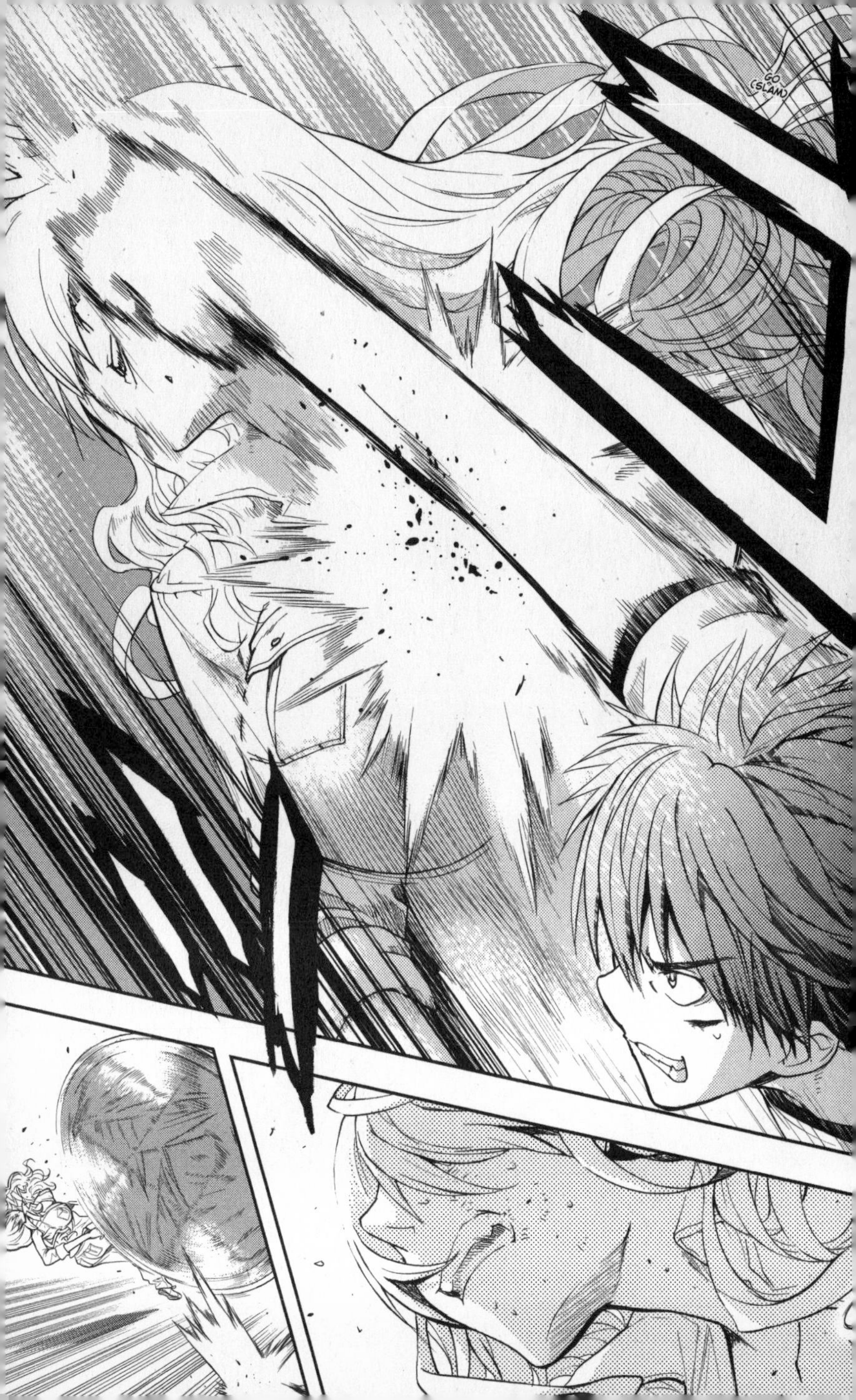
GO (SLAM)

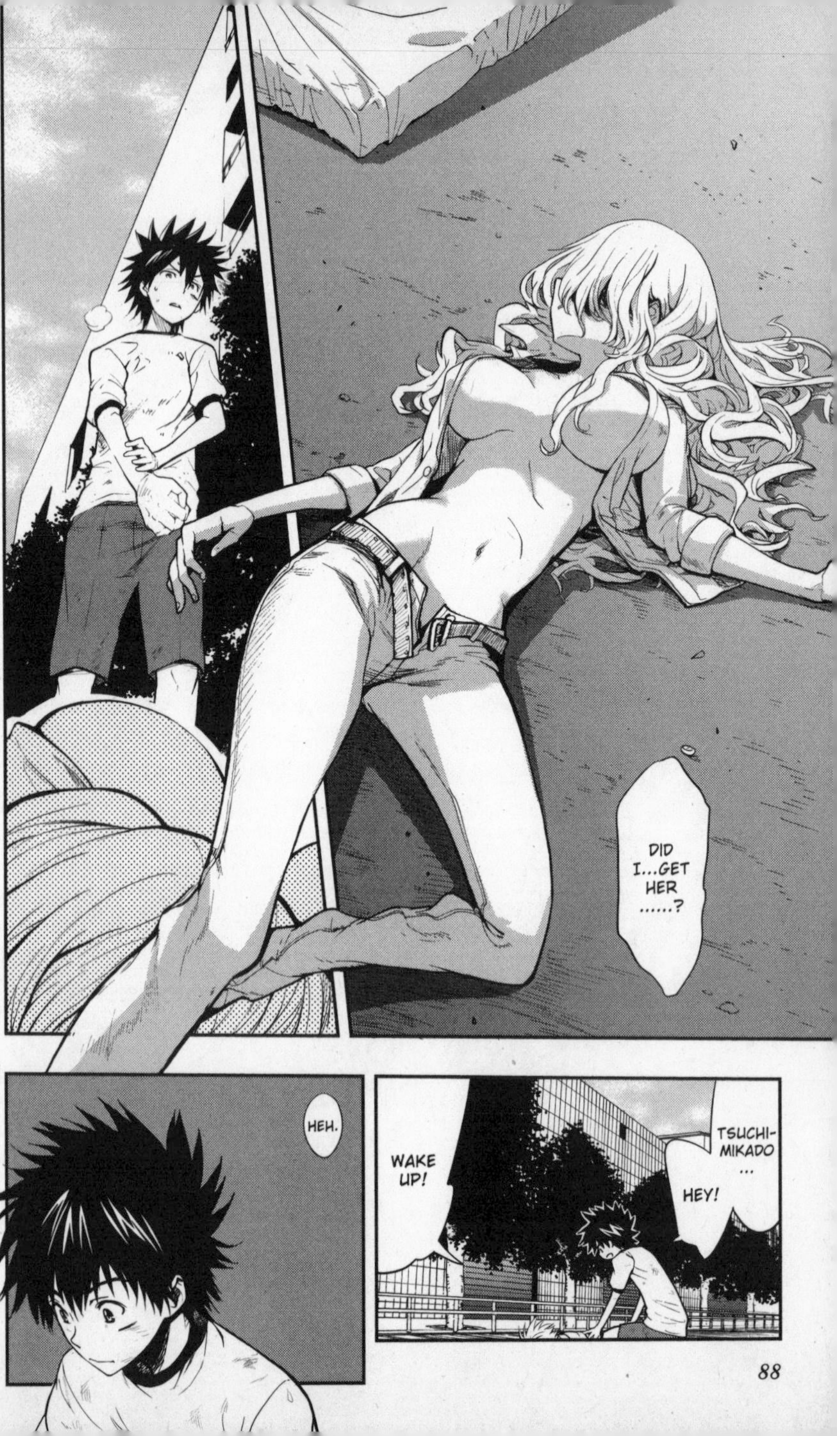
DID I...GET HER ......?
TSUCHI-MIKADO ...
HEY!
WAKE UP!
HEH.

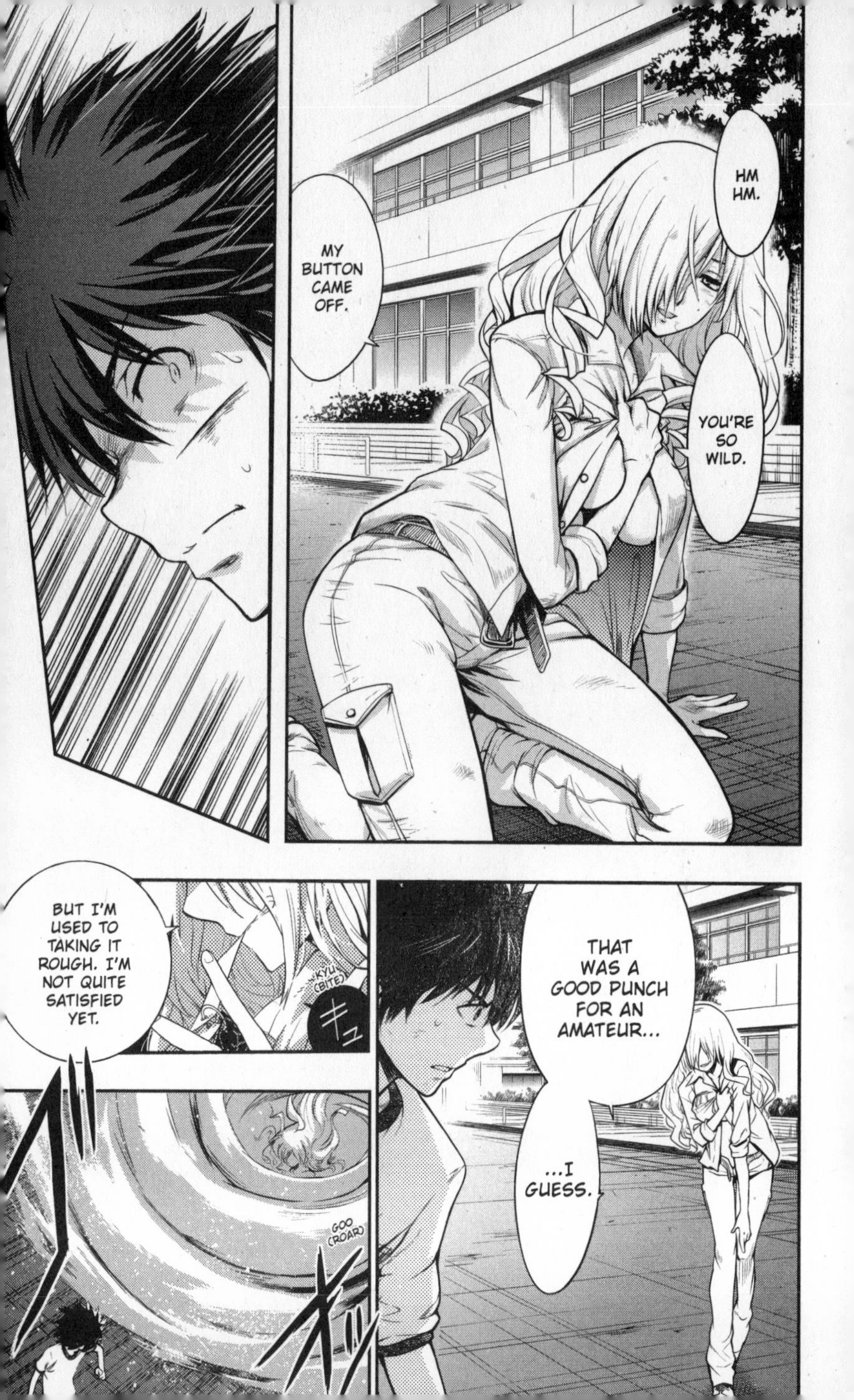
HM HM.
MY BUTTON CAME OFF.
YOU'RE SO WILD.
THAT WAS A GOOD PUNCH FOR AN AMATEUR...
...I GUESS.
BUT I'M USED TO TAKING IT ROUGH. I'M NOT QUITE SATISFIED YET.
KYU (BITE)
GOO (ROAR)

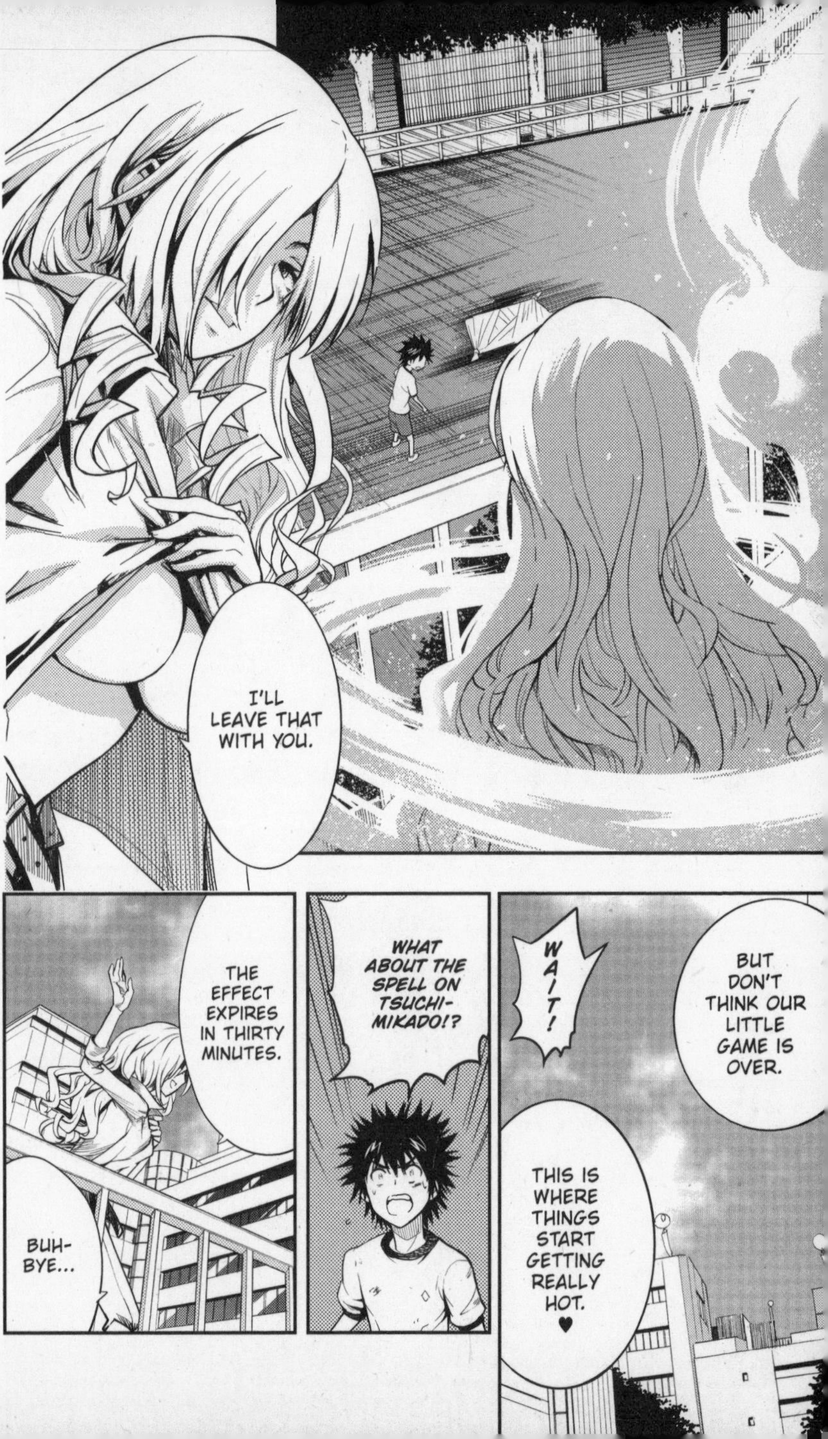
I'LL LEAVE THAT WITH YOU.
BUT DON'T THINK OUR LITTLE GAME IS OVER.
THIS IS WHERE THINGS START GETTING REALLY HOT. ♥
WAIT!
WHAT ABOUT THE SPELL ON TSUCHI-MIKADO!?
THE EFFECT EXPIRES IN THIRTY MINUTES.
BUH-BYE...

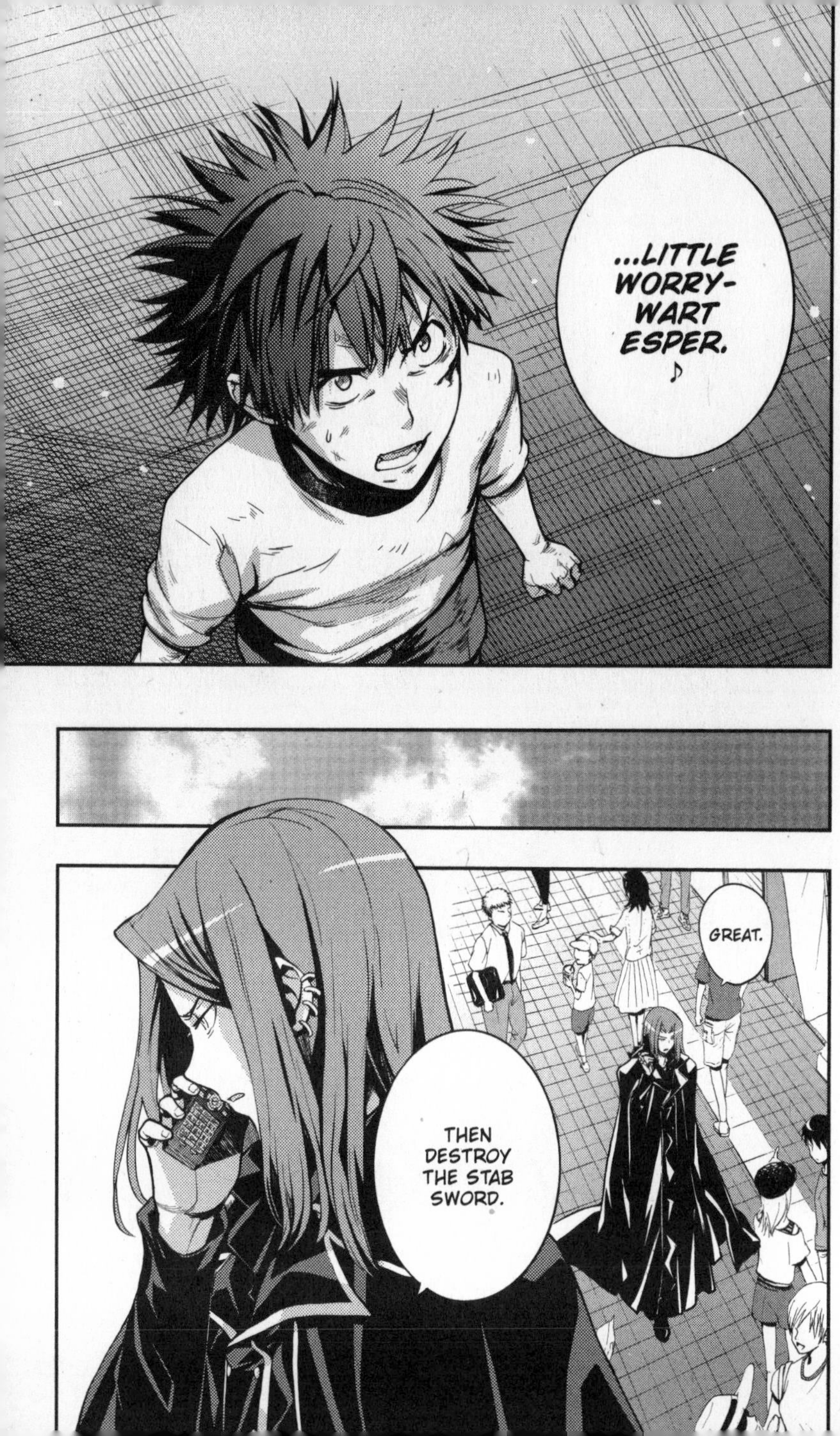
...LITTLE WORRY-WART ESPER. ♪
GREAT.
THEN DESTROY THE STAB SWORD.

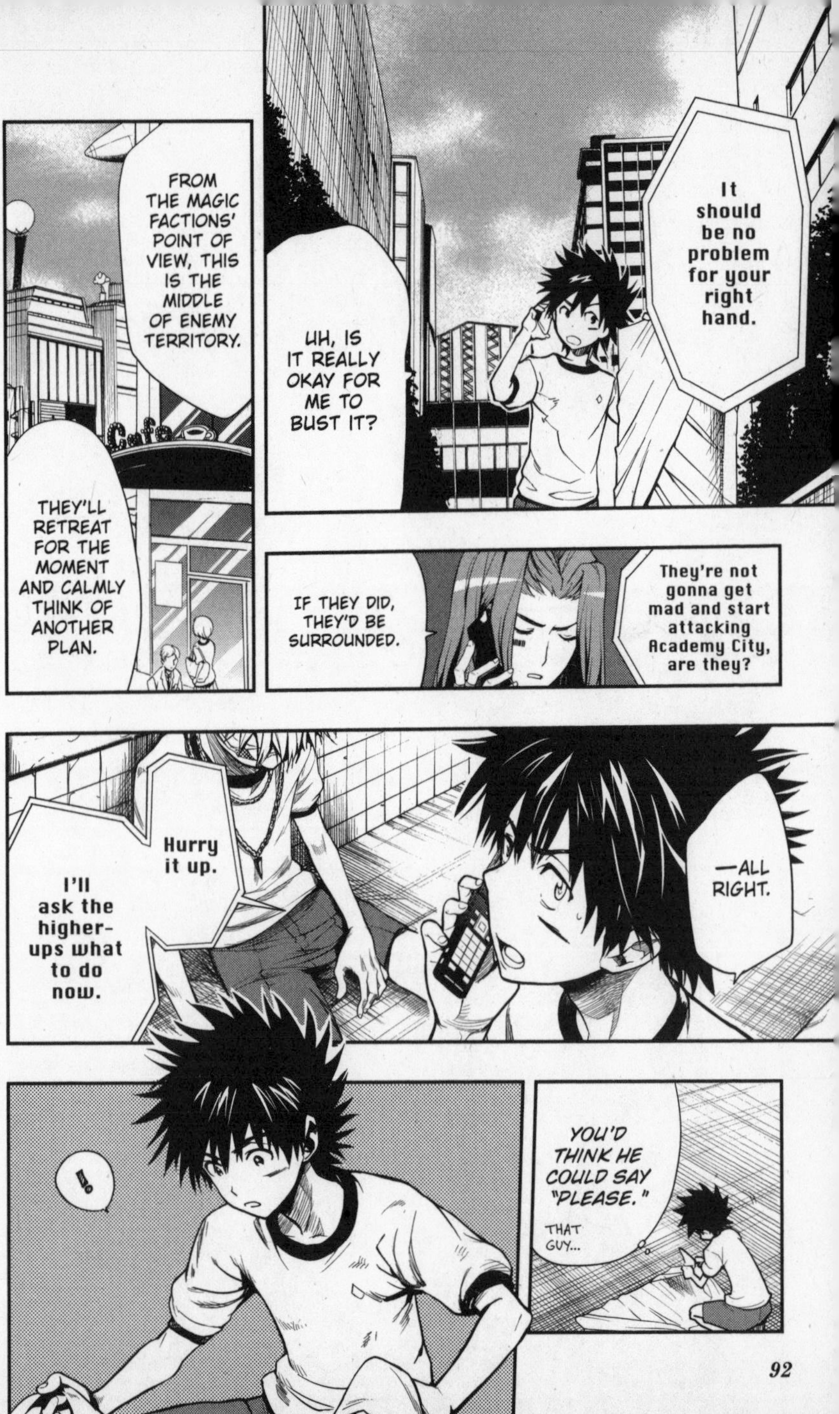
It should be no problem for your right hand.
UH, IS IT REALLY OKAY FOR ME TO BUST IT?
They're not gonna get mad and start attacking Academy City, are they?
IF THEY DID, THEY'D BE SURROUNDED.
FROM THE MAGIC FACTIONS' POINT OF VIEW, THIS IS THE MIDDLE OF ENEMY TERRITORY.
THEY'LL RETREAT FOR THE MOMENT AND CALMLY THINK OF ANOTHER PLAN.
—ALL RIGHT.
Hurry it up.
I'll ask the higher-ups what to do now.
YOU'D THINK HE COULD SAY "PLEASE."
THAT GUY...
!?

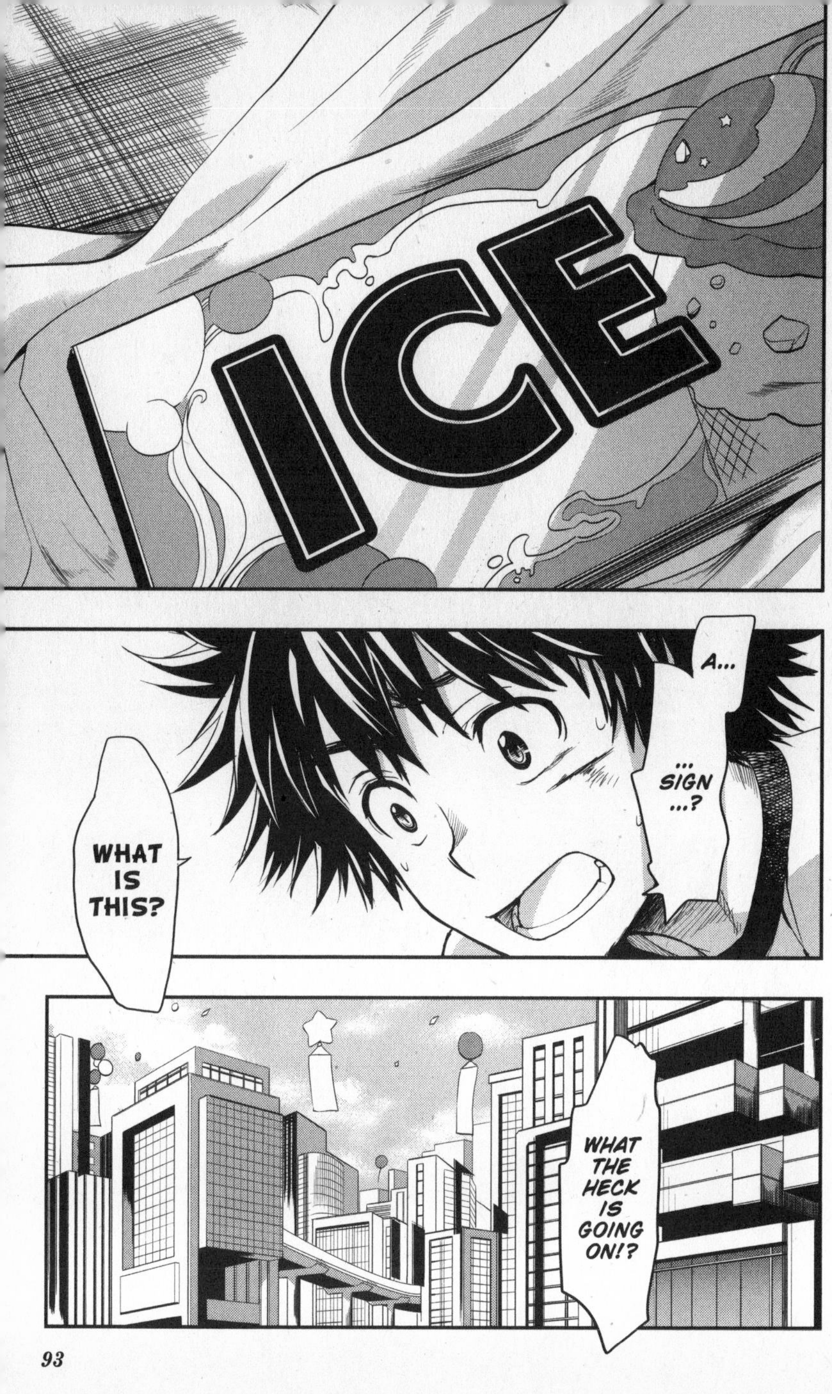
ICE
A...
...SIGN...?
WHAT IS THIS?
WHAT THE HECK IS GOING ON!?

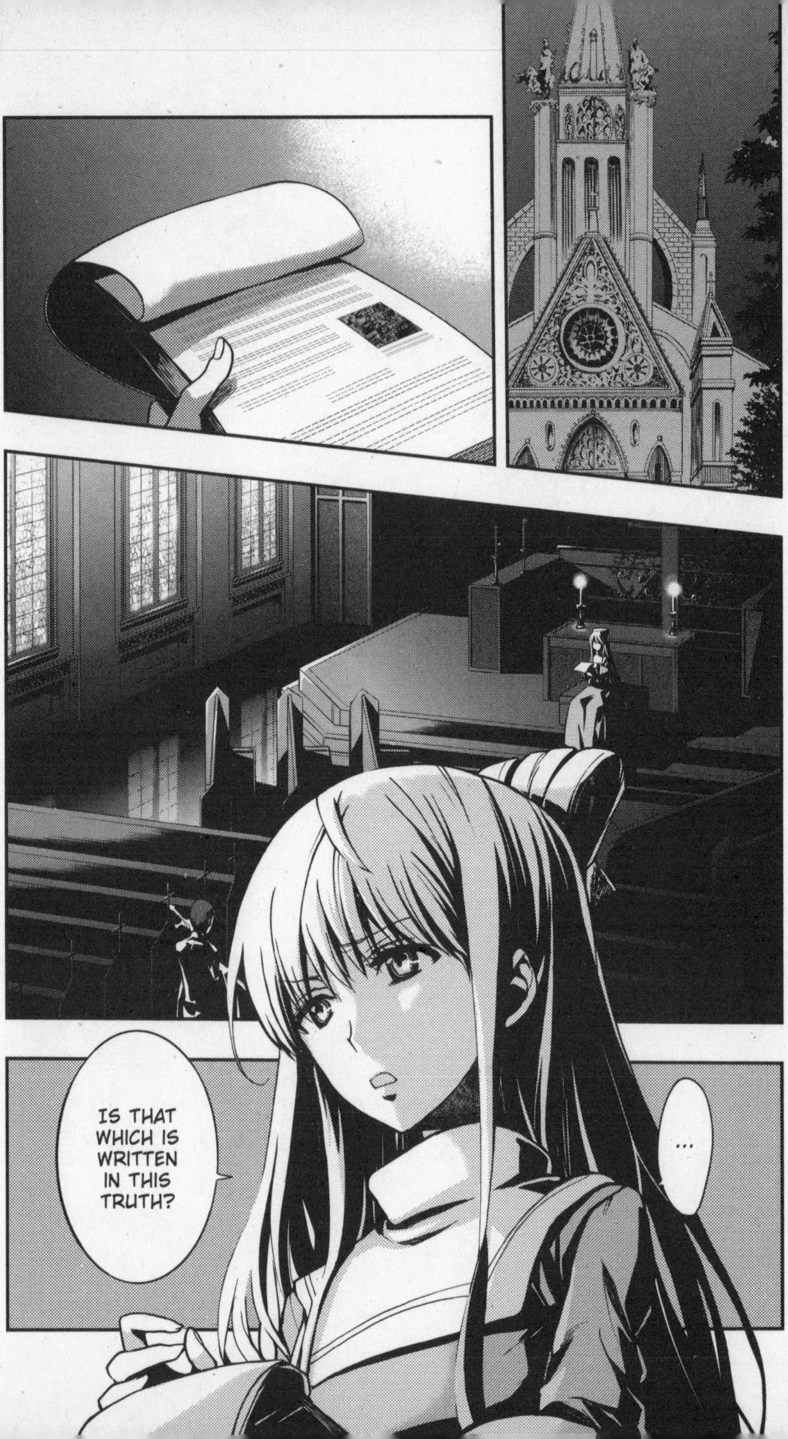
...
IS THAT WHICH IS WRITTEN IN THIS TRUTH?

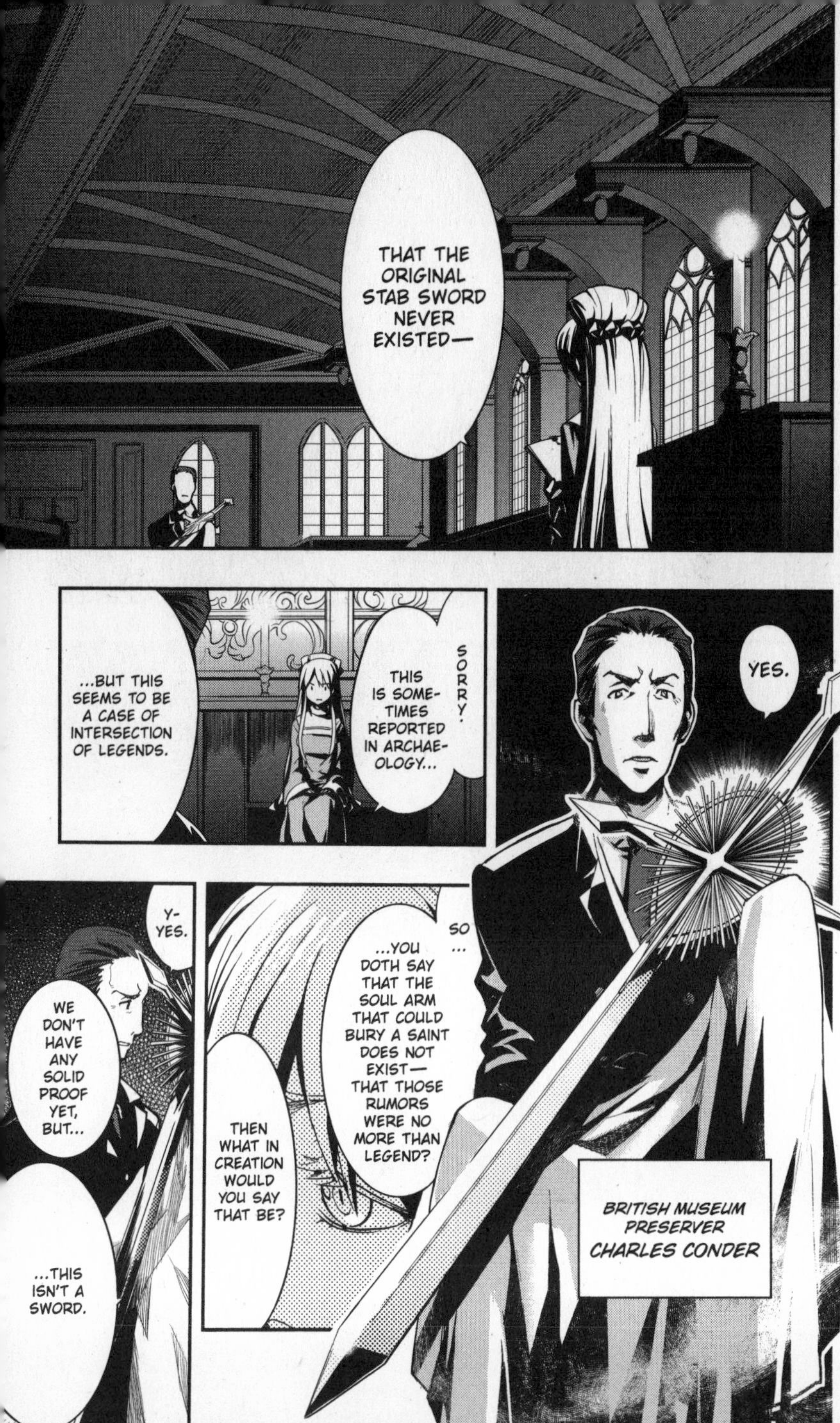
THAT THE ORIGINAL STAB SWORD NEVER EXISTED—
YES.
BRITISH MUSEUM PRESERVER CHARLES CONDER
SORRY.
THIS IS SOMETIMES REPORTED IN ARCHAEOLOGY...
...BUT THIS SEEMS TO BE A CASE OF INTERSECTION OF LEGENDS.
SO...
...YOU DOTH SAY THAT THE SOUL ARM THAT COULD BURY A SAINT DOES NOT EXIST—THAT THOSE RUMORS WERE NO MORE THAN LEGEND?
THEN WHAT IN CREATION WOULD YOU SAY THAT BE?
Y-YES.
WE DON'T HAVE ANY SOLID PROOF YET, BUT...
...THIS ISN'T A SWORD.

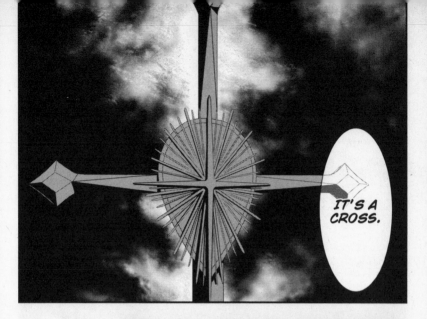

IT'S A
CROSS.

IT APPEARS
TO BE
SOMETHING
CALLED
THE CROCE
DI PIETRO
IN LOCAL
PARLANCE.

...IF SUCH IS
TRUE, THEN
'TWOULD
FUNDAMENTALLY
CHANGE WHAT
THEIR "DEAL" IN
ACADEMY CITY
IS...

PETER'S
CROSS!?

P...

GATA
(CLATTER)

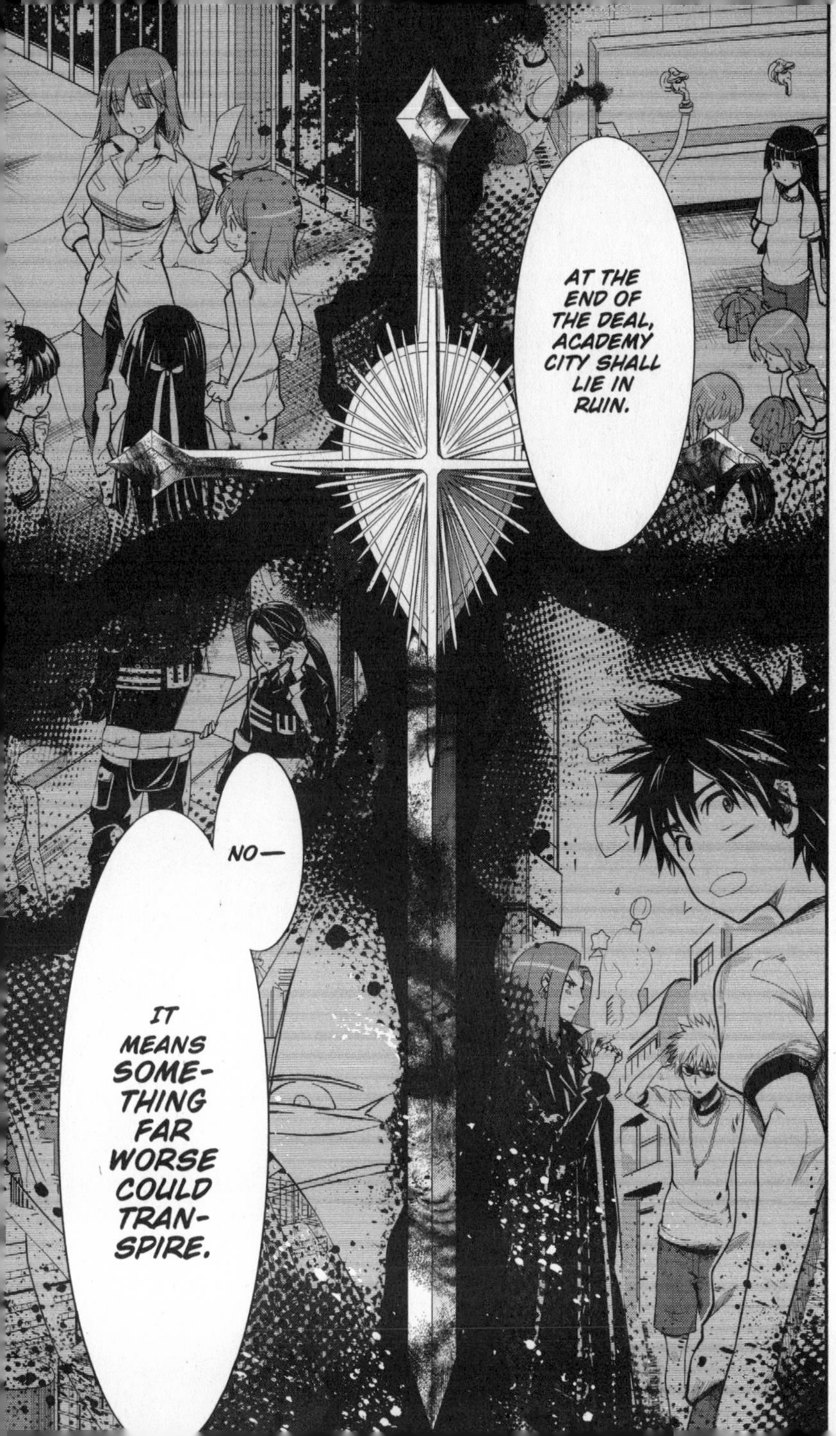
AT THE END OF THE DEAL, ACADEMY CITY SHALL LIE IN RUIN.
NO—
IT MEANS SOME-THING FAR WORSE COULD TRAN-SPIRE.

A Certain Magical Index

#74 THE DEAL

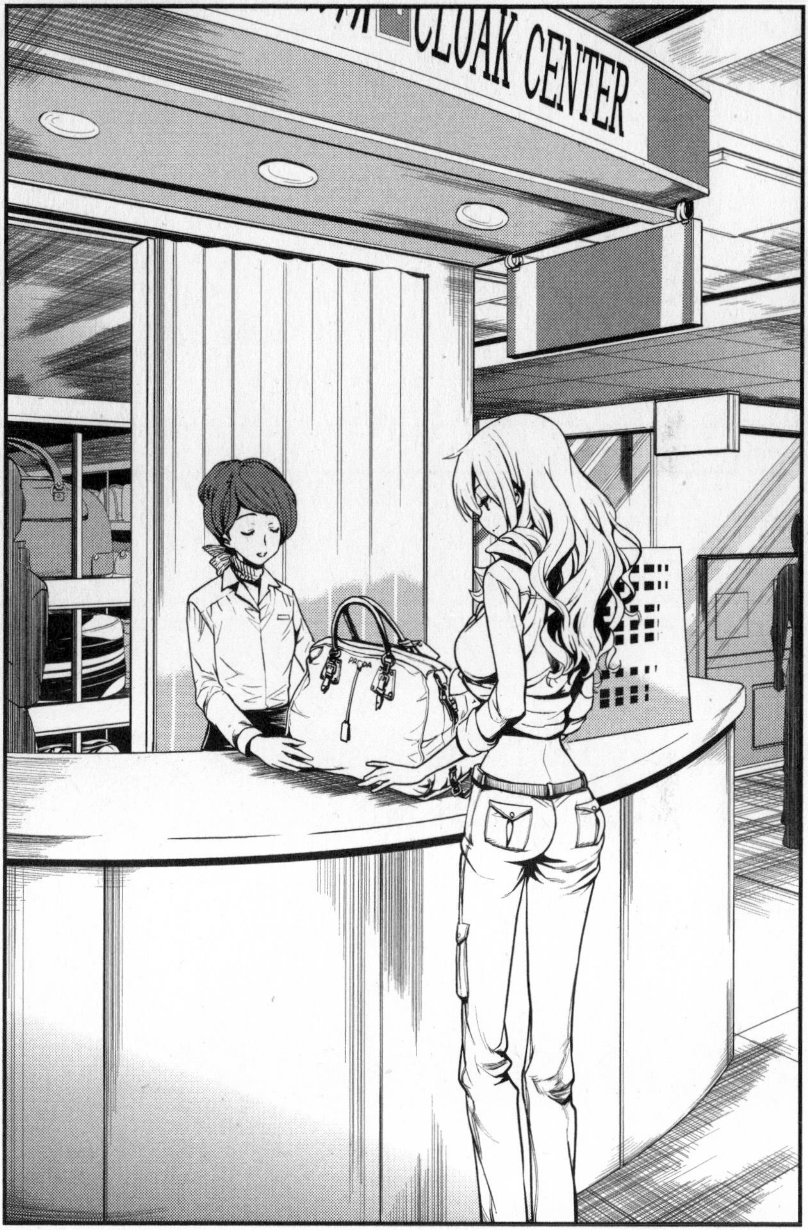
CLOAK CENTER
PRADA

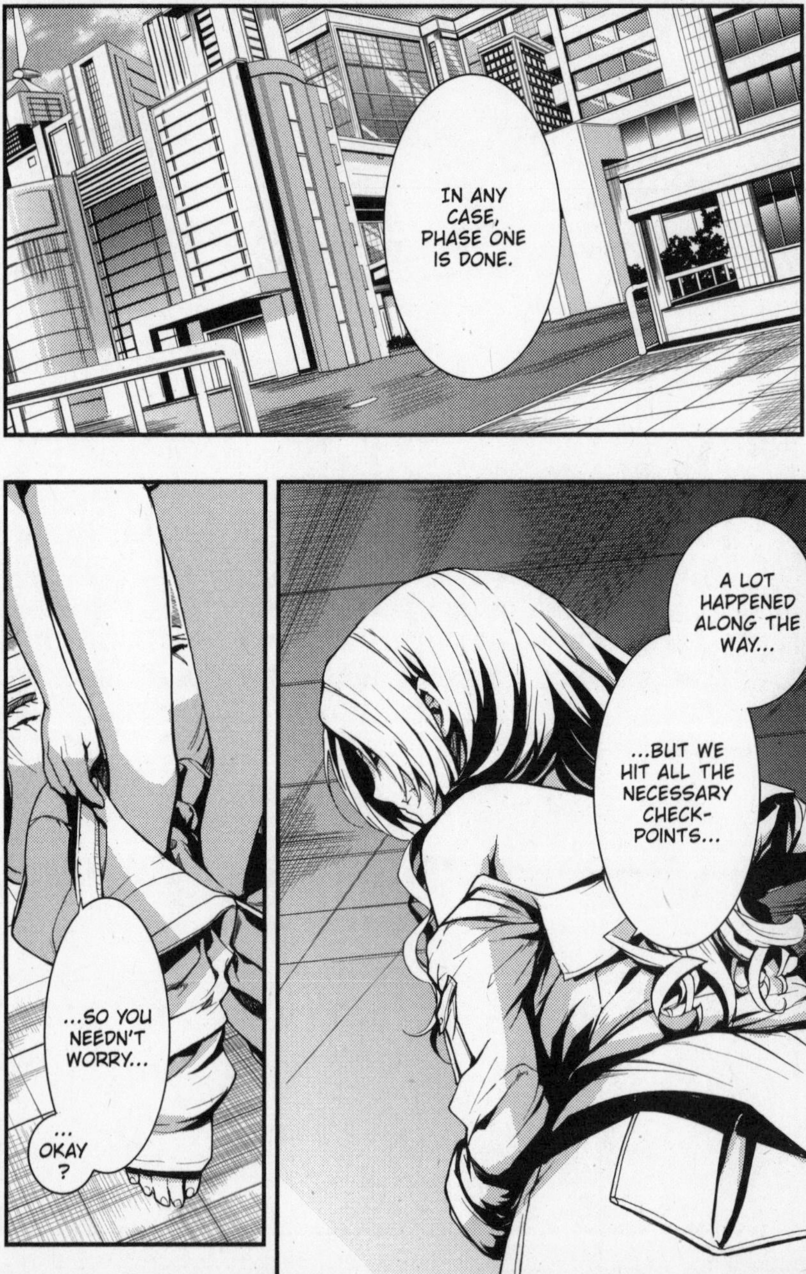
IN ANY CASE, PHASE ONE IS DONE.
A LOT HAPPENED ALONG THE WAY...
...BUT WE HIT ALL THE NECESSARY CHECK-POINTS...
...SO YOU NEEDN'T WORRY...
...OKAY?

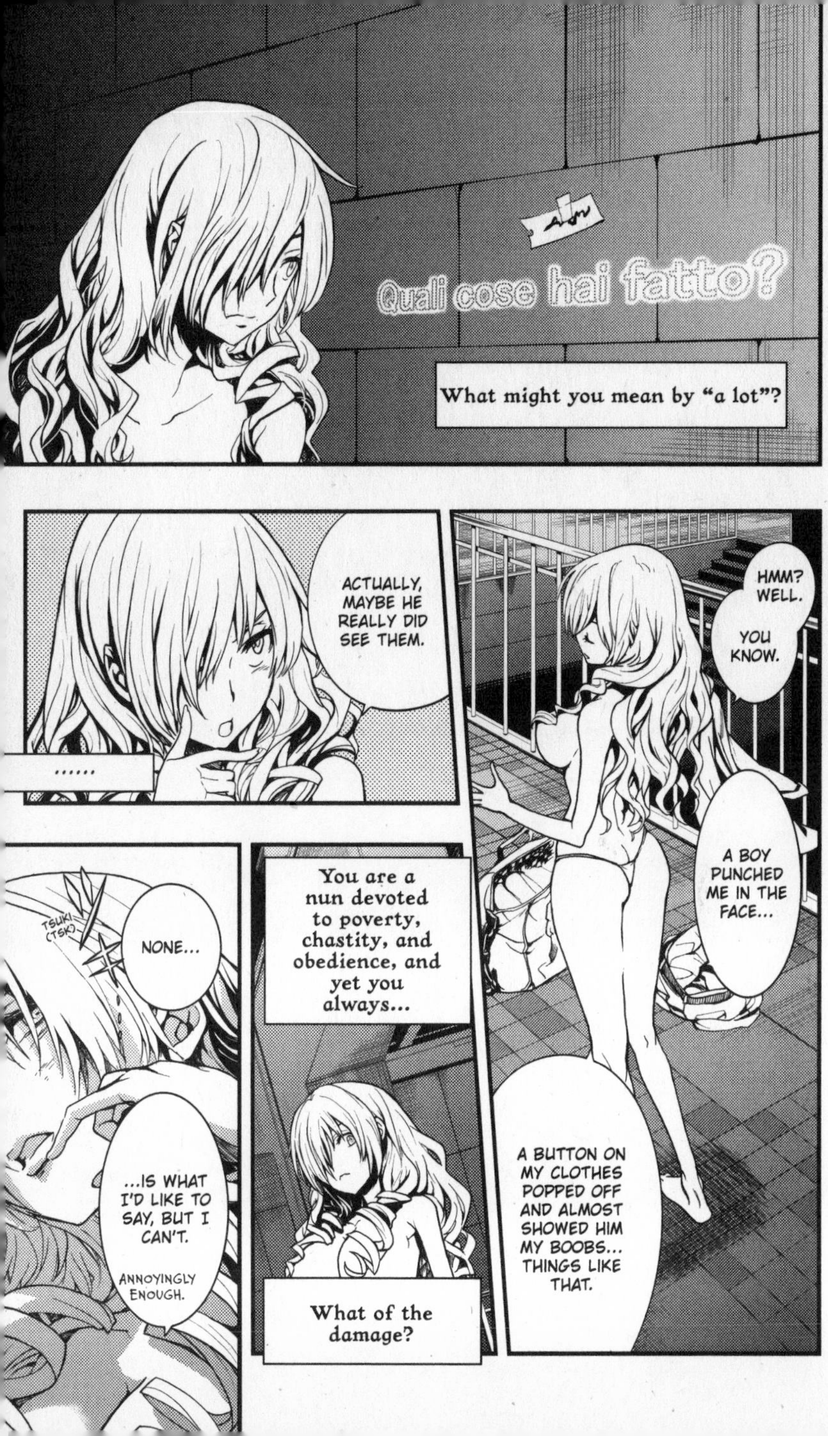
Quali cose hai fatto?
What might you mean by "a lot"?
HMM? WELL.
YOU KNOW.
A BOY PUNCHED ME IN THE FACE...
A BUTTON ON MY CLOTHES POPPED OFF AND ALMOST SHOWED HIM MY BOOBS... THINGS LIKE THAT.
ACTUALLY, MAYBE HE REALLY DID SEE THEM.
......
You are a nun devoted to poverty, chastity, and obedience, and yet you always...
What of the damage?
TSUKI (TSK)
NONE...
...IS WHAT I'D LIKE TO SAY, BUT I CAN'T.
ANNOYINGLY ENOUGH.

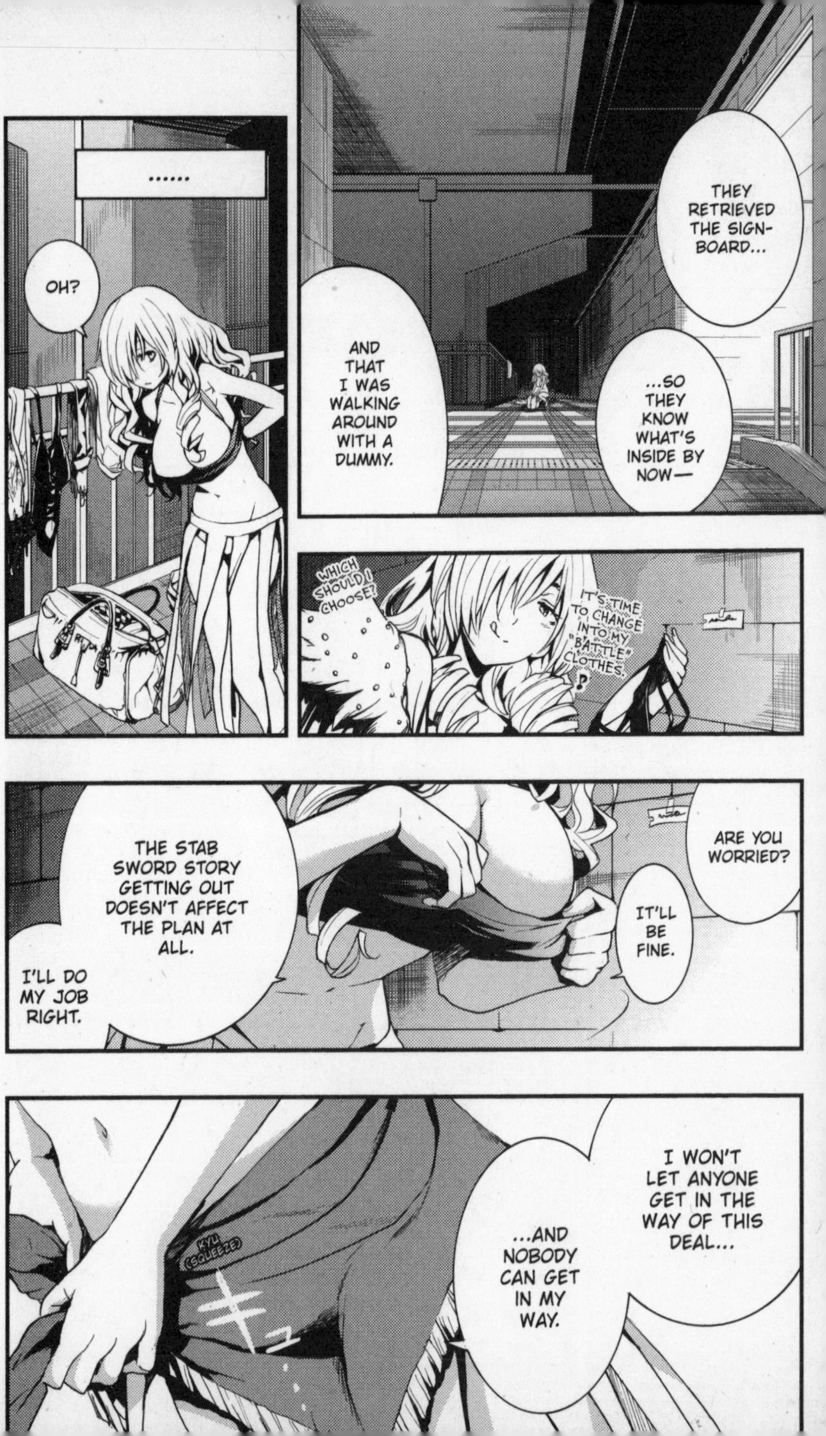
THEY RETRIEVED THE SIGN-BOARD...
...SO THEY KNOW WHAT'S INSIDE BY NOW—
AND THAT I WAS WALKING AROUND WITH A DUMMY.
IT'S TIME TO CHANGE INTO MY "BATTLE" CLOTHES.
!?
WHICH SHOULD I CHOOSE?
......
OH?
ARE YOU WORRIED?
IT'LL BE FINE.
THE STAB SWORD STORY GETTING OUT DOESN'T AFFECT THE PLAN AT ALL.
I'LL DO MY JOB RIGHT.
I WON'T LET ANYONE GET IN THE WAY OF THIS DEAL...
...AND NOBODY CAN GET IN MY WAY.
KYU (SQUEEZE)

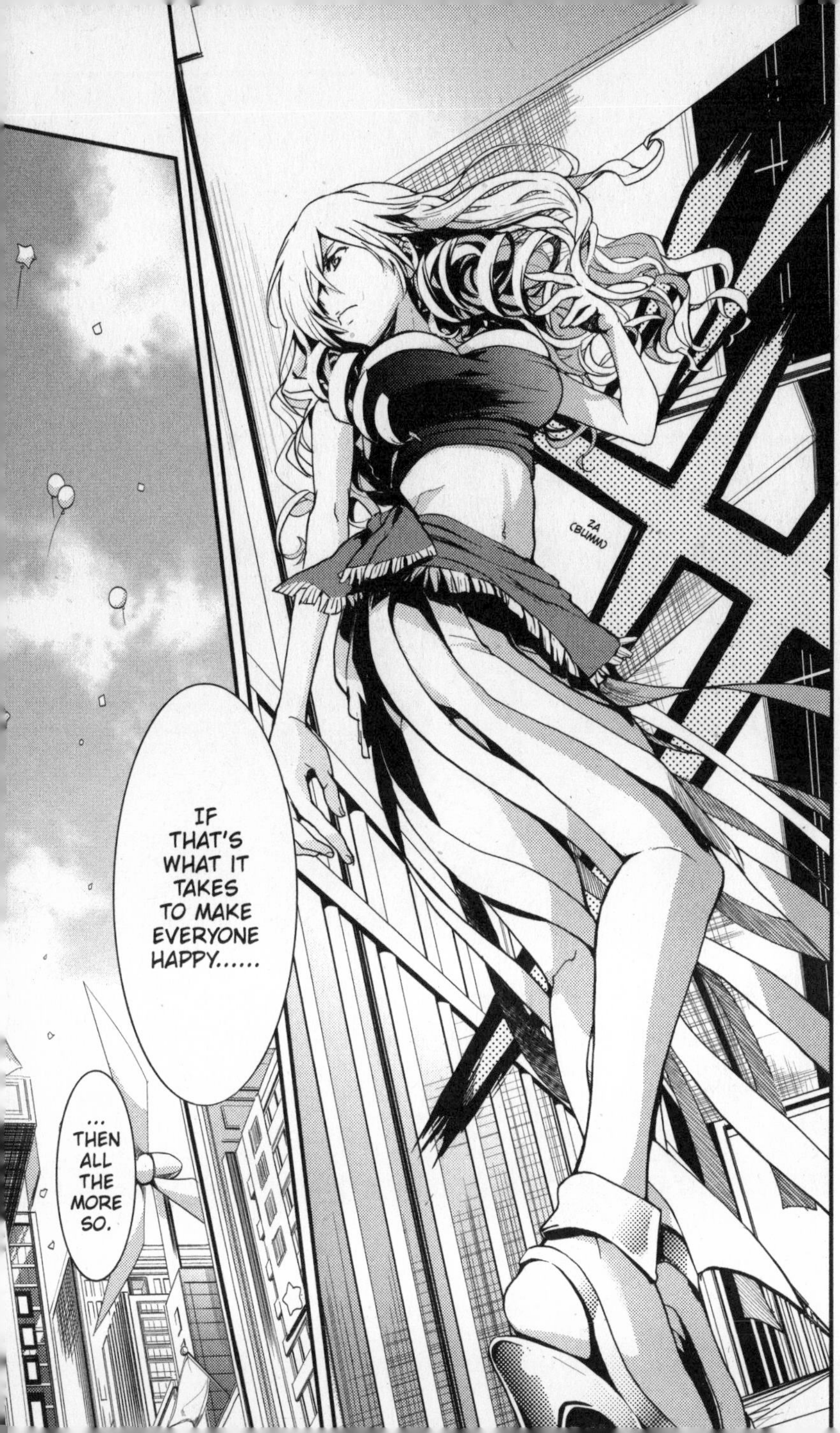
ZA (BLMM)
IF THAT'S WHAT IT TAKES TO MAKE EVERYONE HAPPY......
...THEN ALL THE MORE SO.

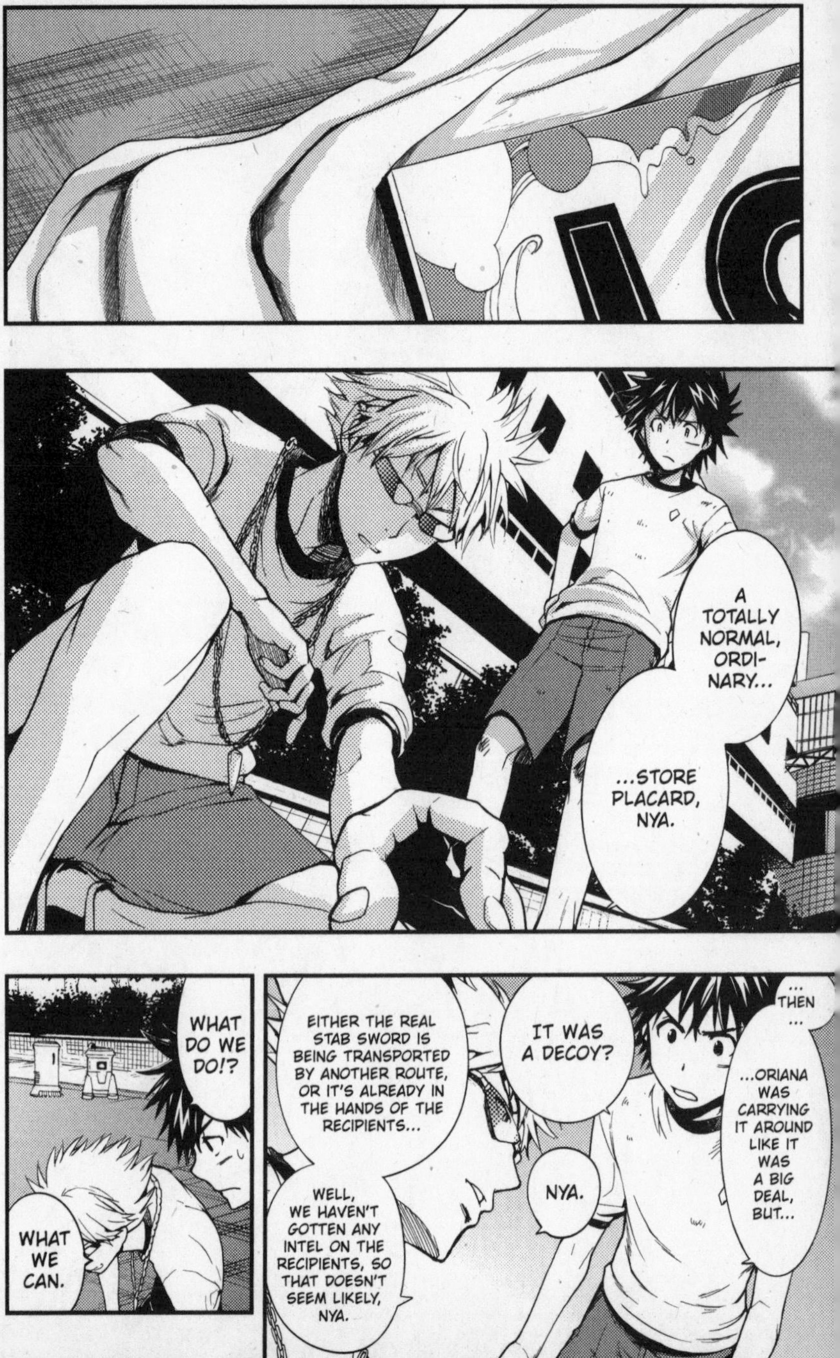
A TOTALLY NORMAL, ORDINARY...
...STORE PLACARD, NYA.
...THEN...
...ORIANA WAS CARRYING IT AROUND LIKE IT WAS A BIG DEAL, BUT...
IT WAS A DECOY?
NYA.
EITHER THE REAL STAB SWORD IS BEING TRANSPORTED BY ANOTHER ROUTE, OR IT'S ALREADY IN THE HANDS OF THE RECIPIENTS...
WELL, WE HAVEN'T GOTTEN ANY INTEL ON THE RECIPIENTS, SO THAT DOESN'T SEEM LIKELY, NYA.
WHAT DO WE DO!?
WHAT WE CAN.

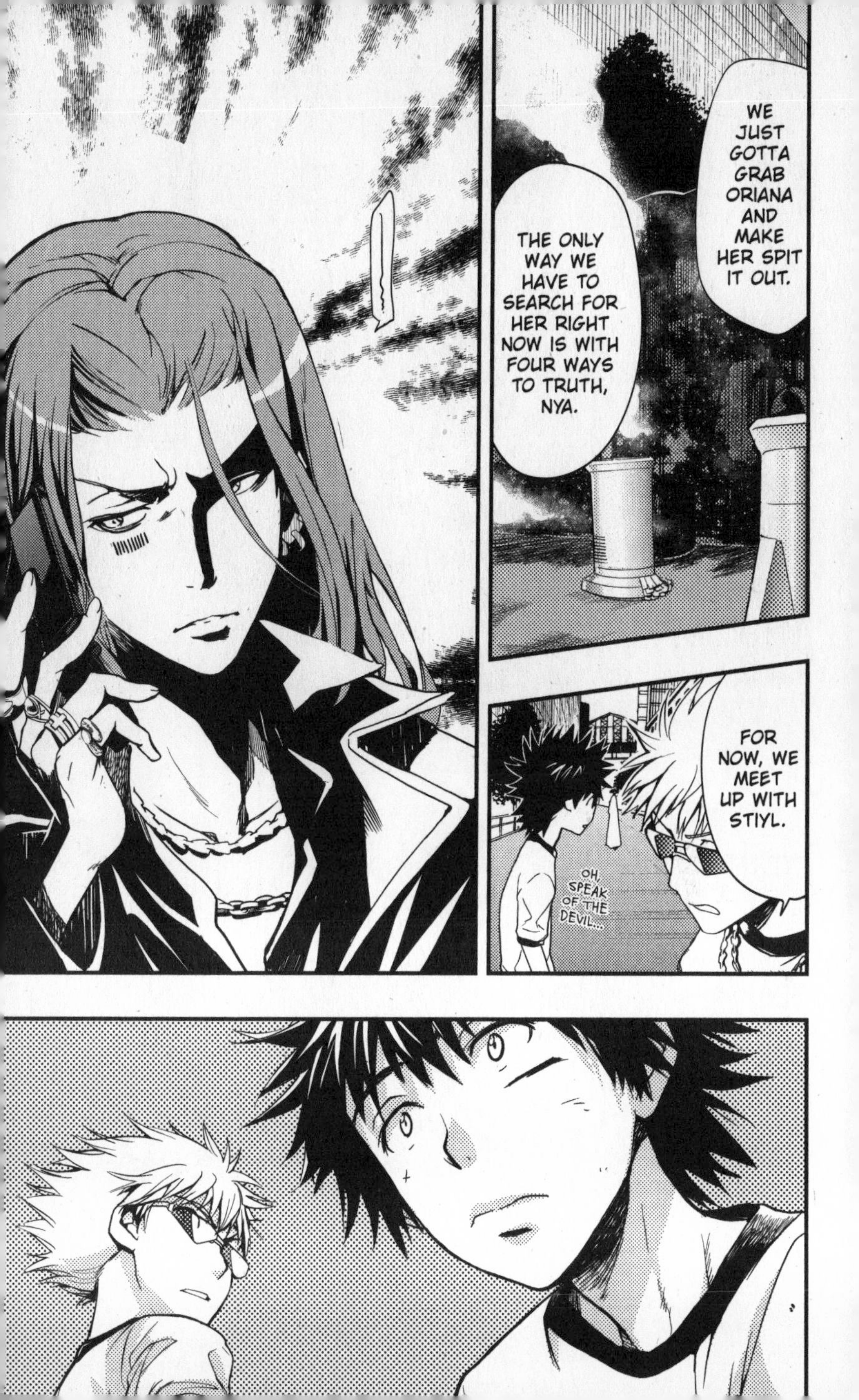
WE JUST GOTTA GRAB ORIANA AND MAKE HER SPIT IT OUT.
THE ONLY WAY WE HAVE TO SEARCH FOR HER RIGHT NOW IS WITH FOUR WAYS TO TRUTH, NYA.
FOR NOW, WE MEET UP WITH STIYL.
OH, SPEAK OF THE DEVIL...

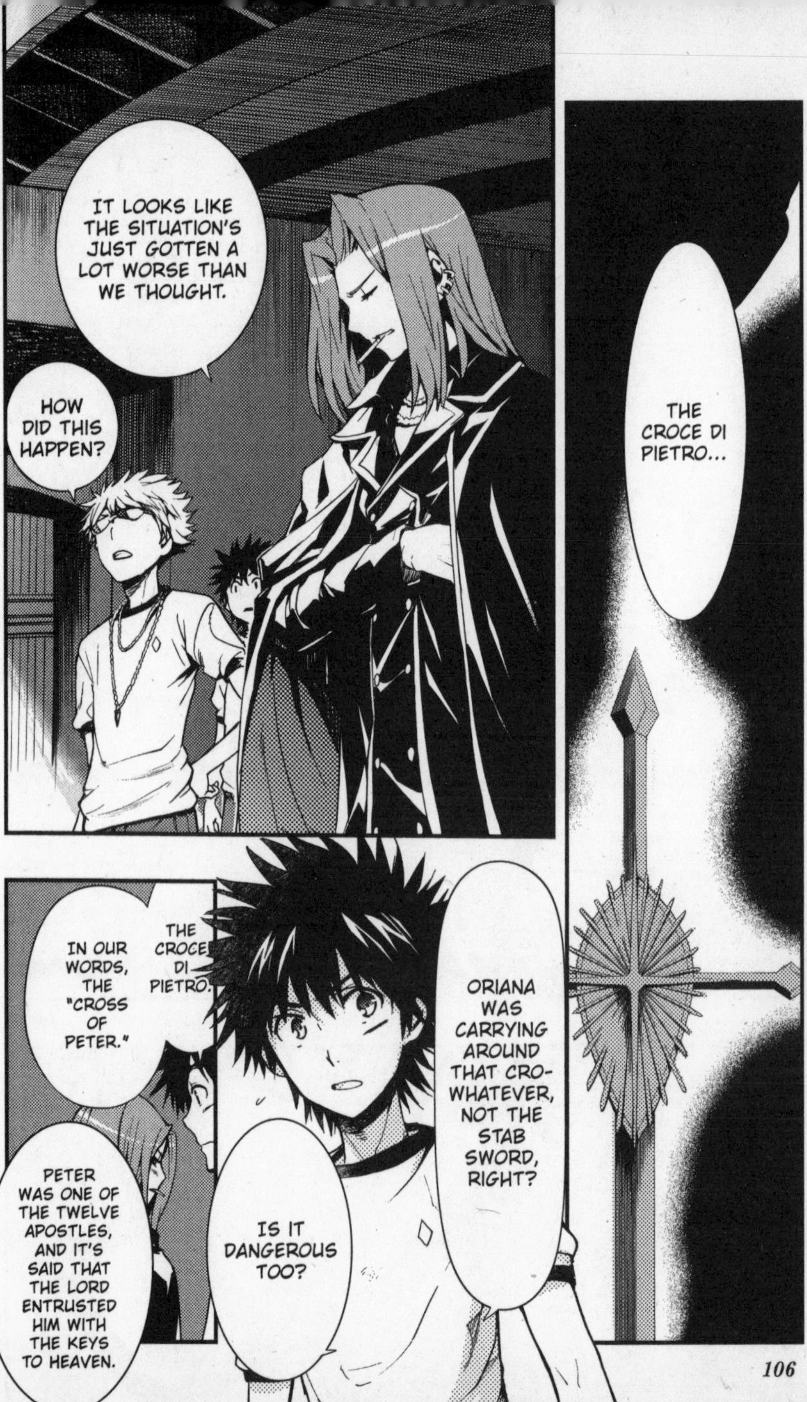
THE CROCE DI PIETRO...
IT LOOKS LIKE THE SITUATION'S JUST GOTTEN A LOT WORSE THAN WE THOUGHT.
HOW DID THIS HAPPEN?
ORIANA WAS CARRYING AROUND THAT CRO-WHATEVER, NOT THE STAB SWORD, RIGHT?
IS IT DANGEROUS TOO?
THE CROCE DI PIETRO.
IN OUR WORDS, THE "CROSS OF PETER."
PETER WAS ONE OF THE TWELVE APOSTLES, AND IT'S SAID THAT THE LORD ENTRUSTED HIM WITH THE KEYS TO HEAVEN.

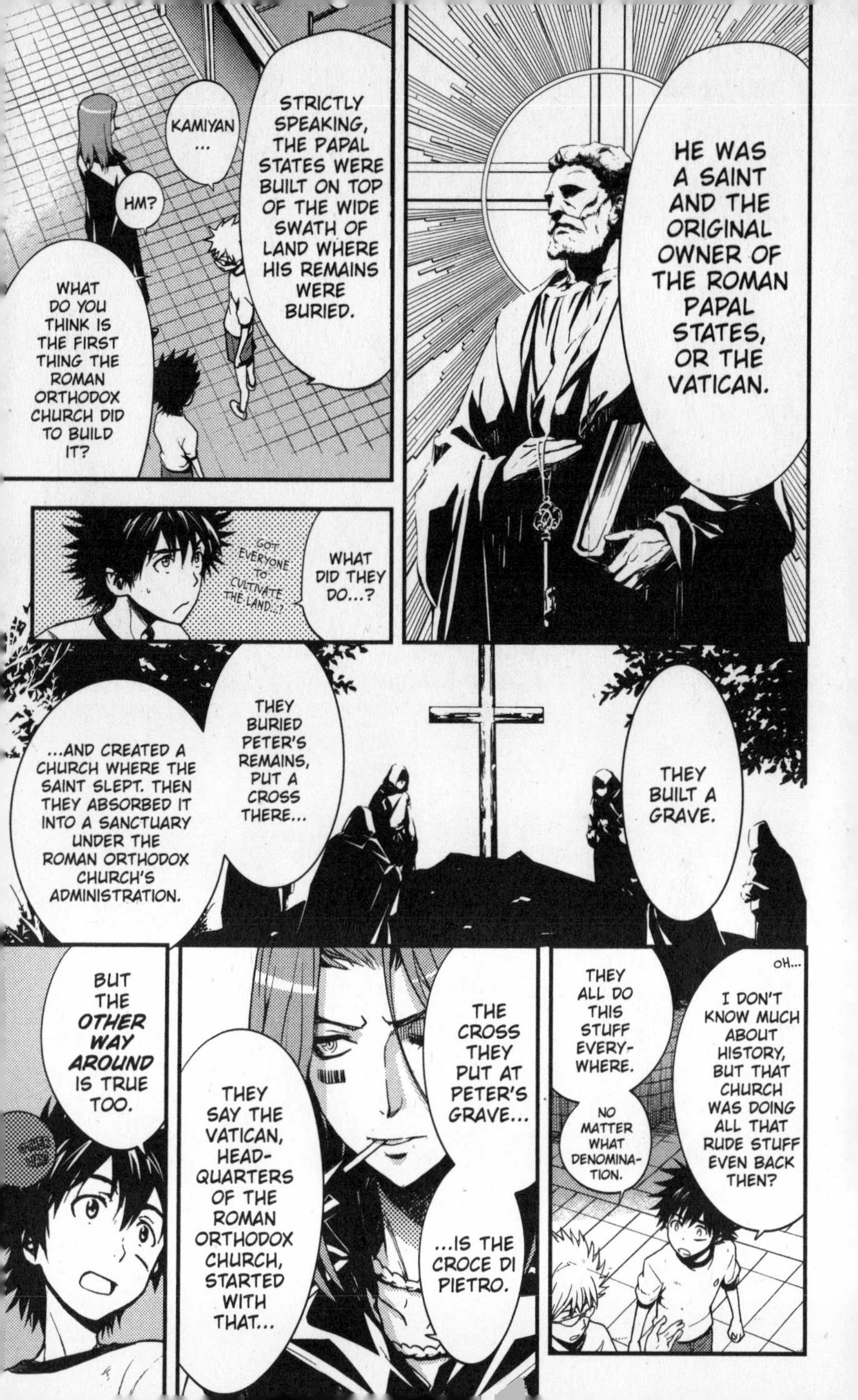
HE WAS A SAINT AND THE ORIGINAL OWNER OF THE ROMAN PAPAL STATES, OR THE VATICAN.
STRICTLY SPEAKING, THE PAPAL STATES WERE BUILT ON TOP OF THE WIDE SWATH OF LAND WHERE HIS REMAINS WERE BURIED.
KAMIYAN...
HM?
WHAT DO YOU THINK IS THE FIRST THING THE ROMAN ORTHODOX CHURCH DID TO BUILD IT?
WHAT DID THEY DO...?
GOT EVERYONE TO CULTIVATE THE LAND...?
THEY BUILT A GRAVE.
THEY BURIED PETER'S REMAINS, PUT A CROSS THERE...
...AND CREATED A CHURCH WHERE THE SAINT SLEPT. THEN THEY ABSORBED IT INTO A SANCTUARY UNDER THE ROMAN ORTHODOX CHURCH'S ADMINISTRATION.
OH...
I DON'T KNOW MUCH ABOUT HISTORY, BUT THAT CHURCH WAS DOING ALL THAT RUDE STUFF EVEN BACK THEN?
THEY ALL DO THIS STUFF EVERYWHERE.
NO MATTER WHAT DENOMINATION.
THE CROSS THEY PUT AT PETER'S GRAVE...
...IS THE CROCE DI PIETRO.
THEY SAY THE VATICAN, HEADQUARTERS OF THE ROMAN ORTHODOX CHURCH, STARTED WITH THAT...
BUT THE *OTHER WAY AROUND* IS TRUE TOO.
OTHER WAY

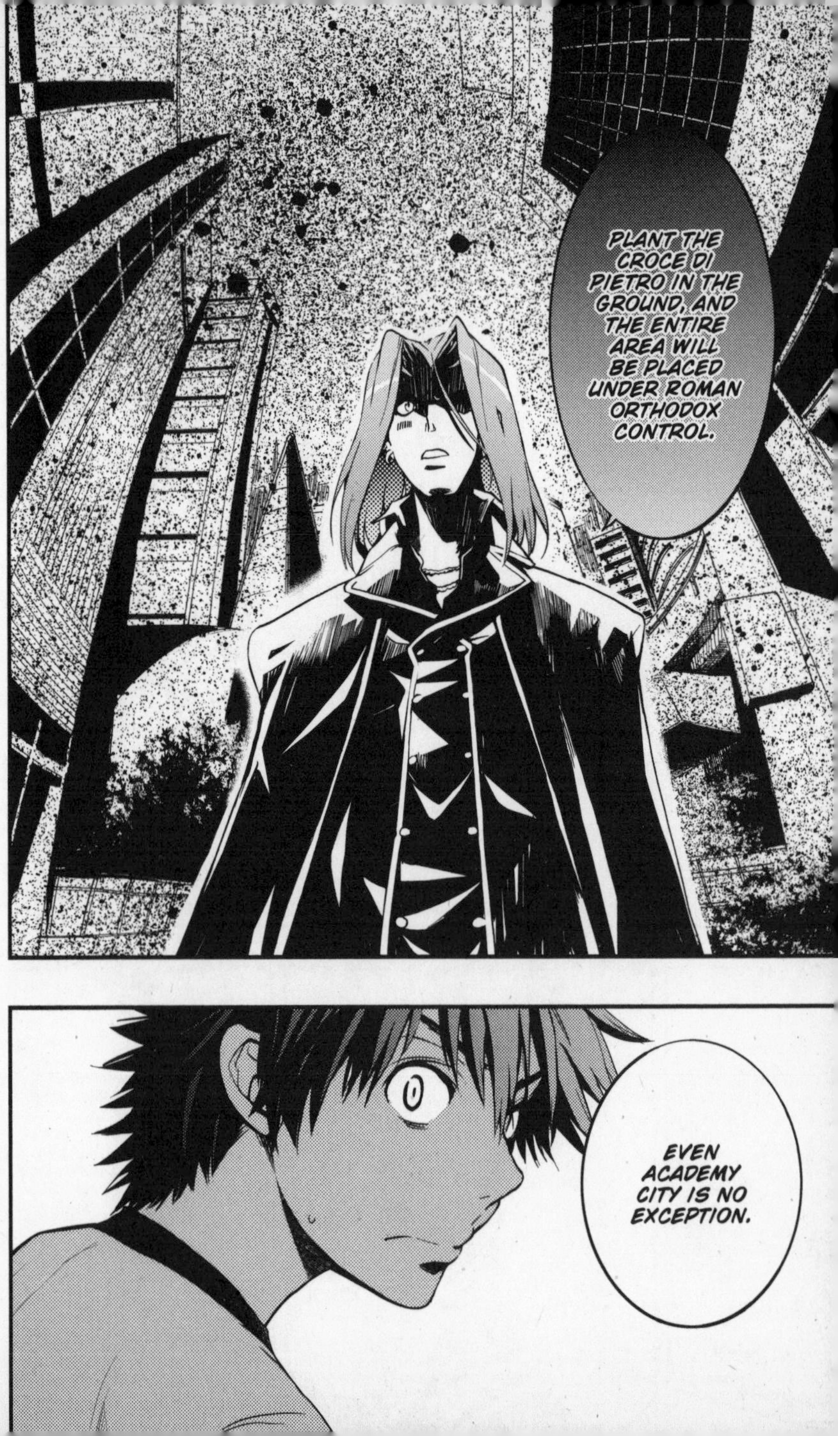
PLANT THE CROCE DI PIETRO IN THE GROUND, AND THE ENTIRE AREA WILL BE PLACED UNDER ROMAN ORTHODOX CONTROL.
EVEN ACADEMY CITY IS NO EXCEPTION.

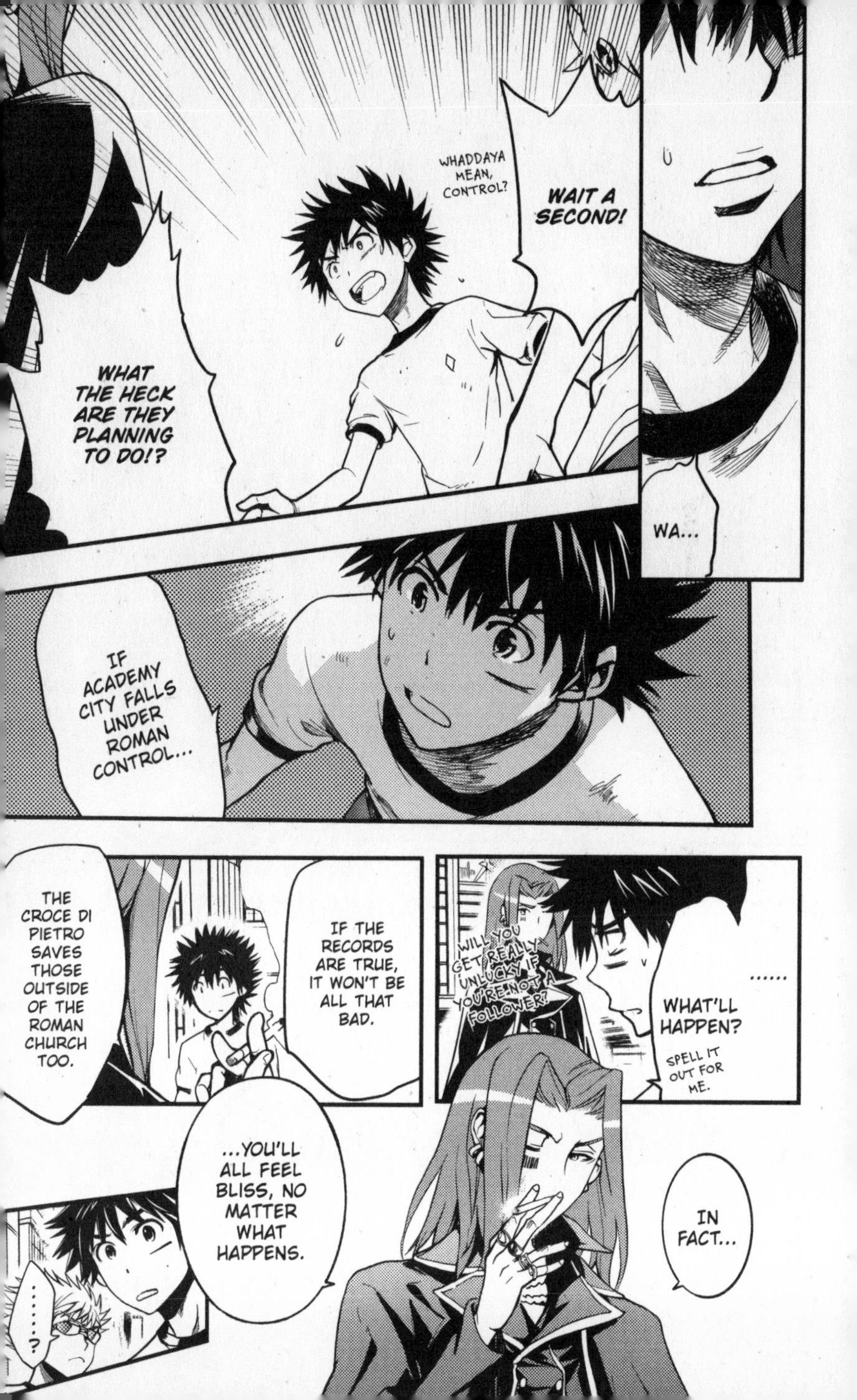
WA...
WAIT A SECOND!
WHADDAYA MEAN, CONTROL?
WHAT THE HECK ARE THEY PLANNING TO DO!?
IF ACADEMY CITY FALLS UNDER ROMAN CONTROL...
......
WHAT'LL HAPPEN?
SPELL IT OUT FOR ME.
WILL YOU GET REALLY UNLUCKY IF YOU'RE NOT A FOLLOWER?
IF THE RECORDS ARE TRUE, IT WON'T BE ALL THAT BAD.
THE CROCE DI PIETRO SAVES THOSE OUTSIDE OF THE ROMAN CHURCH TOO.
IN FACT...
...YOU'LL ALL FEEL BLISS, NO MATTER WHAT HAPPENS.
......?

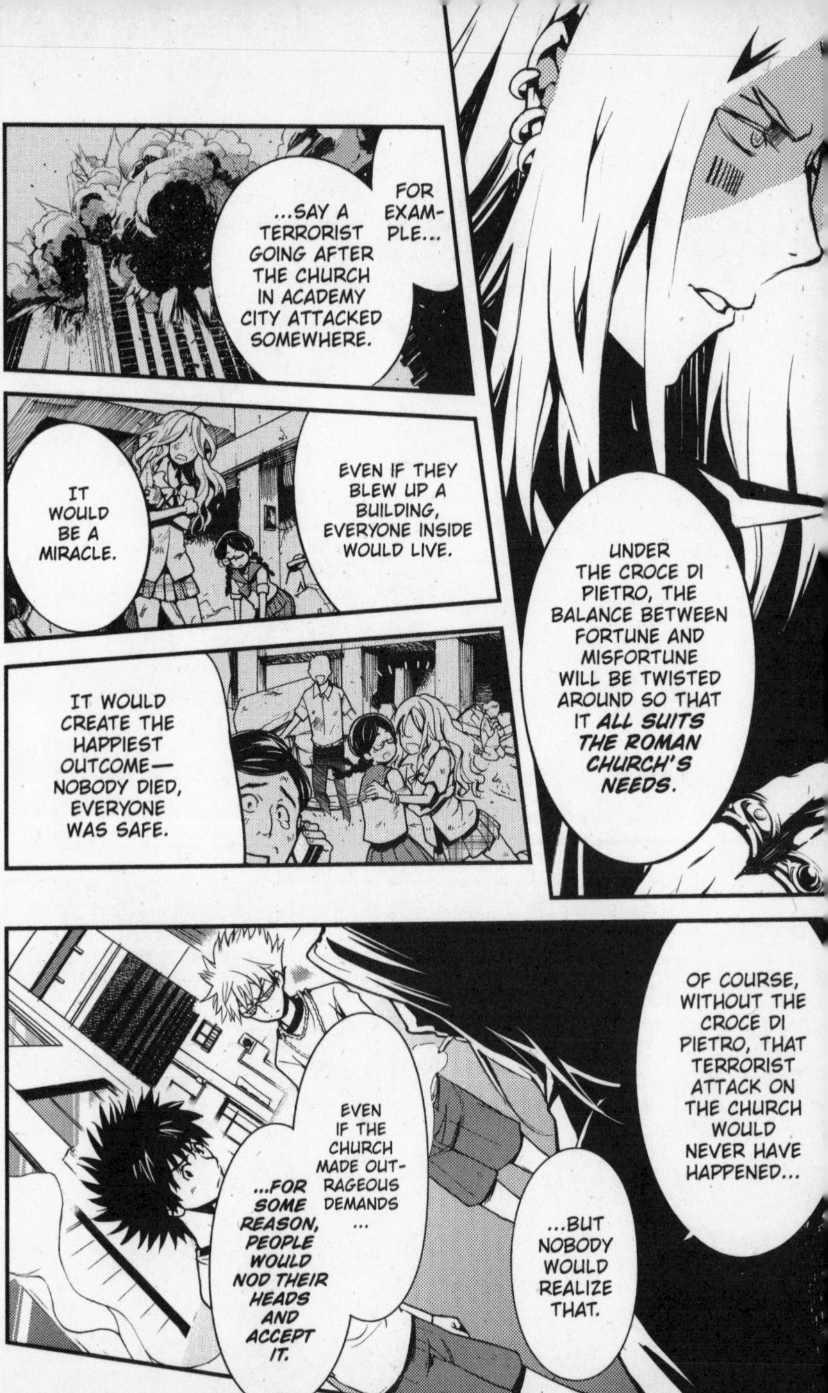
UNDER THE CROCE DI PIETRO, THE BALANCE BETWEEN FORTUNE AND MISFORTUNE WILL BE TWISTED AROUND SO THAT IT ***ALL SUITS THE ROMAN CHURCH'S NEEDS.***
FOR EXAMPLE...
...SAY A TERRORIST GOING AFTER THE CHURCH IN ACADEMY CITY ATTACKED SOMEWHERE.
EVEN IF THEY BLEW UP A BUILDING, EVERYONE INSIDE WOULD LIVE.
IT WOULD BE A MIRACLE.
IT WOULD CREATE THE HAPPIEST OUTCOME—NOBODY DIED, EVERYONE WAS SAFE.
OF COURSE, WITHOUT THE CROCE DI PIETRO, THAT TERRORIST ATTACK ON THE CHURCH WOULD NEVER HAVE HAPPENED...
...BUT NOBODY WOULD REALIZE THAT.
EVEN IF THE CHURCH MADE OUTRAGEOUS DEMANDS...
...FOR SOME REASON, PEOPLE WOULD NOD THEIR HEADS AND ACCEPT IT.

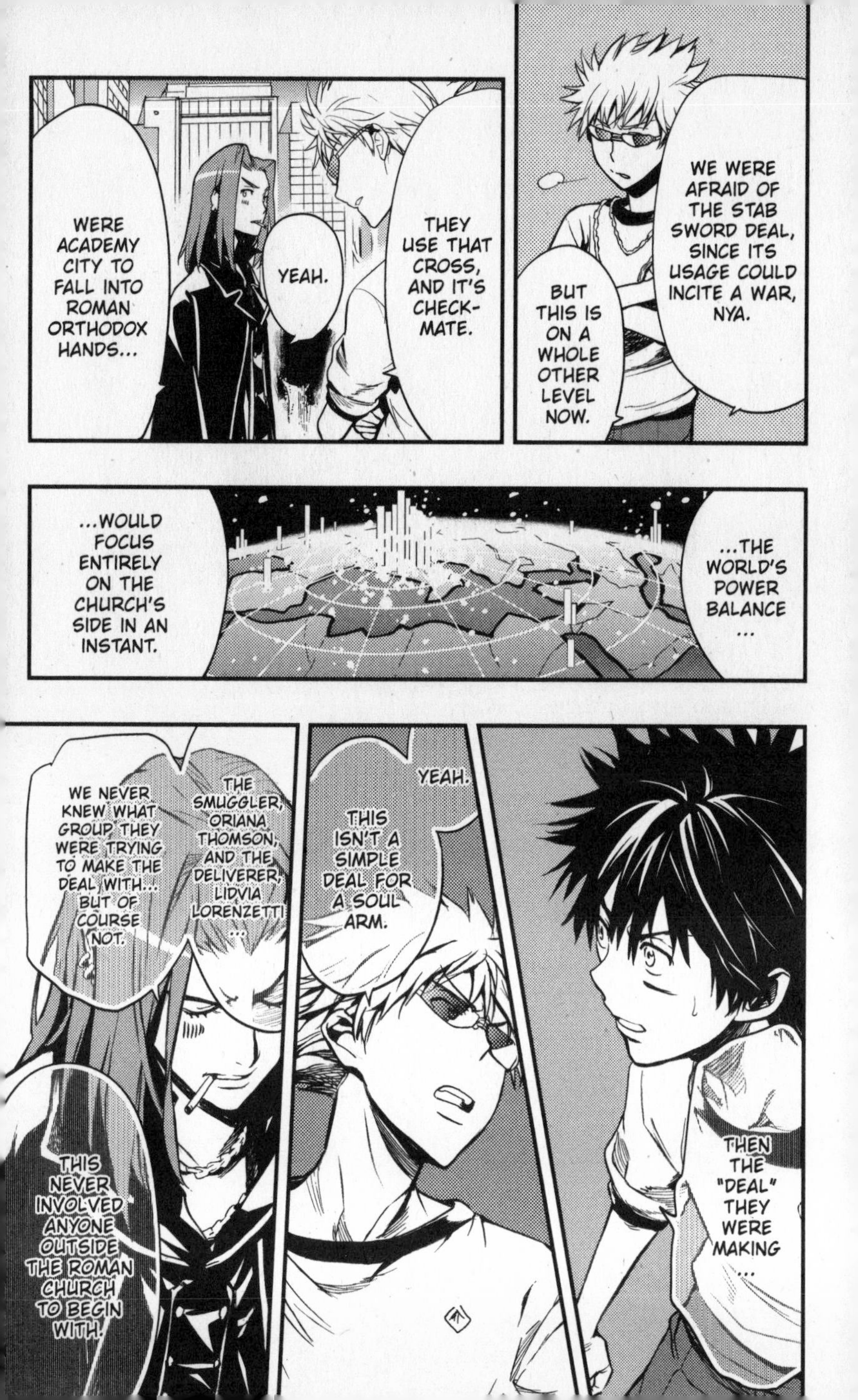
WE WERE AFRAID OF THE STAB SWORD DEAL, SINCE ITS USAGE COULD INCITE A WAR, NYA.
BUT THIS IS ON A WHOLE OTHER LEVEL NOW.
THEY USE THAT CROSS, AND IT'S CHECK-MATE.
YEAH.
WERE ACADEMY CITY TO FALL INTO ROMAN ORTHODOX HANDS...
...THE WORLD'S POWER BALANCE ...
...WOULD FOCUS ENTIRELY ON THE CHURCH'S SIDE IN AN INSTANT.
THEN THE "DEAL" THEY WERE MAKING ...
YEAH.
THIS ISN'T A SIMPLE DEAL FOR A SOUL ARM.
THE SMUGGLER, ORIANA THOMSON, AND THE DELIVERER, LIDVIA LORENZETTI ...
WE NEVER KNEW WHAT GROUP THEY WERE TRYING TO MAKE THE DEAL WITH... BUT OF COURSE NOT.
THIS NEVER INVOLVED ANYONE OUTSIDE THE ROMAN CHURCH TO BEGIN WITH.

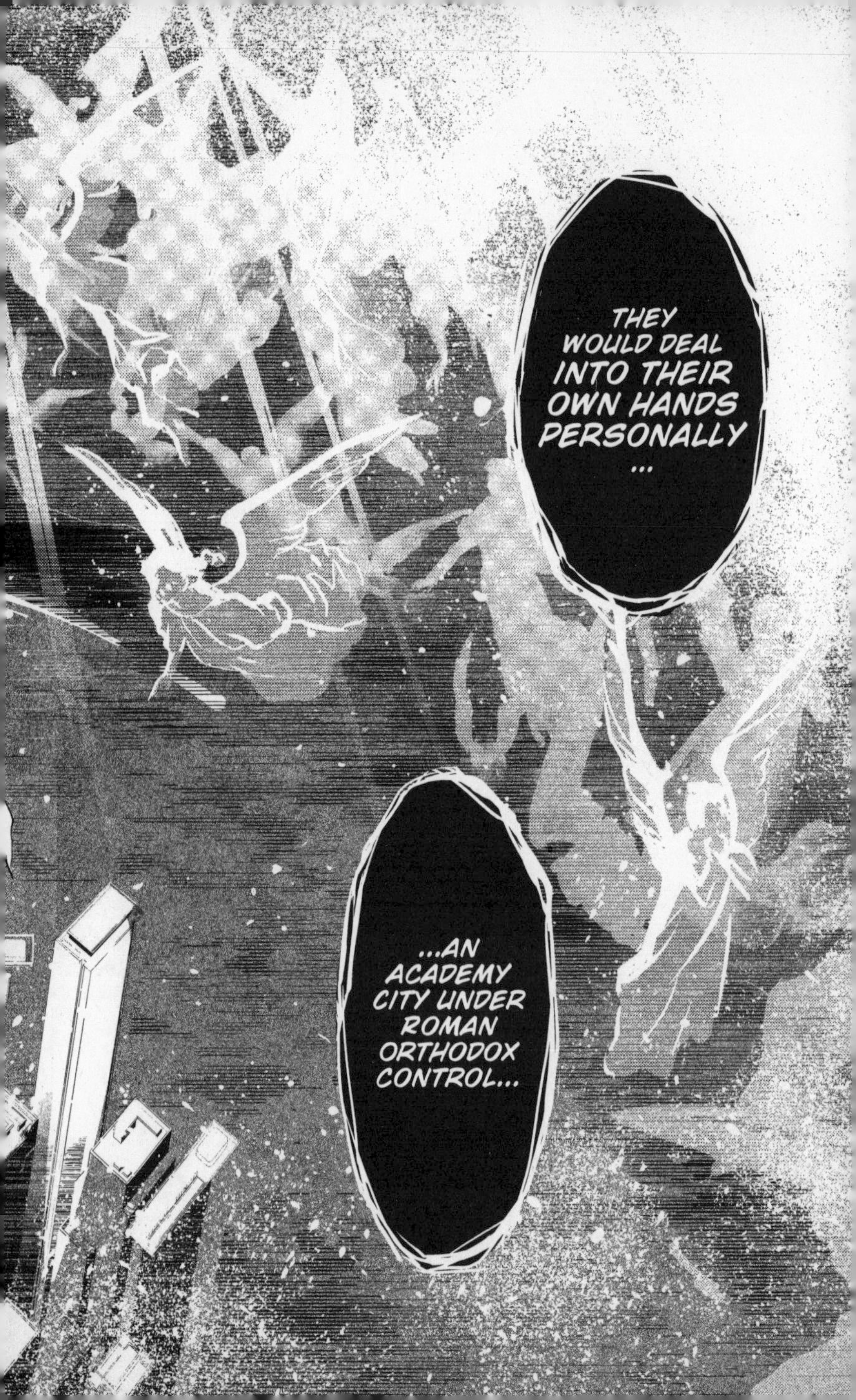
THEY WOULD DEAL INTO THEIR OWN HANDS PERSONALLY ...
...AN ACADEMY CITY UNDER ROMAN ORTHODOX CONTROL...

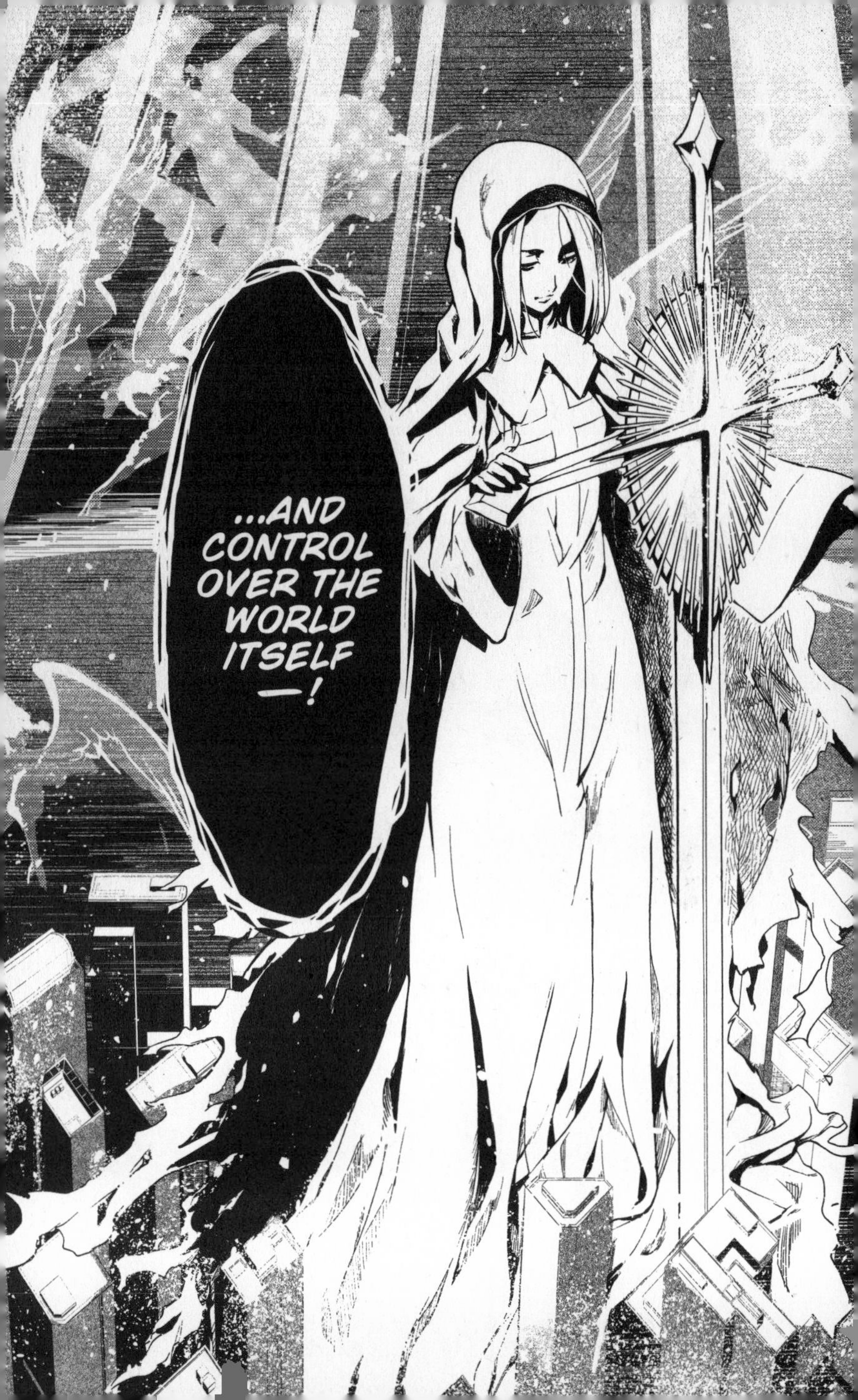
...AND CONTROL OVER THE WORLD ITSELF —!

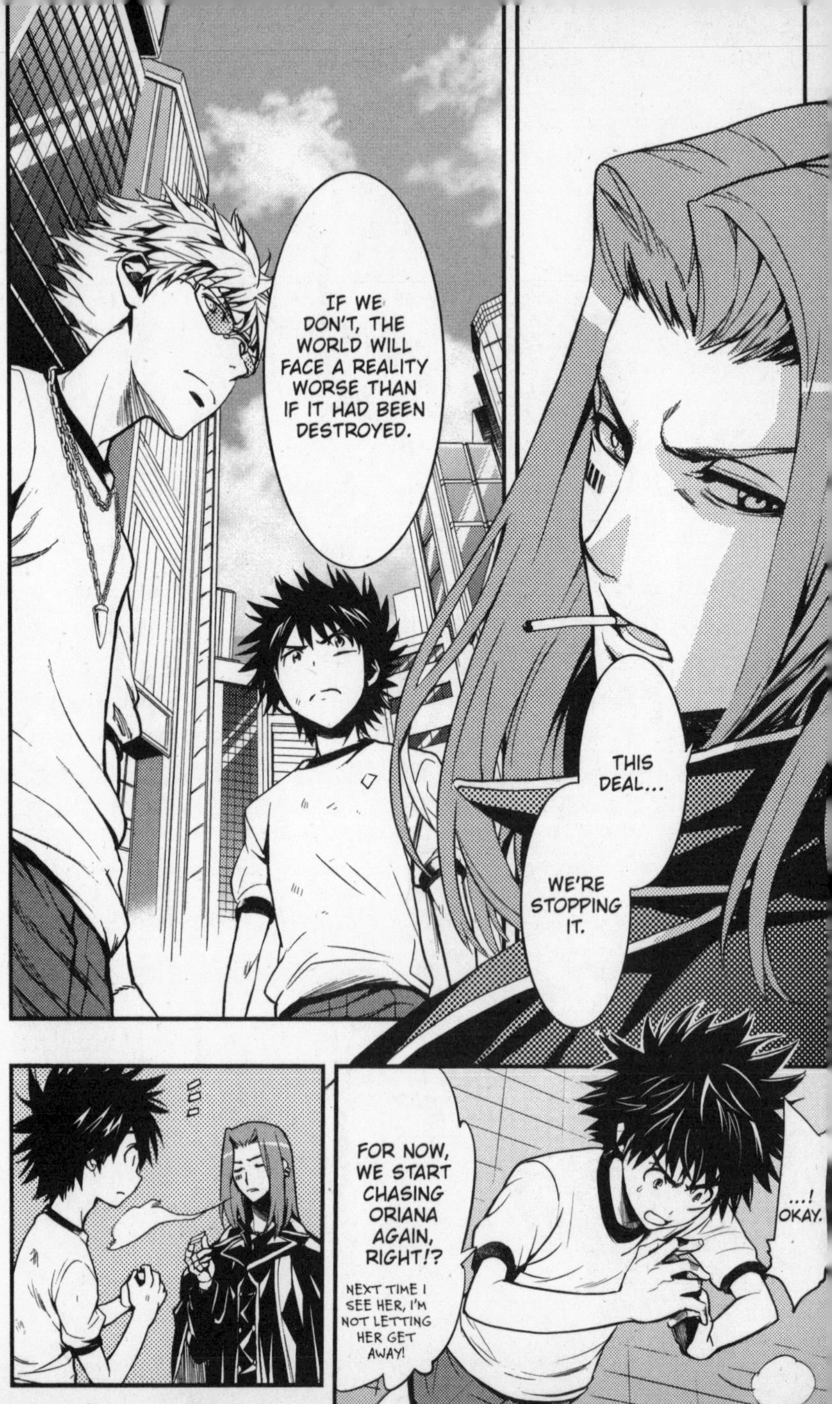
THIS DEAL...
WE'RE STOPPING IT.
IF WE DON'T, THE WORLD WILL FACE A REALITY WORSE THAN IF IT HAD BEEN DESTROYED.
...! OKAY.
FOR NOW, WE START CHASING ORIANA AGAIN, RIGHT!?
NEXT TIME I SEE HER, I'M NOT LETTING HER GET AWAY!

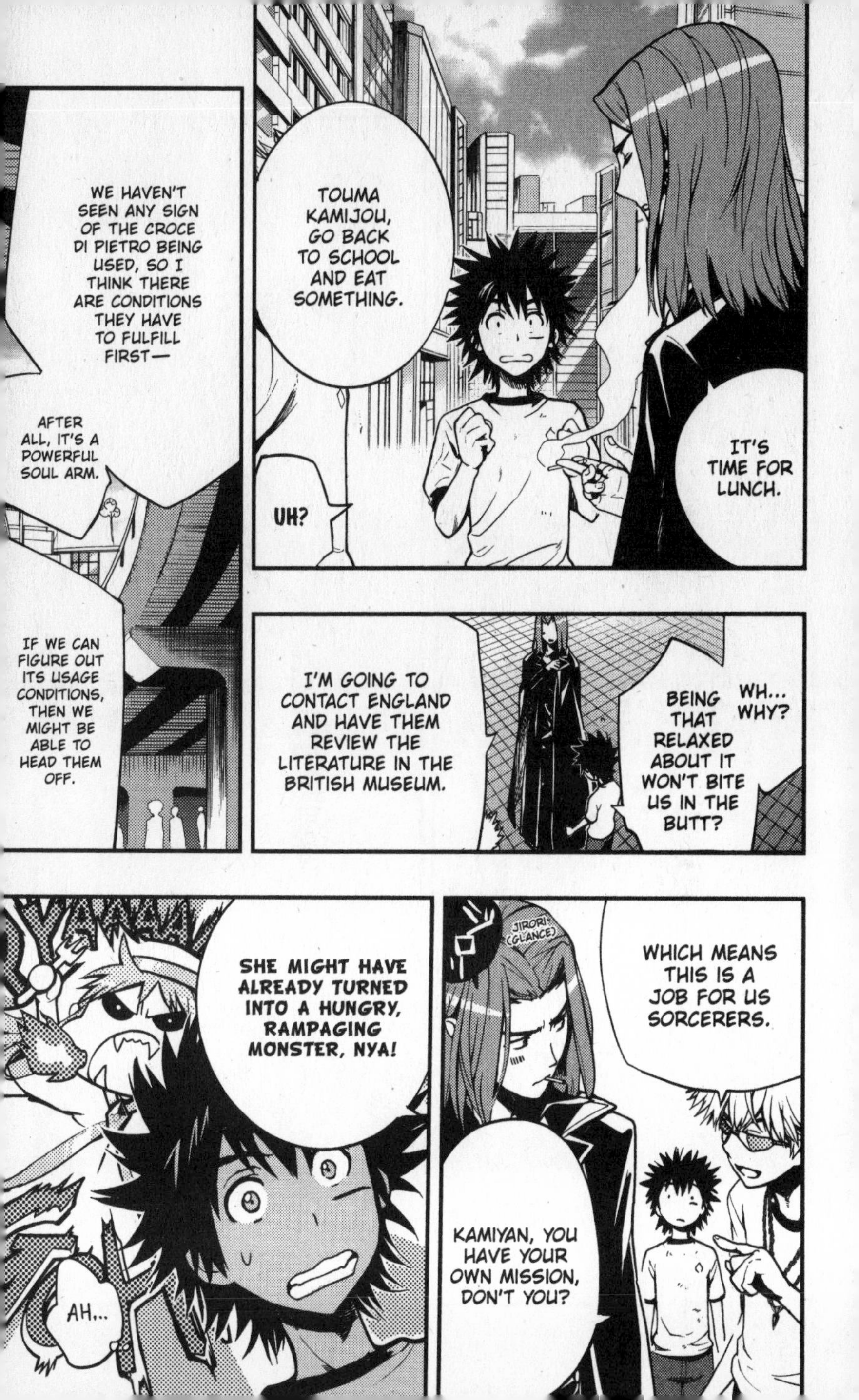
IT'S TIME FOR LUNCH.
TOUMA KAMIJOU, GO BACK TO SCHOOL AND EAT SOMETHING.
UH?
WH... WHY?
BEING THAT RELAXED ABOUT IT WON'T BITE US IN THE BUTT?
I'M GOING TO CONTACT ENGLAND AND HAVE THEM REVIEW THE LITERATURE IN THE BRITISH MUSEUM.
WE HAVEN'T SEEN ANY SIGN OF THE CROCE DI PIETRO BEING USED, SO I THINK THERE ARE CONDITIONS THEY HAVE TO FULFILL FIRST—
AFTER ALL, IT'S A POWERFUL SOUL ARM.
IF WE CAN FIGURE OUT ITS USAGE CONDITIONS, THEN WE MIGHT BE ABLE TO HEAD THEM OFF.
JIRORI (GLANCE)
WHICH MEANS THIS IS A JOB FOR US SORCERERS.
KAMIYAN, YOU HAVE YOUR OWN MISSION, DON'T YOU?
SHE MIGHT HAVE ALREADY TURNED INTO A HUNGRY, RAMPAGING MONSTER, NYA!
AH...

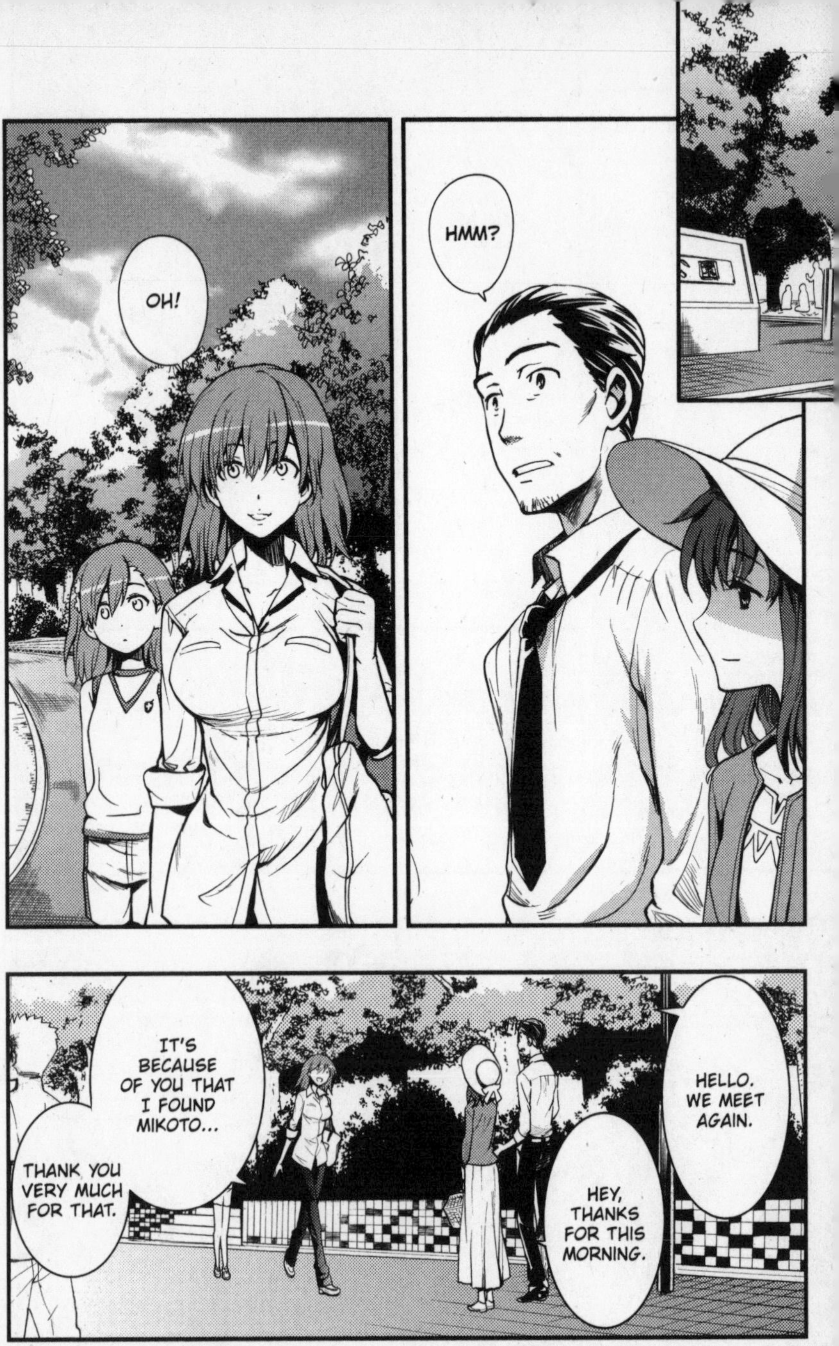
HMM?
OH!
HELLO. WE MEET AGAIN.
HEY, THANKS FOR THIS MORNING.
IT'S BECAUSE OF YOU THAT I FOUND MIKOTO...
THANK YOU VERY MUCH FOR THAT.

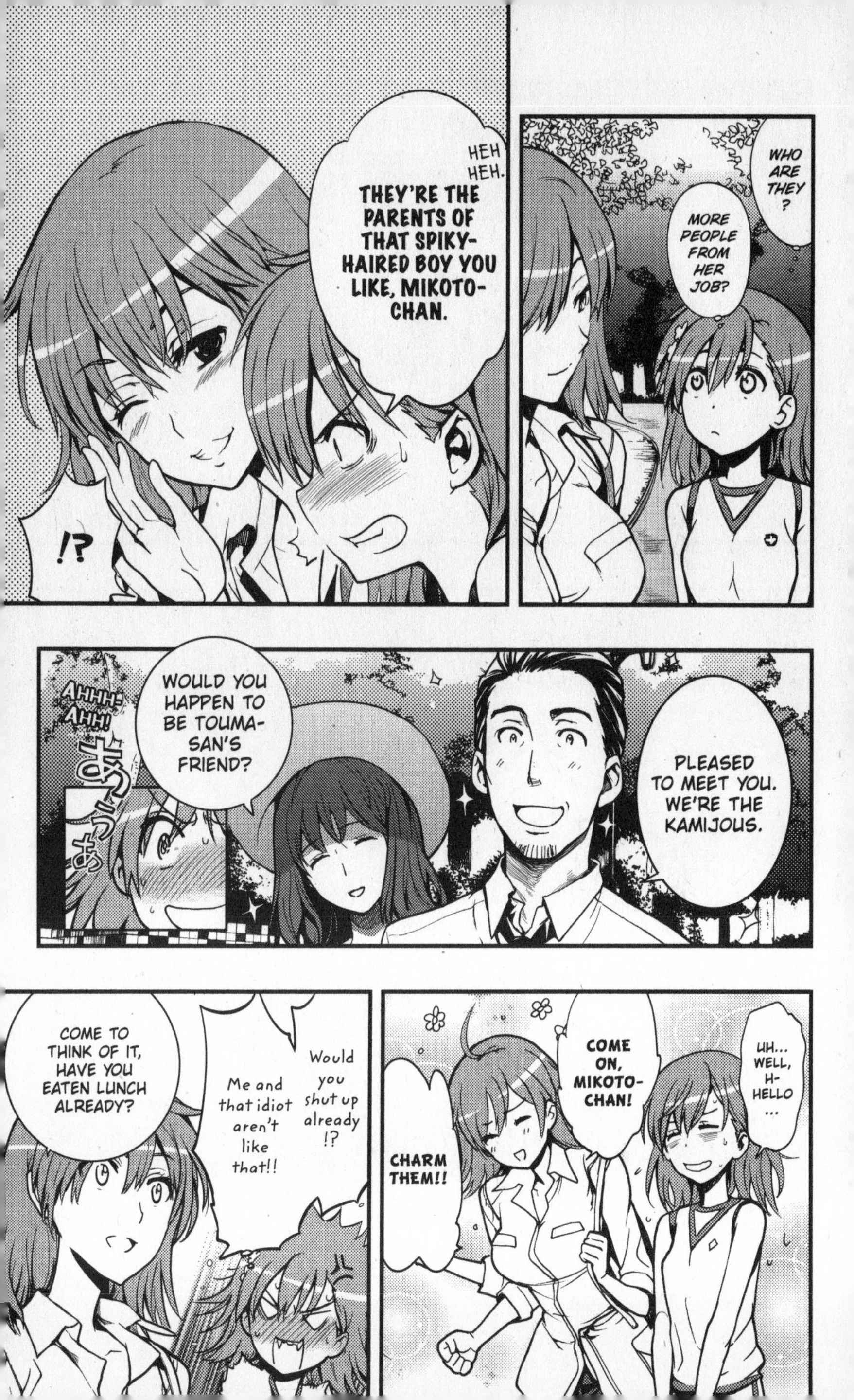
WHO ARE THEY?
MORE PEOPLE FROM HER JOB?
HEH HEH.
THEY'RE THE PARENTS OF THAT SPIKY-HAIRED BOY YOU LIKE, MIKOTO-CHAN.
!?
PLEASED TO MEET YOU. WE'RE THE KAMIJOUS.
WOULD YOU HAPPEN TO BE TOUMA-SAN'S FRIEND?
AHHH- AHH!
UH... WELL, H-HELLO...
COME ON, MIKOTO-CHAN!
CHARM THEM!!
Would you shut up already!?
Me and that idiot aren't like that!!
COME TO THINK OF IT, HAVE YOU EATEN LUNCH ALREADY?

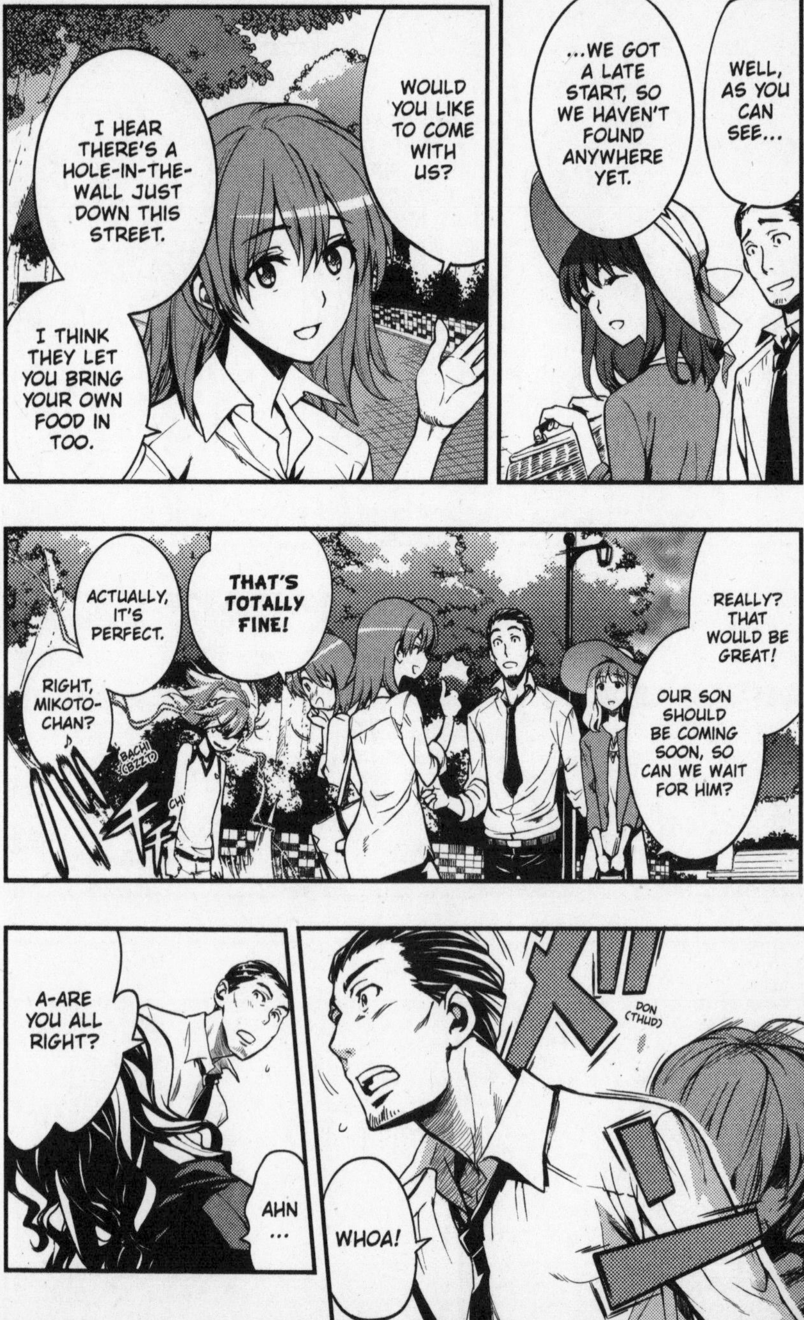
WELL, AS YOU CAN SEE...
...WE GOT A LATE START, SO WE HAVEN'T FOUND ANYWHERE YET.
WOULD YOU LIKE TO COME WITH US?
I HEAR THERE'S A HOLE-IN-THE-WALL JUST DOWN THIS STREET.
I THINK THEY LET YOU BRING YOUR OWN FOOD IN TOO.
REALLY? THAT WOULD BE GREAT!
OUR SON SHOULD BE COMING SOON, SO CAN WE WAIT FOR HIM?
THAT'S TOTALLY FINE!
ACTUALLY, IT'S PERFECT.
RIGHT, MIKOTO-CHAN? ♪
BACHI (BZZT)
CHI
DON (THUD)
WHOA!
A-ARE YOU ALL RIGHT?
AHN ...

I'M SO SORRY! I'M NOT USED TO THESE CROWDS...

BA (WHIP)

ZUGOGOGOGO (RUMBLE)

FWAH...!?

D-DEAR!!?

OH, WELL, THANK YOU FOR YOUR CONSIDER-ATION. ♥

EXCUSE ME!

NO, NO, NO, I'M JUST GLAD YOU'RE NOT HURT!!!

HAH... ACADEMY CITY REALLY IS AMAZING...

BOSO
(MUTTER)

...FIG-
URES.

THE
APPLE
DOESN'T
FALL FAR
FROM
THE
TREE.

I-I'M
SORRY
~!!!

TH-THIS
ISN'T WHAT IT
LOOKS LIKE!

I WAS CERTAINLY
NOT ENTRANCED
BY THAT WOMAN'S
CHEST AND LEGS
AT ALL...IT WAS
JUST...WELL...

I believe I told
you to avoid
contact with
civilians as much
as possible.

...Still,
waiting
is a
pain,
isn't
it—?

I
am.

That
was an
unavoid-
able
situa-
tion.

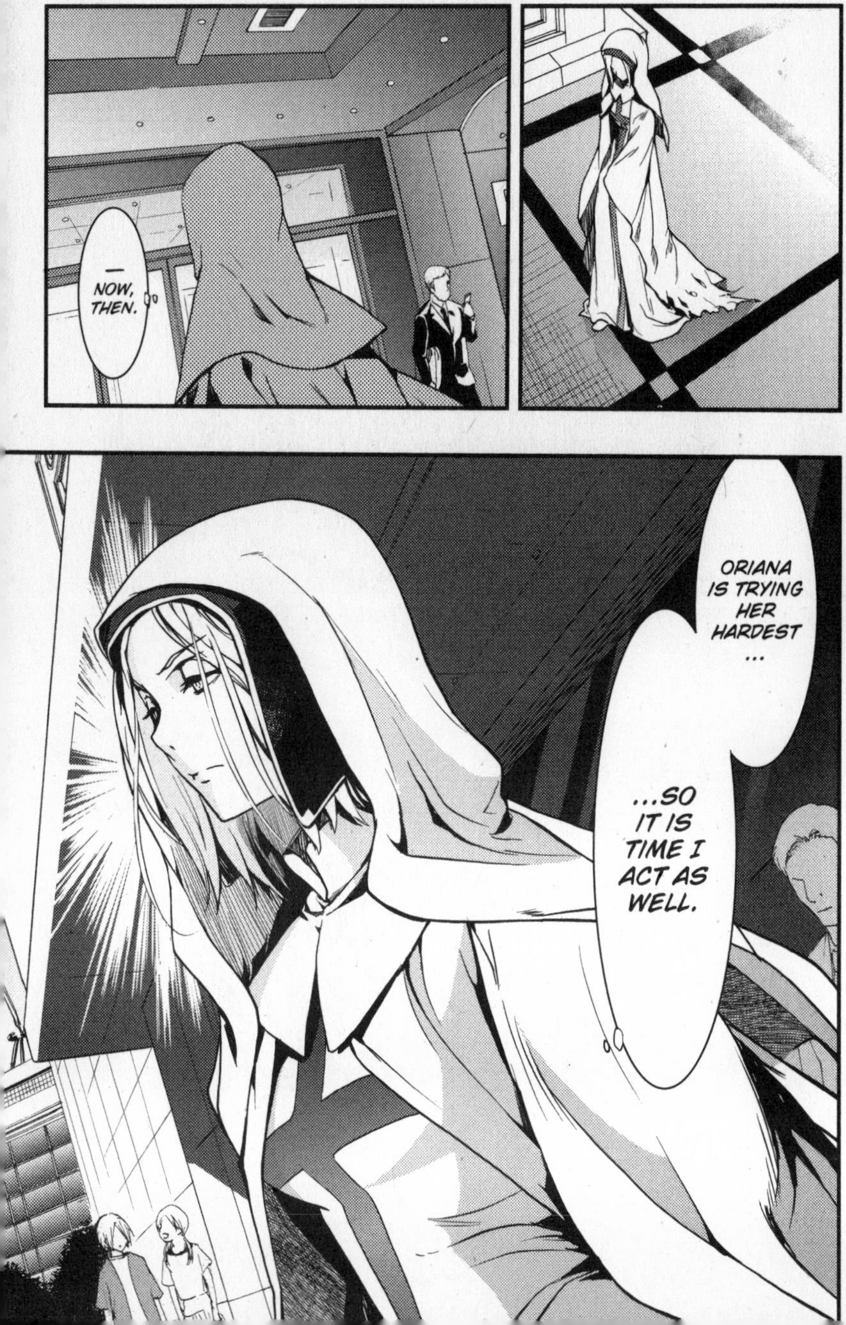
— NOW, THEN.
ORIANA IS TRYING HER HARDEST ...
...SO IT IS TIME I ACT AS WELL.

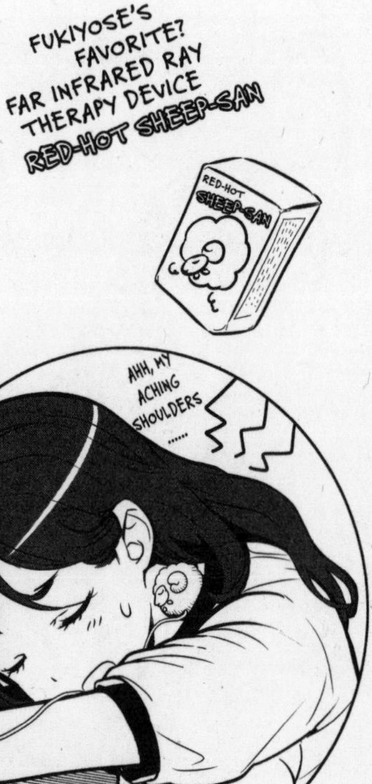
FUKIYOSE'S FAVORITE? FAR INFRARED RAY THERAPY DEVICE RED-HOT SHEEP-SAN
RED-HOT SHEEP-SAN
AHH, MY ACHING SHOULDERS ......

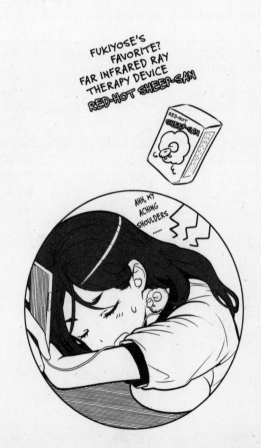

#75 LUNCH BREAK

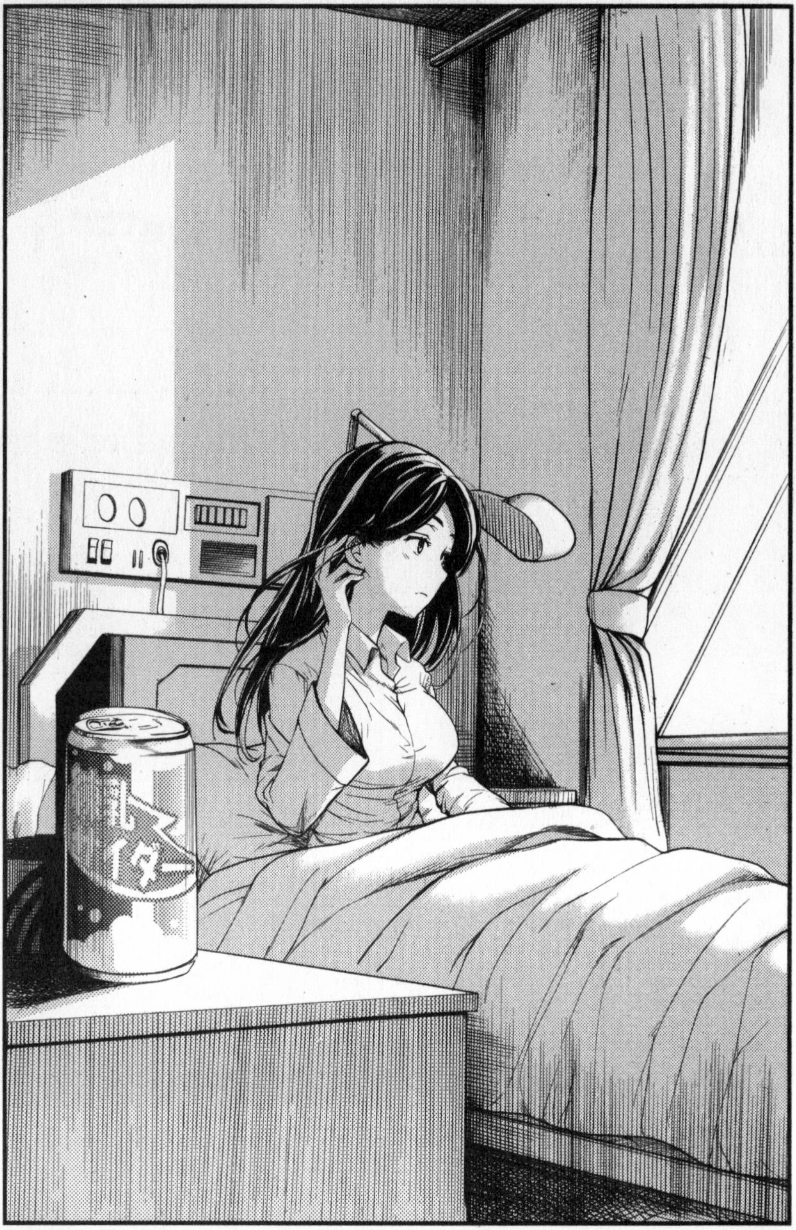

CAN: CONDENSED MILK SODA

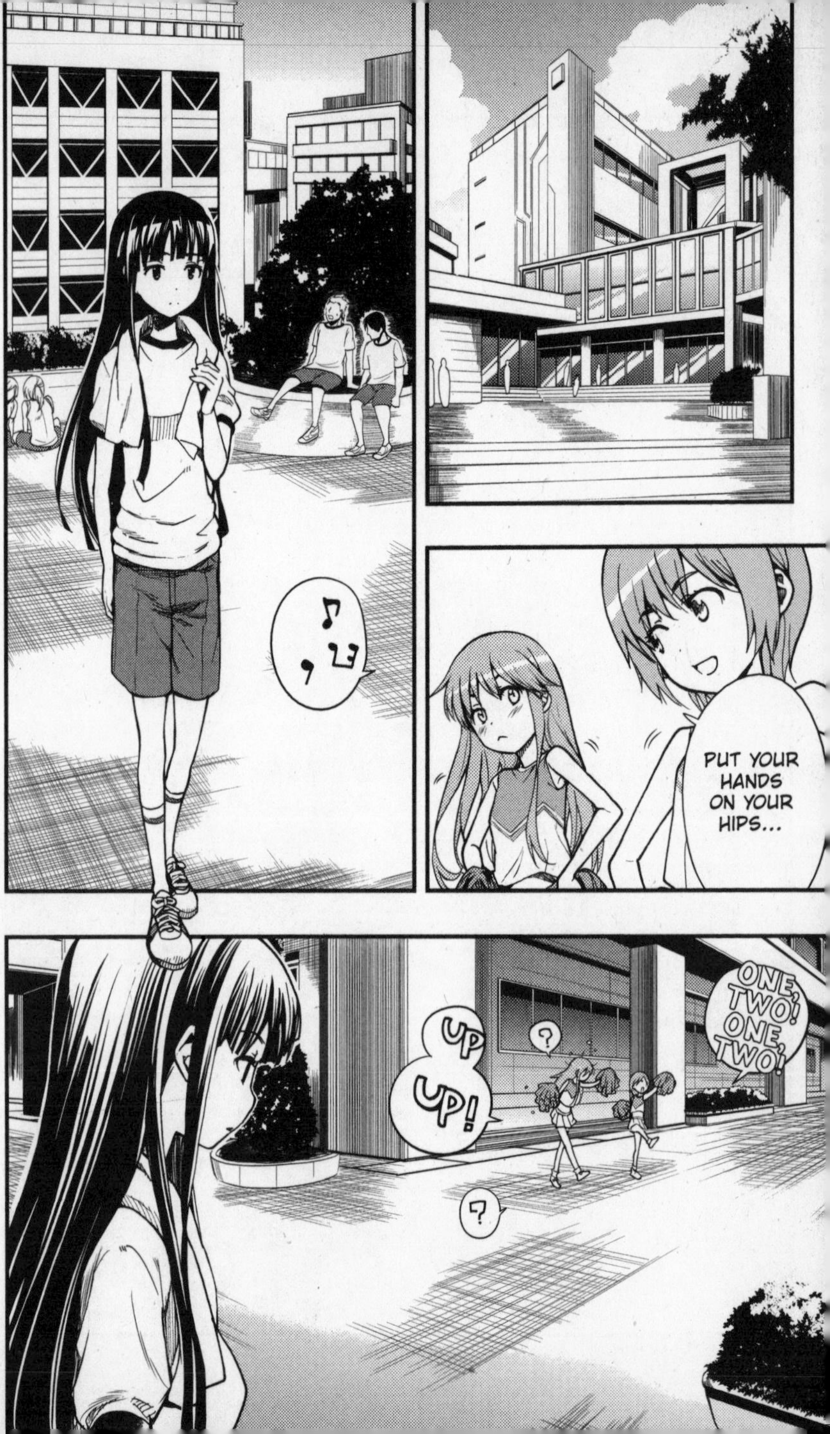
PUT YOUR HANDS ON YOUR HIPS...
♪
ONE, TWO! ONE, TWO!
?
UP UP!
?

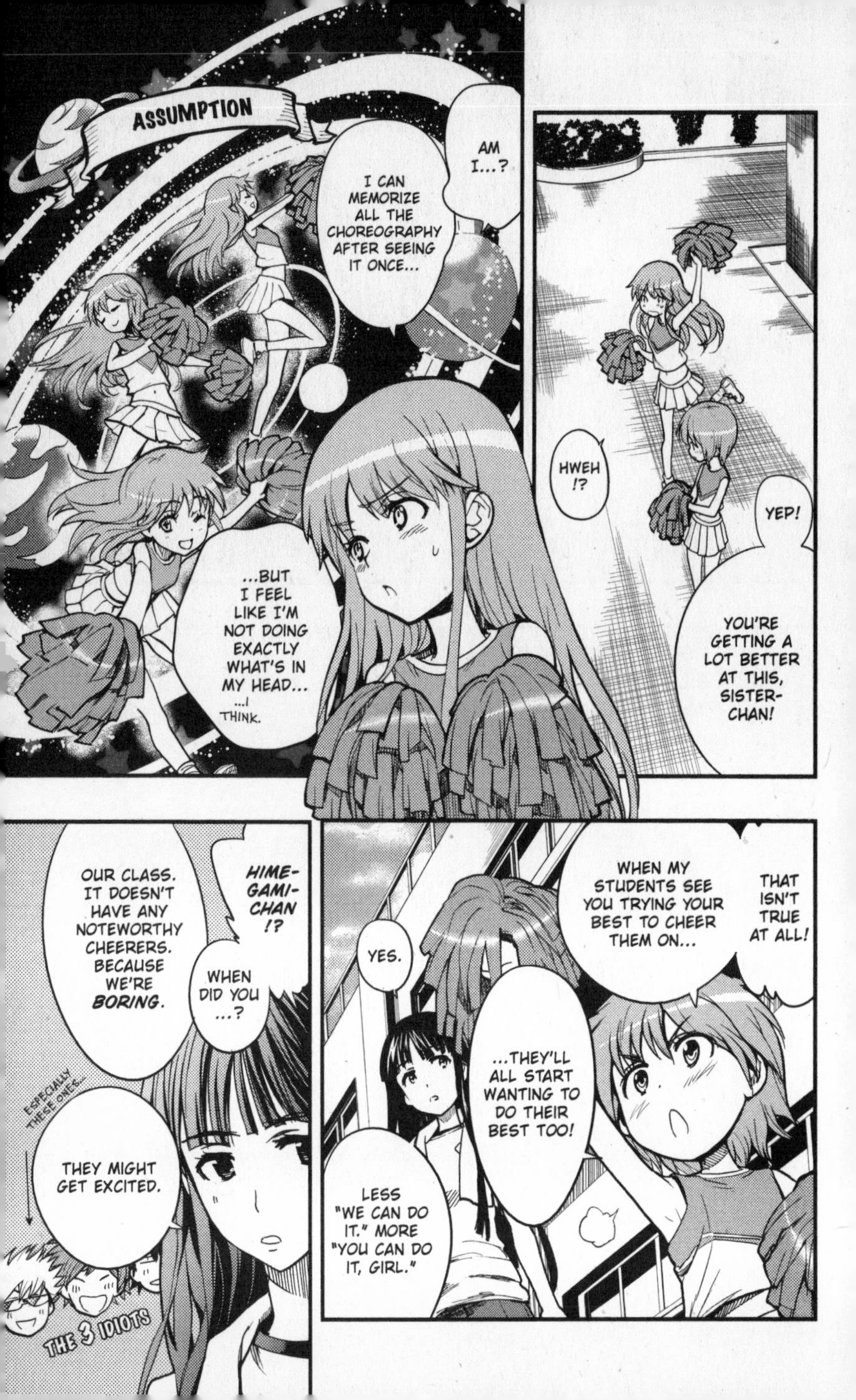

YOU'RE GETTING A LOT BETTER AT THIS, SISTER-CHAN!
HWEH !?
YEP!
ASSUMPTION
AM I...?
I CAN MEMORIZE ALL THE CHOREOGRAPHY AFTER SEEING IT ONCE...
...BUT I FEEL LIKE I'M NOT DOING EXACTLY WHAT'S IN MY HEAD...
...I THINK.
THAT ISN'T TRUE AT ALL!
WHEN MY STUDENTS SEE YOU TRYING YOUR BEST TO CHEER THEM ON...
...THEY'LL ALL START WANTING TO DO THEIR BEST TOO!
YES.
LESS "WE CAN DO IT." MORE "YOU CAN DO IT, GIRL."
HIME-GAMI-CHAN !?
WHEN DID YOU ...?
OUR CLASS. IT DOESN'T HAVE ANY NOTEWORTHY CHEERERS. BECAUSE WE'RE BORING.
THEY MIGHT GET EXCITED.
ESPECIALLY THESE ONES...
THE 3 IDIOTS

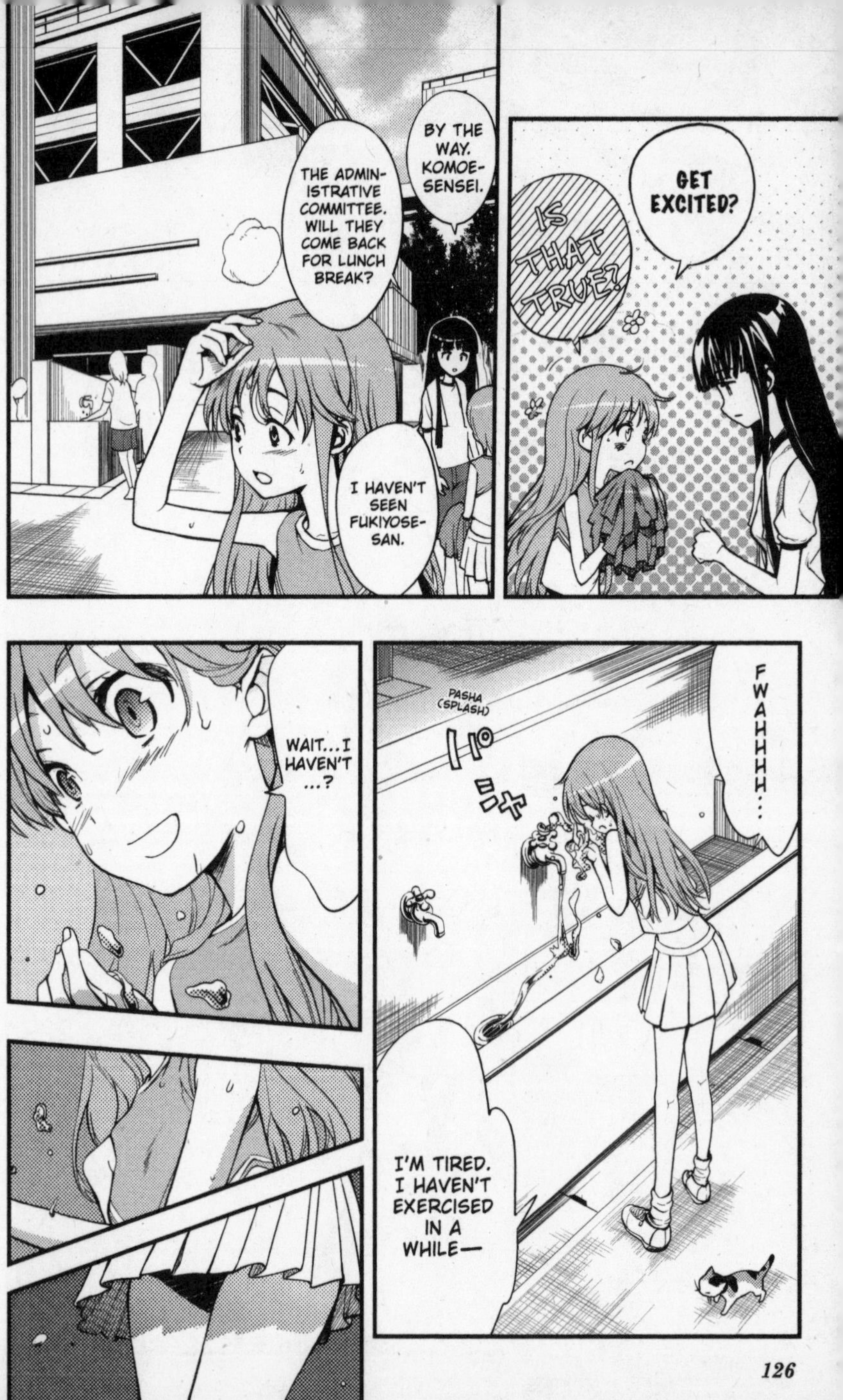
GET EXCITED?
IS THAT TRUE?
BY THE WAY. KOMOE-SENSEI.
THE ADMINISTRATIVE COMMITTEE. WILL THEY COME BACK FOR LUNCH BREAK?
I HAVEN'T SEEN FUKIYOSE-SAN.
FWAHHHH...
PASHA (SPLASH)
I'M TIRED. I HAVEN'T EXERCISED IN A WHILE—
WAIT...I HAVEN'T ...?

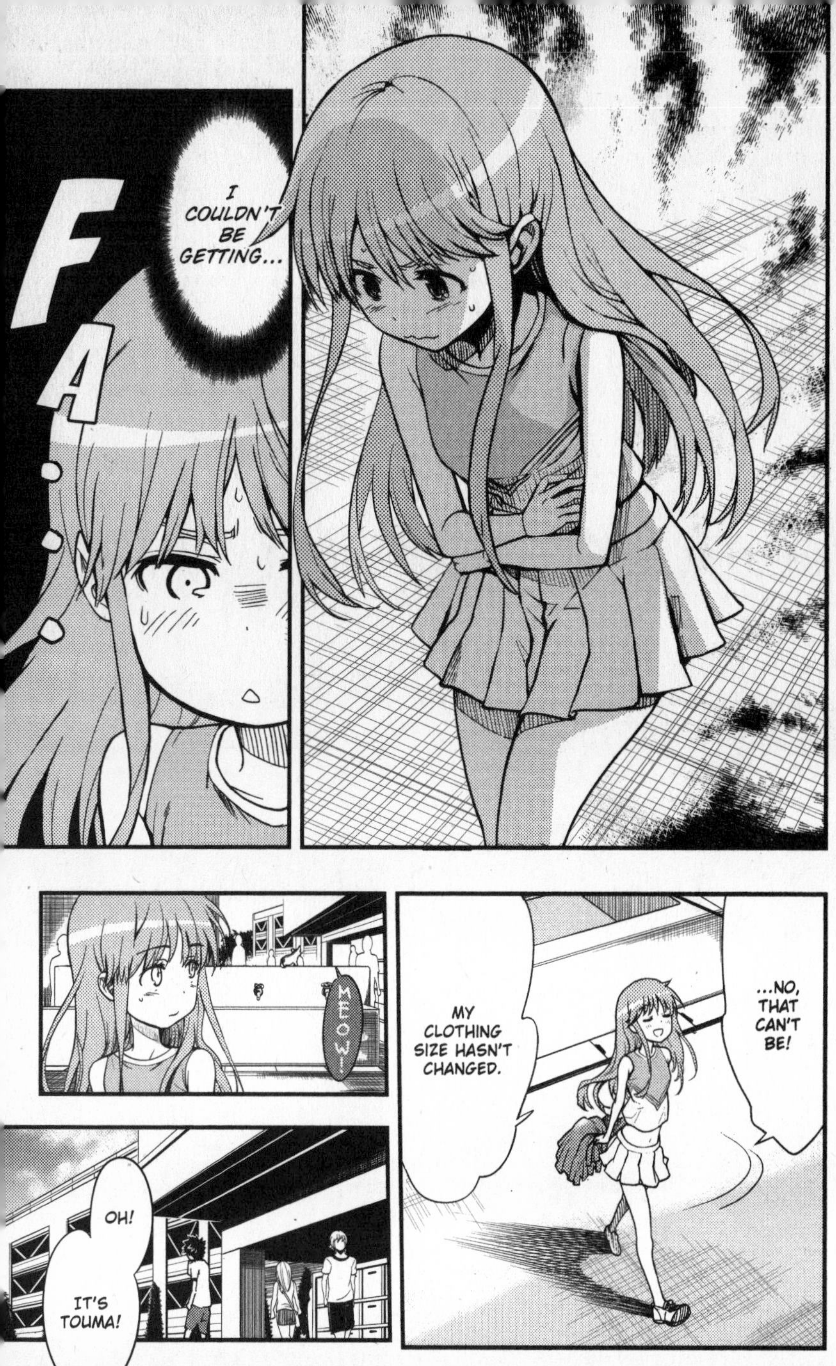
I COULDN'T BE GETTING...
FA...
...NO, THAT CAN'T BE!
MY CLOTHING SIZE HASN'T CHANGED.
MEOW!
OH!
IT'S TOUMA!

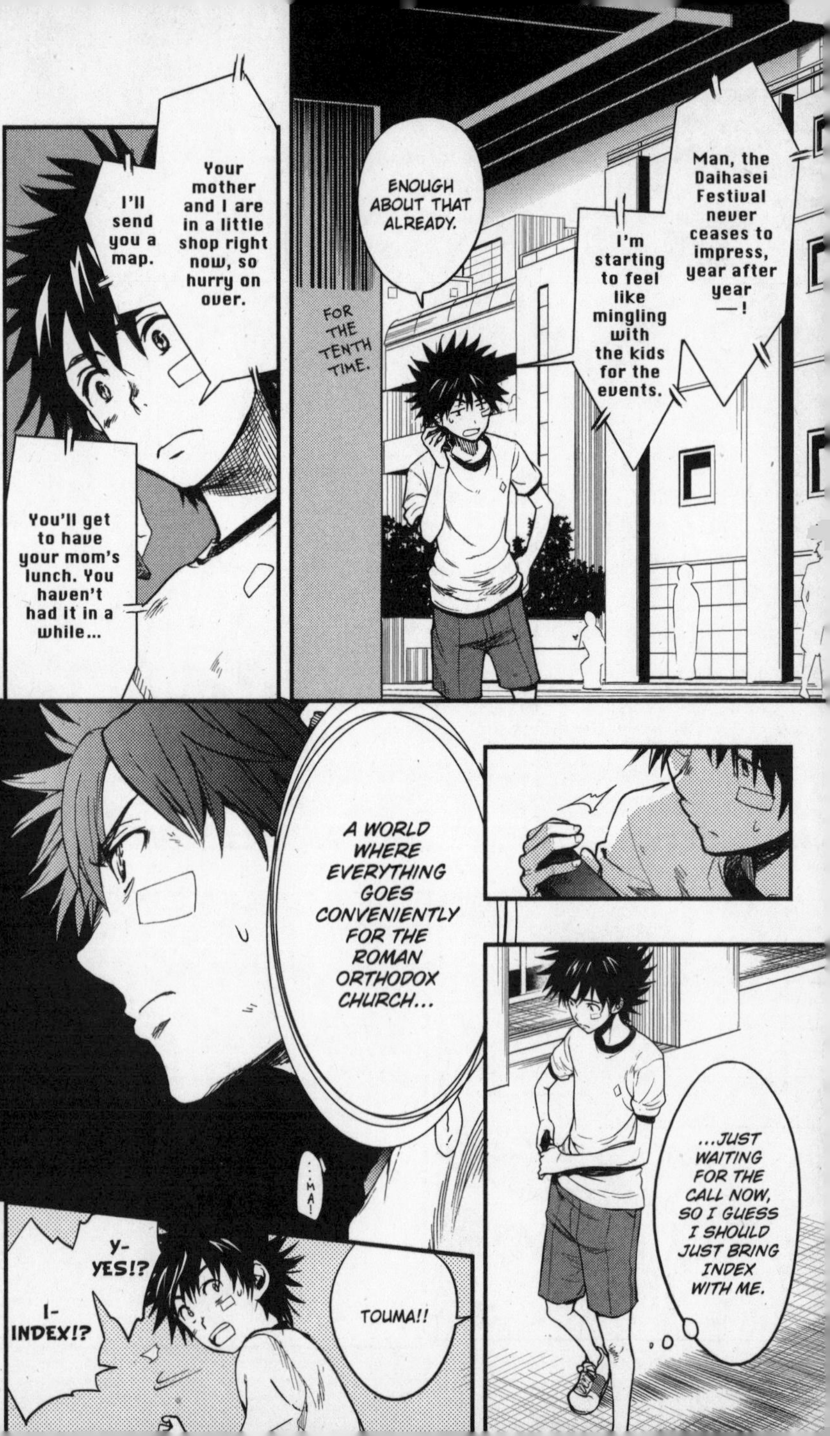

Man, the Daihasei Festival never ceases to impress, year after year —!
I'm starting to feel like mingling with the kids for the events.
ENOUGH ABOUT THAT ALREADY.
FOR THE TENTH TIME.
Your mother and I are in a little shop right now, so hurry on over.
I'll send you a map.
You'll get to have your mom's lunch. You haven't had it in a while...
...JUST WAITING FOR THE CALL NOW, SO I GUESS I SHOULD JUST BRING INDEX WITH ME.
A WORLD WHERE EVERYTHING GOES CONVENIENTLY FOR THE ROMAN ORTHODOX CHURCH...
...MA!
TOUMA!!
Y-YES!?
I-INDEX!?

YO!

I'VE BEEN CALLING YOU FOR A WHILE NOW.

SORRY, SORRY!

HEY, HOW LONG ARE YOU GONNA WEAR THOSE CLOTHES?

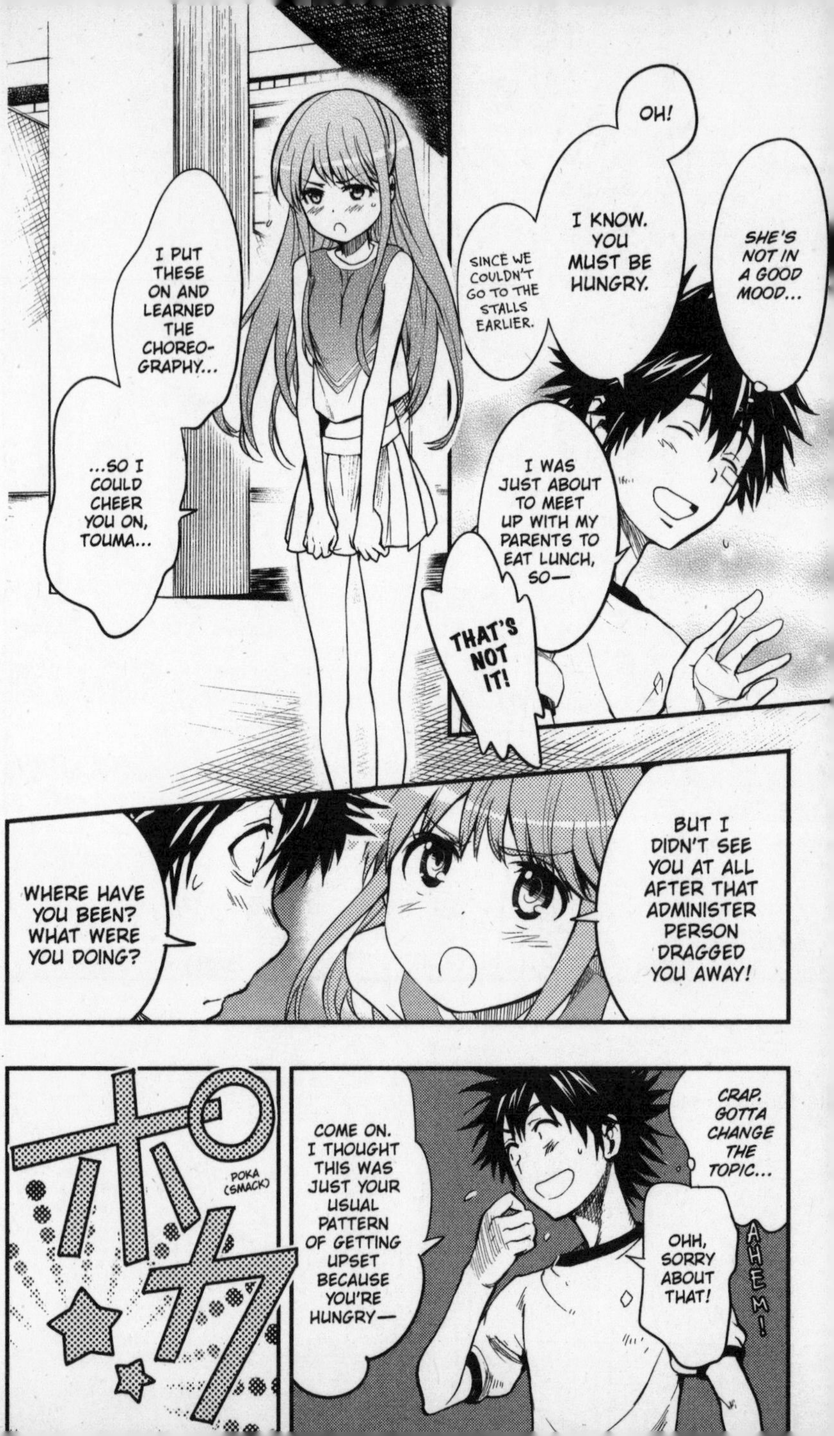
SHE'S NOT IN A GOOD MOOD...
OH!
I KNOW. YOU MUST BE HUNGRY.
SINCE WE COULDN'T GO TO THE STALLS EARLIER.
I WAS JUST ABOUT TO MEET UP WITH MY PARENTS TO EAT LUNCH, SO—
THAT'S NOT IT!
I PUT THESE ON AND LEARNED THE CHOREOGRAPHY...
...SO I COULD CHEER YOU ON, TOUMA...
BUT I DIDN'T SEE YOU AT ALL AFTER THAT ADMINISTER PERSON DRAGGED YOU AWAY!
WHERE HAVE YOU BEEN? WHAT WERE YOU DOING?
CRAP. GOTTA CHANGE THE TOPIC...
AHEM!
OHH, SORRY ABOUT THAT!
COME ON. I THOUGHT THIS WAS JUST YOUR USUAL PATTERN OF GETTING UPSET BECAUSE YOU'RE HUNGRY—
POKA (SMACK)

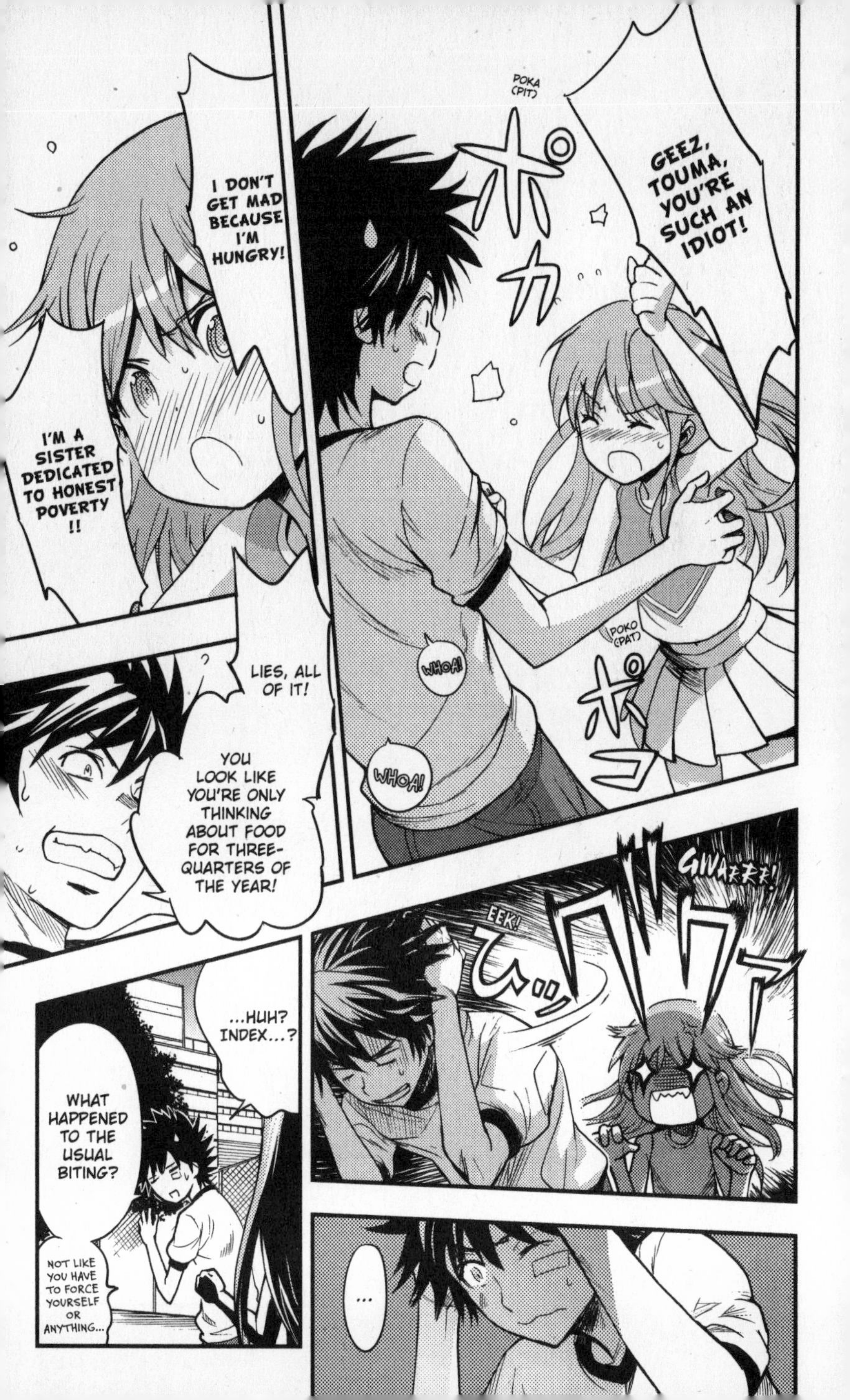
POKA (PIT)
GEEZ, TOUMA, YOU'RE SUCH AN IDIOT!
POKO (PAT)
WHOA!
WHOA!
I DON'T GET MAD BECAUSE I'M HUNGRY!
I'M A SISTER DEDICATED TO HONEST POVERTY !!
LIES, ALL OF IT!
YOU LOOK LIKE YOU'RE ONLY THINKING ABOUT FOOD FOR THREE-QUARTERS OF THE YEAR!
GWARRR!
EEK!
...HUH? INDEX...?
WHAT HAPPENED TO THE USUAL BITING?
NOT LIKE YOU HAVE TO FORCE YOURSELF OR ANYTHING...
...

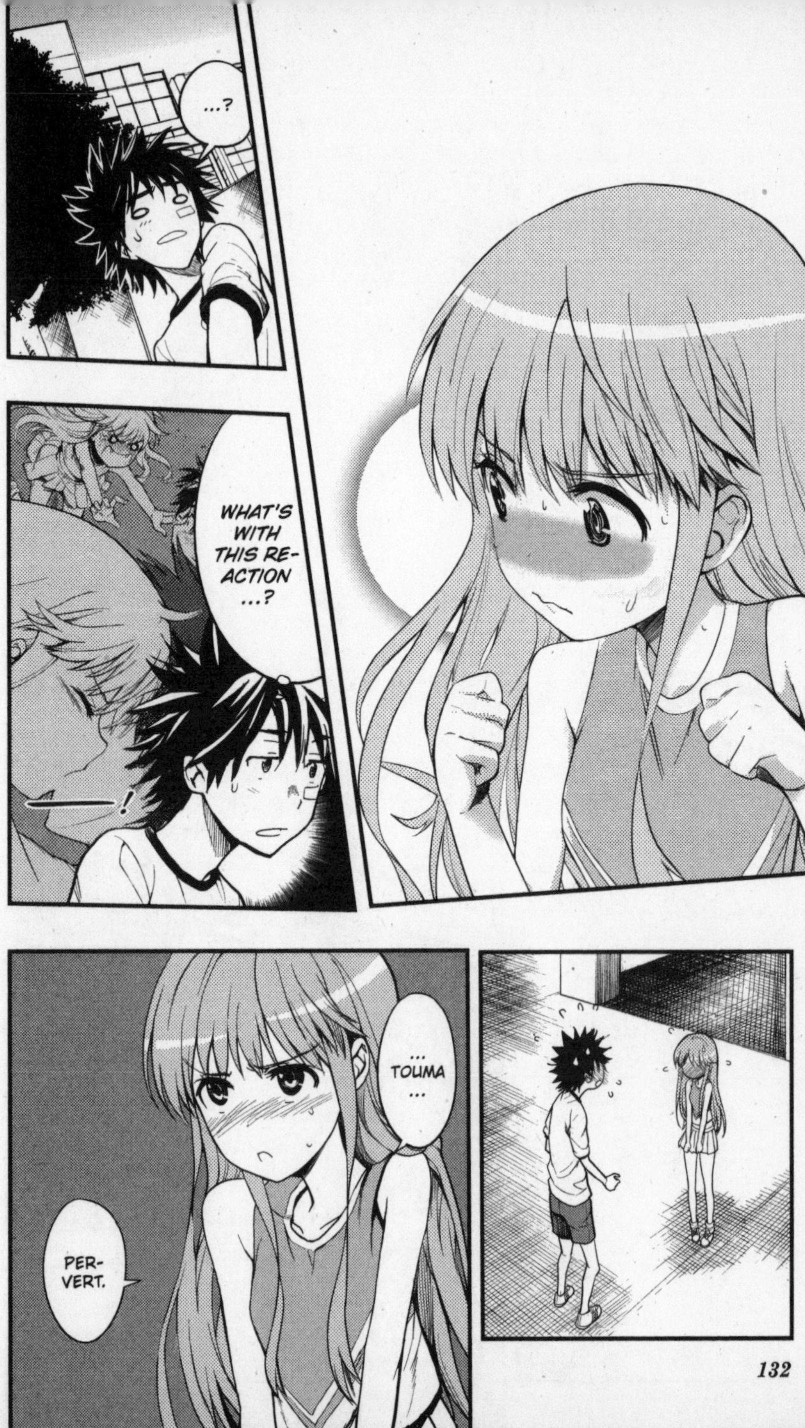
...?
WHAT'S WITH THIS RE-ACTION ...?
——!
... TOUMA ...
PER-VERT.

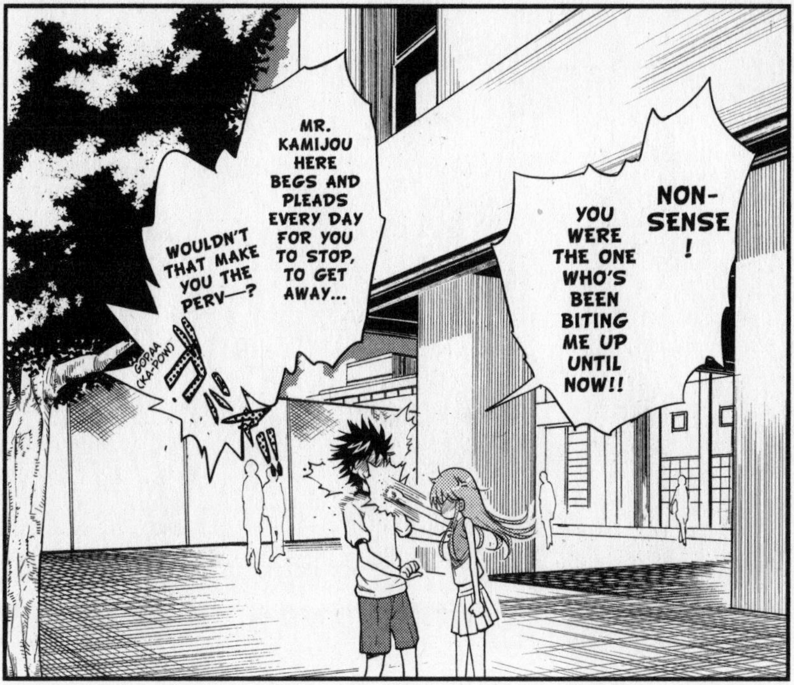
NON-SENSE!
YOU WERE THE ONE WHO'S BEEN BITING ME UP UNTIL NOW!!
MR. KAMIJOU HERE BEGS AND PLEADS EVERY DAY FOR YOU TO STOP, TO GET AWAY...
WOULDN'T THAT MAKE YOU THE PERV—?
GOPAA (KA-POW)

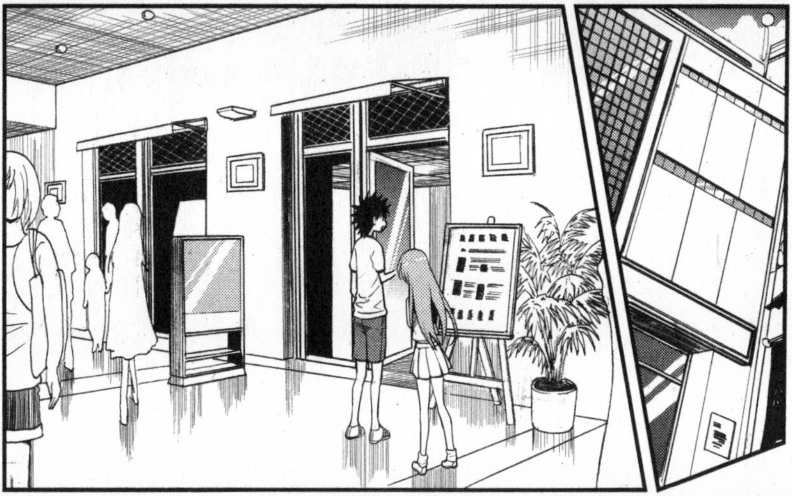

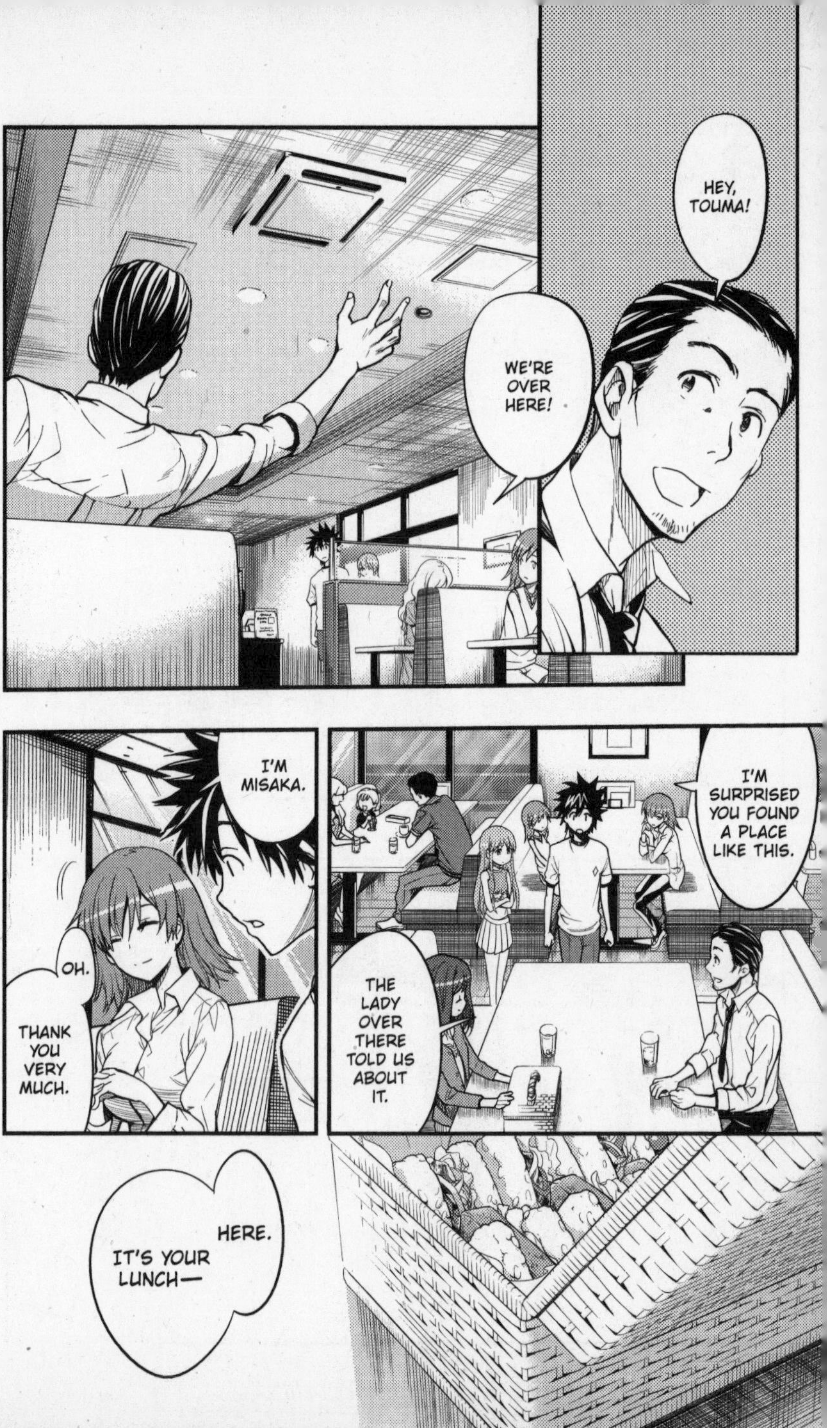
HEY, TOUMA!
WE'RE OVER HERE!
I'M SURPRISED YOU FOUND A PLACE LIKE THIS.
THE LADY OVER THERE TOLD US ABOUT IT.
I'M MISAKA.
OH.
THANK YOU VERY MUCH.
HERE.
IT'S YOUR LUNCH—

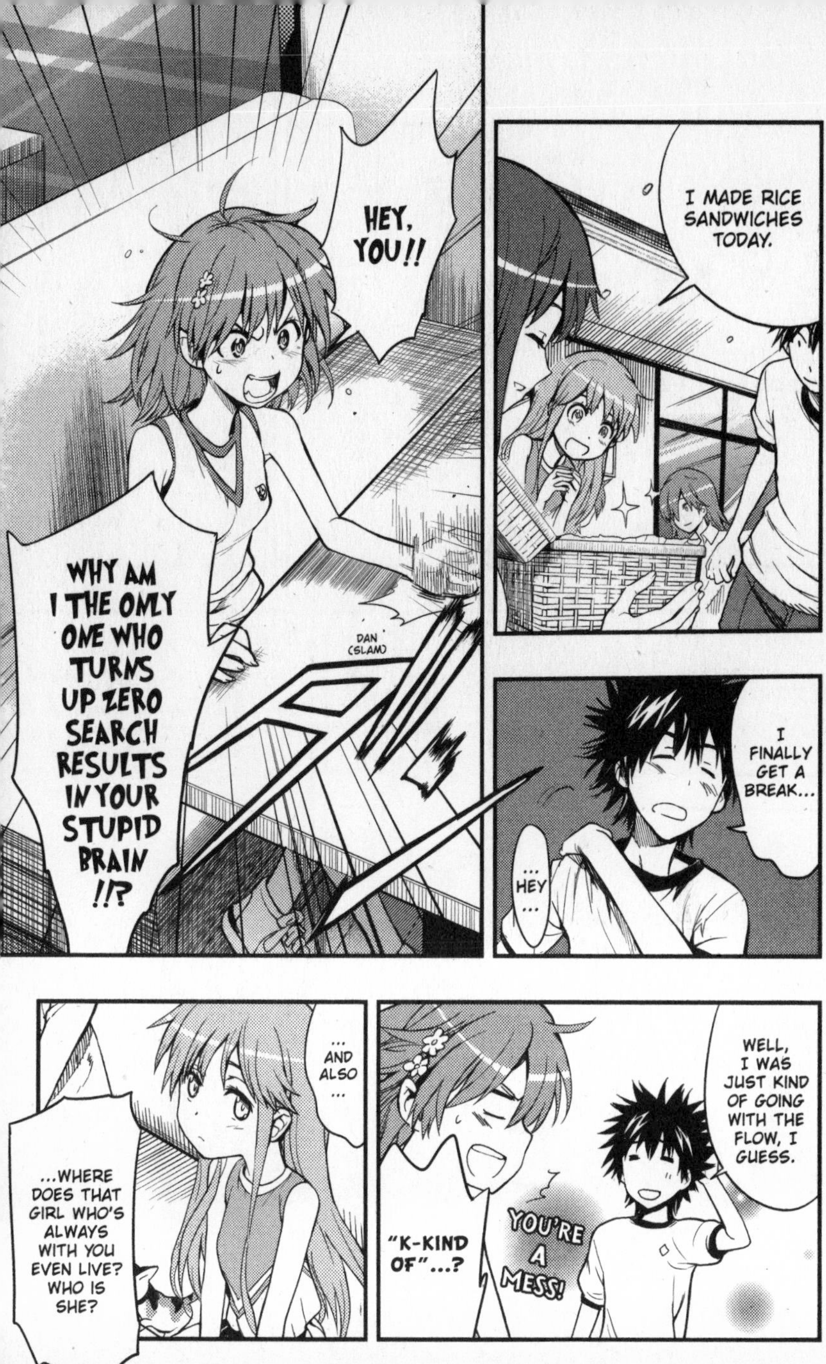
I MADE RICE SANDWICHES TODAY.
I FINALLY GET A BREAK...
...HEY...
HEY, YOU!!
DAN (SLAM)
WHY AM I THE ONLY ONE WHO TURNS UP ZERO SEARCH RESULTS IN YOUR STUPID BRAIN!!?
WELL, I WAS JUST KIND OF GOING WITH THE FLOW, I GUESS.
YOU'RE A MESS!
“K-KIND OF”...?
...AND ALSO...
...WHERE DOES THAT GIRL WHO'S ALWAYS WITH YOU EVEN LIVE? WHO IS SHE?

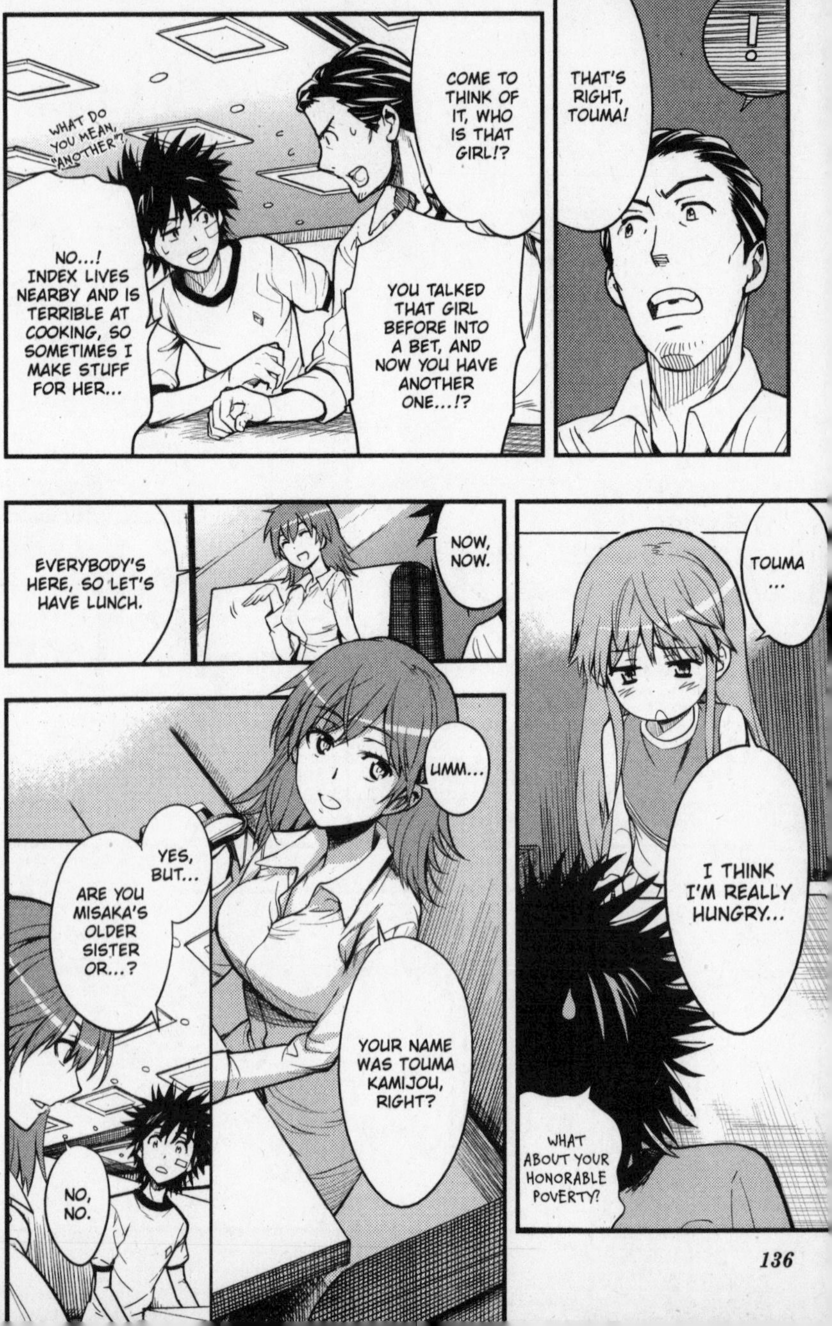
!
THAT'S RIGHT, TOUMA!
COME TO THINK OF IT, WHO IS THAT GIRL!?
YOU TALKED THAT GIRL BEFORE INTO A BET, AND NOW YOU HAVE ANOTHER ONE...!?
WHAT DO YOU MEAN, "ANOTHER"?
NO...! INDEX LIVES NEARBY AND IS TERRIBLE AT COOKING, SO SOMETIMES I MAKE STUFF FOR HER...
TOUMA...
I THINK I'M REALLY HUNGRY...
WHAT ABOUT YOUR HONORABLE POVERTY?
NOW, NOW.
EVERYBODY'S HERE, SO LET'S HAVE LUNCH.
UMM...
YOUR NAME WAS TOUMA KAMIJOU, RIGHT?
YES, BUT... ARE YOU MISAKA'S OLDER SISTER OR...?
NO, NO.

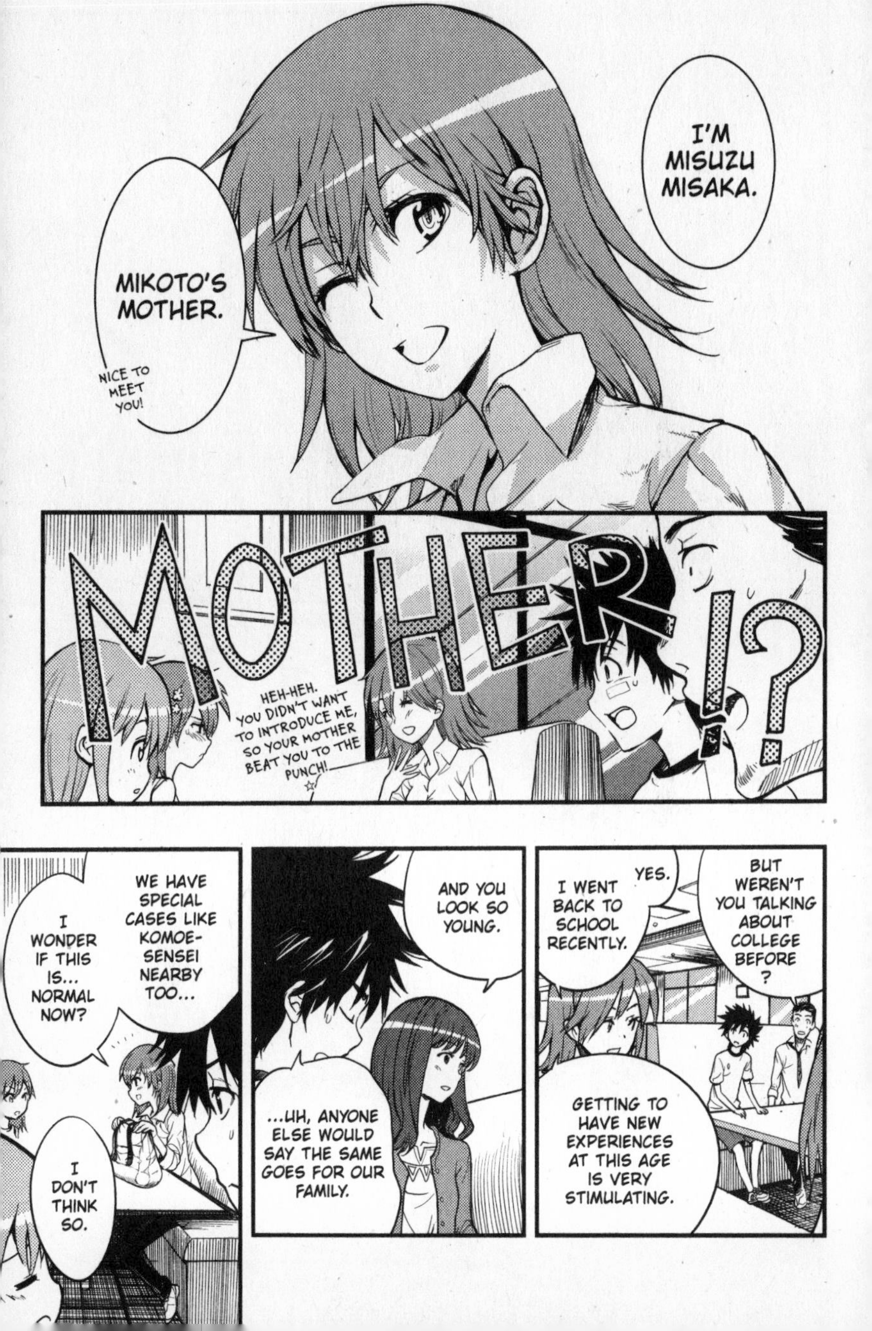

I'M MISUZU MISAKA.
MIKOTO'S MOTHER.
NICE TO MEET YOU!
MOTHER!?
HEH-HEH. YOU DIDN'T WANT TO INTRODUCE ME, SO YOUR MOTHER BEAT YOU TO THE PUNCH! ☆
BUT WEREN'T YOU TALKING ABOUT COLLEGE BEFORE?
YES.
I WENT BACK TO SCHOOL RECENTLY.
GETTING TO HAVE NEW EXPERIENCES AT THIS AGE IS VERY STIMULATING.
AND YOU LOOK SO YOUNG.
...UH, ANYONE ELSE WOULD SAY THE SAME GOES FOR OUR FAMILY.
WE HAVE SPECIAL CASES LIKE KOMOE-SENSEI NEARBY TOO...
I WONDER IF THIS IS... NORMAL NOW?
I DON'T THINK SO.

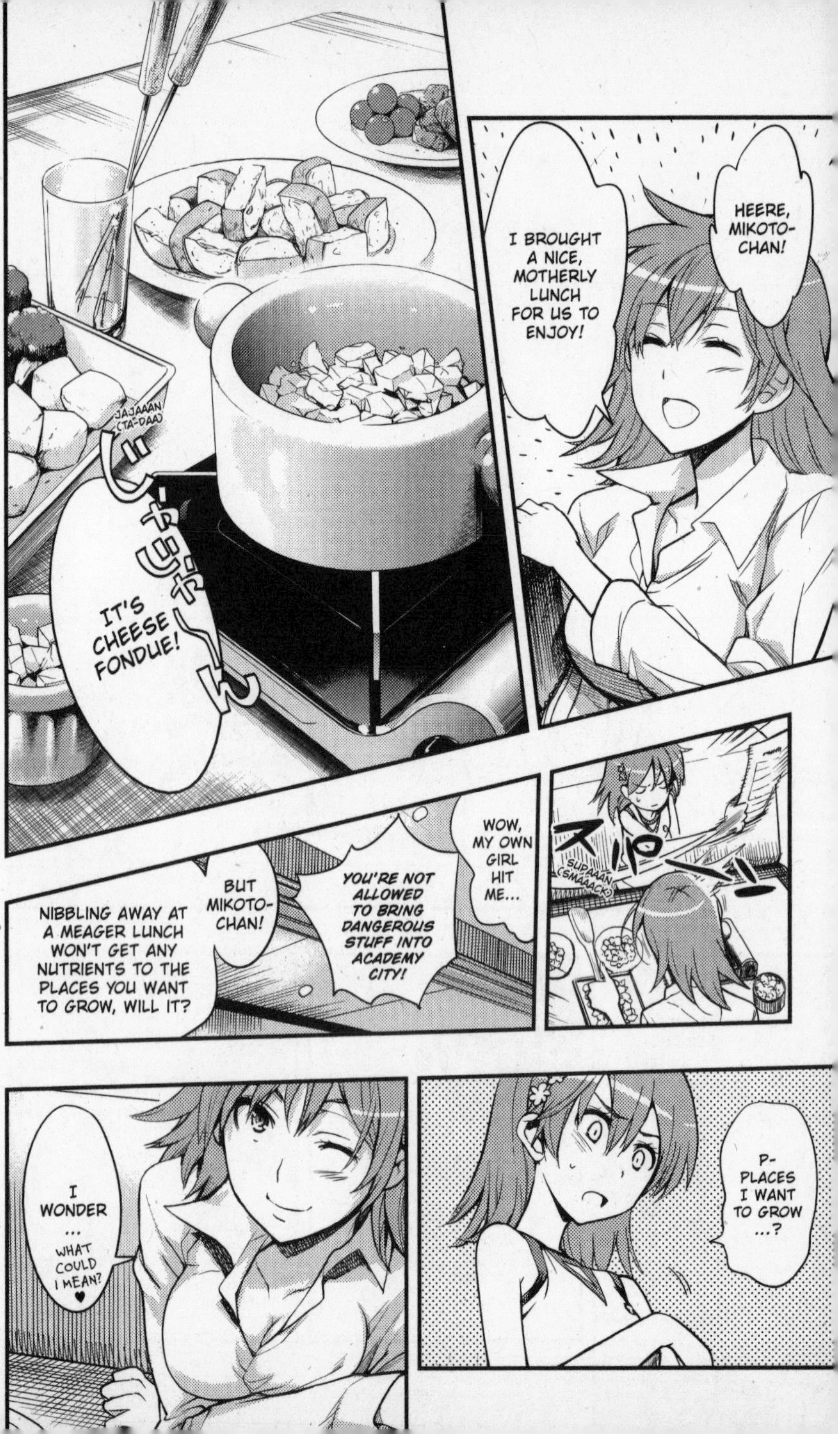
HEERE, MIKOTO-CHAN!
I BROUGHT A NICE, MOTHERLY LUNCH FOR US TO ENJOY!
JAJAAAN (TA-DAA)
IT'S CHEESE FONDUE!
SUPAAAN (SMAAACK)
WOW, MY OWN GIRL HIT ME...
YOU'RE NOT ALLOWED TO BRING DANGEROUS STUFF INTO ACADEMY CITY!
BUT MIKOTO-CHAN!
NIBBLING AWAY AT A MEAGER LUNCH WON'T GET ANY NUTRIENTS TO THE PLACES YOU WANT TO GROW, WILL IT?
P-PLACES I WANT TO GROW ...?
I WONDER ... WHAT COULD I MEAN? ♥

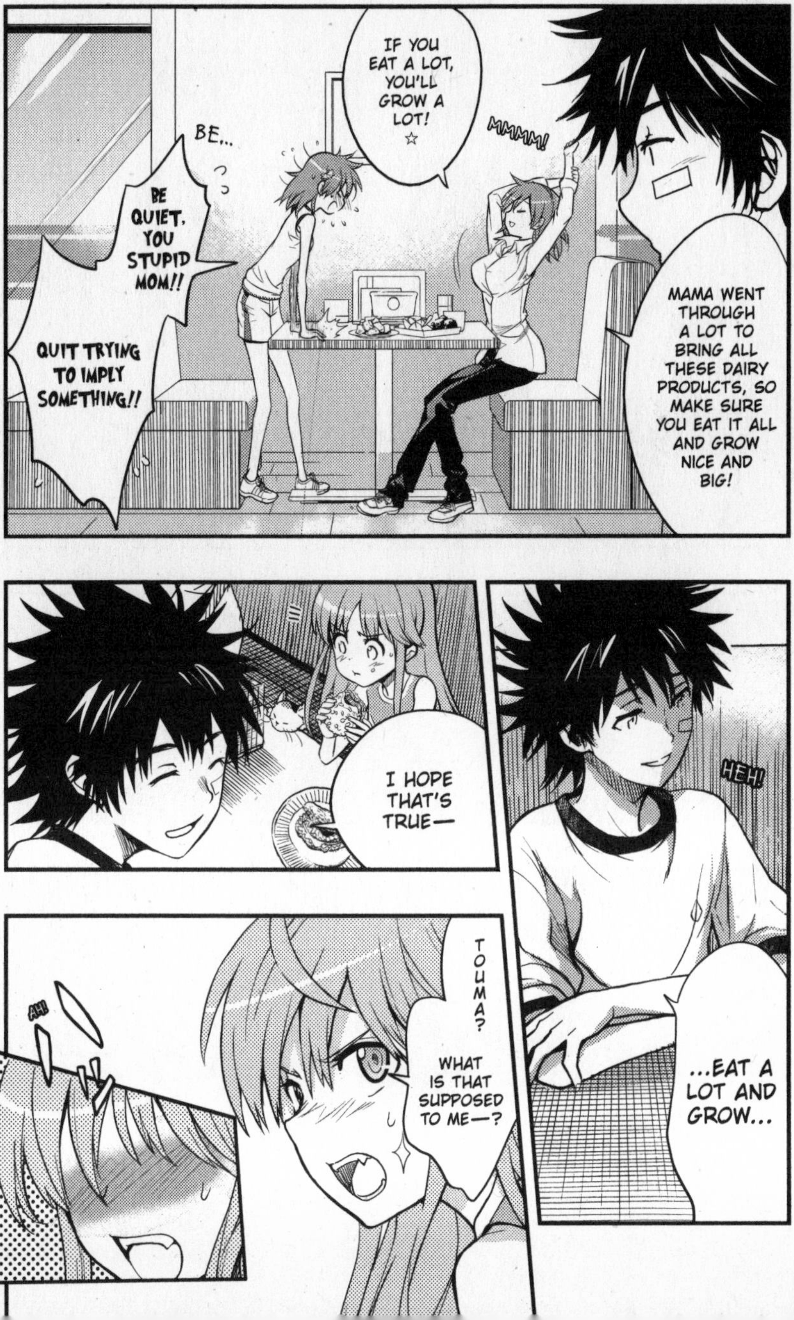
MAMA WENT THROUGH A LOT TO BRING ALL THESE DAIRY PRODUCTS, SO MAKE SURE YOU EAT IT ALL AND GROW NICE AND BIG!
IF YOU EAT A LOT, YOU'LL GROW A LOT! ☆
MMMM!
BE...
BE QUIET, YOU STUPID MOM!!
QUIT TRYING TO IMPLY SOMETHING!!
HEH!
...EAT A LOT AND GROW...
I HOPE THAT'S TRUE—
TOUMA?
WHAT IS THAT SUPPOSED TO ME—?
AH!

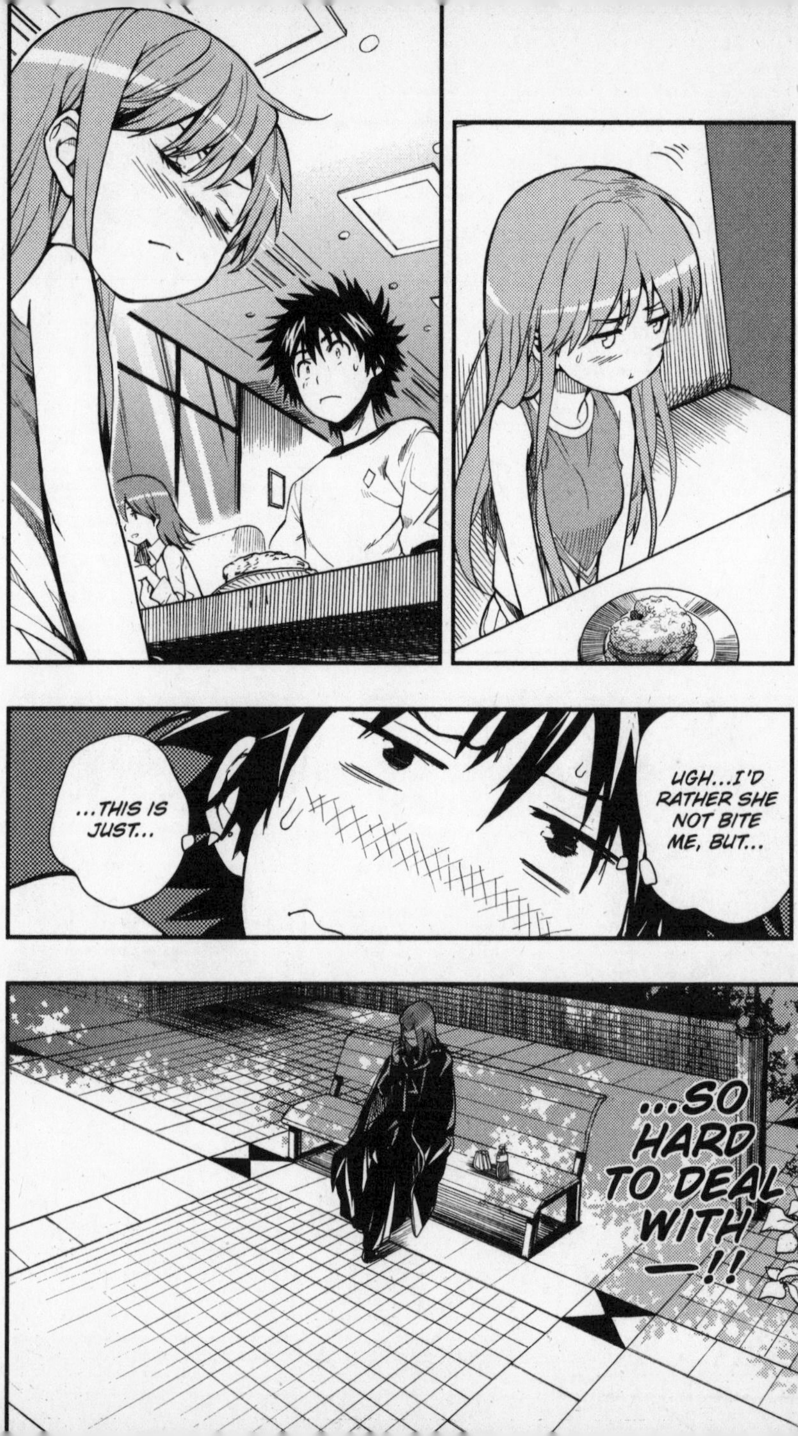
UGH...I'D RATHER SHE NOT BITE ME, BUT...
...THIS IS JUST...
...SO HARD TO DEAL WITH—!!

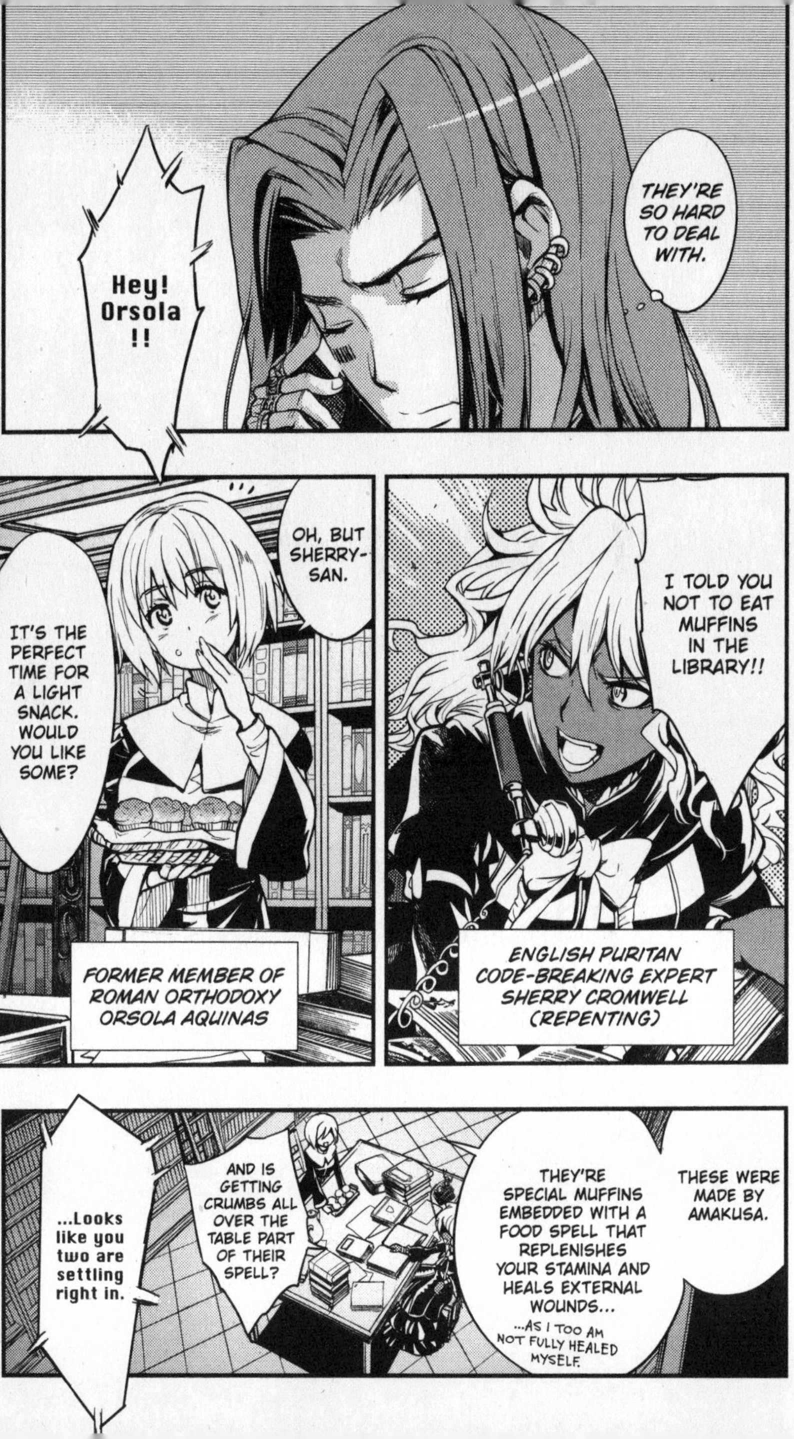
THEY'RE SO HARD TO DEAL WITH.
Hey! Orsola!!
I TOLD YOU NOT TO EAT MUFFINS IN THE LIBRARY!!
ENGLISH PURITAN CODE-BREAKING EXPERT SHERRY CROMWELL (REPENTING)
OH, BUT SHERRY-SAN.
IT'S THE PERFECT TIME FOR A LIGHT SNACK. WOULD YOU LIKE SOME?
FORMER MEMBER OF ROMAN ORTHODOXY ORSOLA AQUINAS
THESE WERE MADE BY AMAKUSA.
THEY'RE SPECIAL MUFFINS EMBEDDED WITH A FOOD SPELL THAT REPLENISHES YOUR STAMINA AND HEALS EXTERNAL WOUNDS...
...AS I TOO AM NOT FULLY HEALED MYSELF.
AND IS GETTING CRUMBS ALL OVER THE TABLE PART OF THEIR SPELL?
...Looks like you two are settling right in.

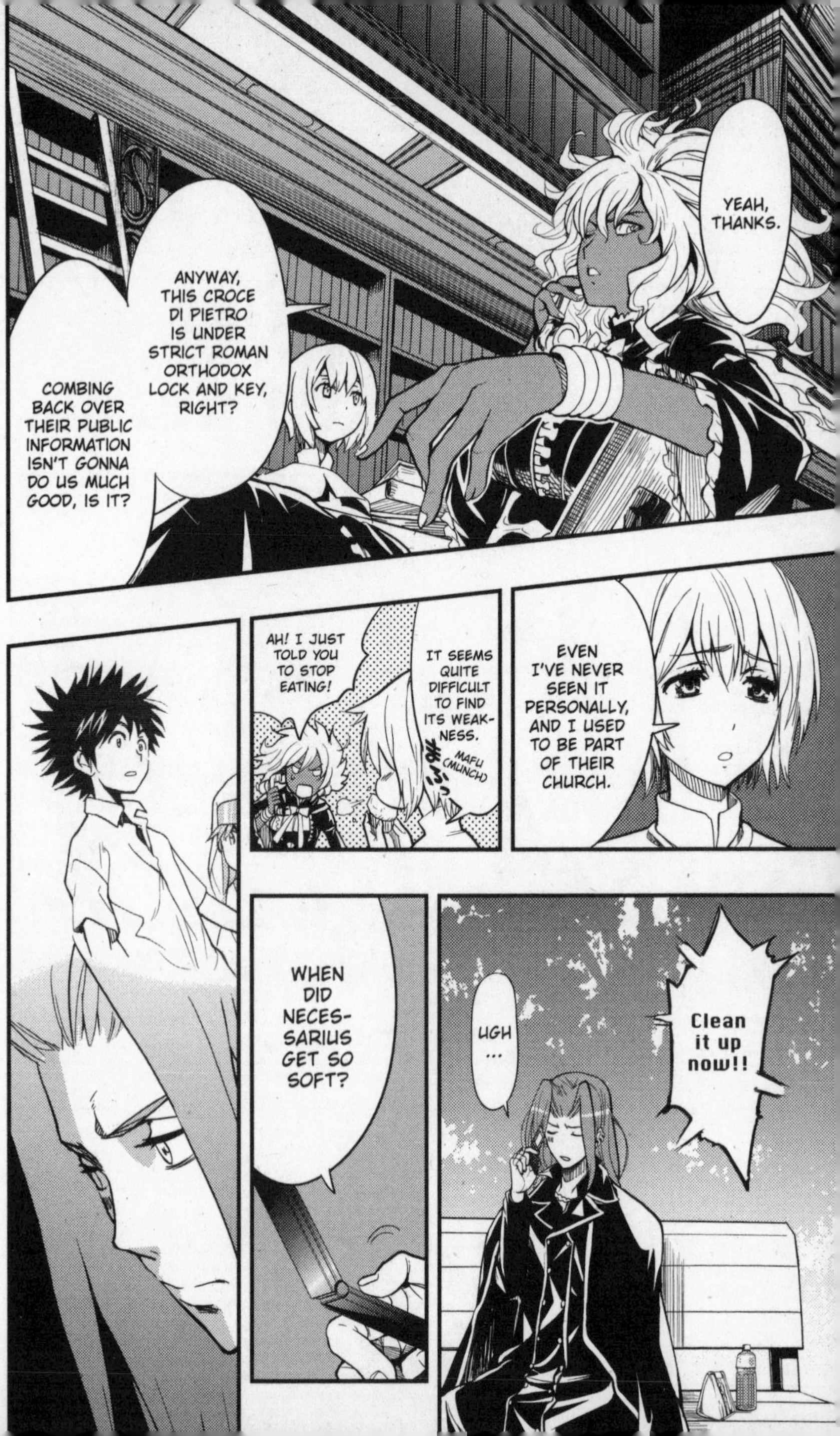
YEAH, THANKS.
ANYWAY, THIS CROCE DI PIETRO IS UNDER STRICT ROMAN ORTHODOX LOCK AND KEY, RIGHT?
COMBING BACK OVER THEIR PUBLIC INFORMATION ISN'T GONNA DO US MUCH GOOD, IS IT?
EVEN I'VE NEVER SEEN IT PERSONALLY, AND I USED TO BE PART OF THEIR CHURCH.
IT SEEMS QUITE DIFFICULT TO FIND ITS WEAK-NESS.
MAFU (MUNCH)
AH! I JUST TOLD YOU TO STOP EATING!
Clean it up now!!
UGH...
WHEN DID NECES-SARIUS GET SO SOFT?

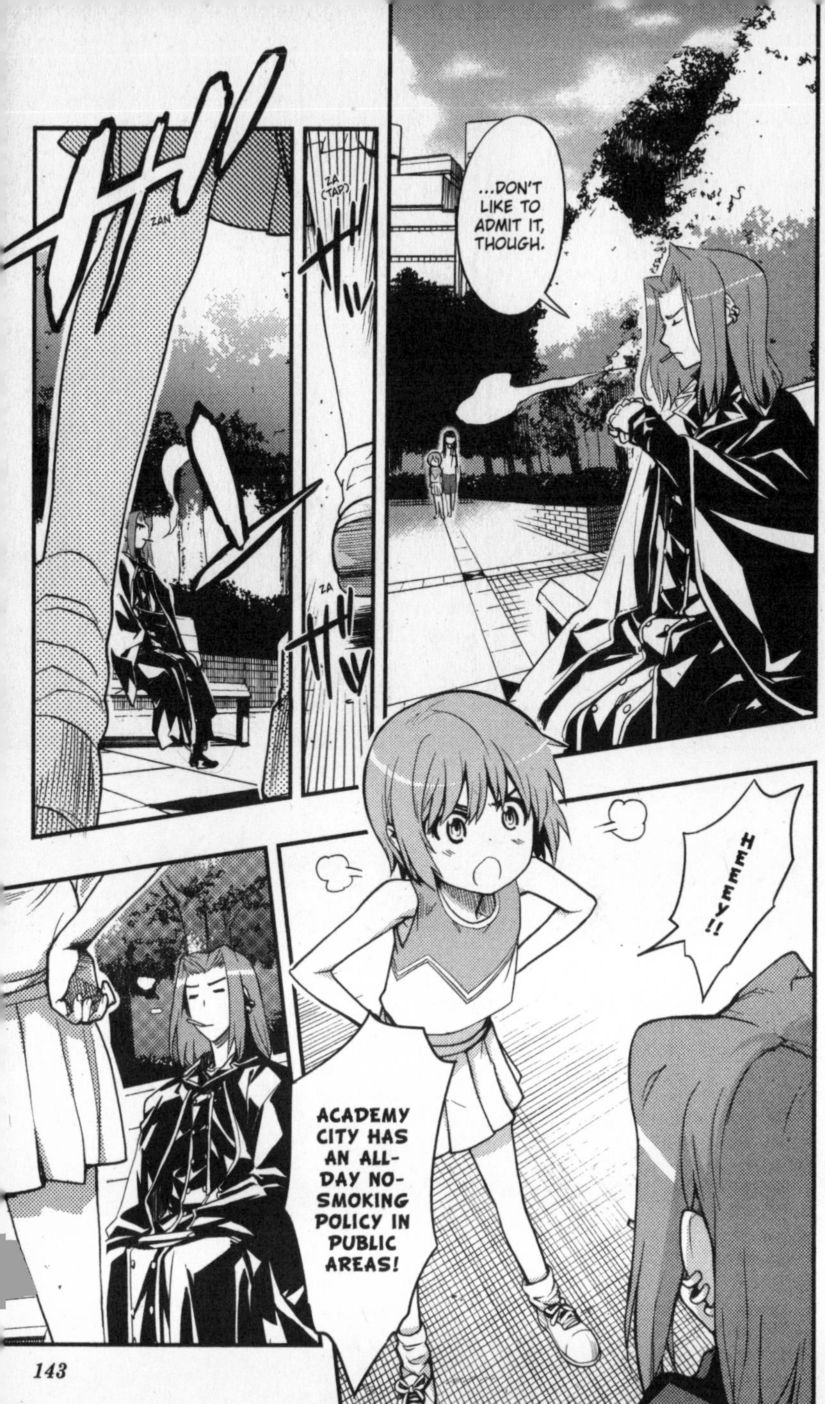
...DON'T LIKE TO ADMIT IT, THOUGH.
ZA (TAP)
ZA
ZAN
HEEEEY!!
ACADEMY CITY HAS AN ALL-DAY NO-SMOKING POLICY IN PUBLIC AREAS!

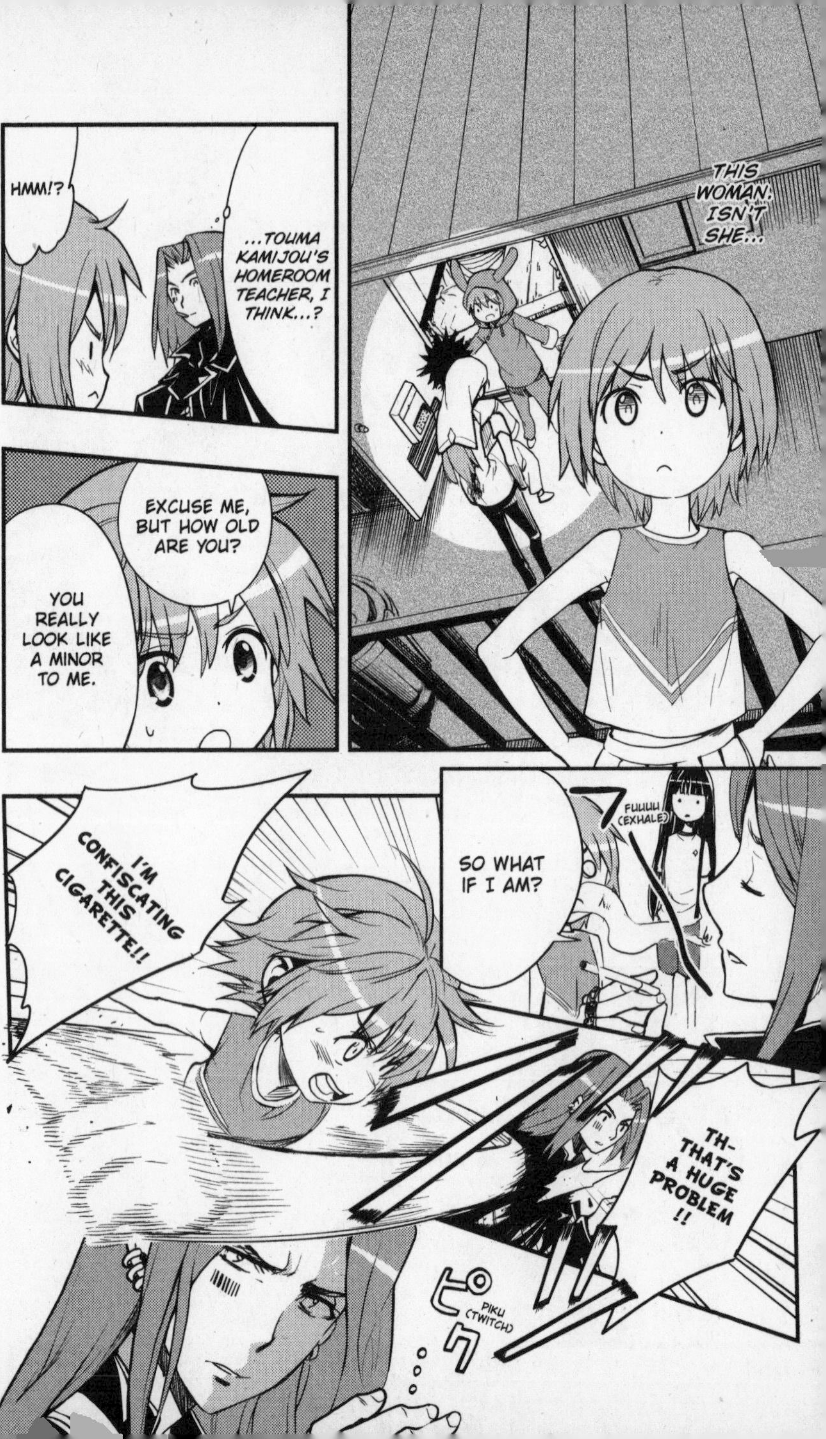
THIS WOMAN. ISN'T SHE...
...TOUMA KAMIJOU'S HOMEROOM TEACHER, I THINK...?
HMM!?
EXCUSE ME, BUT HOW OLD ARE YOU?
YOU REALLY LOOK LIKE A MINOR TO ME.
FUUUU (EXHALE)
SO WHAT IF I AM?
I'M CONFISCATING THIS CIGARETTE!!
TH-THAT'S A HUGE PROBLEM!!
PIKU (TWITCH)

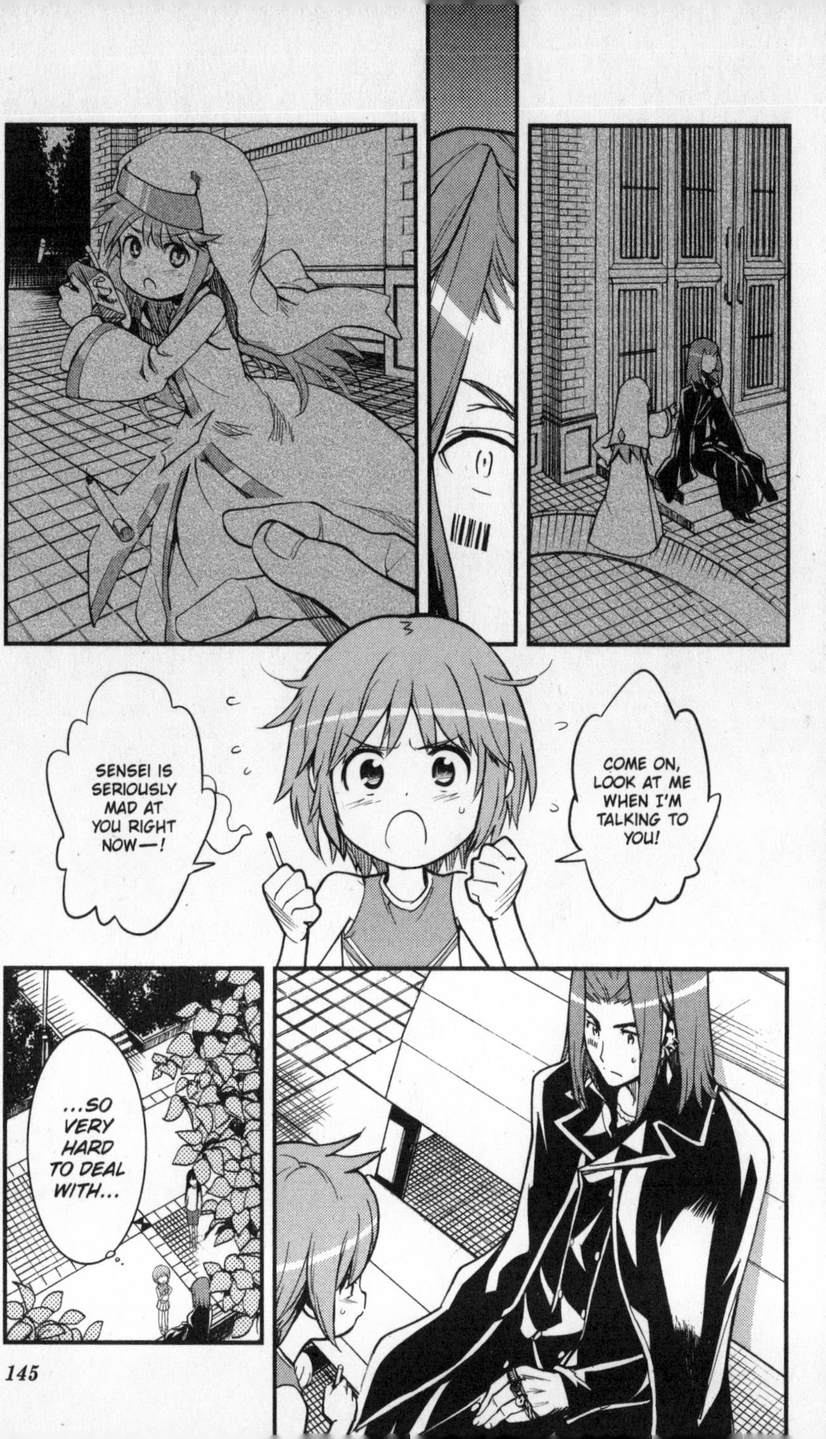
COME ON, LOOK AT ME WHEN I'M TALKING TO YOU!
SENSEI IS SERIOUSLY MAD AT YOU RIGHT NOW—!
...SO VERY HARD TO DEAL WITH...

A Certain Magical Index

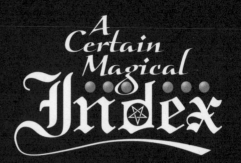

#76 PURSUIT AGAIN

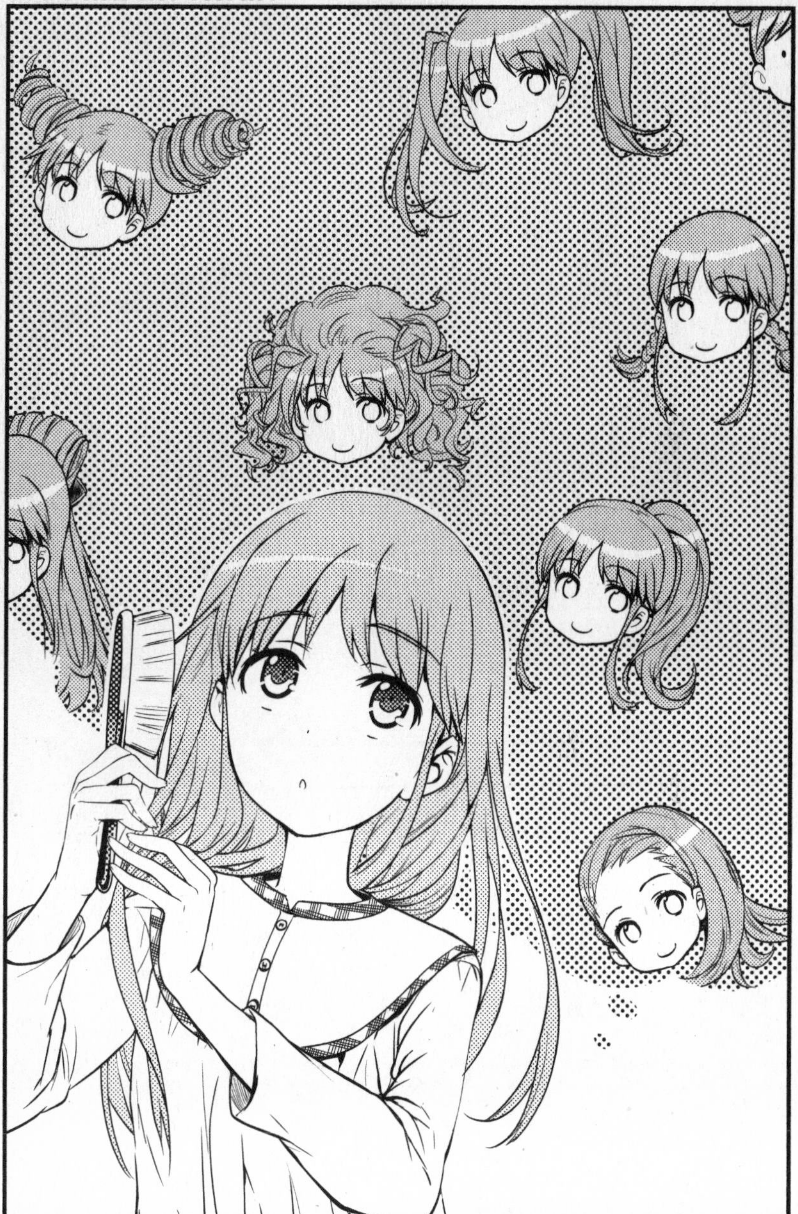

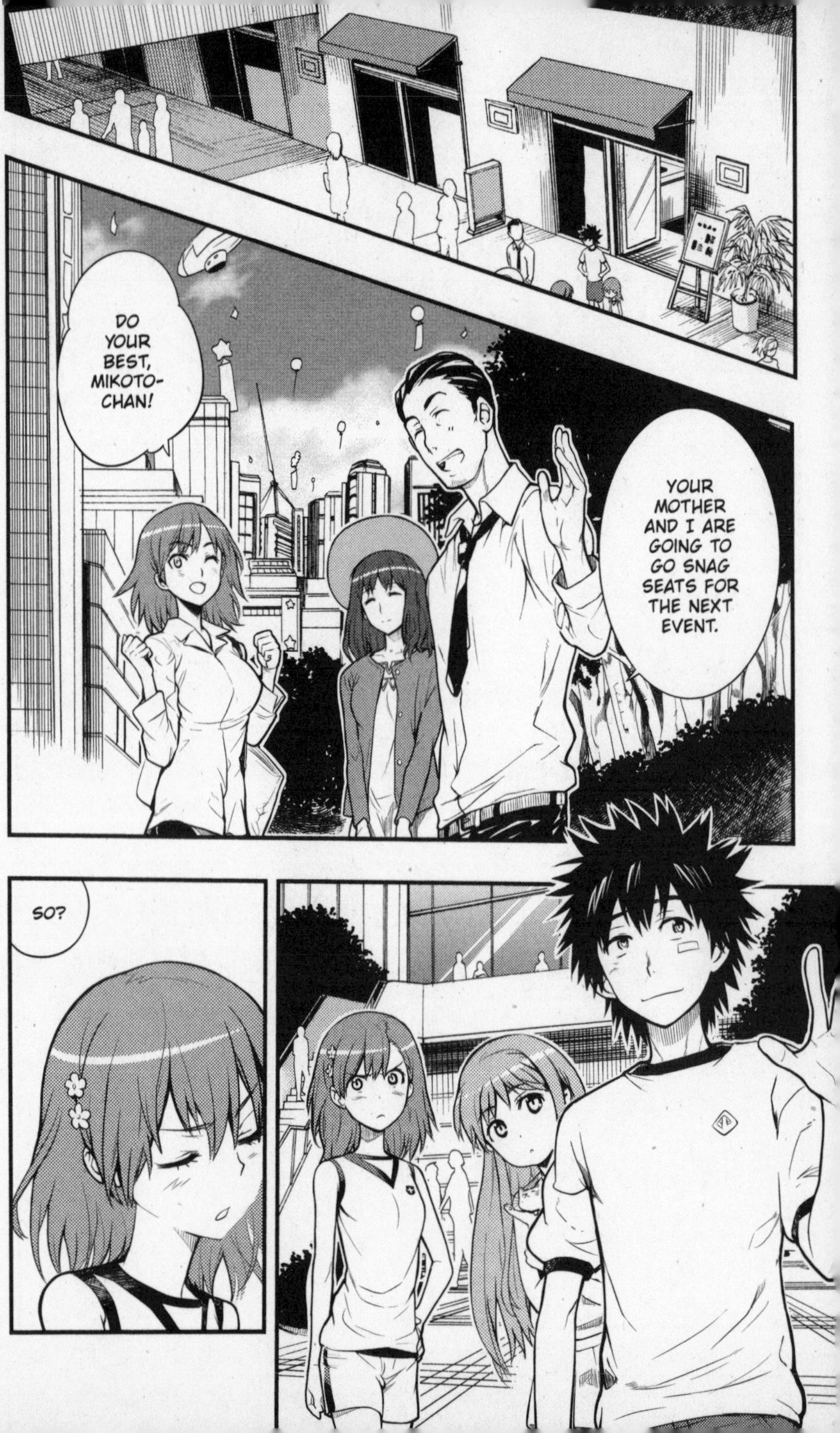
YOUR MOTHER AND I ARE GOING TO GO SNAG SEATS FOR THE NEXT EVENT.
DO YOUR BEST, MIKOTO-CHAN!
SO?

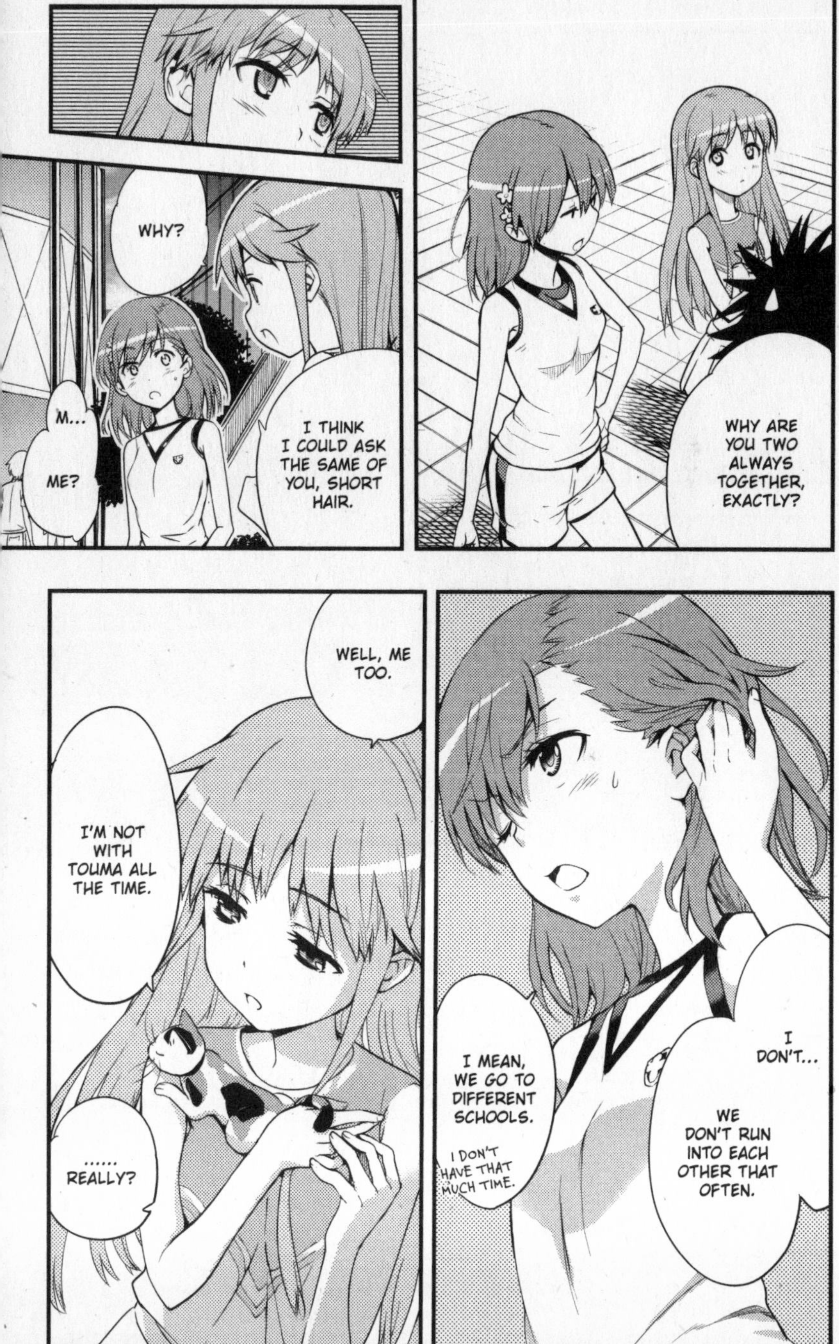
WHY ARE YOU TWO ALWAYS TOGETHER, EXACTLY?
WHY?
I THINK I COULD ASK THE SAME OF YOU, SHORT HAIR.
M... ME?
I DON'T...
WE DON'T RUN INTO EACH OTHER THAT OFTEN.
I MEAN, WE GO TO DIFFERENT SCHOOLS.
I DON'T HAVE THAT MUCH TIME.
WELL, ME TOO.
I'M NOT WITH TOUMA ALL THE TIME.
......REALLY?

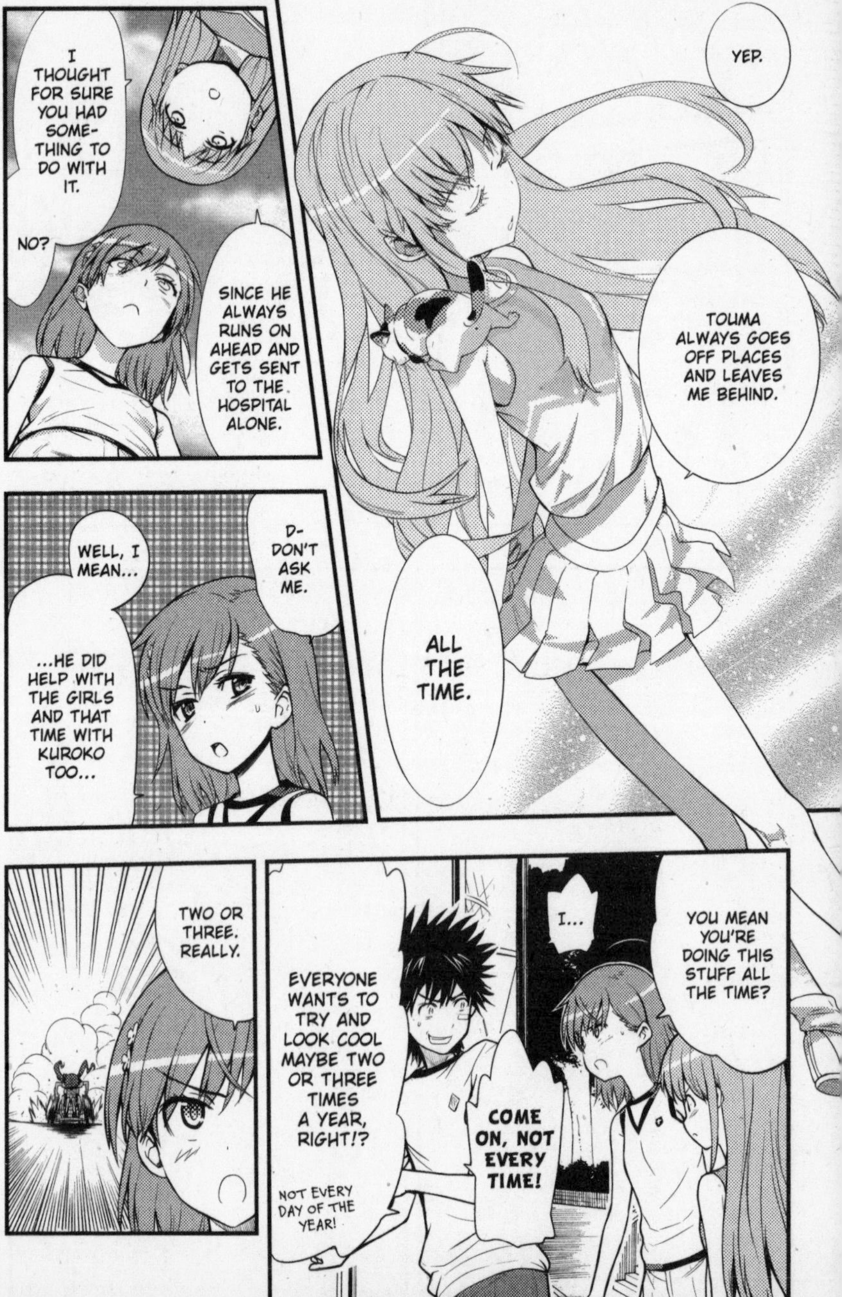
YEP.
TOUMA ALWAYS GOES OFF PLACES AND LEAVES ME BEHIND.
ALL THE TIME.
SINCE HE ALWAYS RUNS ON AHEAD AND GETS SENT TO THE HOSPITAL ALONE.
I THOUGHT FOR SURE YOU HAD SOME-THING TO DO WITH IT.
NO?
D-DON'T ASK ME.
WELL, I MEAN...
...HE DID HELP WITH THE GIRLS AND THAT TIME WITH KUROKO TOO...
YOU MEAN YOU'RE DOING THIS STUFF ALL THE TIME?
I...
COME ON, NOT EVERY TIME!
EVERYONE WANTS TO TRY AND LOOK COOL MAYBE TWO OR THREE TIMES A YEAR, RIGHT!?
NOT EVERY DAY OF THE YEAR!
TWO OR THREE. REALLY.

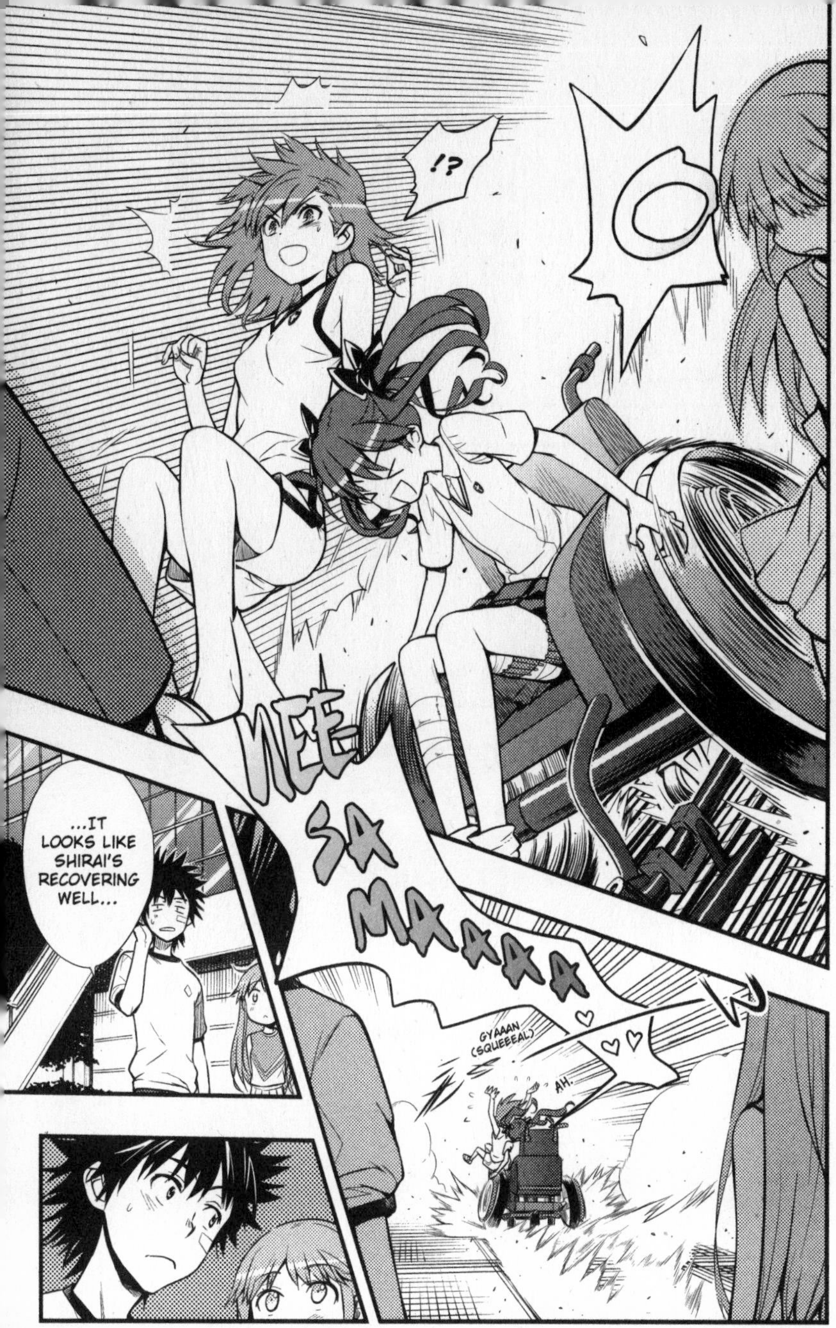
!?
NEE-SA MAAAAA
GYAAAN (SQUEEEAL)
AH.
...IT LOOKS LIKE SHIRAI'S RECOVERING WELL...

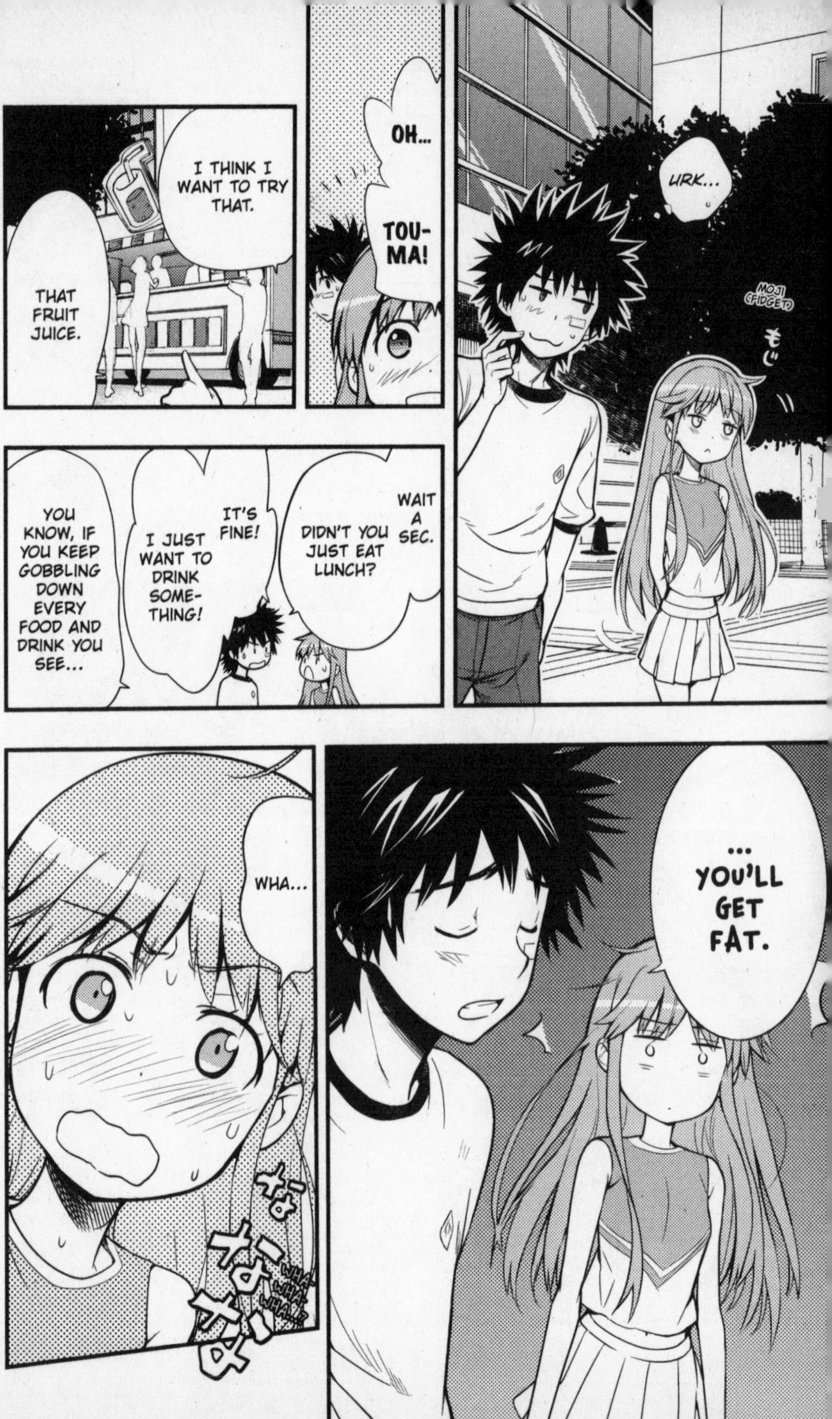
URK...
MOJI (FIDGET)
もじ
OH...
TOU-MA!
I THINK I WANT TO TRY THAT.
THAT FRUIT JUICE.
WAIT A SEC.
DIDN'T YOU JUST EAT LUNCH?
IT'S FINE!
I JUST WANT TO DRINK SOME-THING!
YOU KNOW, IF YOU KEEP GOBBLING DOWN EVERY FOOD AND DRINK YOU SEE...
... YOU'LL GET FAT.
WHA...
なななな
WHA-WHA-WHA...?

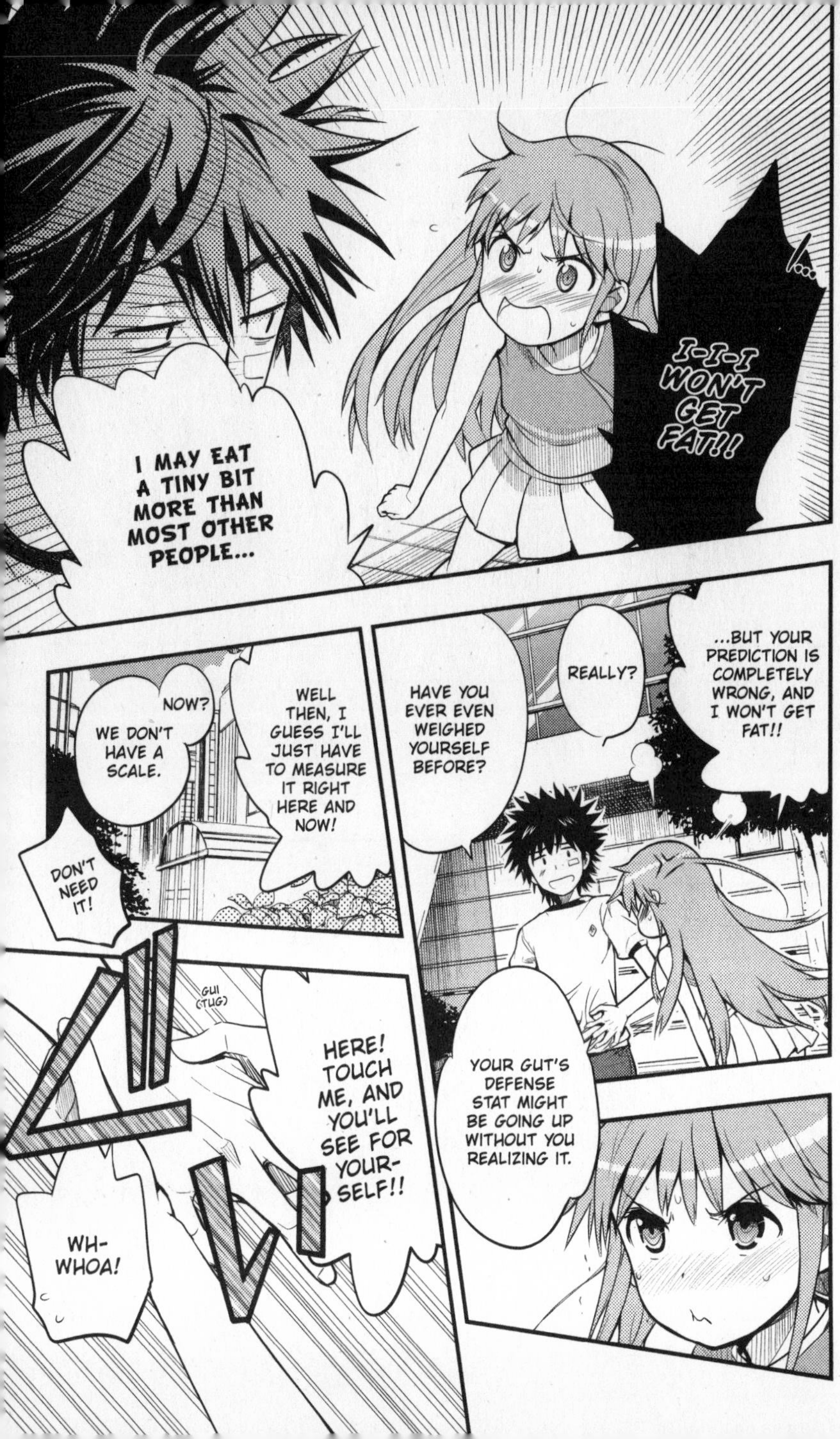
I...
I-I-I WON'T GET FAT!!
I MAY EAT A TINY BIT MORE THAN MOST OTHER PEOPLE...
...BUT YOUR PREDICTION IS COMPLETELY WRONG, AND I WON'T GET FAT!!
REALLY?
HAVE YOU EVER EVEN WEIGHED YOURSELF BEFORE?
YOUR GUT'S DEFENSE STAT MIGHT BE GOING UP WITHOUT YOU REALIZING IT.
WELL THEN, I GUESS I'LL JUST HAVE TO MEASURE IT RIGHT HERE AND NOW!
NOW?
WE DON'T HAVE A SCALE.
DON'T NEED IT!
GUI (TUG)
HERE! TOUCH ME, AND YOU'LL SEE FOR YOURSELF!!
WH-WHOA!

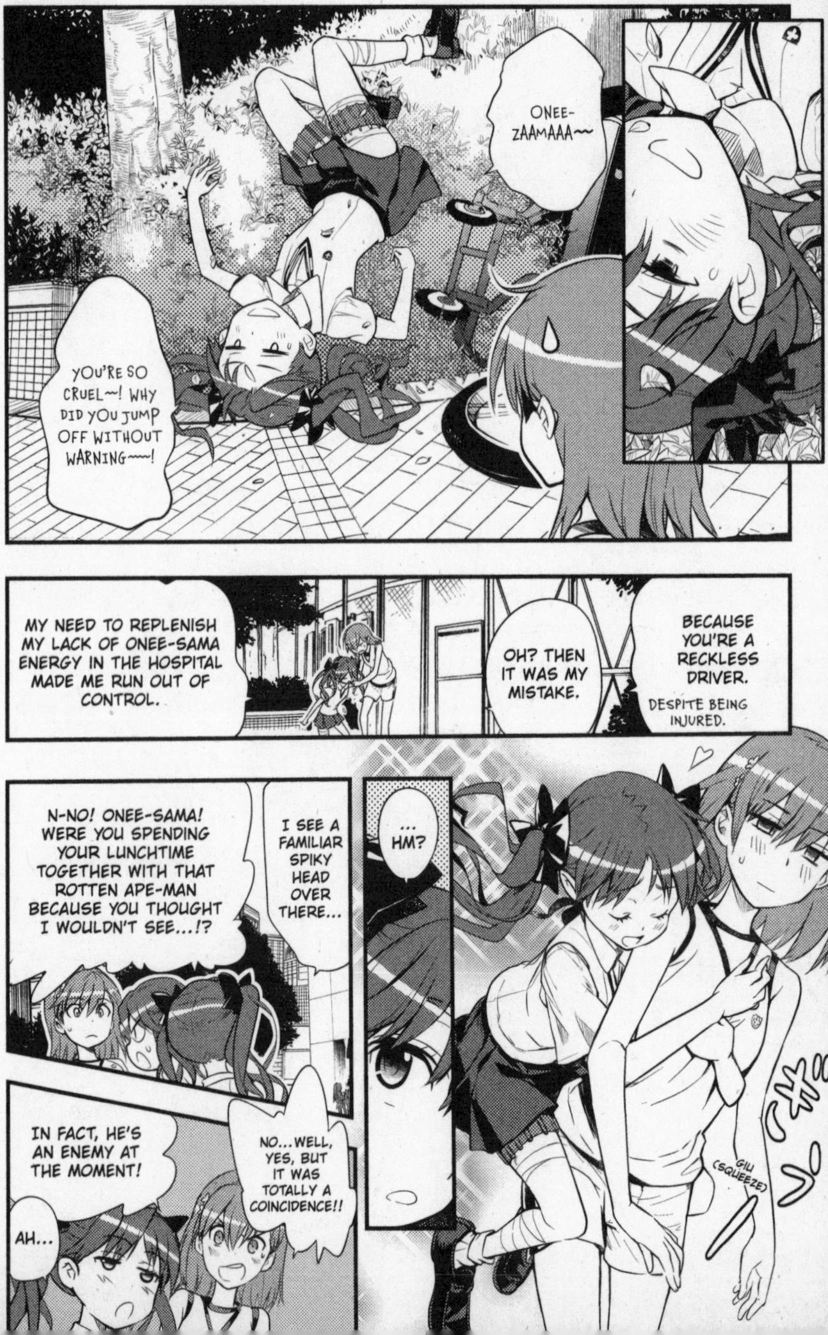
ONEE-ZAAMAAA~~
YOU'RE SO CRUEL~! WHY DID YOU JUMP OFF WITHOUT WARNING~~~!
BECAUSE YOU'RE A RECKLESS DRIVER.
DESPITE BEING INJURED.
OH? THEN IT WAS MY MISTAKE.
MY NEED TO REPLENISH MY LACK OF ONEE-SAMA ENERGY IN THE HOSPITAL MADE ME RUN OUT OF CONTROL.
GIU (SQUEEZE)
... HM?
I SEE A FAMILIAR SPIKY HEAD OVER THERE...
N-NO! ONEE-SAMA! WERE YOU SPENDING YOUR LUNCHTIME TOGETHER WITH THAT ROTTEN APE-MAN BECAUSE YOU THOUGHT I WOULDN'T SEE...!?
NO...WELL, YES, BUT IT WAS TOTALLY A COINCIDENCE!!
IN FACT, HE'S AN ENEMY AT THE MOMENT!
AH...

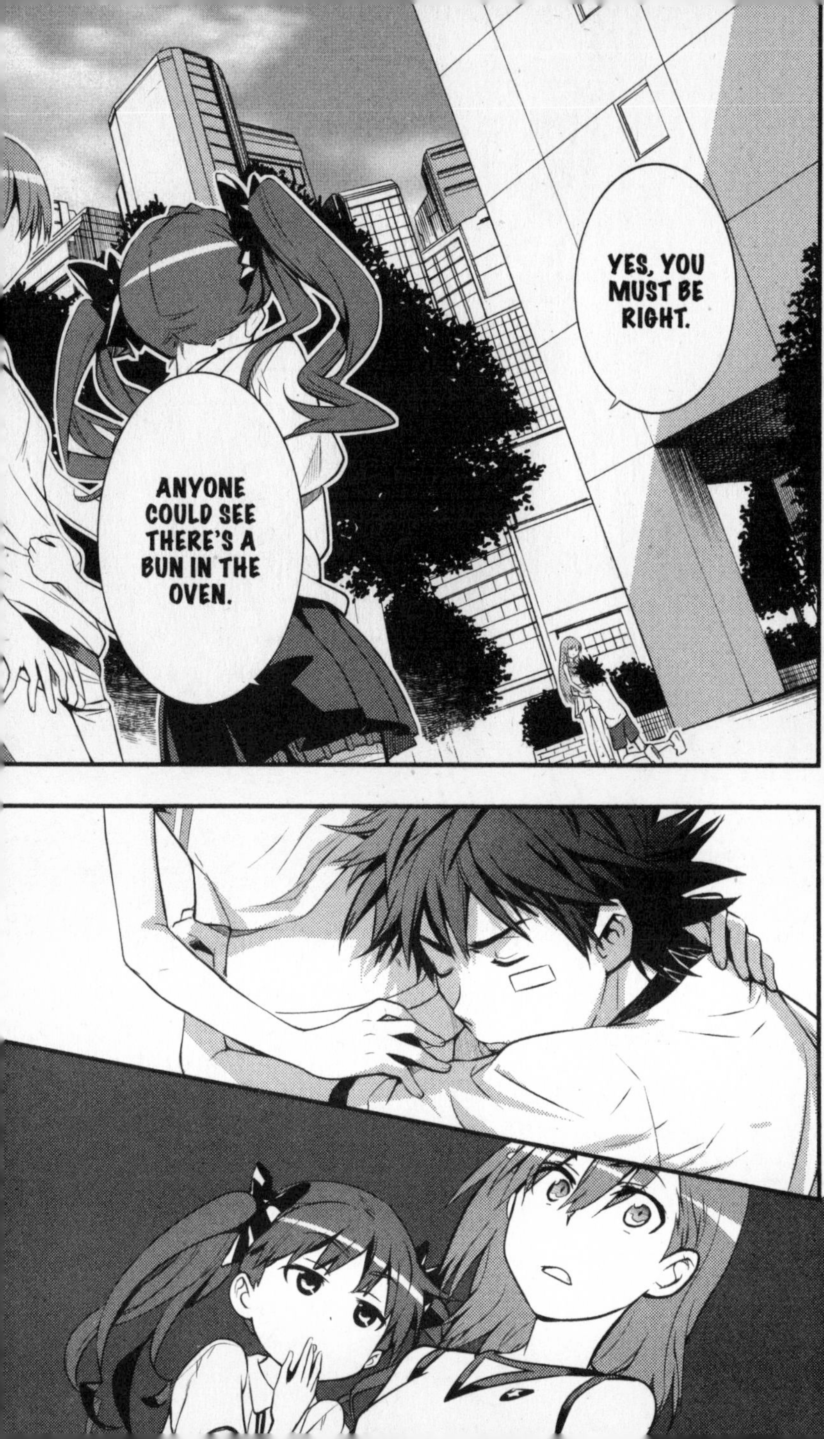
ANYONE COULD SEE THERE'S A BUN IN THE OVEN.
YES, YOU MUST BE RIGHT.

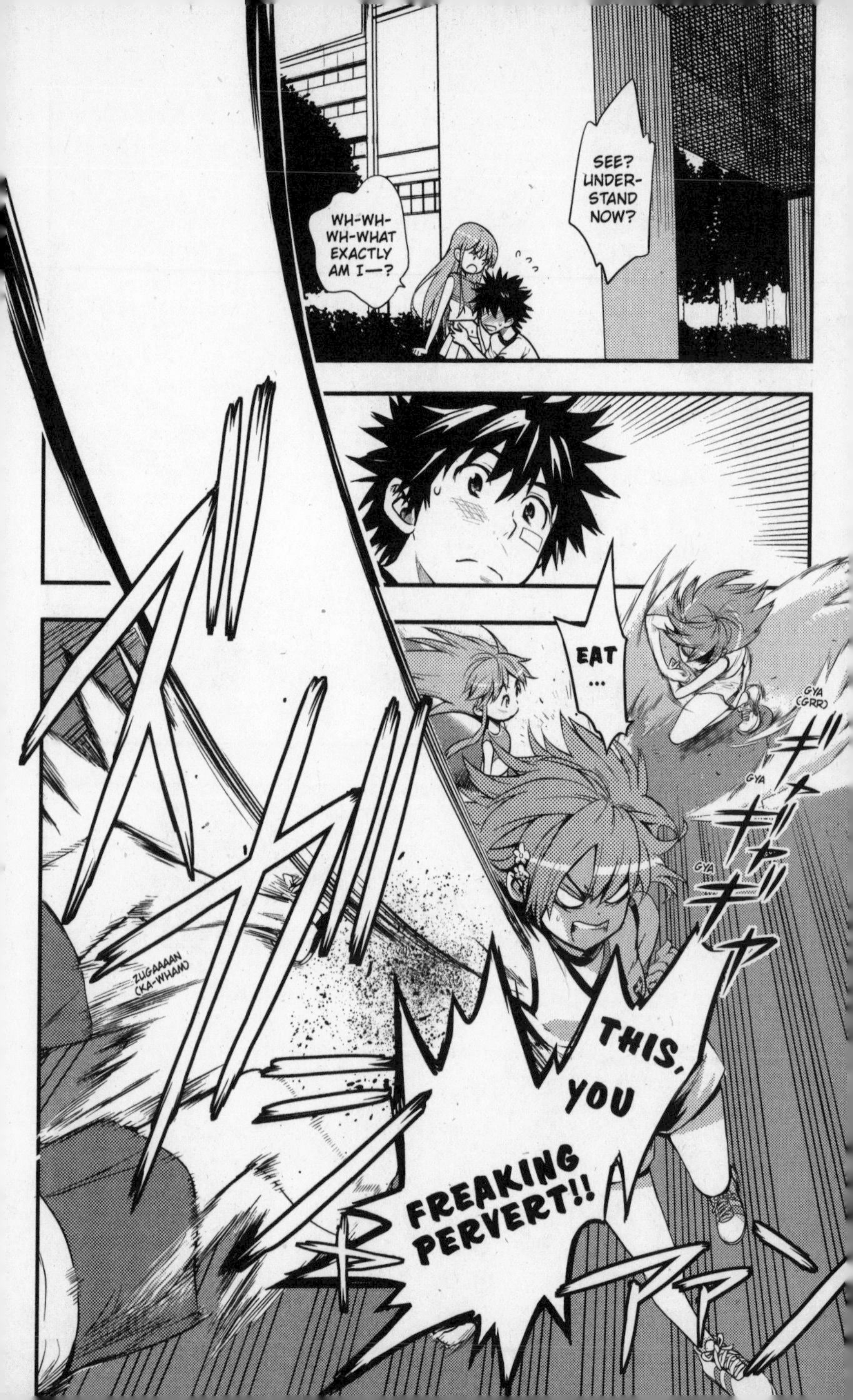
SEE? UNDER-STAND NOW?
WH-WH-WH-WHAT EXACTLY AM I—?
EAT ...
GYA (GRR)
GYA
GYA
THIS, YOU FREAKING PERVERT!!
ZUGAAAAN (KA-WHAM)

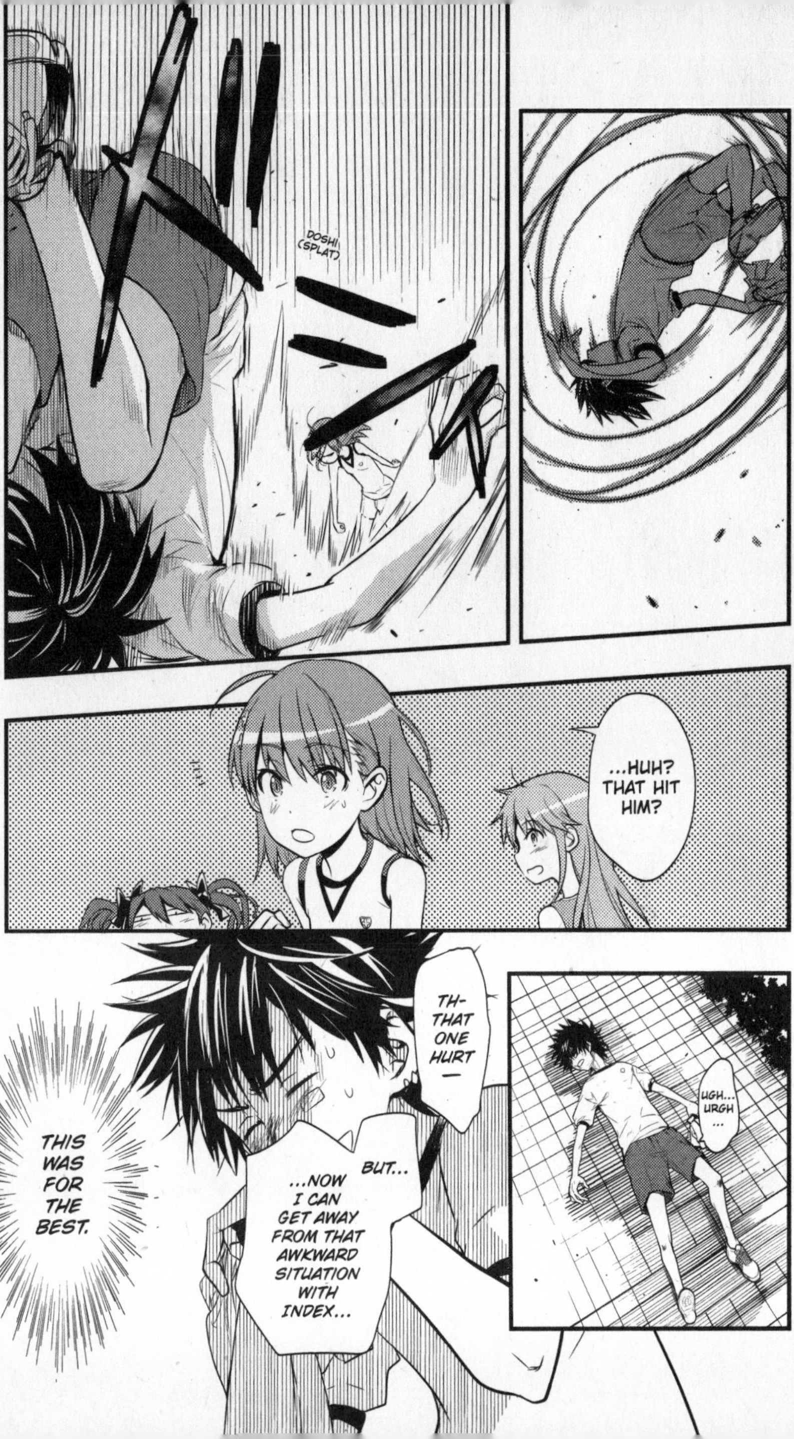
DOSHI (SPLAT)
...HUH? THAT HIT HIM?
UGH... URGH...
TH-THAT ONE HURT—
BUT...
...NOW I CAN GET AWAY FROM THAT AWKWARD SITUATION WITH INDEX...
THIS WAS FOR THE BEST.

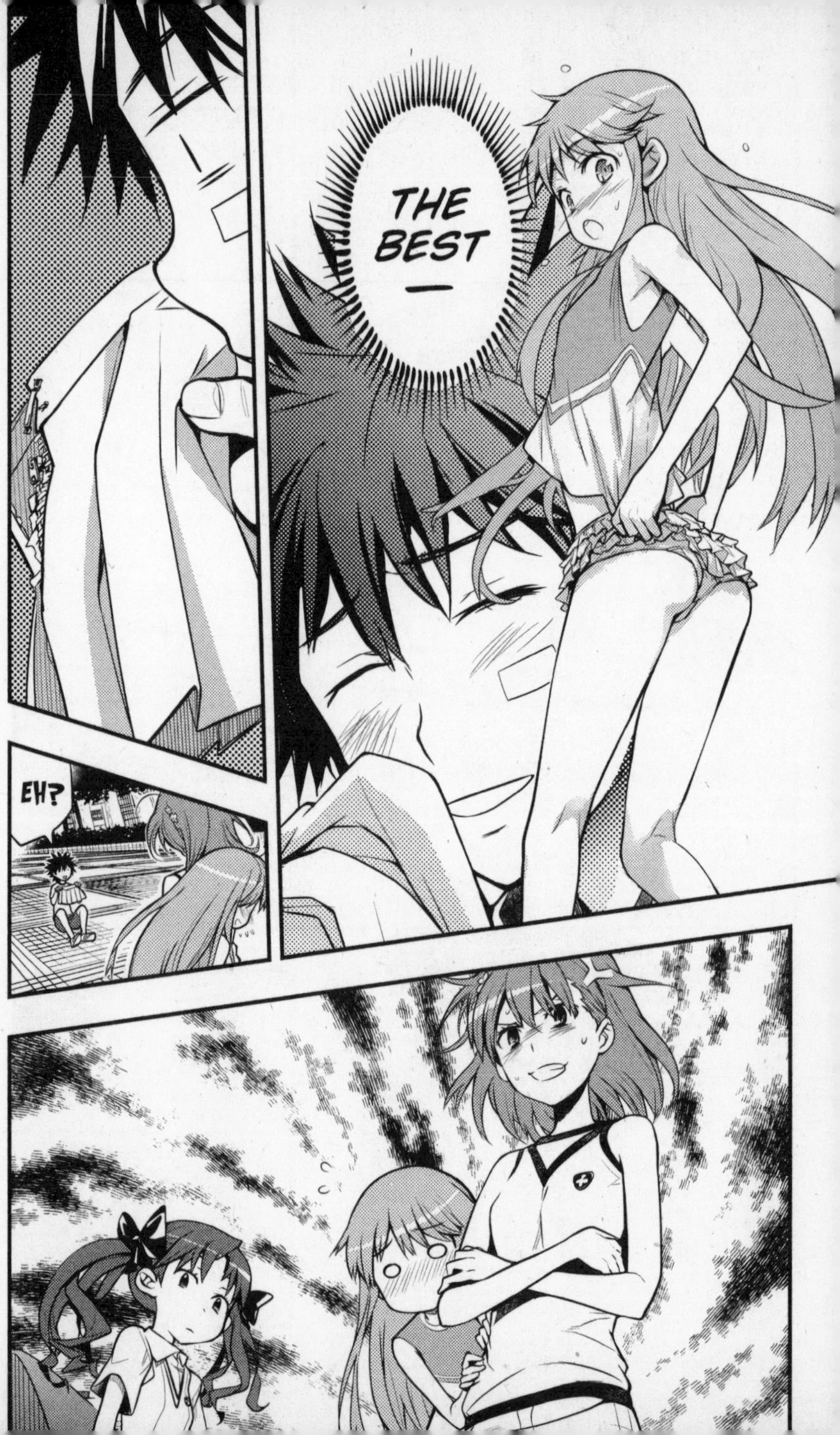
THE BEST —
EH?

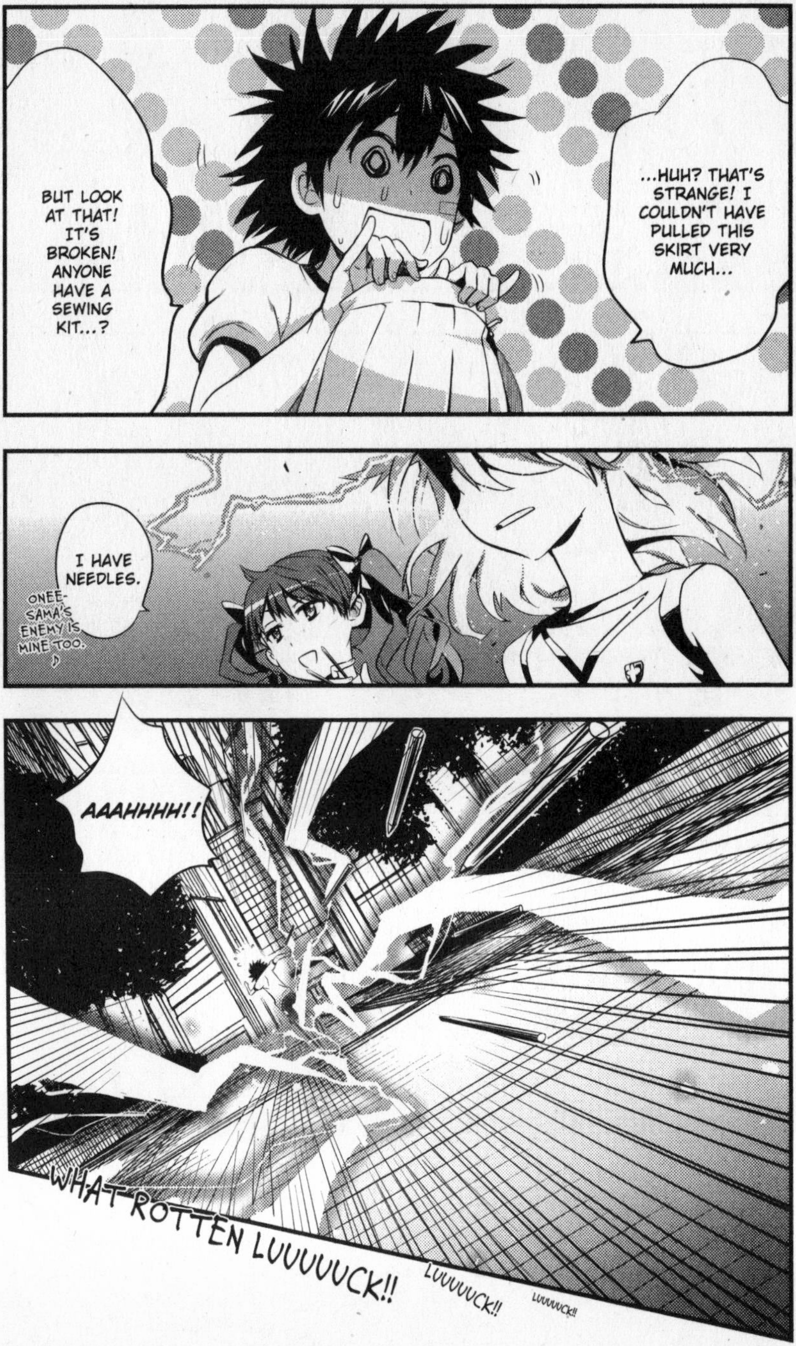
...HUH? THAT'S STRANGE! I COULDN'T HAVE PULLED THIS SKIRT VERY MUCH...
BUT LOOK AT THAT! IT'S BROKEN! ANYONE HAVE A SEWING KIT...?
I HAVE NEEDLES.
ONEE-SAMA'S ENEMY IS MINE TOO. ♪
AAAHHHH!!
WHAT ROTTEN LUUUUUCK!!
LUUUUUCK!!
LUUUUUCK!!

HM...

PASSWORD

●●●*****

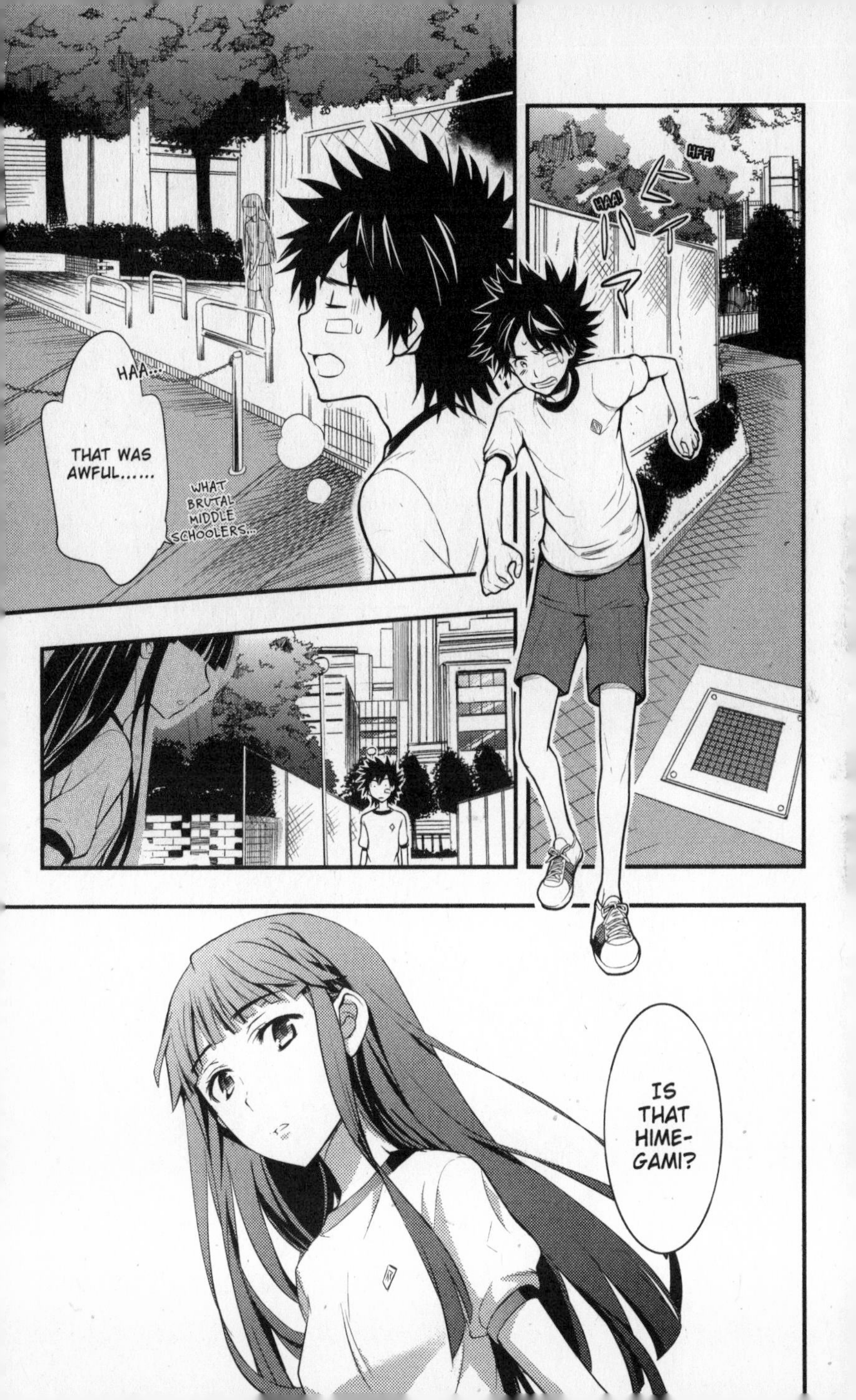
HFF!
HAA!
HAA...
THAT WAS AWFUL......
WHAT BRUTAL MIDDLE SCHOOLERS...
IS THAT HIME-GAMI?

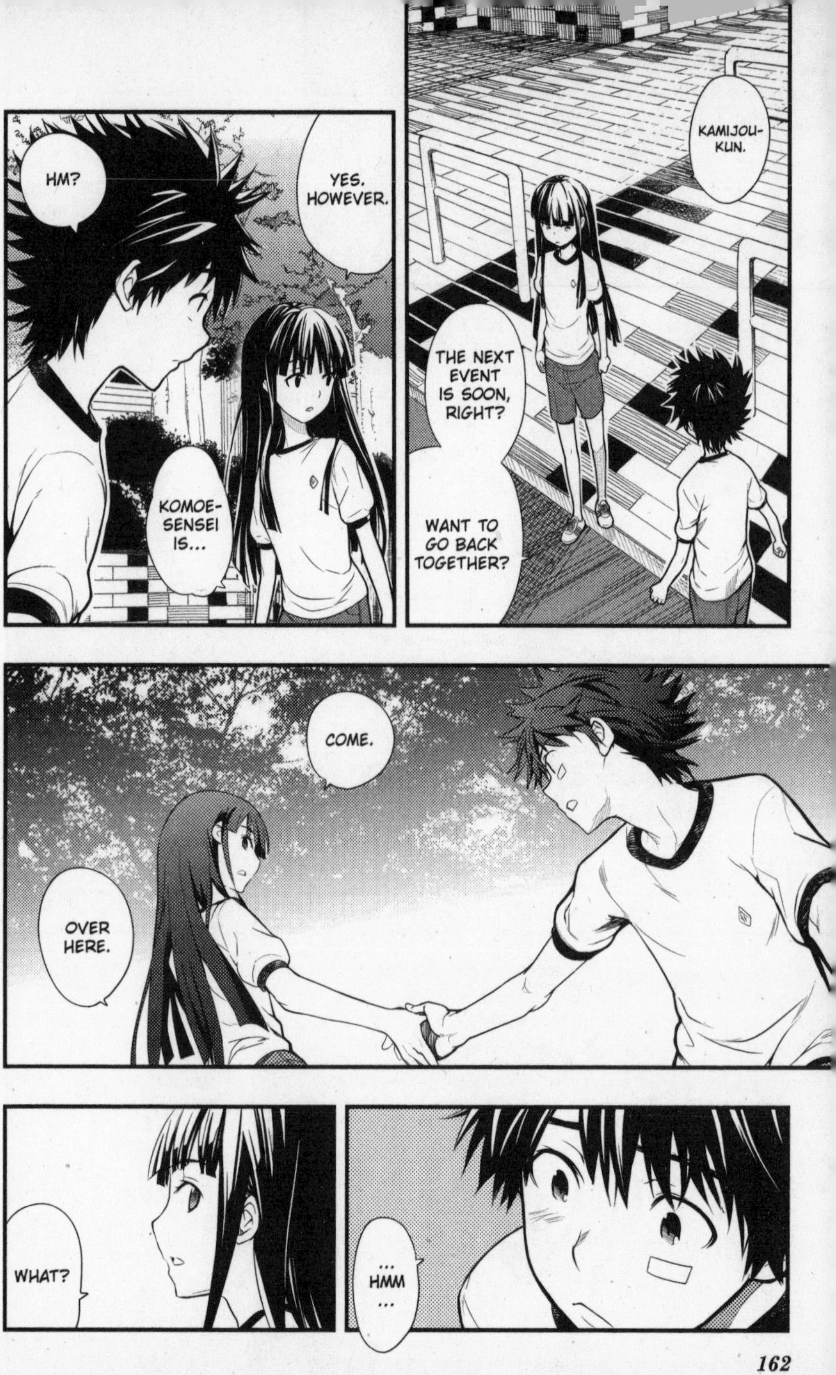
KAMIJOU-KUN.
THE NEXT EVENT IS SOON, RIGHT?
WANT TO GO BACK TOGETHER?
YES. HOWEVER.
HM?
KOMOE-SENSEI IS...
COME.
OVER HERE.
...HMM...
WHAT?

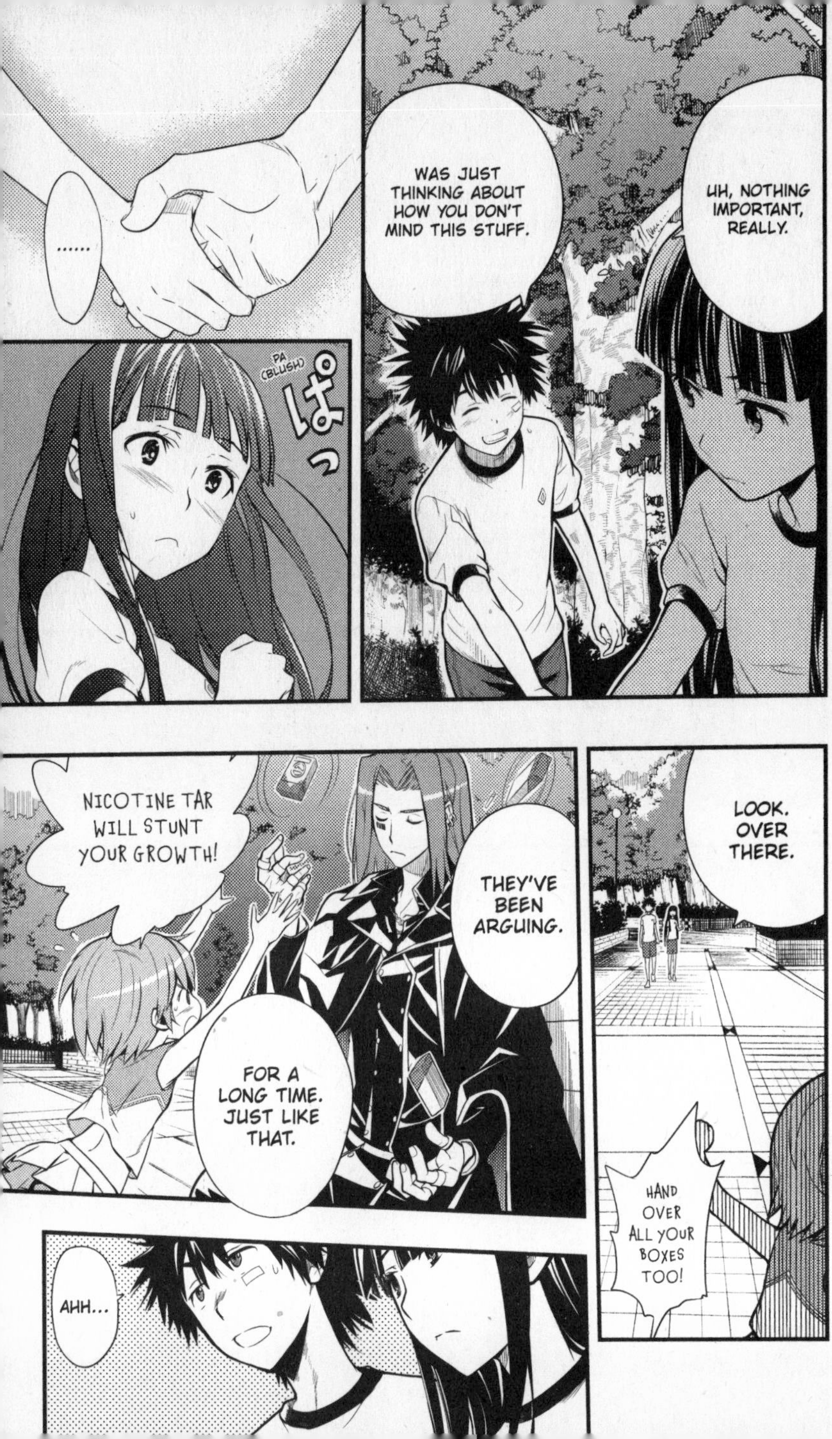
UH, NOTHING IMPORTANT, REALLY.
WAS JUST THINKING ABOUT HOW YOU DON'T MIND THIS STUFF.
......
PA (BLUSH)
ぱっ
LOOK. OVER THERE.
HAND OVER ALL YOUR BOXES TOO!
THEY'VE BEEN ARGUING.
FOR A LONG TIME. JUST LIKE THAT.
NICOTINE TAR WILL STUNT YOUR GROWTH!
AHH...

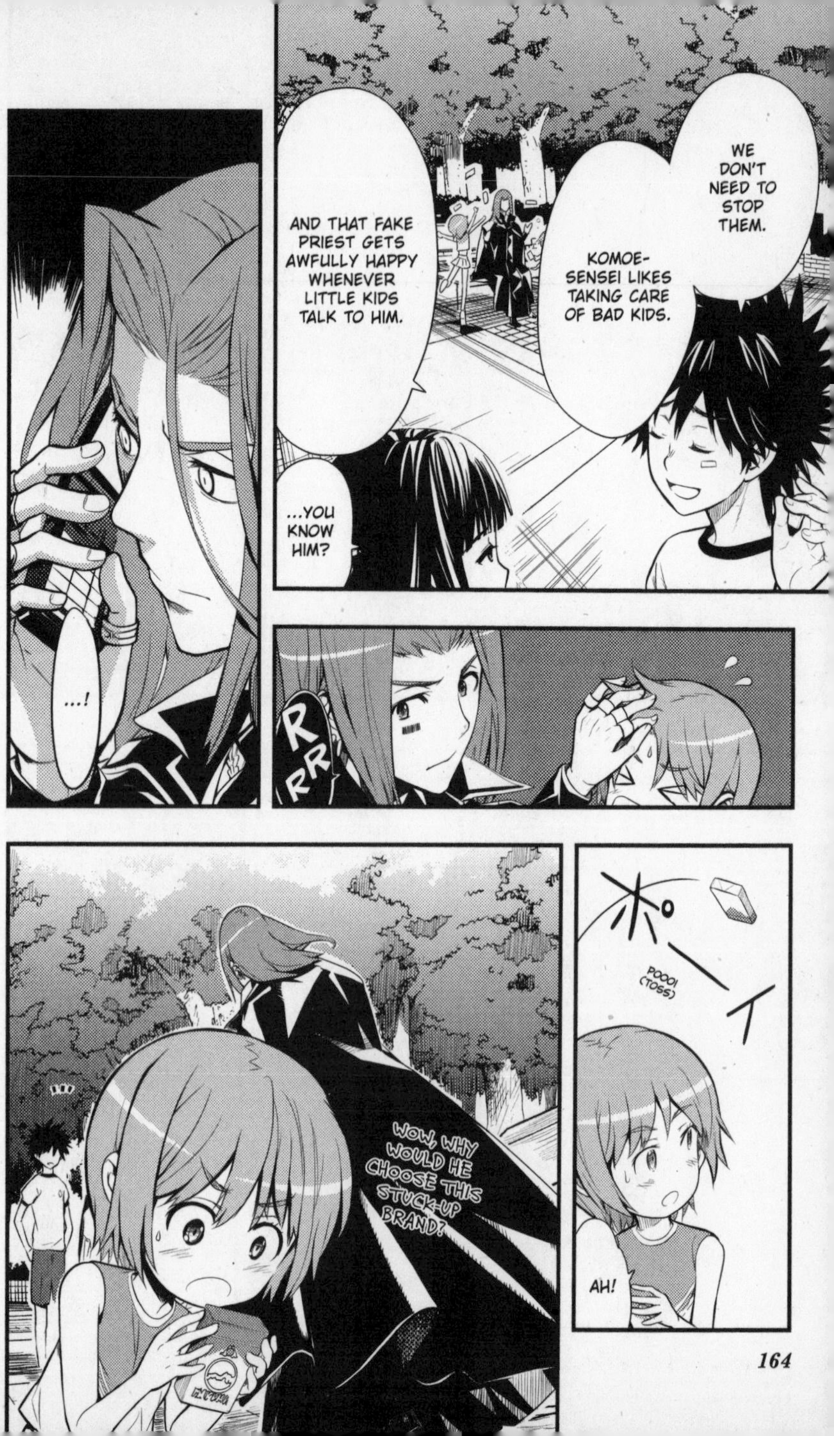
WE DON'T NEED TO STOP THEM.
KOMOE-SENSEI LIKES TAKING CARE OF BAD KIDS.
AND THAT FAKE PRIEST GETS AWFULLY HAPPY WHENEVER LITTLE KIDS TALK TO HIM.
...YOU KNOW HIM?
...!
RRR
POOOI (TOSS)
AH!
WOW, WHY WOULD HE CHOOSE THIS STUCK-UP BRAND?

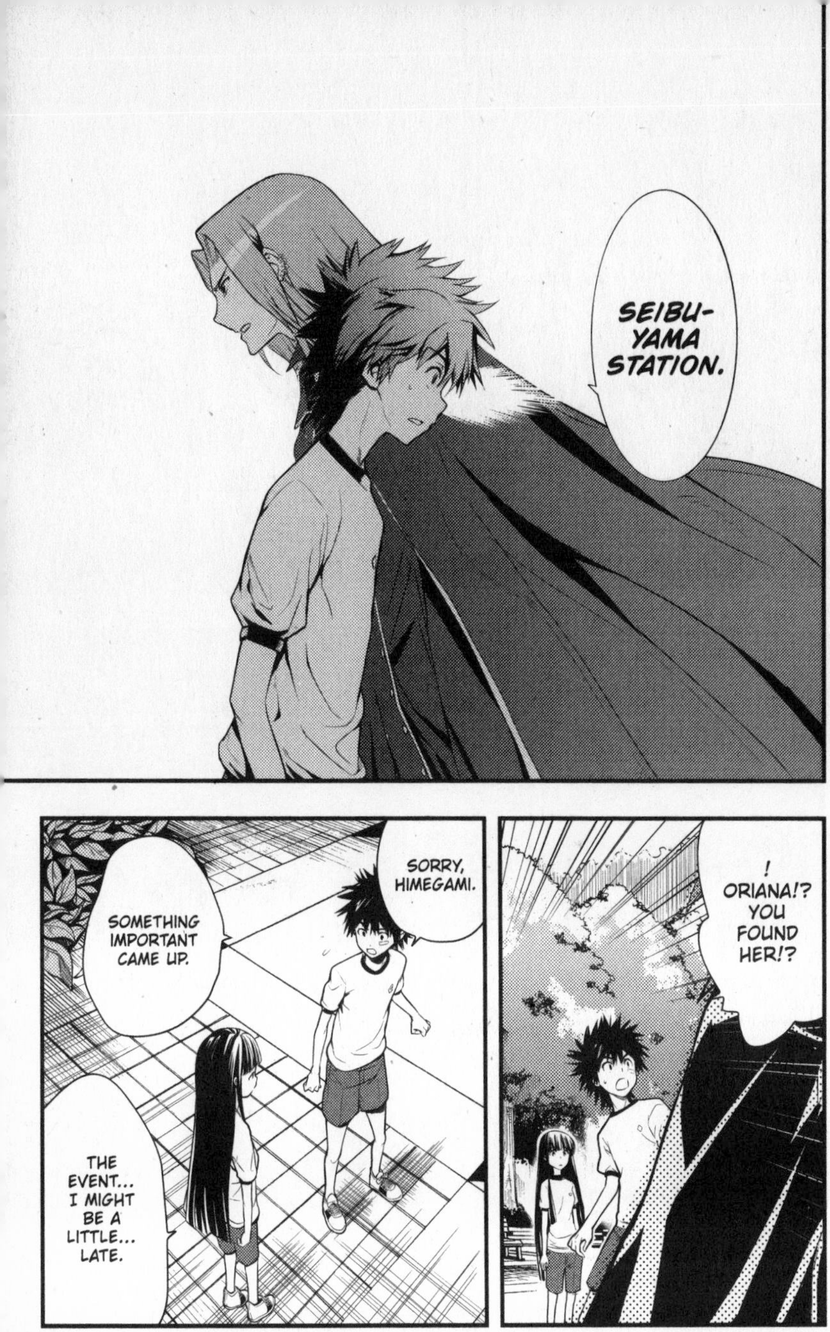
SEIBU-YAMA STATION.
!
ORIANA!? YOU FOUND HER!?
SORRY, HIMEGAMI.
SOMETHING IMPORTANT CAME UP.
THE EVENT... I MIGHT BE A LITTLE... LATE.

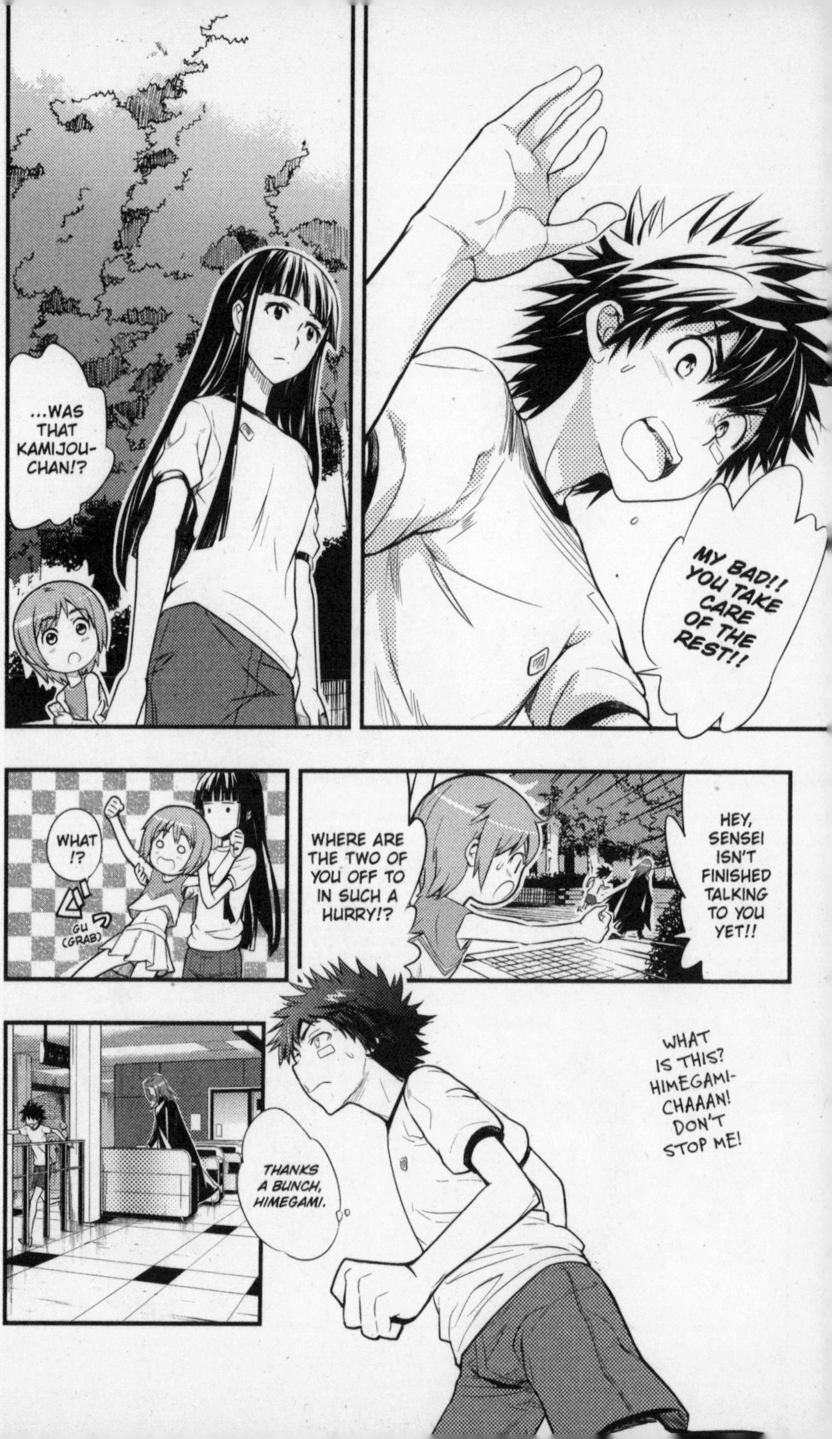
MY BAD!! YOU TAKE CARE OF THE REST!!
...WAS THAT KAMIJOU-CHAN!?
HEY, SENSEI ISN'T FINISHED TALKING TO YOU YET!!
WHERE ARE THE TWO OF YOU OFF TO IN SUCH A HURRY!?
WHAT!?
GU (GRAB)
WHAT IS THIS? HIMEGAMI-CHAAAN! DON'T STOP ME!
THANKS A BUNCH, HIMEGAMI.

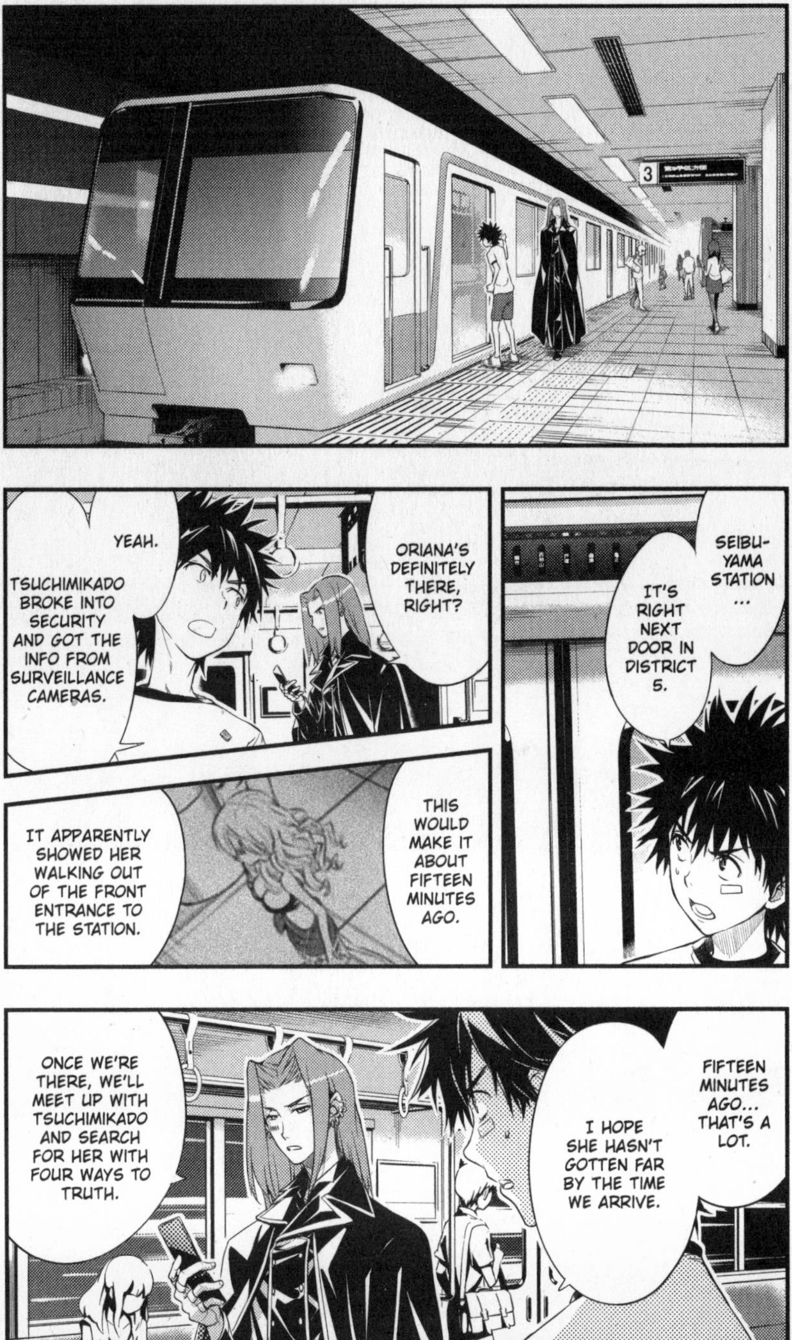
3
SEIBU-YAMA STATION...
IT'S RIGHT NEXT DOOR IN DISTRICT 5.
ORIANA'S DEFINITELY THERE, RIGHT?
YEAH.
TSUCHIMIKADO BROKE INTO SECURITY AND GOT THE INFO FROM SURVEILLANCE CAMERAS.
IT APPARENTLY SHOWED HER WALKING OUT OF THE FRONT ENTRANCE TO THE STATION.
THIS WOULD MAKE IT ABOUT FIFTEEN MINUTES AGO.
FIFTEEN MINUTES AGO... THAT'S A LOT.
I HOPE SHE HASN'T GOTTEN FAR BY THE TIME WE ARRIVE.
ONCE WE'RE THERE, WE'LL MEET UP WITH TSUCHIMIKADO AND SEARCH FOR HER WITH FOUR WAYS TO TRUTH.

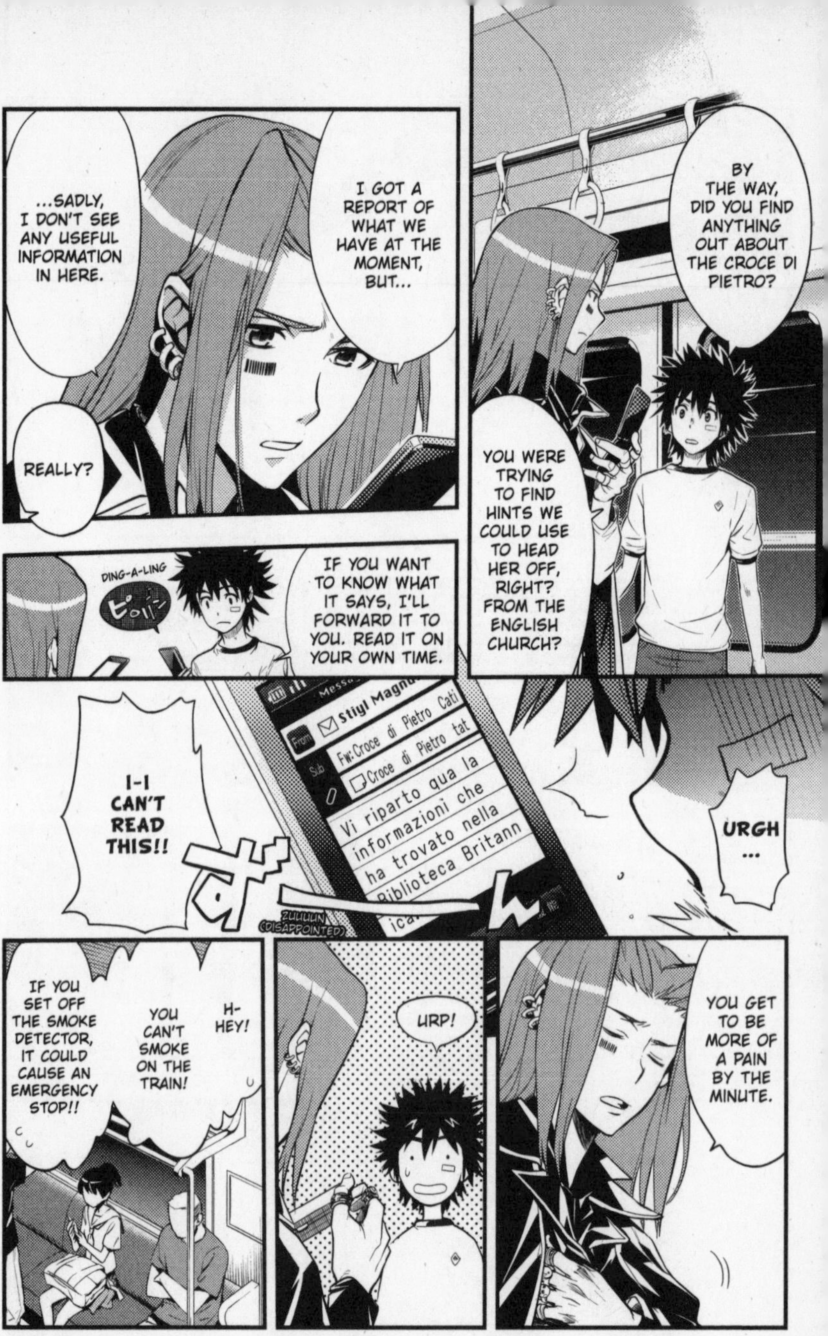
BY THE WAY, DID YOU FIND ANYTHING OUT ABOUT THE CROCE DI PIETRO?
YOU WERE TRYING TO FIND HINTS WE COULD USE TO HEAD HER OFF, RIGHT? FROM THE ENGLISH CHURCH?
I GOT A REPORT OF WHAT WE HAVE AT THE MOMENT, BUT...
...SADLY, I DON'T SEE ANY USEFUL INFORMATION IN HERE.
REALLY?
IF YOU WANT TO KNOW WHAT IT SAYS, I'LL FORWARD IT TO YOU. READ IT ON YOUR OWN TIME.
DING-A-LING
ピロリーン
Stiyl Magnu
From
Fw:Croce di Pietro Cati
Sub
Croce di Pietro tat
Vi riparto qua la
informazioni che
ha trovato nella
Biblioteca Britann
URGH...
I-I CAN'T READ THIS!!
ZUUUUN (DISAPPOINTED)
YOU GET TO BE MORE OF A PAIN BY THE MINUTE.
URP!
H-HEY!
YOU CAN'T SMOKE ON THE TRAIN!
IF YOU SET OFF THE SMOKE DETECTOR, IT COULD CAUSE AN EMERGENCY STOP!!

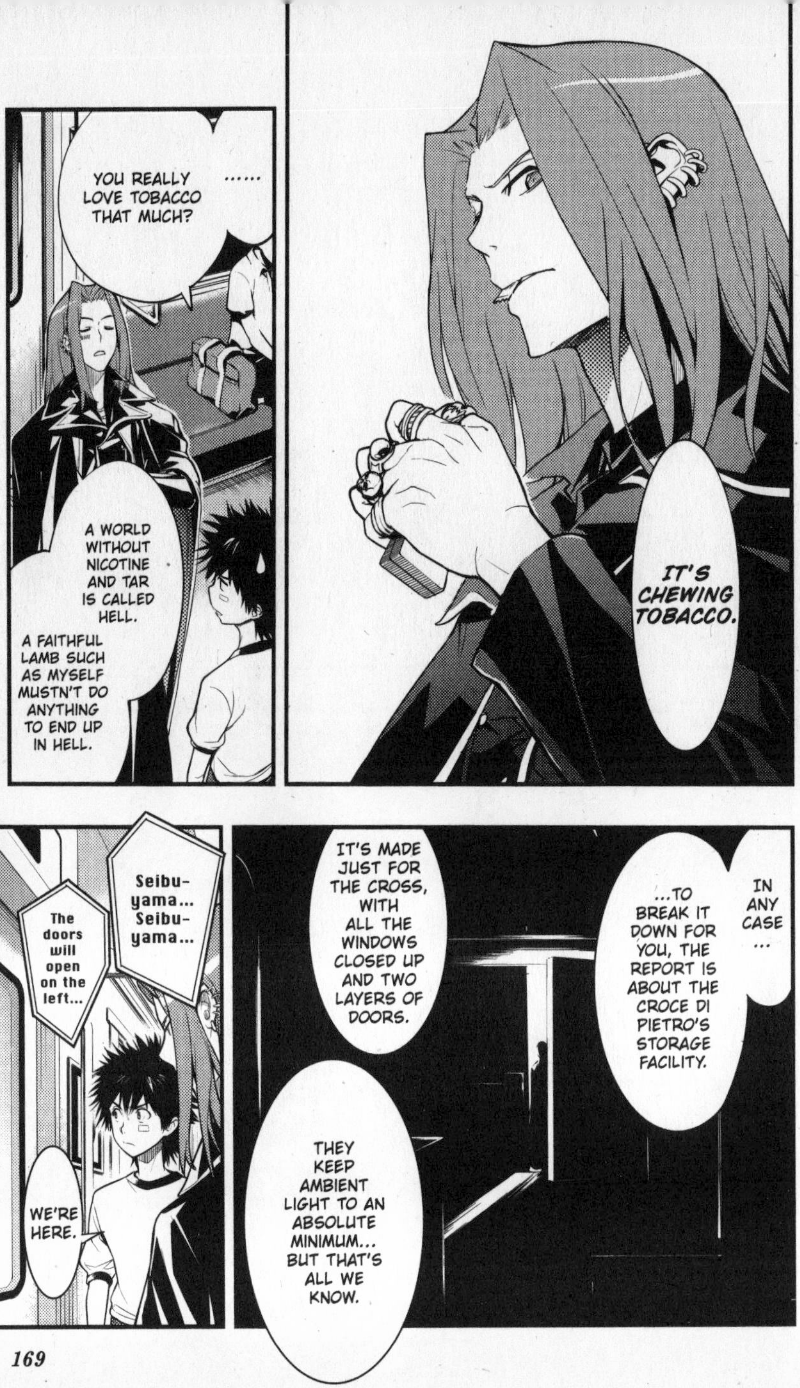
IT'S CHEWING TOBACCO.
......
YOU REALLY LOVE TOBACCO THAT MUCH?
A WORLD WITHOUT NICOTINE AND TAR IS CALLED HELL.
A FAITHFUL LAMB SUCH AS MYSELF MUSTN'T DO ANYTHING TO END UP IN HELL.
IN ANY CASE...
...TO BREAK IT DOWN FOR YOU, THE REPORT IS ABOUT THE CROCE DI PIETRO'S STORAGE FACILITY.
IT'S MADE JUST FOR THE CROSS, WITH ALL THE WINDOWS CLOSED UP AND TWO LAYERS OF DOORS.
THEY KEEP AMBIENT LIGHT TO AN ABSOLUTE MINIMUM... BUT THAT'S ALL WE KNOW.
Seibu-yama... Seibu-yama...
The doors will open on the left...
WE'RE HERE.

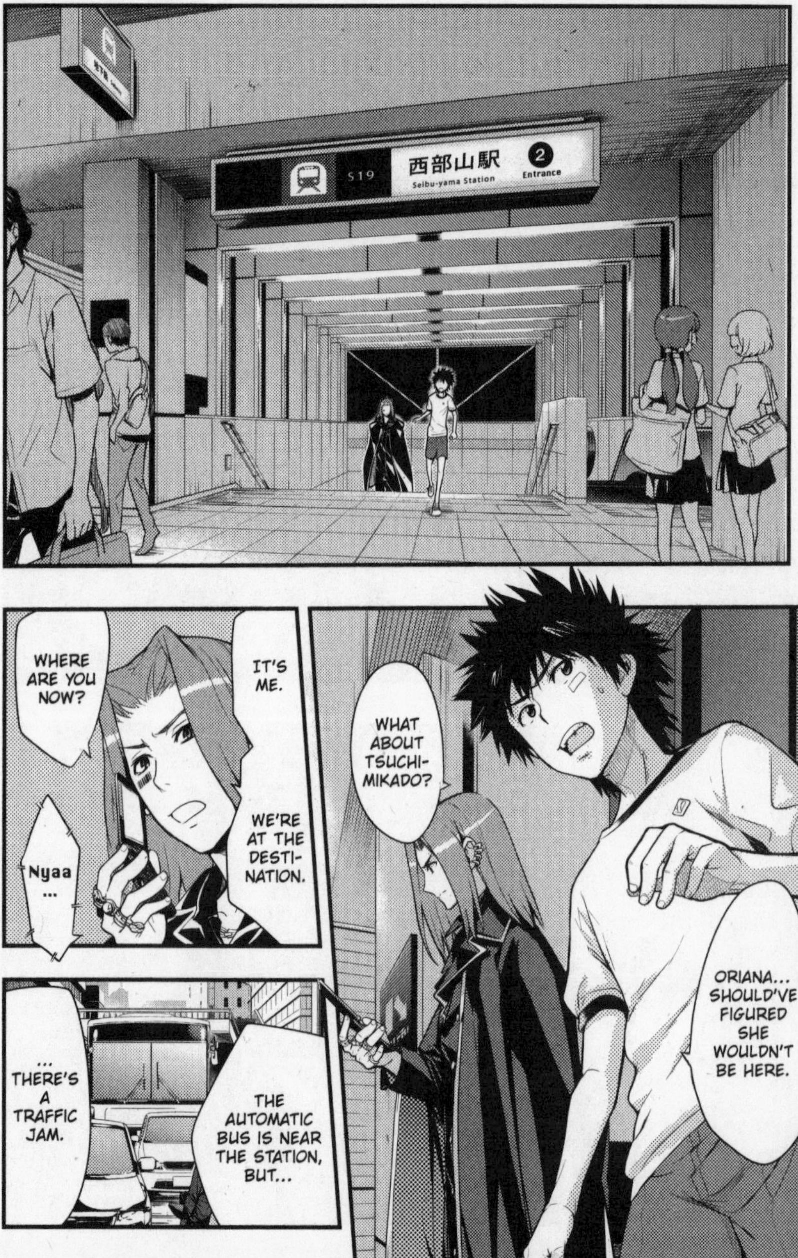
西部山駅
S19
Seibu-yama Station
2
Entrance
WHAT ABOUT TSUCHI-MIKADO?
ORIANA... SHOULD'VE FIGURED SHE WOULDN'T BE HERE.
IT'S ME.
WHERE ARE YOU NOW?
WE'RE AT THE DESTI-NATION.
Nyaa ...
THE AUTOMATIC BUS IS NEAR THE STATION, BUT...
... THERE'S A TRAFFIC JAM.

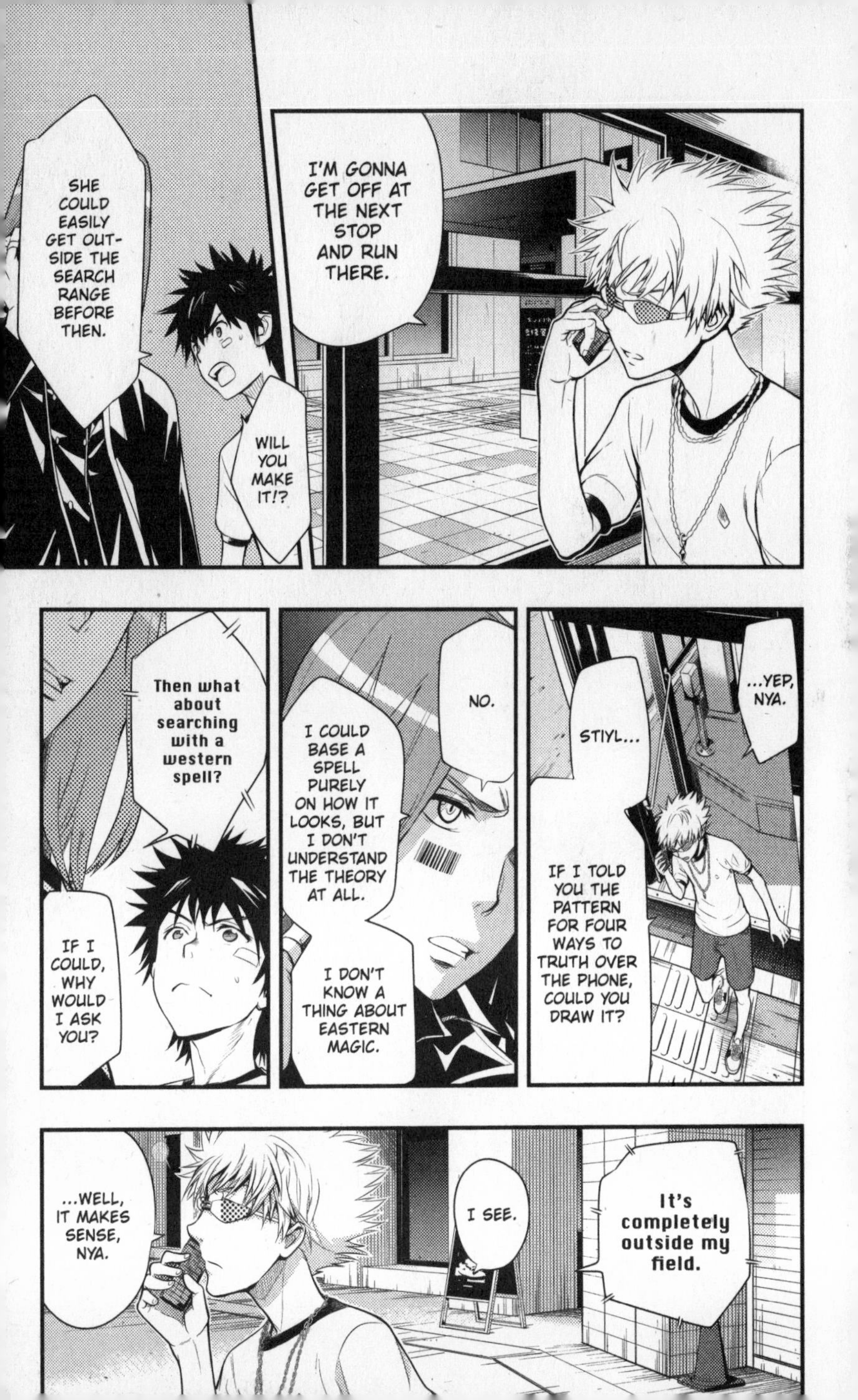
I'M GONNA GET OFF AT THE NEXT STOP AND RUN THERE.
WILL YOU MAKE IT!?
SHE COULD EASILY GET OUT-SIDE THE SEARCH RANGE BEFORE THEN.
...YEP, NYA.
STIYL...
IF I TOLD YOU THE PATTERN FOR FOUR WAYS TO TRUTH OVER THE PHONE, COULD YOU DRAW IT?
NO.
I COULD BASE A SPELL PURELY ON HOW IT LOOKS, BUT I DON'T UNDERSTAND THE THEORY AT ALL.
I DON'T KNOW A THING ABOUT EASTERN MAGIC.
Then what about searching with a western spell?
IF I COULD, WHY WOULD I ASK YOU?
It's completely outside my field.
I SEE.
...WELL, IT MAKES SENSE, NYA.

GOT IT.

I'LL ACTIVATE FOUR WAYS TO TRUTH FROM RIGHT HERE.

ピ・ン！
PIKUN
(JOLT)

AHN!

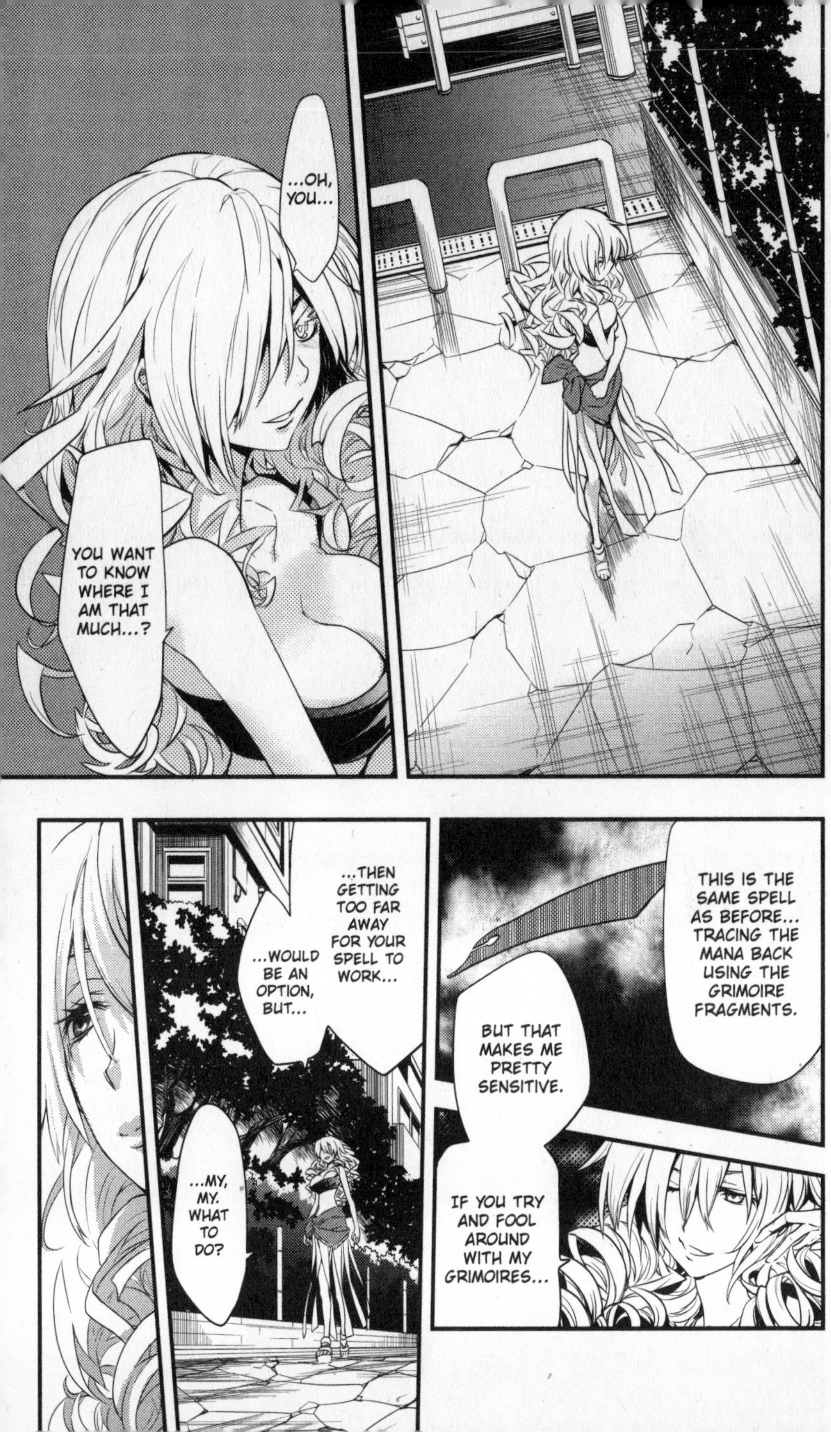
...OH, YOU...
YOU WANT TO KNOW WHERE I AM THAT MUCH...?
THIS IS THE SAME SPELL AS BEFORE... TRACING THE MANA BACK USING THE GRIMOIRE FRAGMENTS.
BUT THAT MAKES ME PRETTY SENSITIVE.
IF YOU TRY AND FOOL AROUND WITH MY GRIMOIRES...
...THEN GETTING TOO FAR AWAY FOR YOUR SPELL TO WORK...
...WOULD BE AN OPTION, BUT...
...MY, MY. WHAT TO DO?

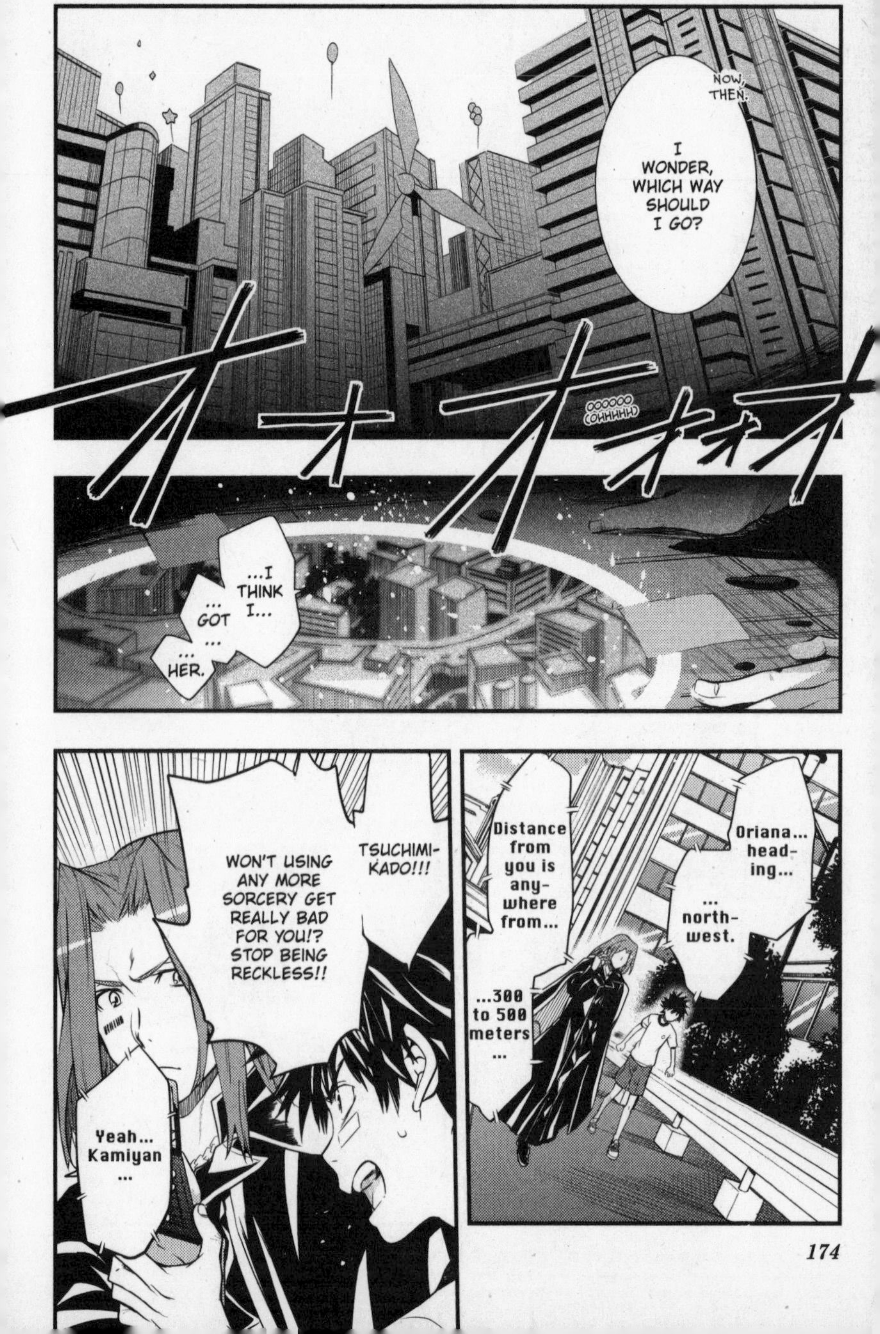
NOW, THEN.
I WONDER, WHICH WAY SHOULD I GO?
OOOOOO (OHHHHH)
...I THINK I...
... GOT ...
... HER.
Oriana... head-ing...
... north-west.
Distance from you is any-where from...
...300 to 500 meters ...
TSUCHIMI-KADO!!!
WON'T USING ANY MORE SORCERY GET REALLY BAD FOR YOU!? STOP BEING RECKLESS!!
Yeah... Kamiyan ...

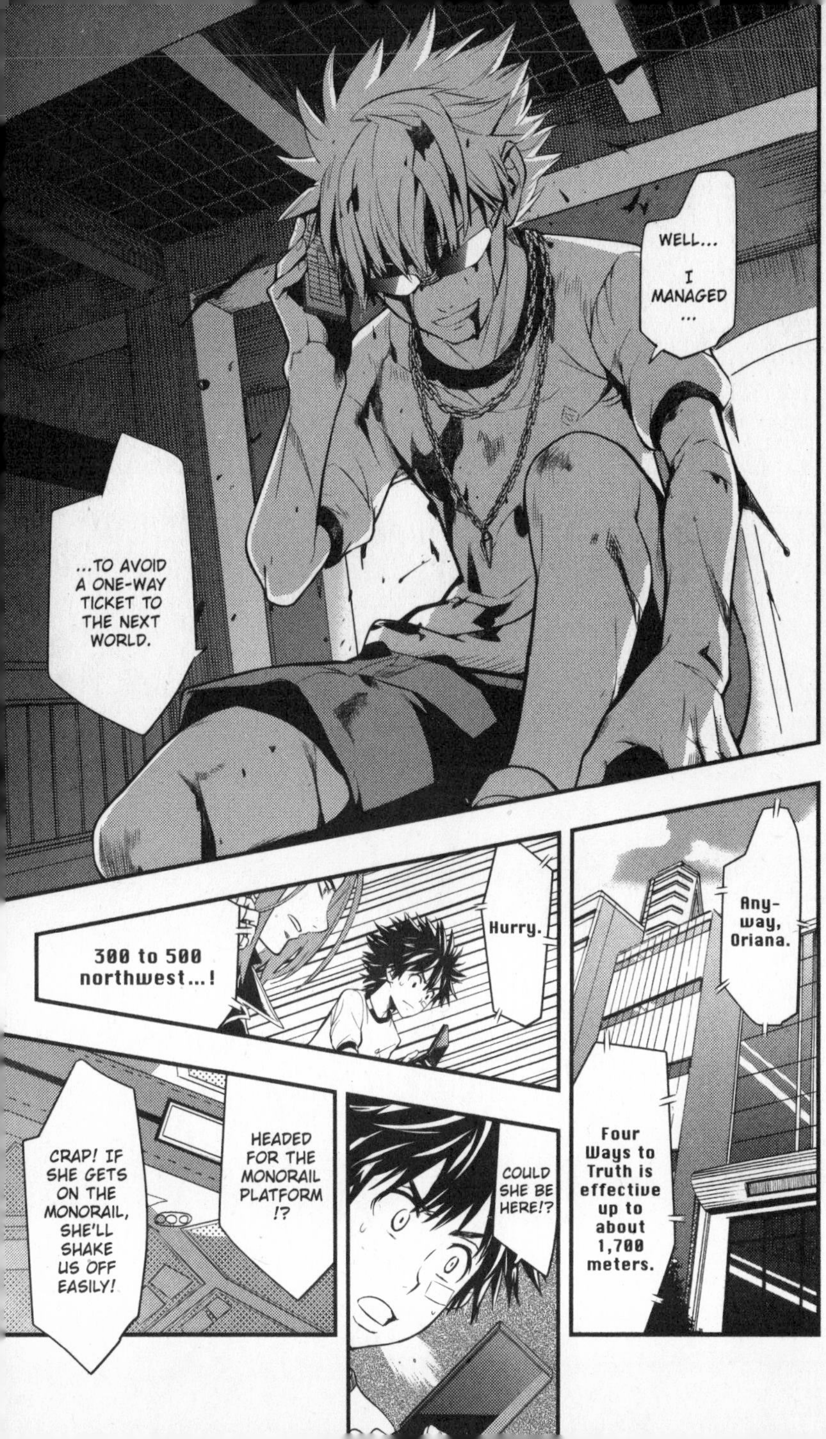
WELL... I MANAGED...
...TO AVOID A ONE-WAY TICKET TO THE NEXT WORLD.
Any-way, Oriana.
Four Ways to Truth is effective up to about 1,700 meters.
Hurry.
300 to 500 northwest...!
COULD SHE BE HERE!?
HEADED FOR THE MONORAIL PLATFORM!?
CRAP! IF SHE GETS ON THE MONORAIL, SHE'LL SHAKE US OFF EASILY!

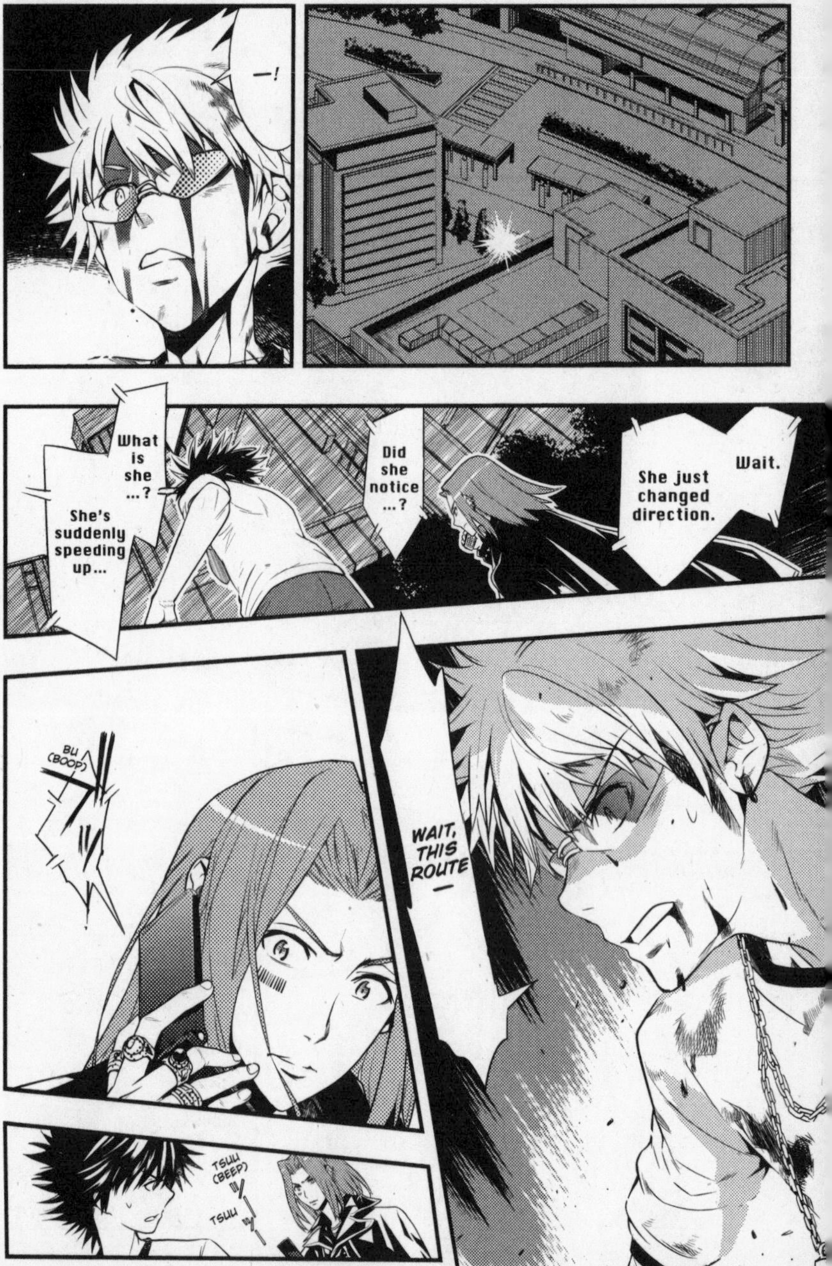
—!
Wait.
She just changed direction.
Did she notice ...?
What is she ...?
She's suddenly speeding up...
WAIT, THIS ROUTE —
BU (BOOP)
TSUU (BEEP)
TSUU

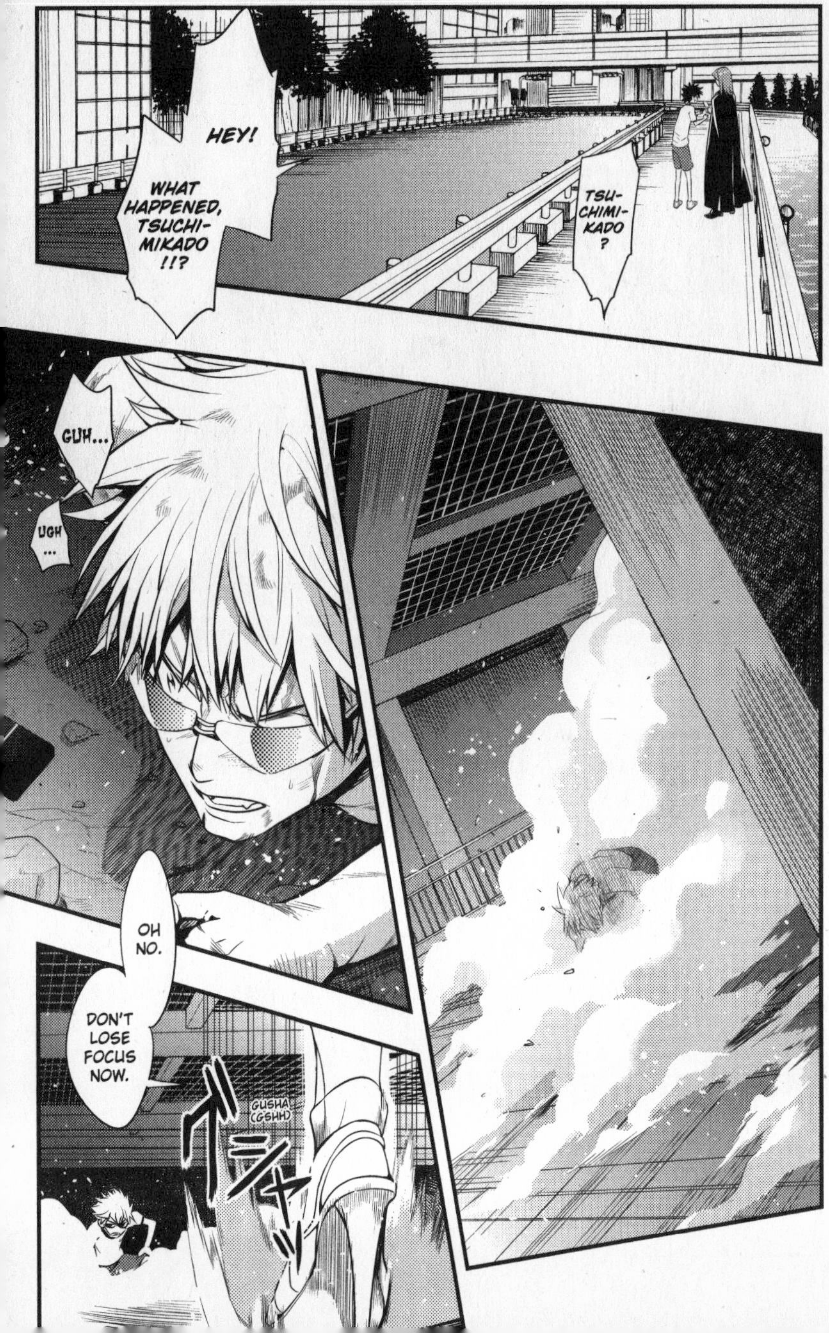
TSU-CHIMI-KADO?
HEY!
WHAT HAPPENED, TSUCHI-MIKADO!!?
GUH...
UGH...
OH NO.
DON'T LOSE FOCUS NOW.
GUSHA (GSHH)

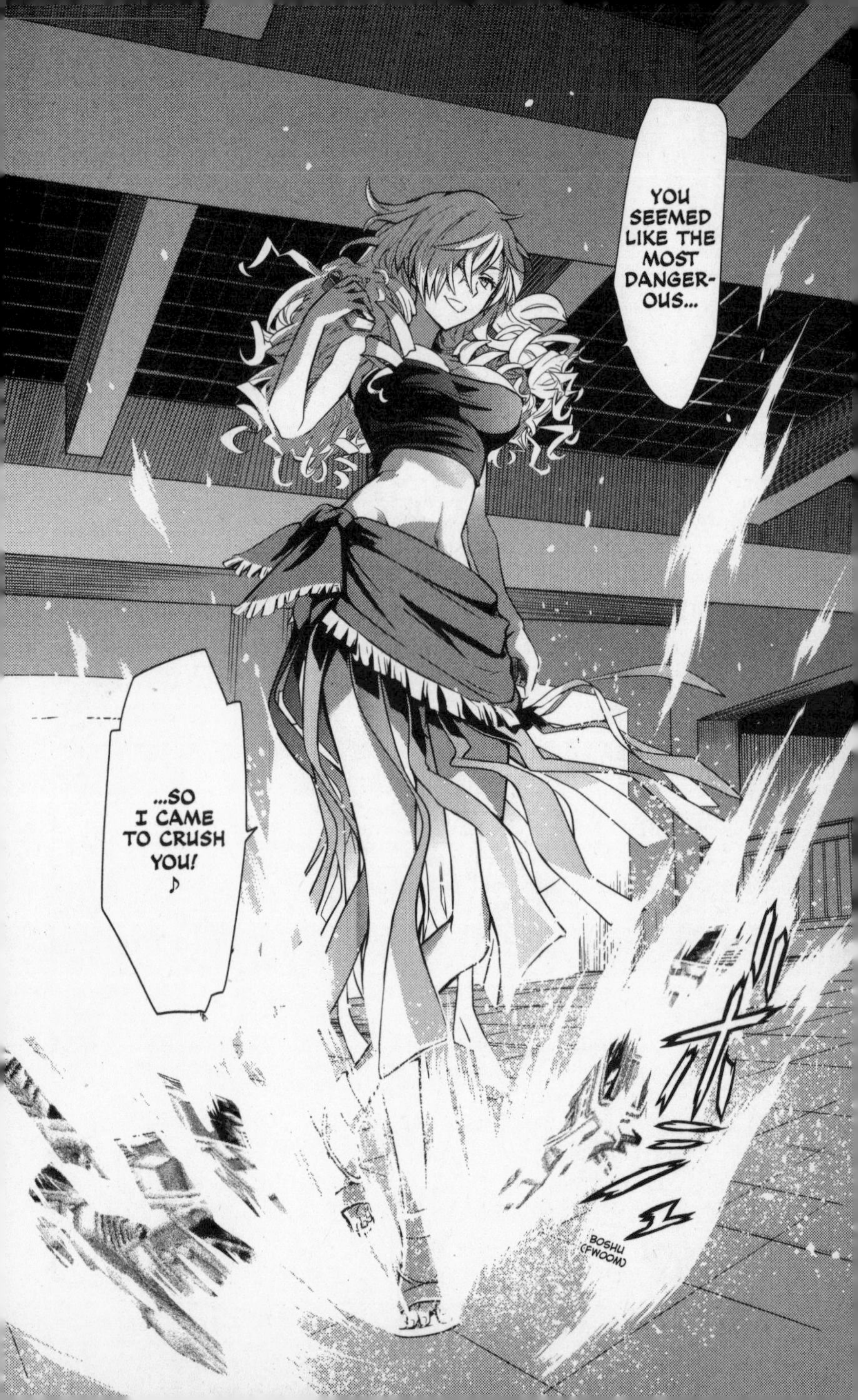
YOU SEEMED LIKE THE MOST DANGER-OUS...
...SO I CAME TO CRUSH YOU! ♪
BOSHU (FWOOM)

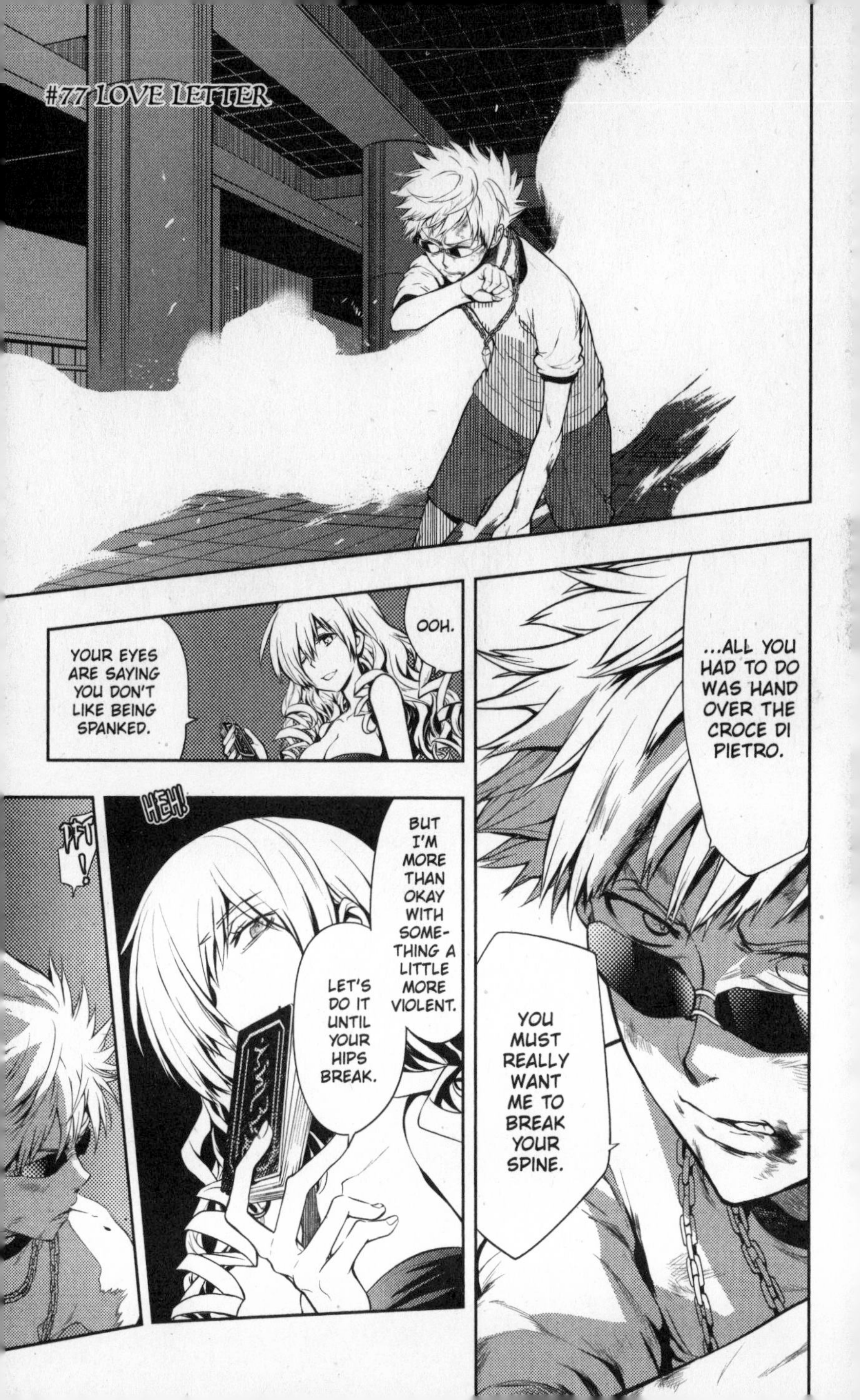
#77 LOVE LETTER
...ALL YOU HAD TO DO WAS HAND OVER THE CROCE DI PIETRO.
YOU MUST REALLY WANT ME TO BREAK YOUR SPINE.
OOH.
YOUR EYES ARE SAYING YOU DON'T LIKE BEING SPANKED.
HEH!
BUT I'M MORE THAN OKAY WITH SOME-THING A LITTLE MORE VIOLENT.
LET'S DO IT UNTIL YOUR HIPS BREAK.
PFFT!

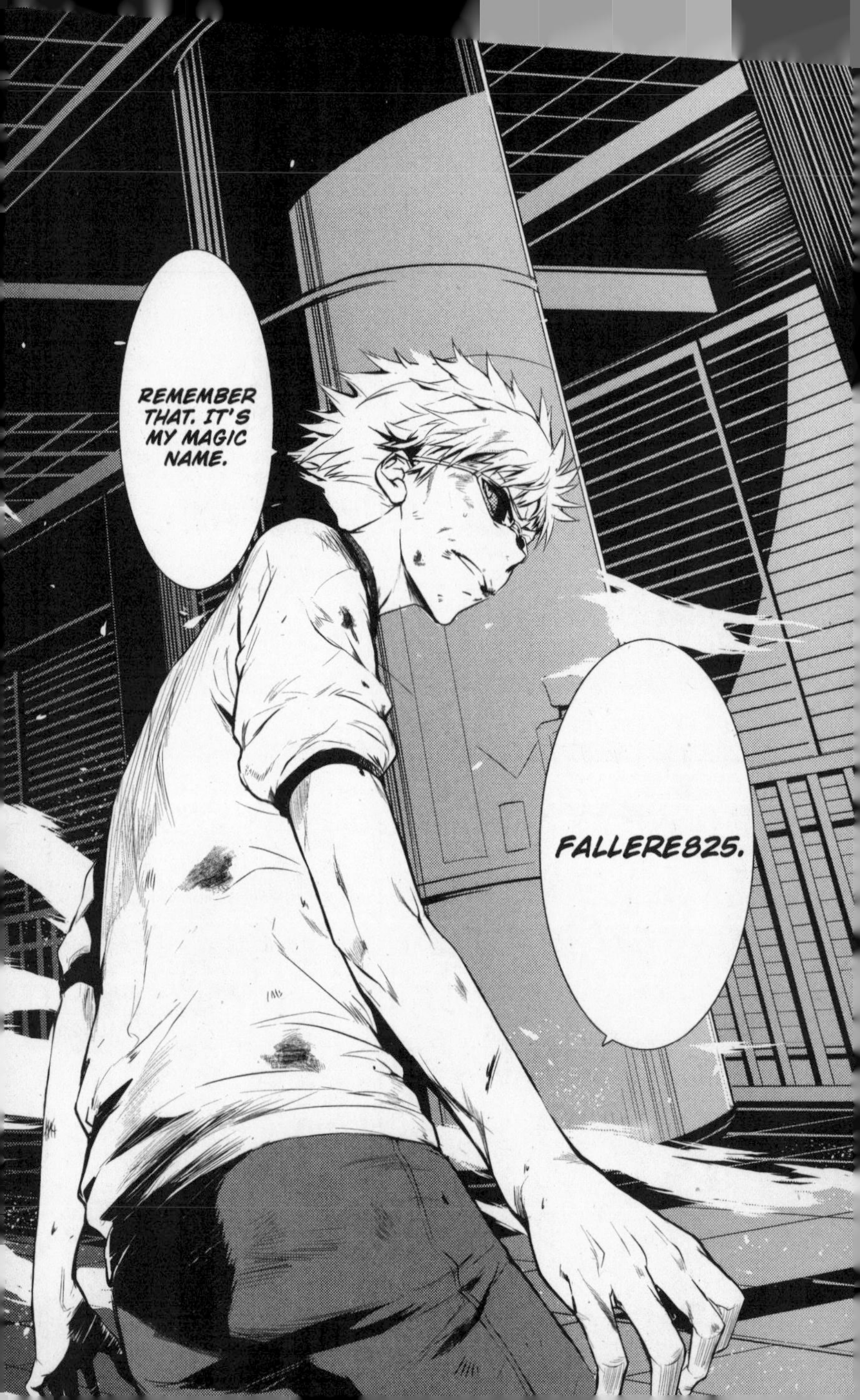
FALLERE825.
REMEMBER THAT. IT'S MY MAGIC NAME.

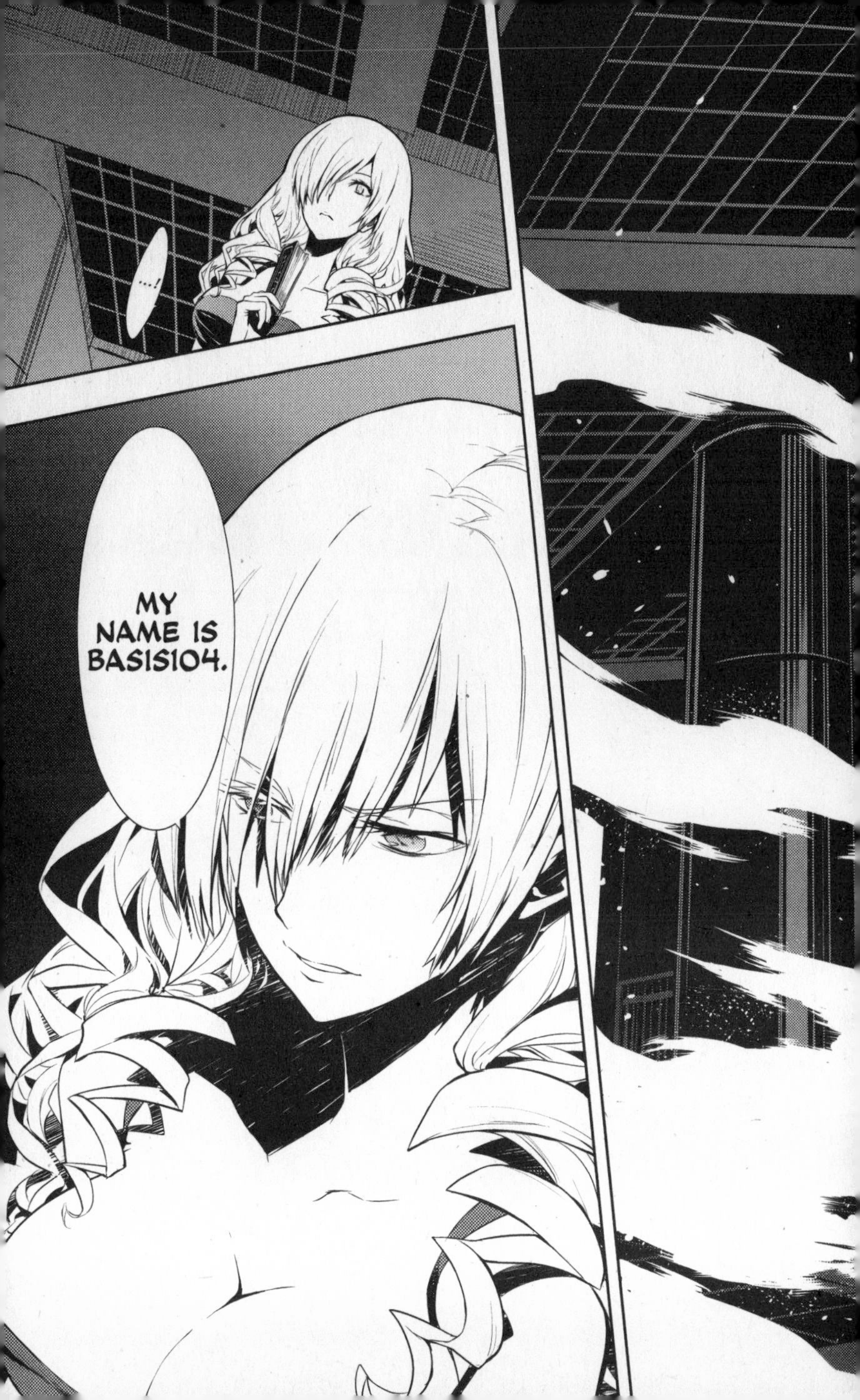
...!
MY NAME IS BASIS104.

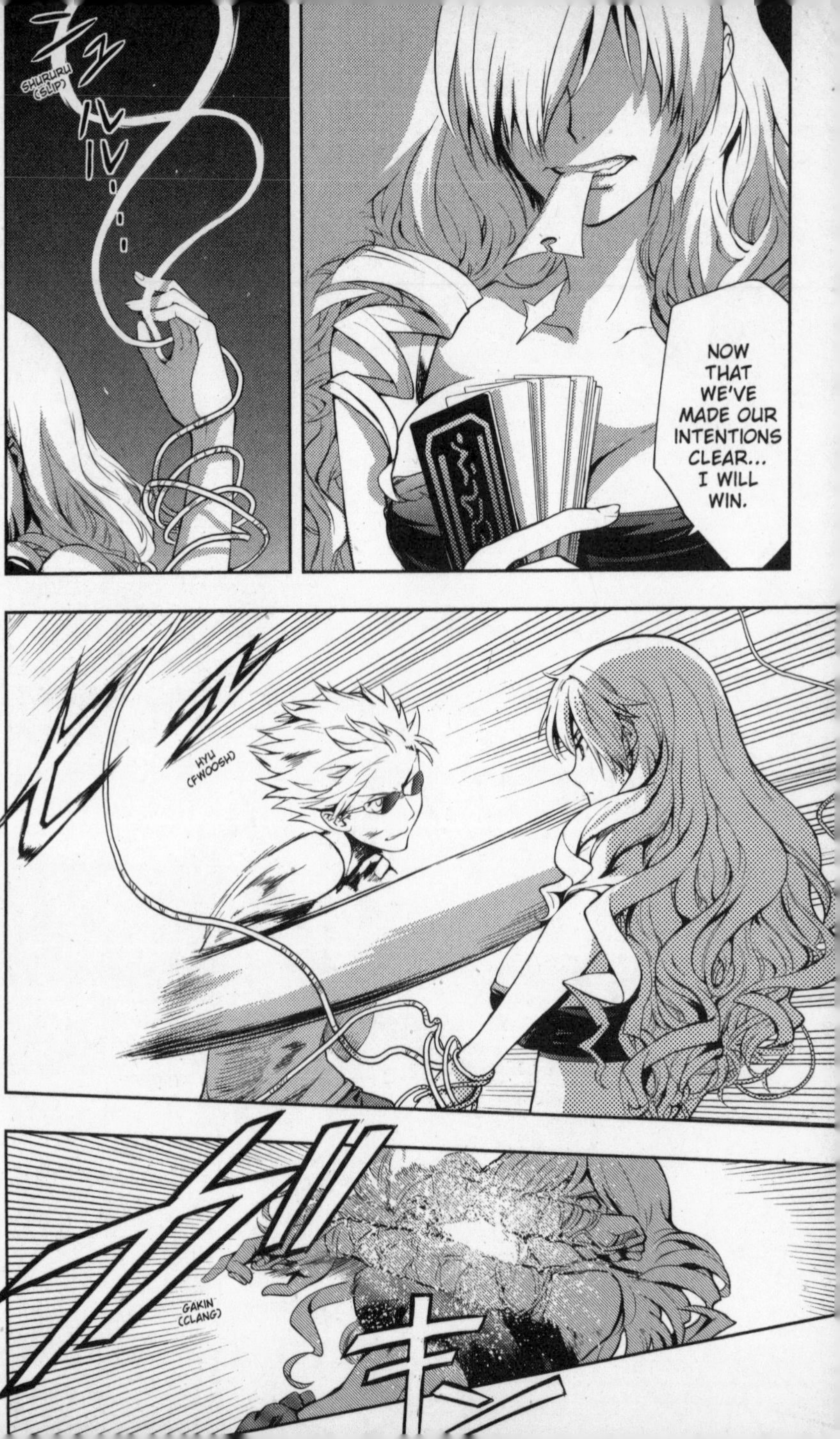
NOW THAT WE'VE MADE OUR INTENTIONS CLEAR... I WILL WIN.
SHURURU (SLIP)
HYU (FWOOSH)
GAKIN (CLANG)

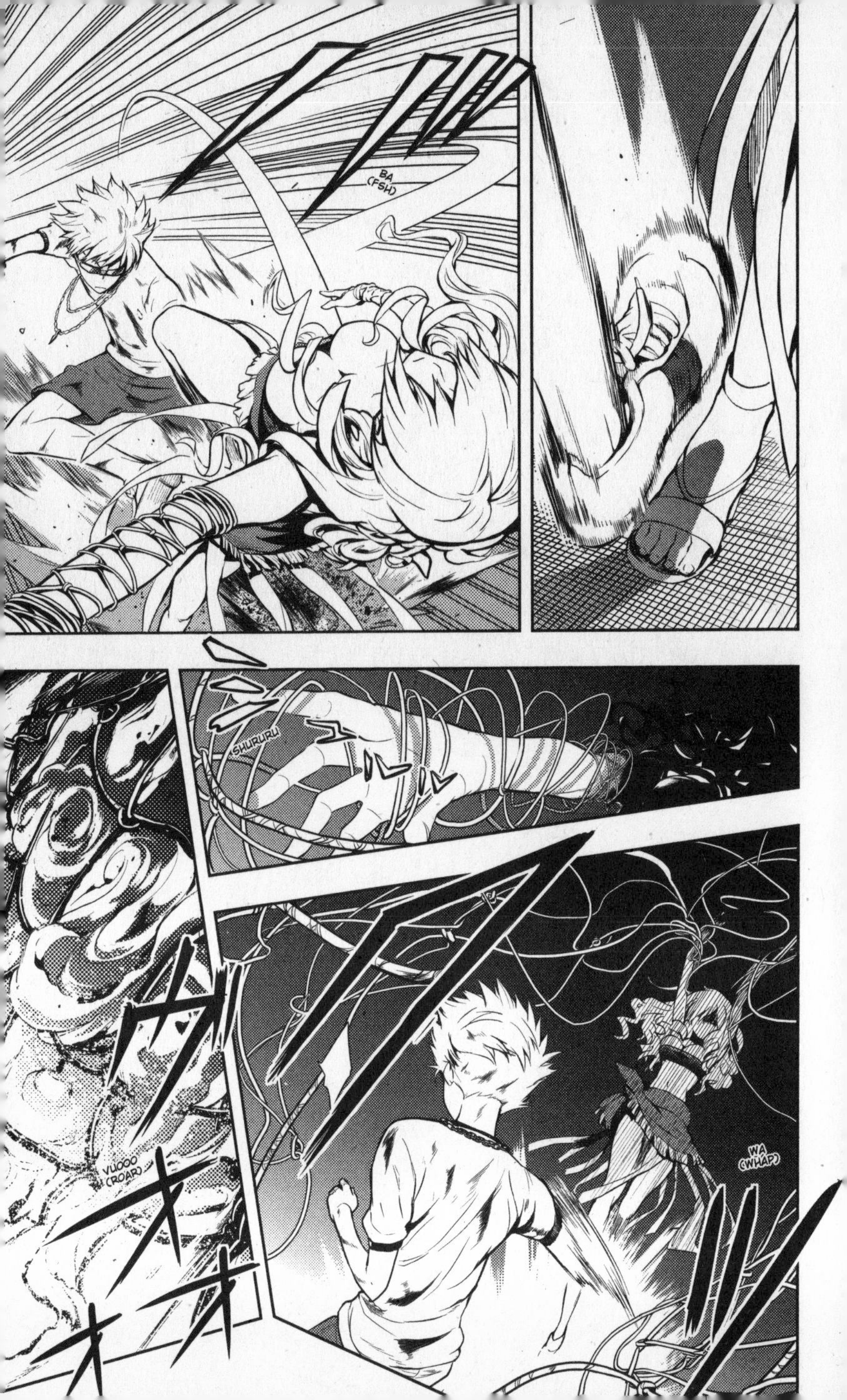
BA
(FSH)
SHURURU
WA
(WHAP)
VUOOO
(ROAR)

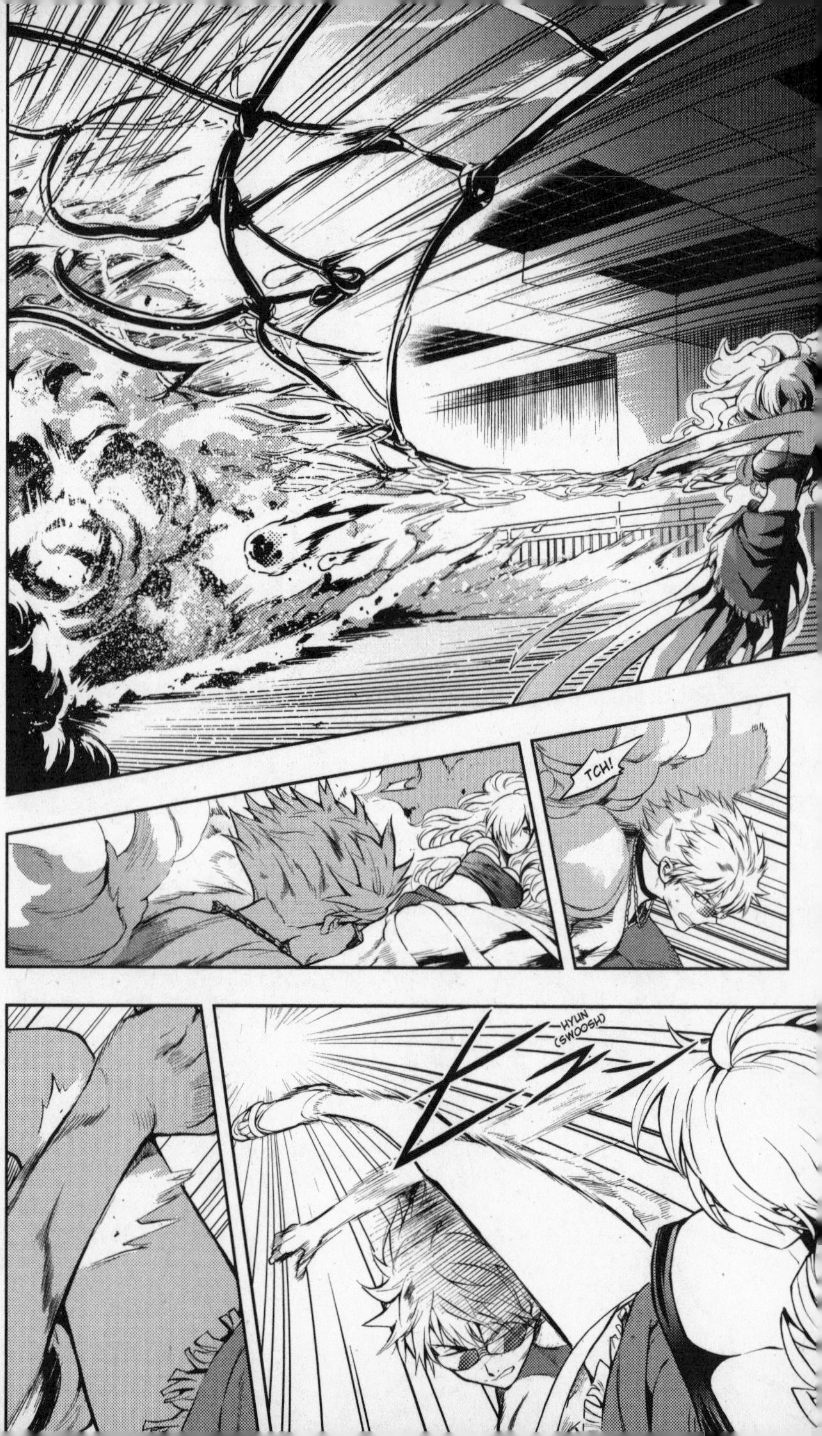
TCH!
HYUN
(SWOOSH)

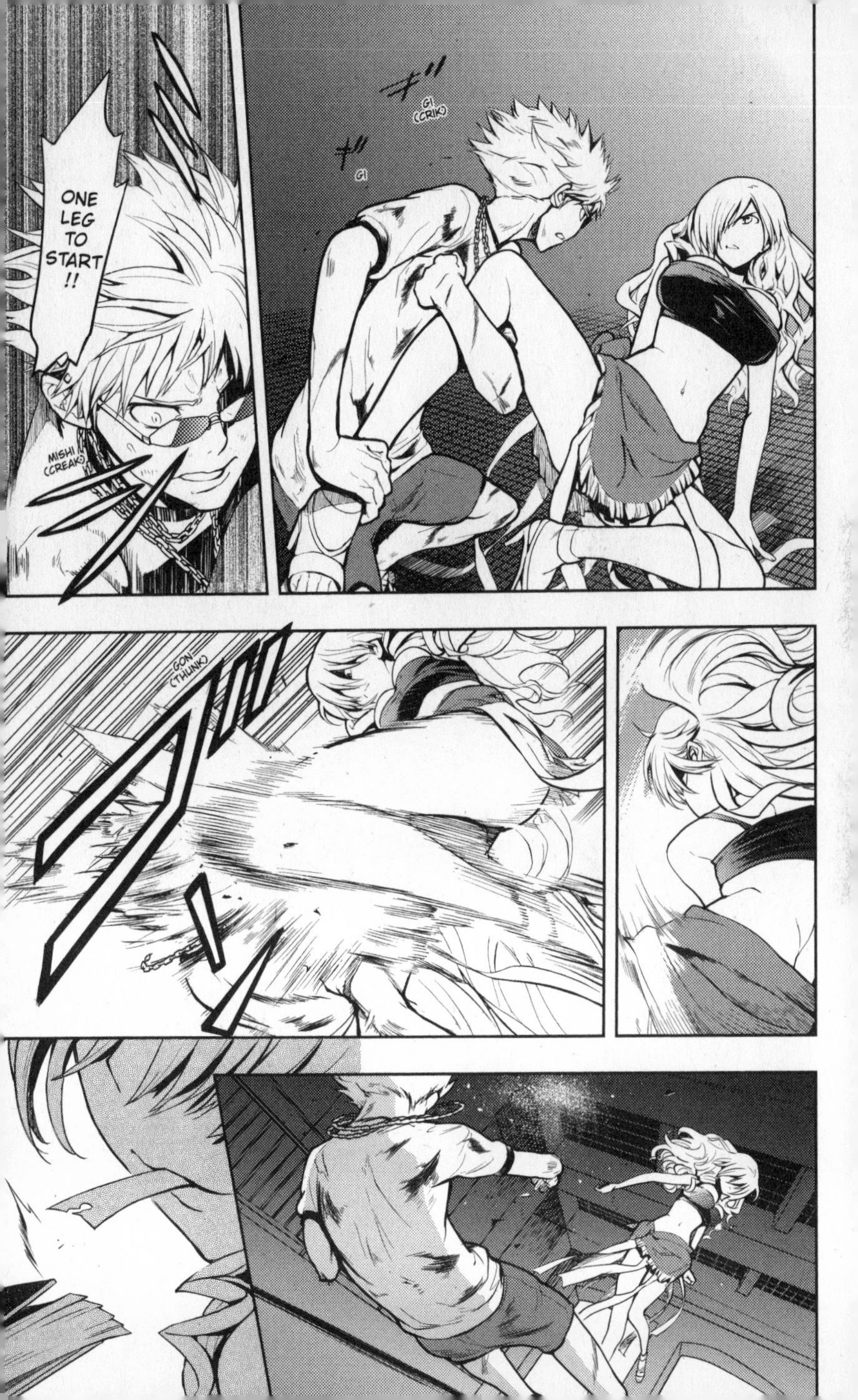
GI (CRIK)
GI
ONE LEG TO START!!
MISHI (CREAK)
GON (THUNK)

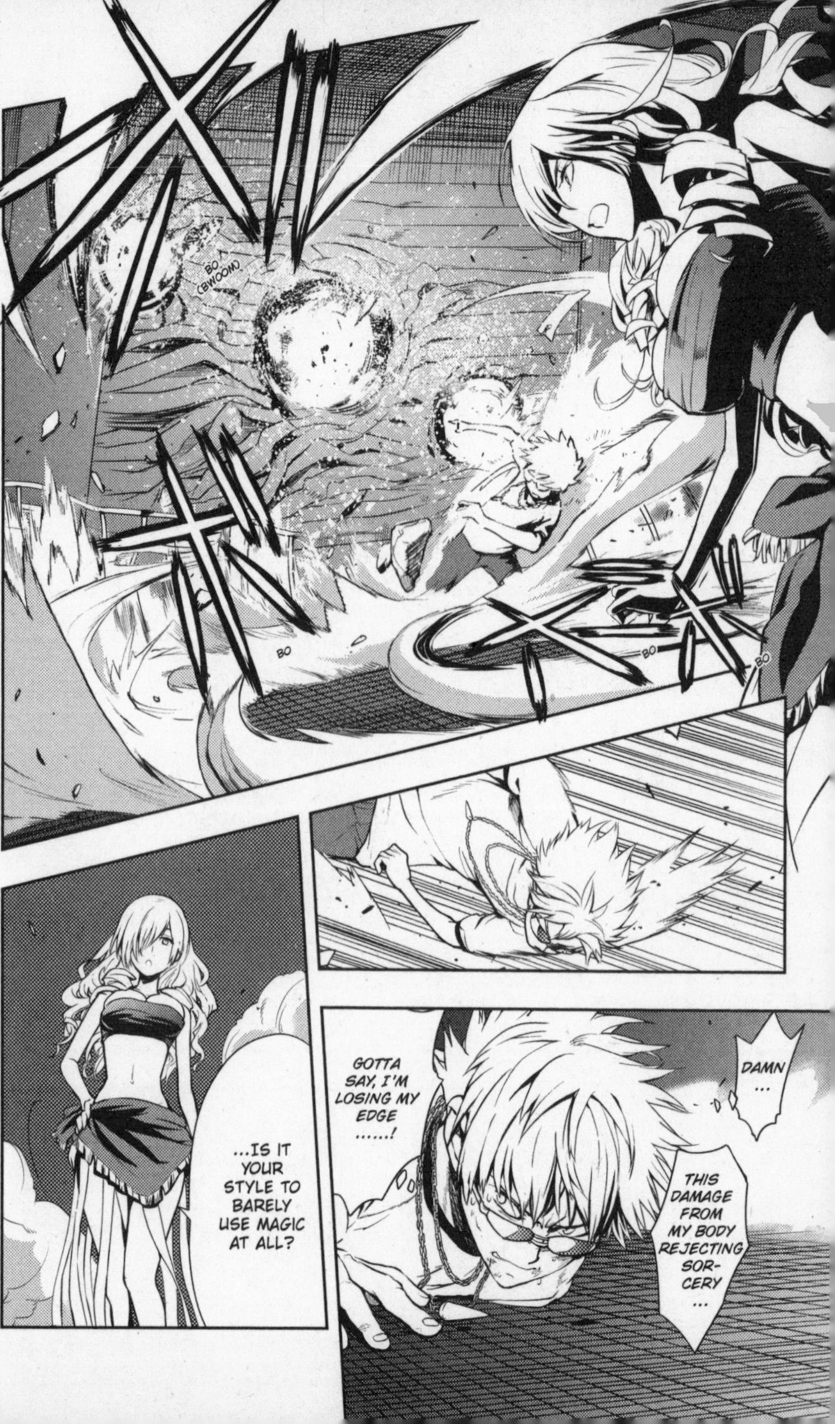
BO (BWOOM)
BO
BO
BO
DAMN...
GOTTA SAY, I'M LOSING MY EDGE ......!
THIS DAMAGE FROM MY BODY REJECTING SOR-CERY...
...IS IT YOUR STYLE TO BARELY USE MAGIC AT ALL?

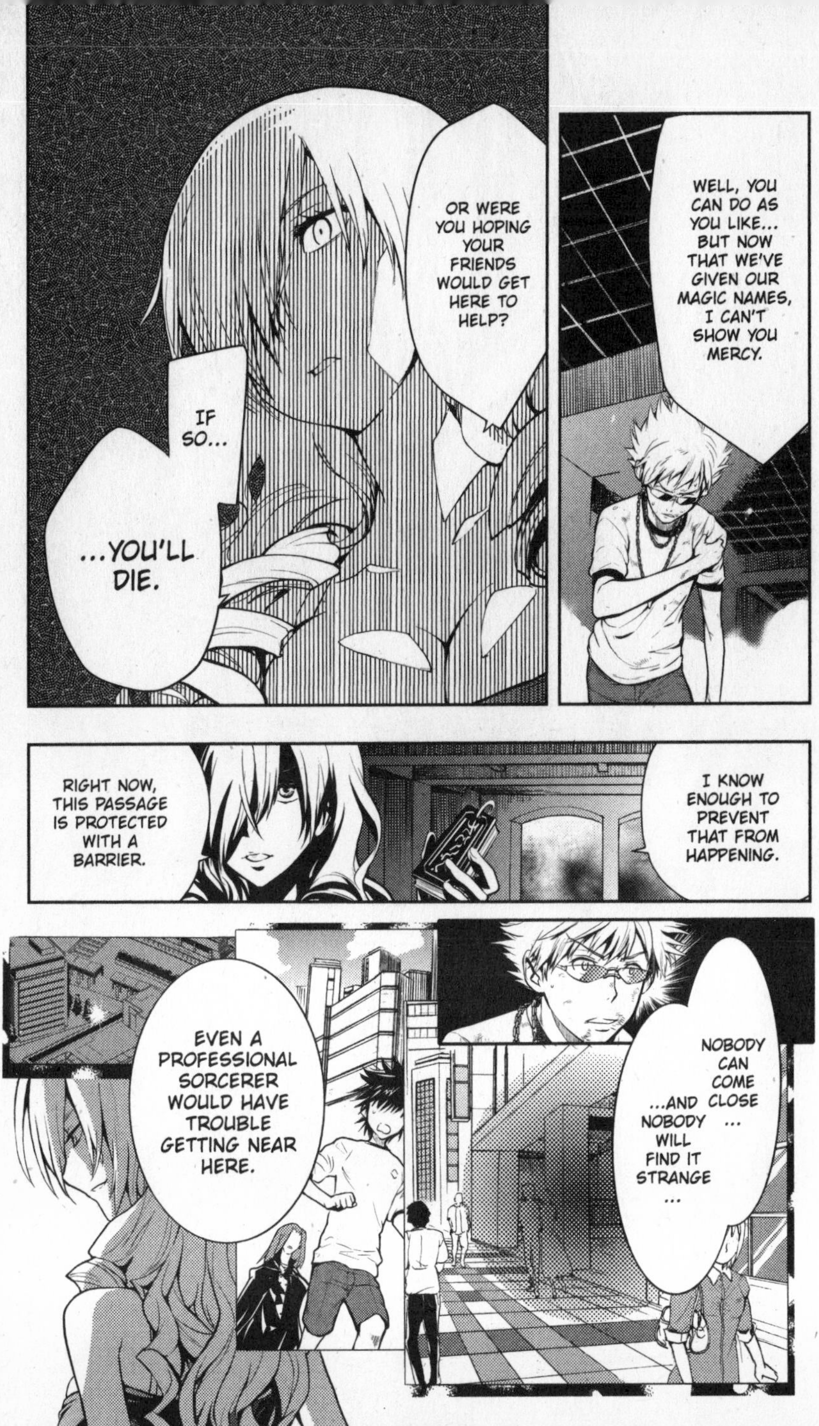
WELL, YOU CAN DO AS YOU LIKE... BUT NOW THAT WE'VE GIVEN OUR MAGIC NAMES, I CAN'T SHOW YOU MERCY.
OR WERE YOU HOPING YOUR FRIENDS WOULD GET HERE TO HELP?
IF SO...
...YOU'LL DIE.
I KNOW ENOUGH TO PREVENT THAT FROM HAPPENING.
RIGHT NOW, THIS PASSAGE IS PROTECTED WITH A BARRIER.
NOBODY CAN COME CLOSE ...
...AND NOBODY WILL FIND IT STRANGE ...
EVEN A PROFESSIONAL SORCERER WOULD HAVE TROUBLE GETTING NEAR HERE.

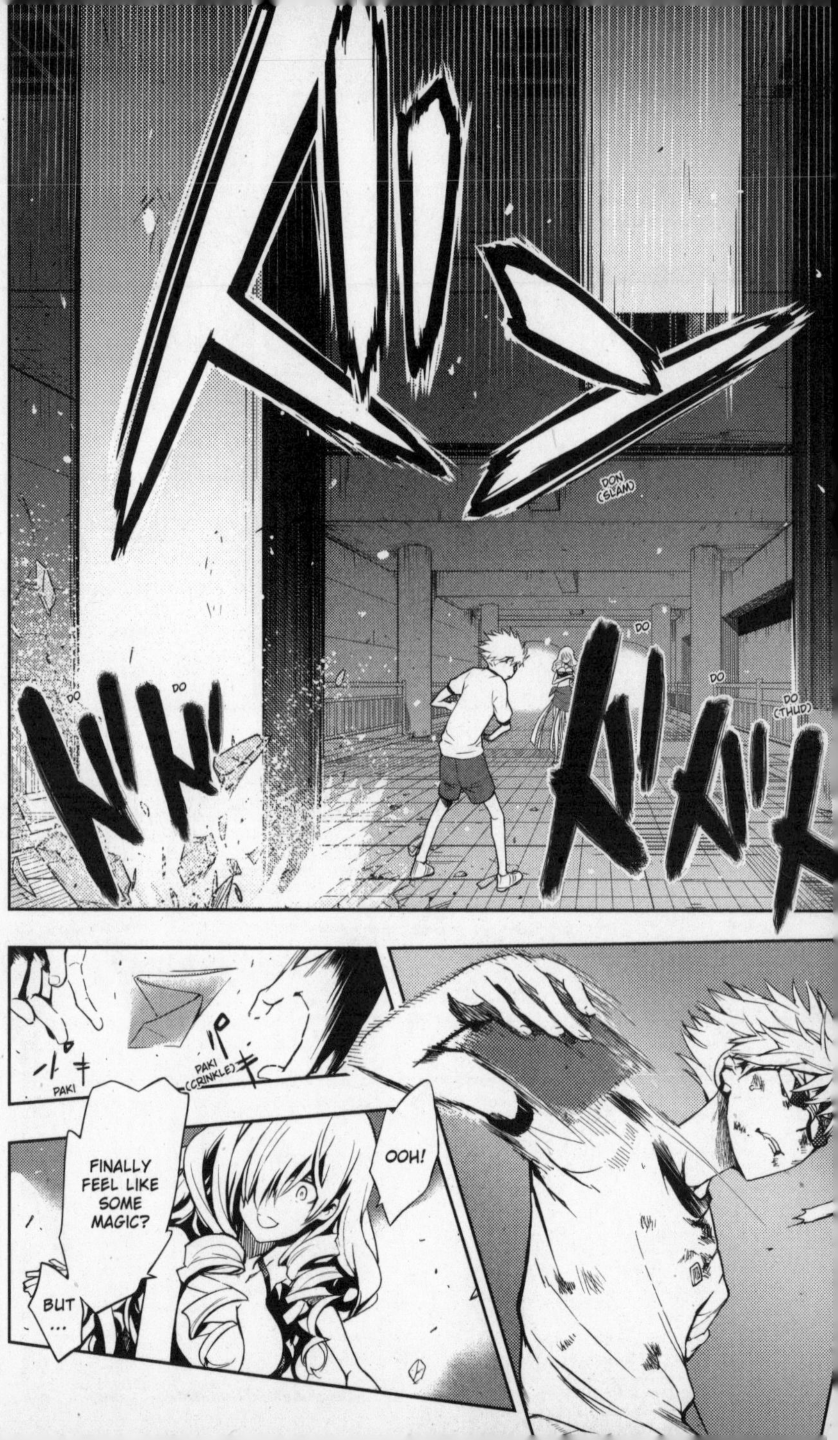
DON (SLAM)
DO
DO
DO (THUD)
DO
DO
PAKI (CRINKLE)
PAKI
OOH!
FINALLY FEEL LIKE SOME MAGIC?
BUT ...

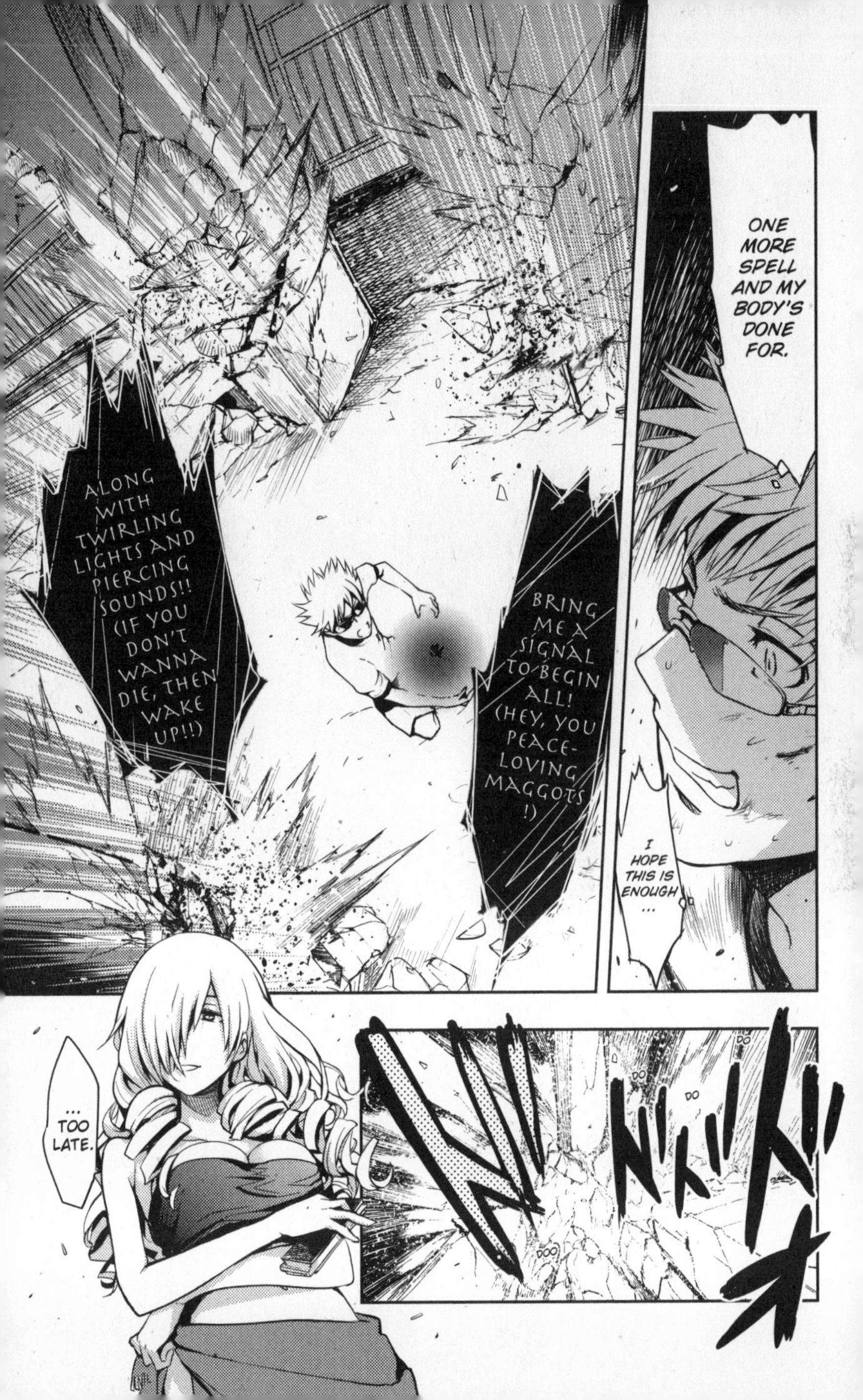
ONE MORE SPELL AND MY BODY'S DONE FOR.
I HOPE THIS IS ENOUGH ...
BRING ME A SIGNAL TO BEGIN ALL! (HEY, YOU PEACE-LOVING MAGGOTS!)
ALONG WITH TWIRLING LIGHTS AND PIERCING SOUNDS!! (IF YOU DON'T WANNA DIE, THEN WAKE UP!!)
DO
DO
DO
DOO
... TOO LATE.

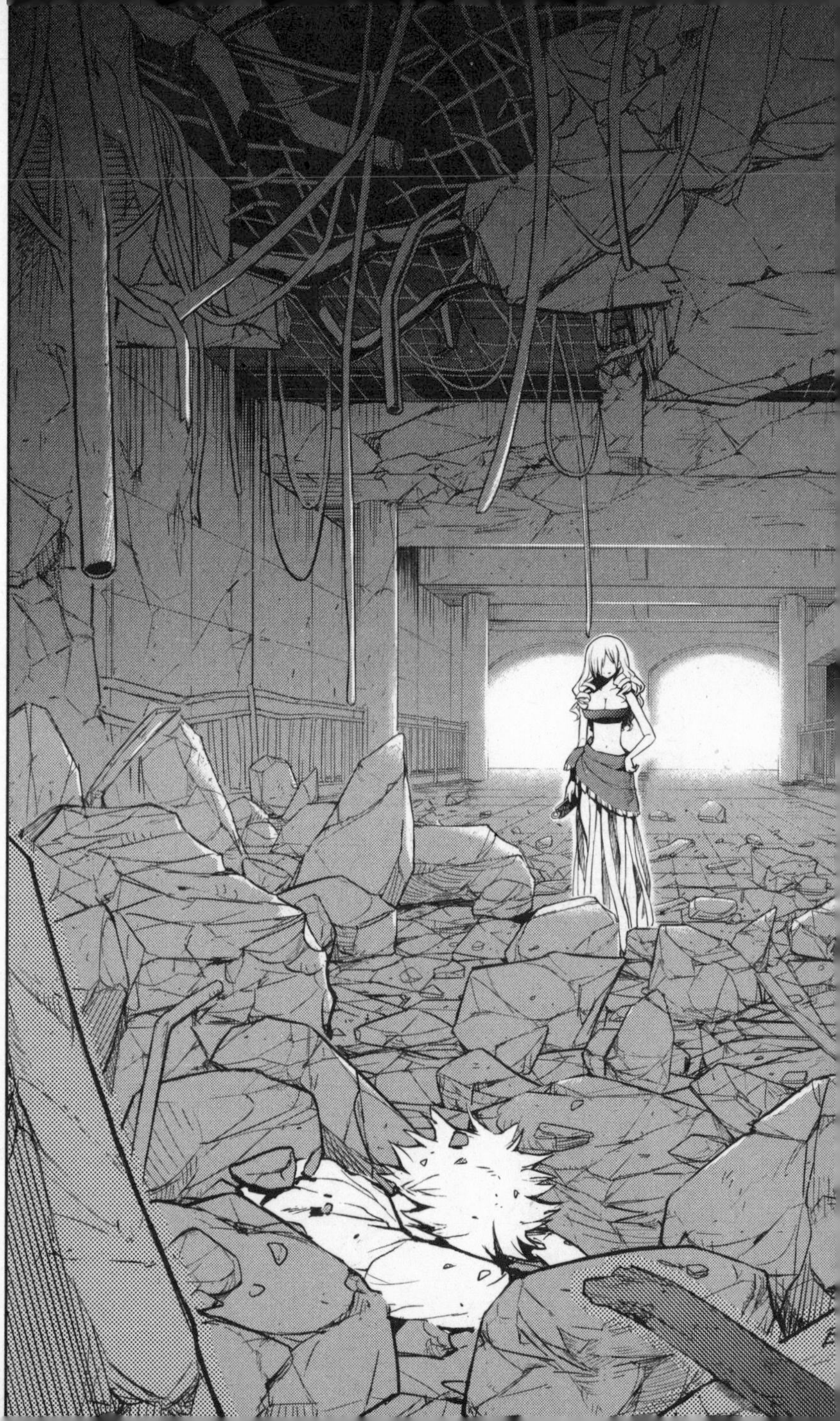

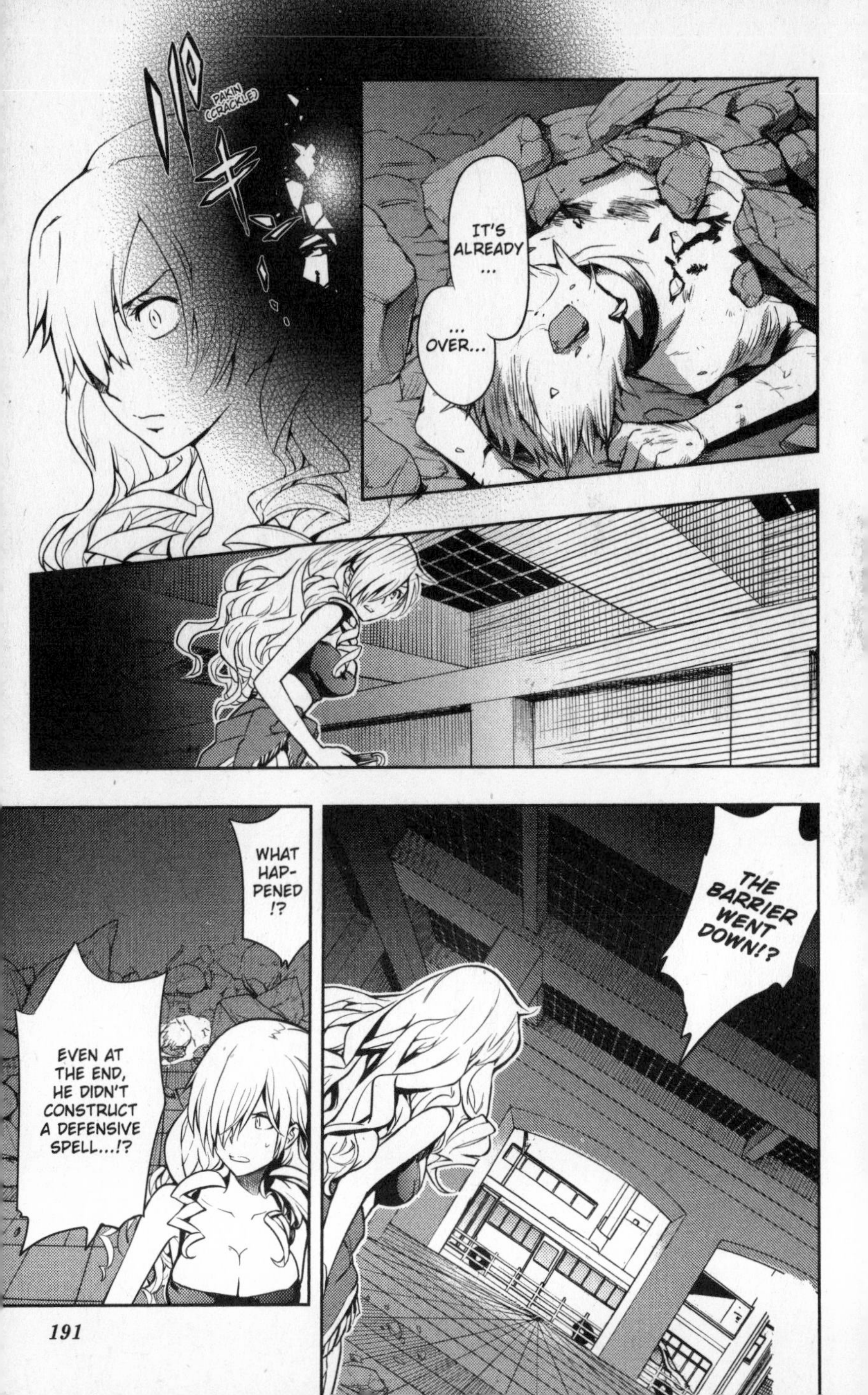
IT'S ALREADY ...
... OVER...
PAKIN (CRACKLE)
THE BARRIER WENT DOWN!?
WHAT HAP-PENED !?
EVEN AT THE END, HE DIDN'T CONSTRUCT A DEFENSIVE SPELL...!?

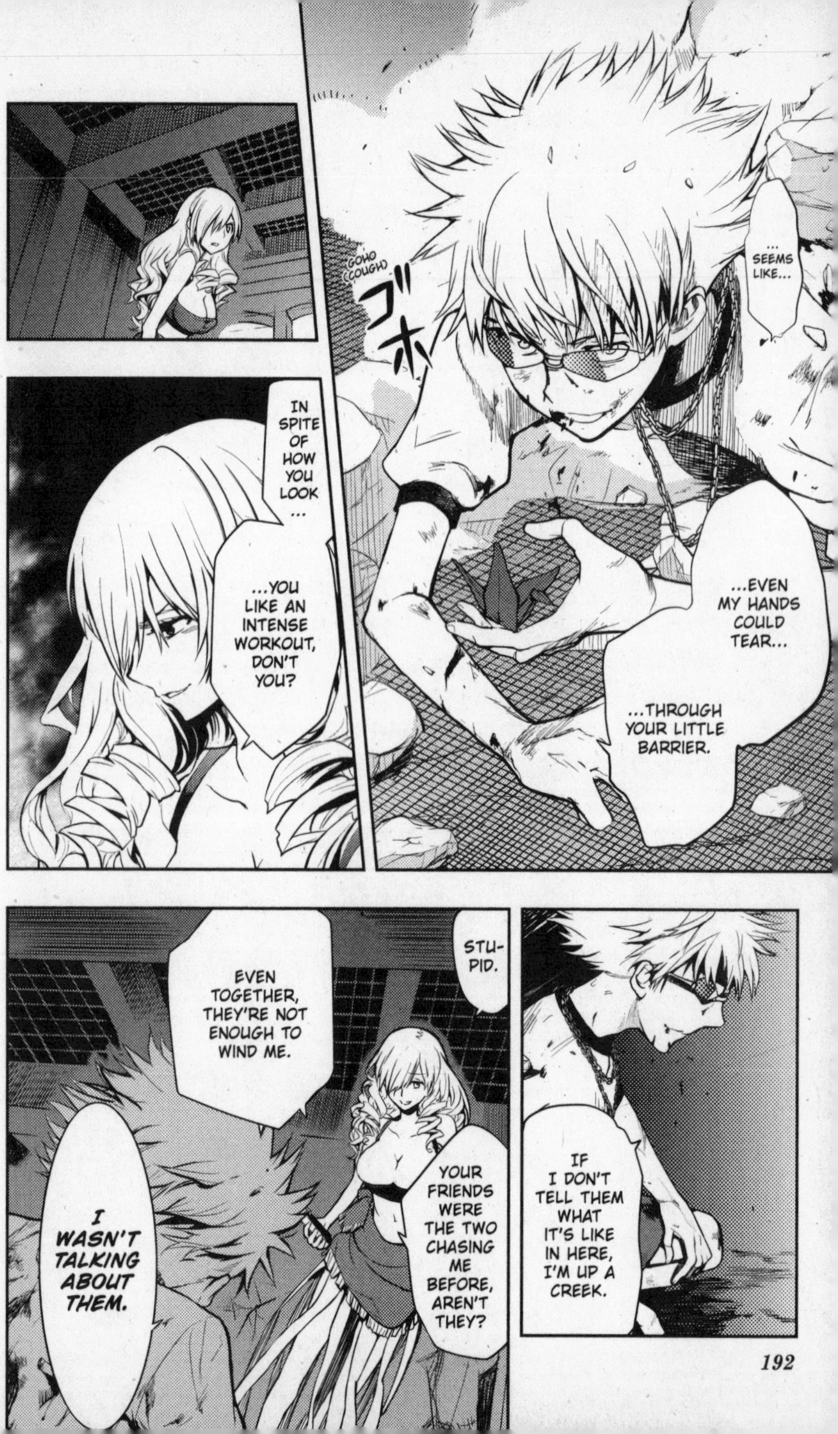

GOHO (COUGH)
ゴホ
...SEEMS LIKE...
...EVEN MY HANDS COULD TEAR...
...THROUGH YOUR LITTLE BARRIER.
IN SPITE OF HOW YOU LOOK...
...YOU LIKE AN INTENSE WORKOUT, DON'T YOU?
IF I DON'T TELL THEM WHAT IT'S LIKE IN HERE, I'M UP A CREEK.
STU-PID.
EVEN TOGETHER, THEY'RE NOT ENOUGH TO WIND ME.
YOUR FRIENDS WERE THE TWO CHASING ME BEFORE, AREN'T THEY?
I WASN'T TALKING ABOUT THEM.

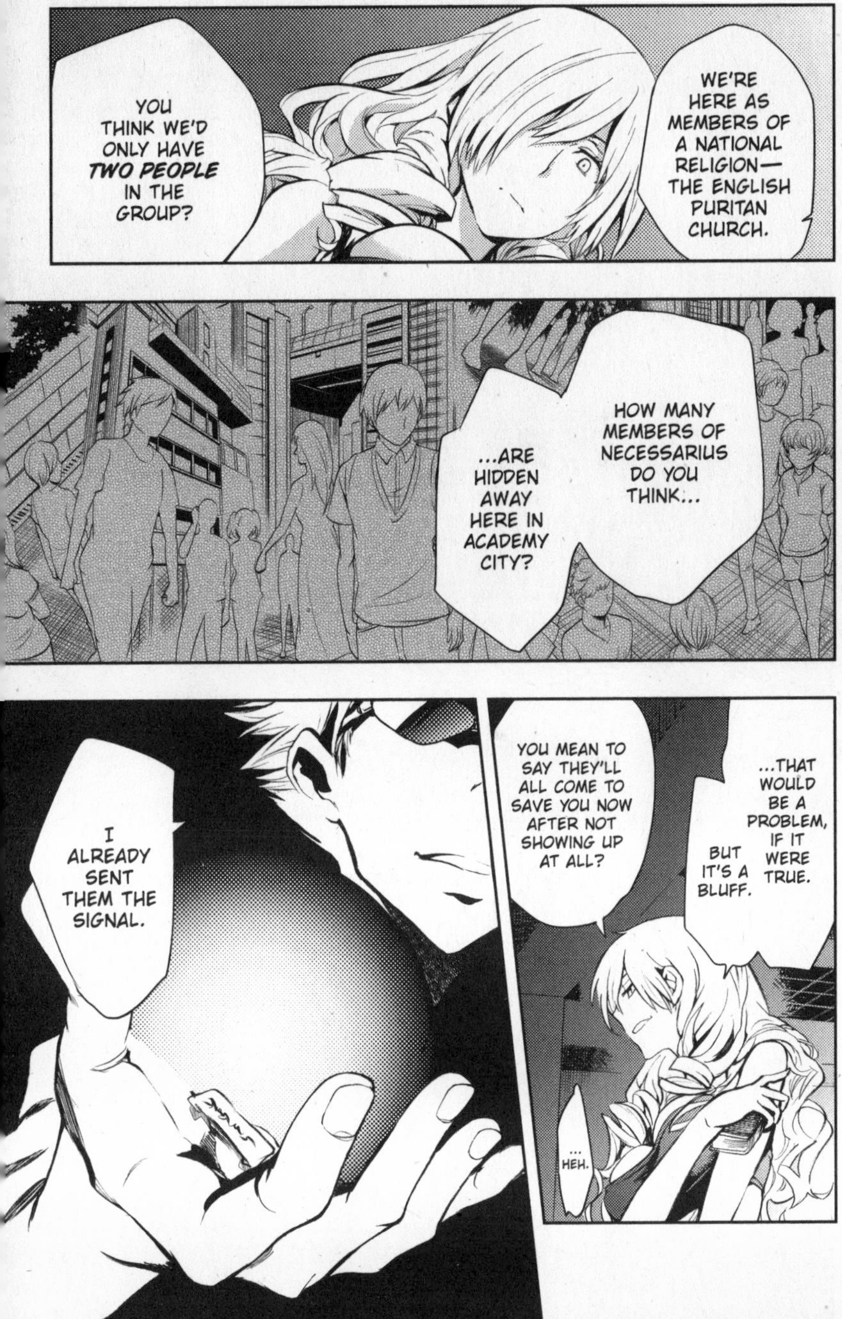
WE'RE HERE AS MEMBERS OF A NATIONAL RELIGION—THE ENGLISH PURITAN CHURCH.
YOU THINK WE'D ONLY HAVE **TWO PEOPLE** IN THE GROUP?
HOW MANY MEMBERS OF NECESSARIUS DO YOU THINK...
...ARE HIDDEN AWAY HERE IN ACADEMY CITY?
...THAT WOULD BE A PROBLEM, IF IT WERE TRUE.
BUT IT'S A BLUFF.
YOU MEAN TO SAY THEY'LL ALL COME TO SAVE YOU NOW AFTER NOT SHOWING UP AT ALL?
...HEH.
I ALREADY SENT THEM THE SIGNAL.

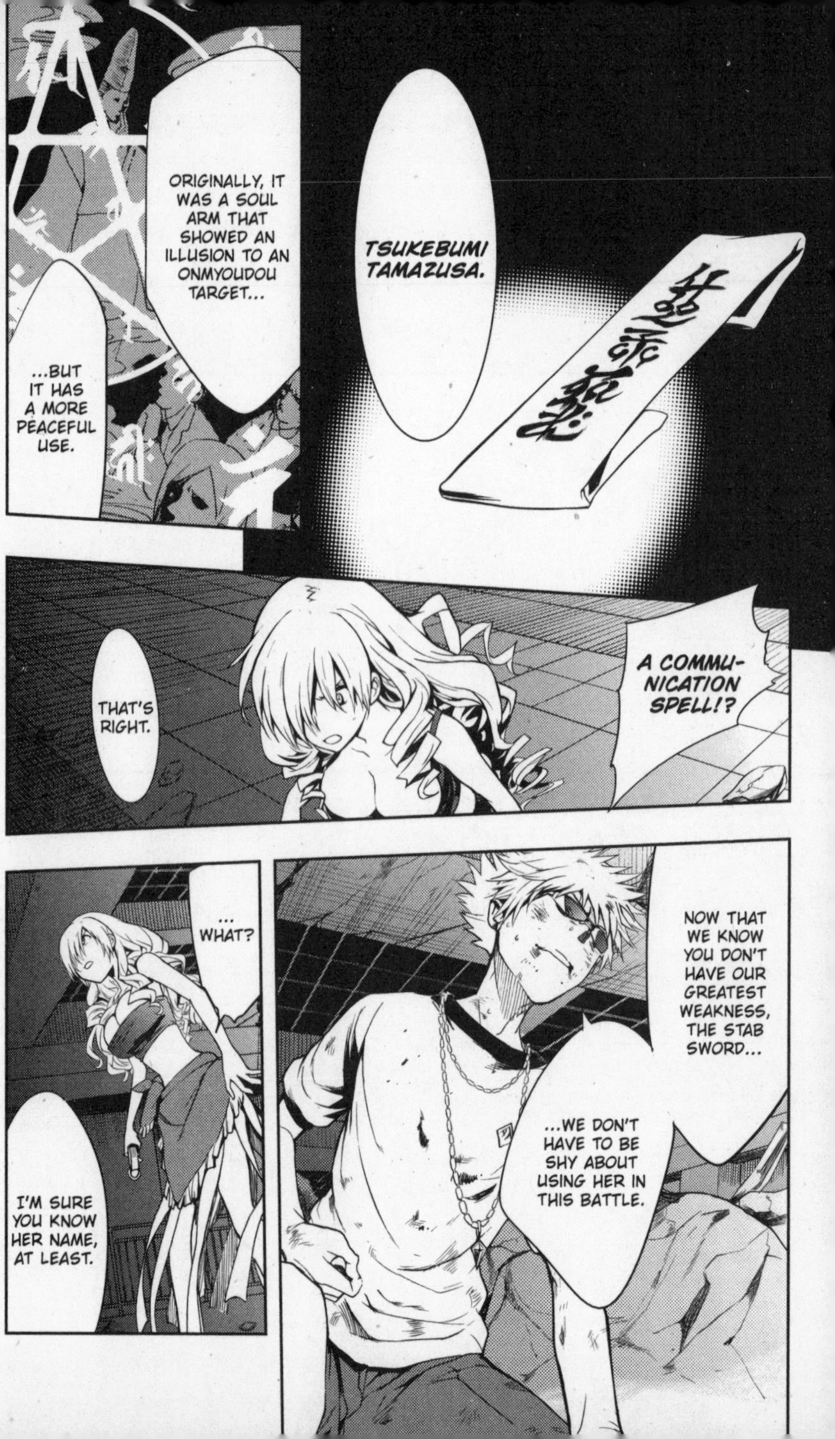
TSUKEBUMI TAMAZUSA.
ORIGINALLY, IT WAS A SOUL ARM THAT SHOWED AN ILLUSION TO AN ONMYOUDOU TARGET...
...BUT IT HAS A MORE PEACEFUL USE.
A COMMU-NICATION SPELL!?
THAT'S RIGHT.
NOW THAT WE KNOW YOU DON'T HAVE OUR GREATEST WEAKNESS, THE STAB SWORD...
...WE DON'T HAVE TO BE SHY ABOUT USING HER IN THIS BATTLE.
... WHAT?
I'M SURE YOU KNOW HER NAME, AT LEAST.

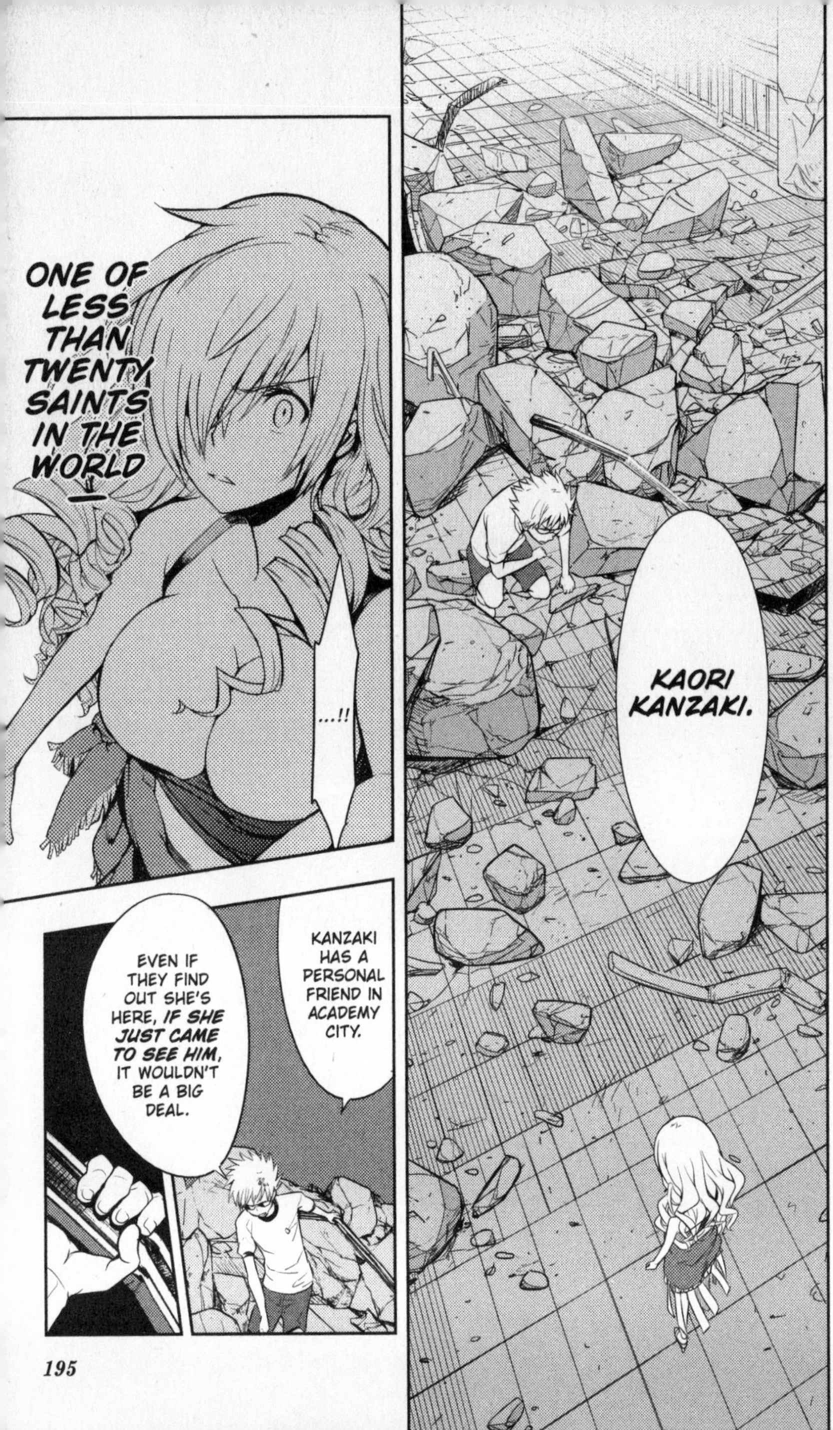
KAORI KANZAKI.
ONE OF LESS THAN TWENTY SAINTS IN THE WORLD—
...!!
KANZAKI HAS A PERSONAL FRIEND IN ACADEMY CITY.
EVEN IF THEY FIND OUT SHE'S HERE, *IF SHE JUST CAME TO SEE HIM*, IT WOULDN'T BE A BIG DEAL.

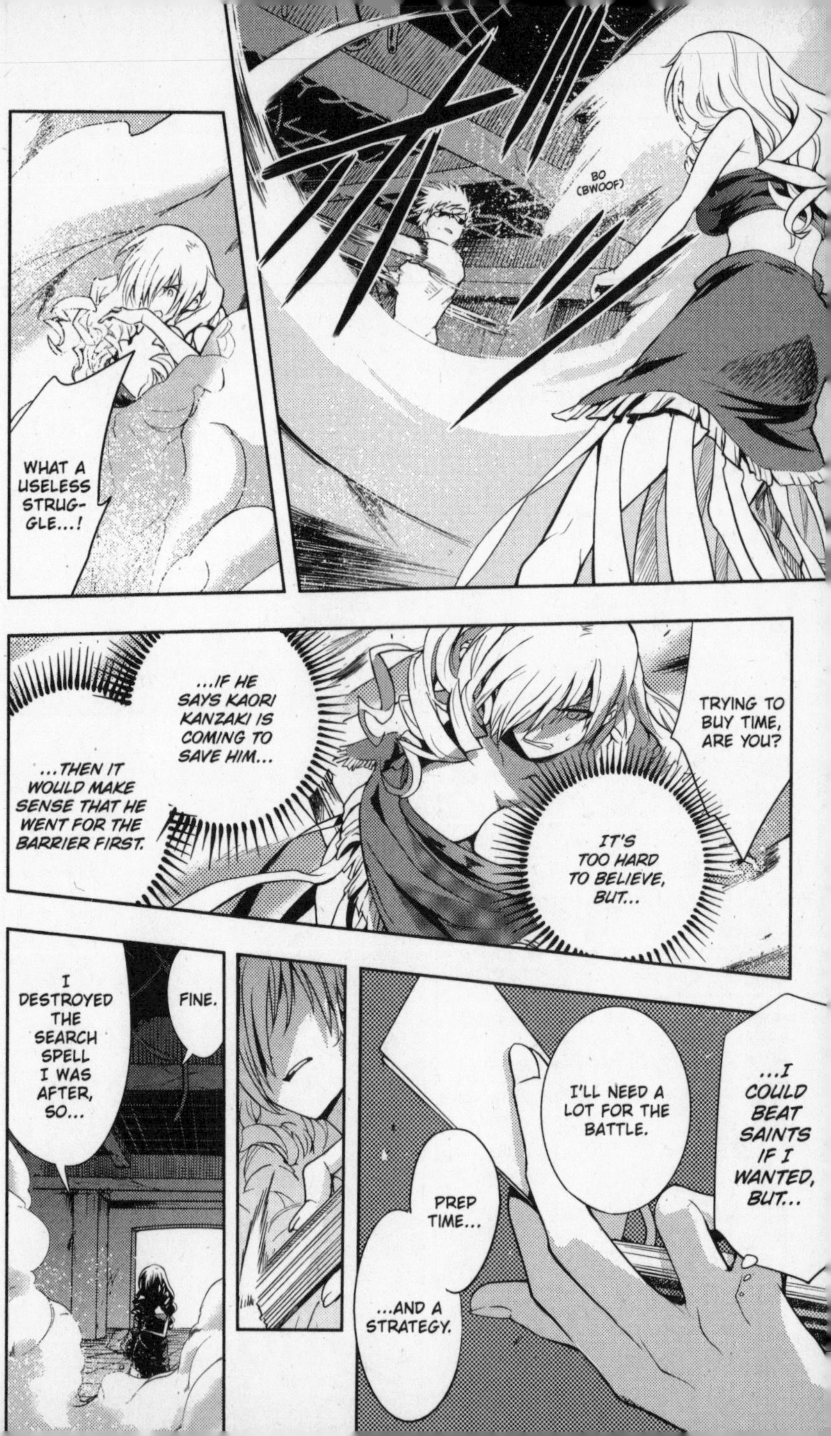
BO
(BWOOF)
WHAT A USELESS STRUGGLE...!
TRYING TO BUY TIME, ARE YOU?
IT'S TOO HARD TO BELIEVE, BUT...
...IF HE SAYS KAORI KANZAKI IS COMING TO SAVE HIM...
...THEN IT WOULD MAKE SENSE THAT HE WENT FOR THE BARRIER FIRST.
...I COULD BEAT SAINTS IF I WANTED, BUT...
I'LL NEED A LOT FOR THE BATTLE.
PREP TIME...
...AND A STRATEGY.
FINE.
I DESTROYED THE SEARCH SPELL I WAS AFTER, SO...

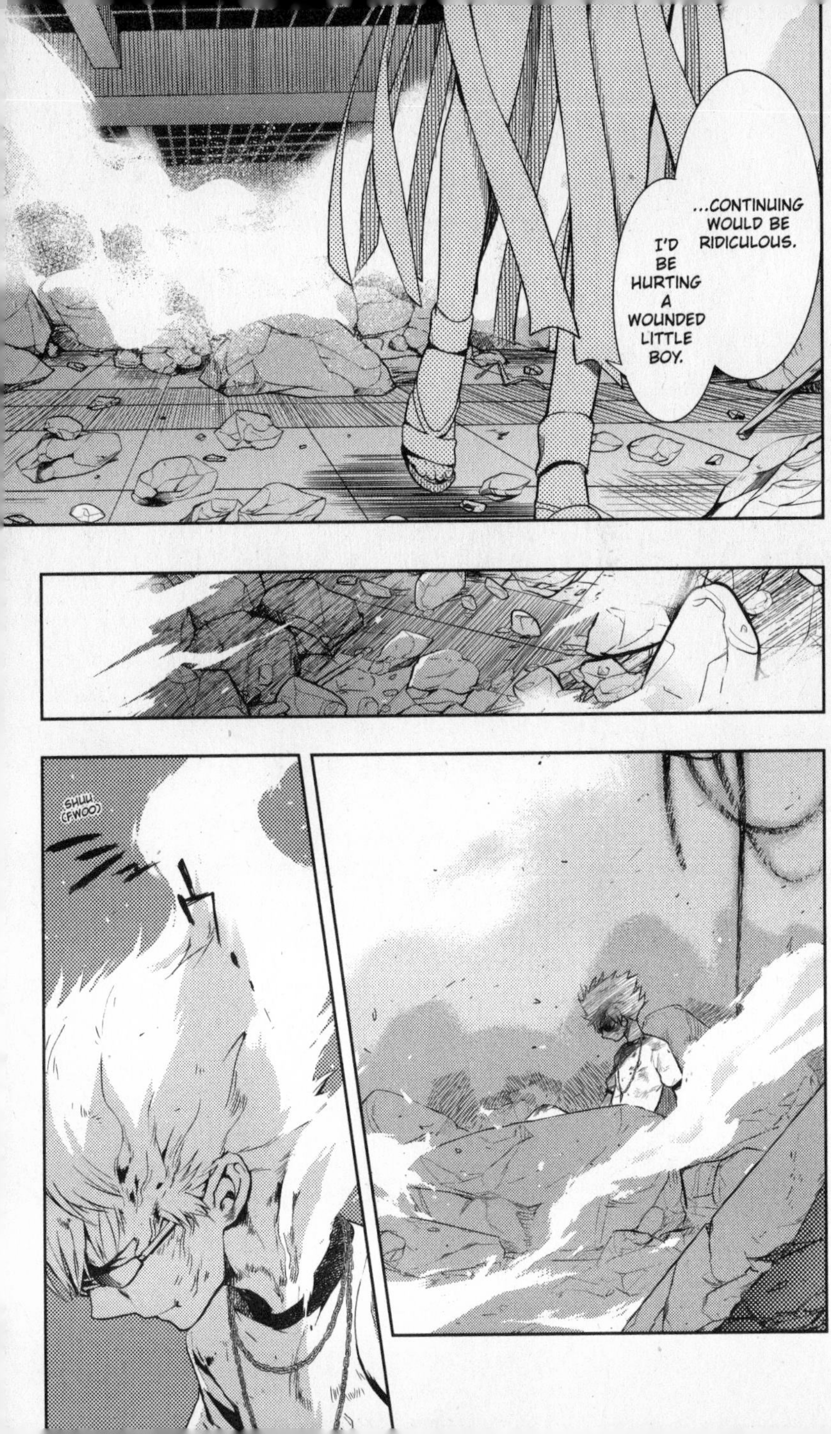
...CONTINUING WOULD BE RIDICULOUS.
I'D BE HURTING A WOUNDED LITTLE BOY.
SHUU (FWOO)

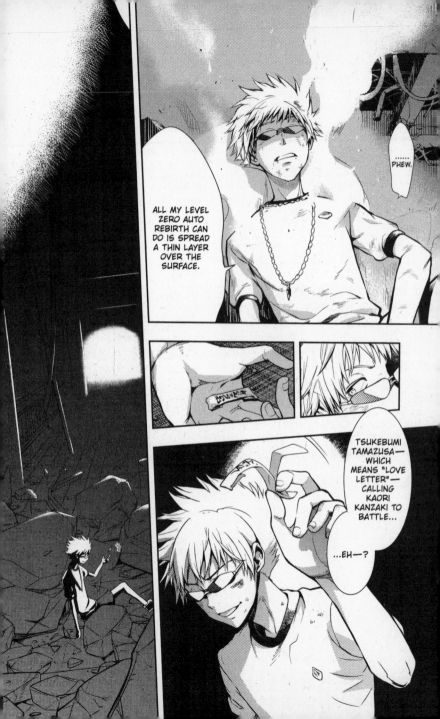

.... PHEW.

ALL MY LEVEL ZERO AUTO REBIRTH CAN DO IS SPREAD A THIN LAYER OVER THE SURFACE.

TSUKEBUMI TAMAZUSA— WHICH MEANS "LOVE LETTER"— CALLING KAORI KANZAKI TO BATTLE...

...EH—?

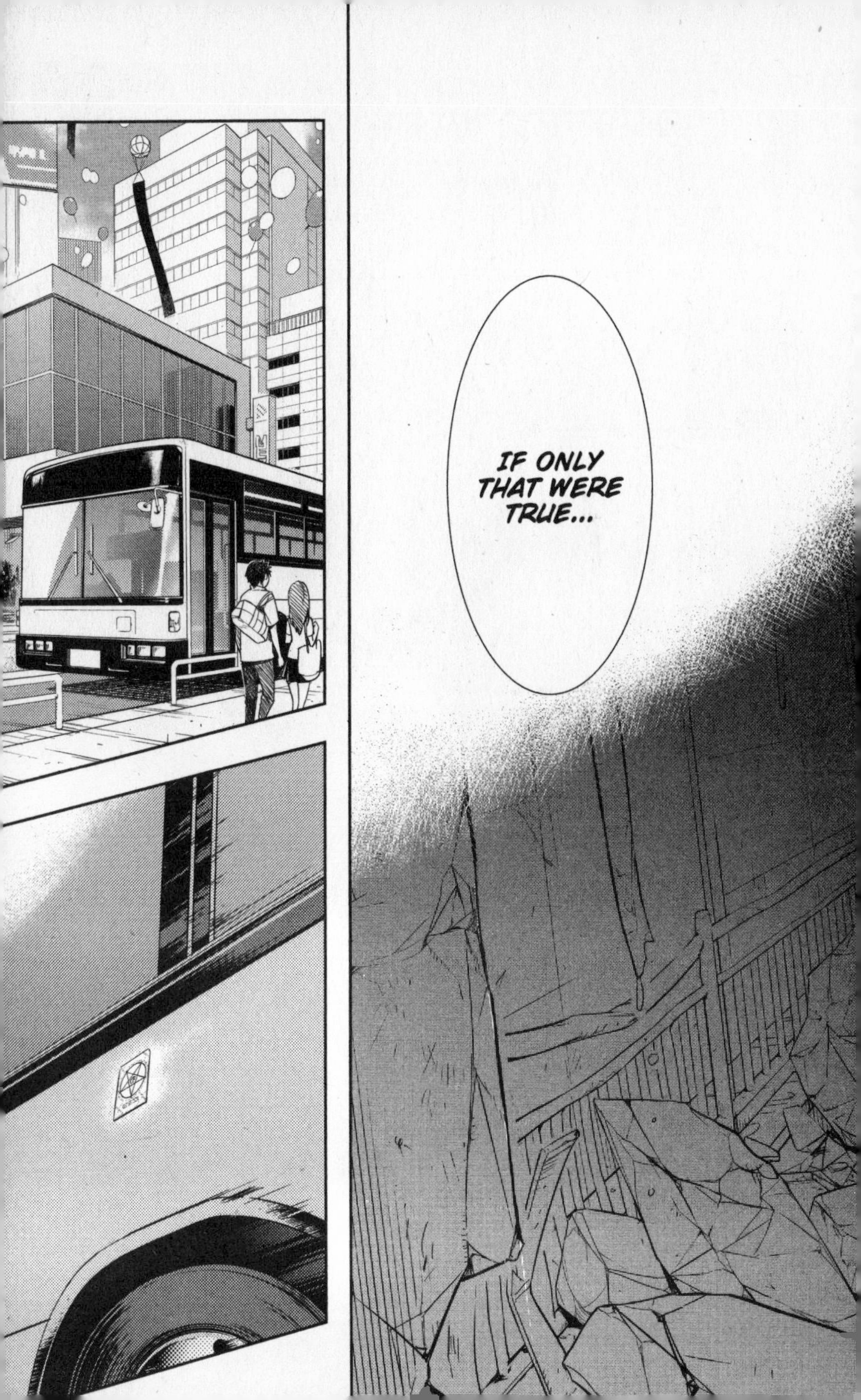
IF ONLY THAT WERE TRUE...

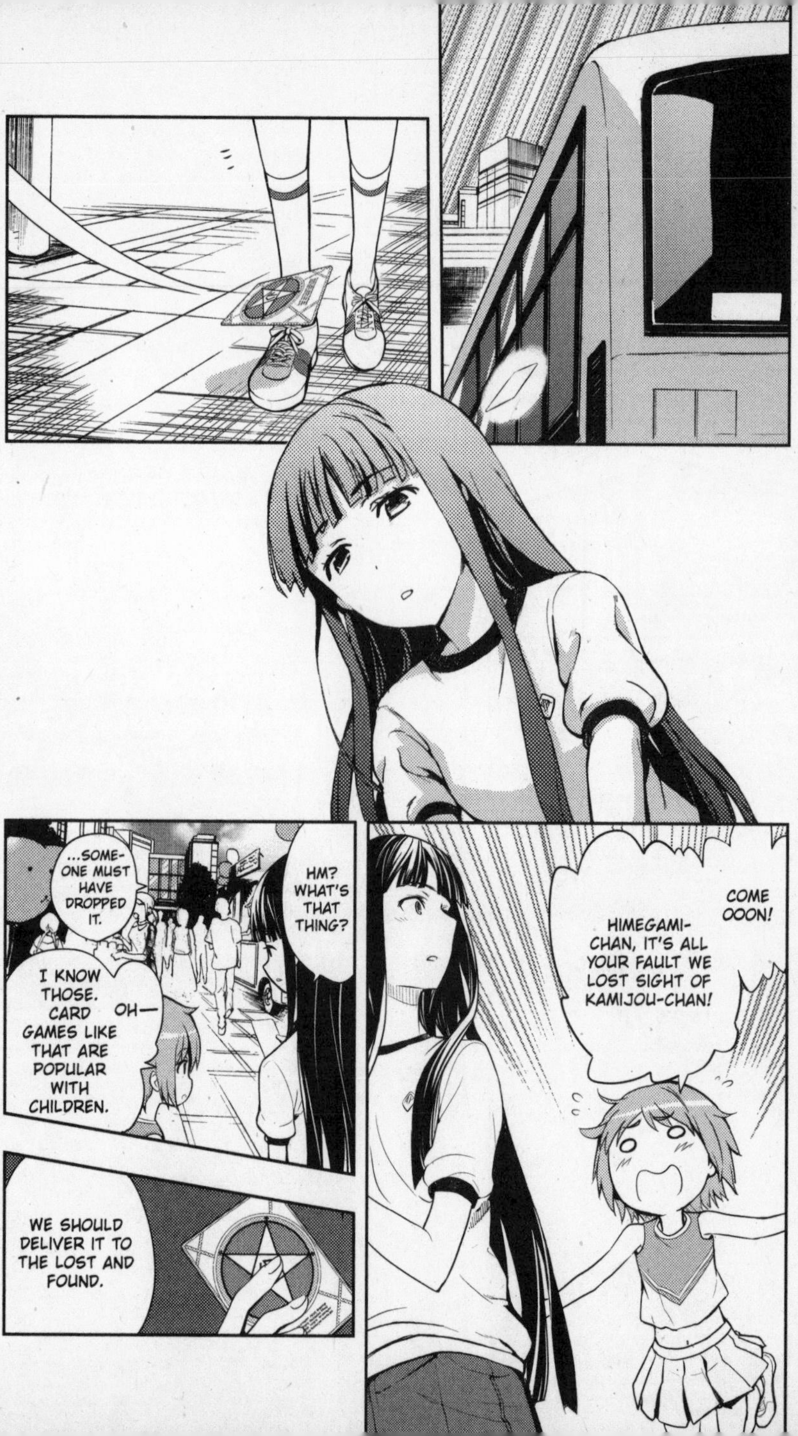
COME OOON!
HIMEGAMI-CHAN, IT'S ALL YOUR FAULT WE LOST SIGHT OF KAMIJOU-CHAN!
HM? WHAT'S THAT THING?
...SOME-ONE MUST HAVE DROPPED IT.
OH—
I KNOW THOSE. CARD GAMES LIKE THAT ARE POPULAR WITH CHILDREN.
WE SHOULD DELIVER IT TO THE LOST AND FOUND.

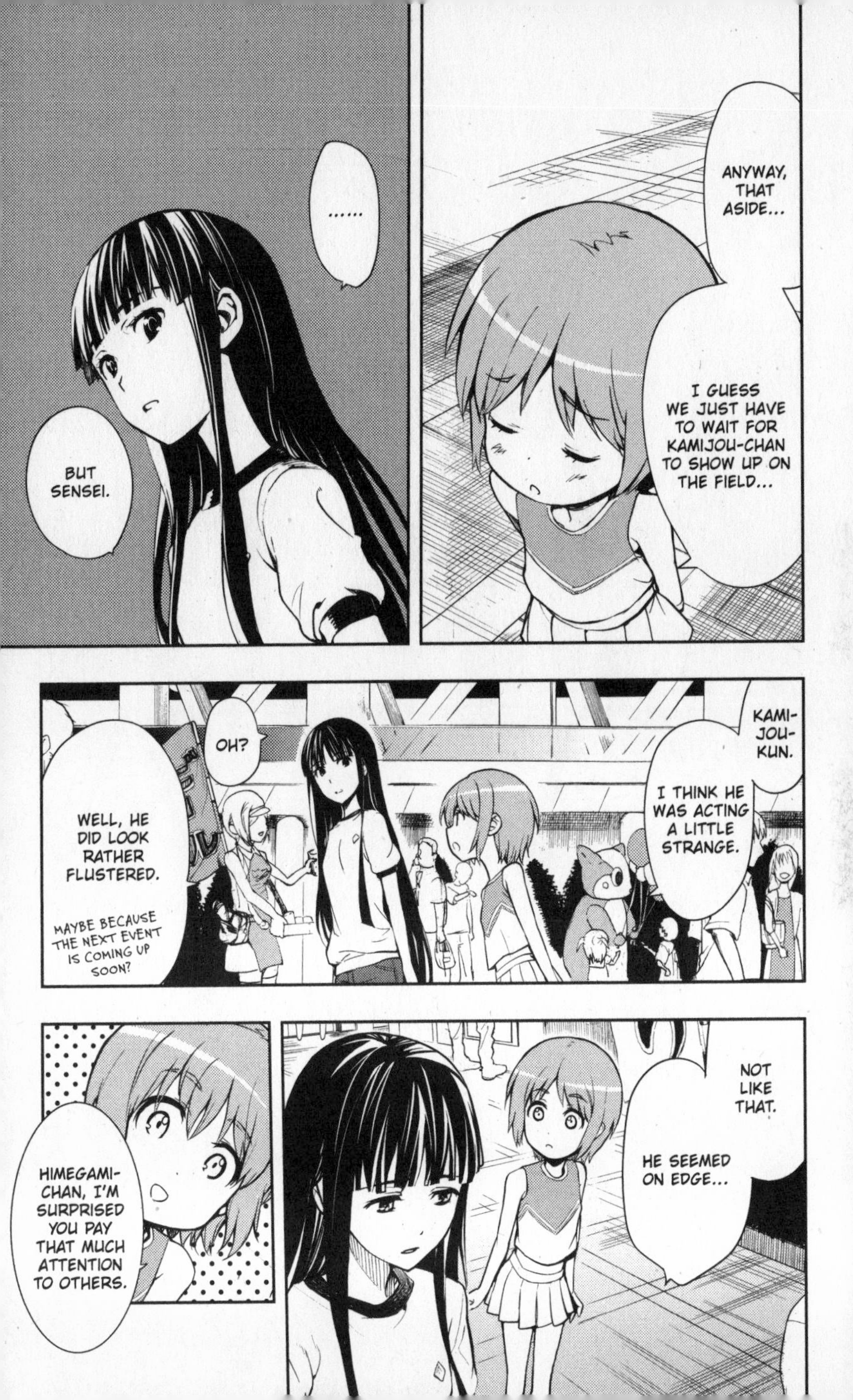
ANYWAY, THAT ASIDE...
I GUESS WE JUST HAVE TO WAIT FOR KAMIJOU-CHAN TO SHOW UP ON THE FIELD...
......
BUT SENSEI.
KAMI-JOU-KUN.
I THINK HE WAS ACTING A LITTLE STRANGE.
OH?
WELL, HE DID LOOK RATHER FLUSTERED.
MAYBE BECAUSE THE NEXT EVENT IS COMING UP SOON?
NOT LIKE THAT.
HE SEEMED ON EDGE...
HIMEGAMI-CHAN, I'M SURPRISED YOU PAY THAT MUCH ATTENTION TO OTHERS.

IS KAMIJOU-CHAN IN PARTICULAR ON YOUR MIND?

...WE'RE NOT VERY CLOSE.

KAMIJOU-KUN AND I...

...MAYBE YOU SHOULD AVOID PUTTING IT LIKE THAT.

WHAT ABOUT THAT?

I GOT IT! HIME-GAMI-CHAN!

IF YOU ...HE'LL HAVE THE ONE IN WRONG TROUBLE. IDEA...

WHY NOT INVITE KAMIJOU-CHAN THERE?

IN A WAY, THE PARADE OF LIGHTS AFTER SUNDOWN IS JUST AS IMPORTANT TO A LOT OF THE STUDENTS AS THE EVENTS.

A NIGHT PARADE...

SIGN: NIGHT PARADE

NO IT WOULDN'T —!

IF I WERE TO SUDDENLY INVITE HIM ...

...IT WOULD PUT KAMIJOU-KUN AT A LOSS.

I CAN'T.

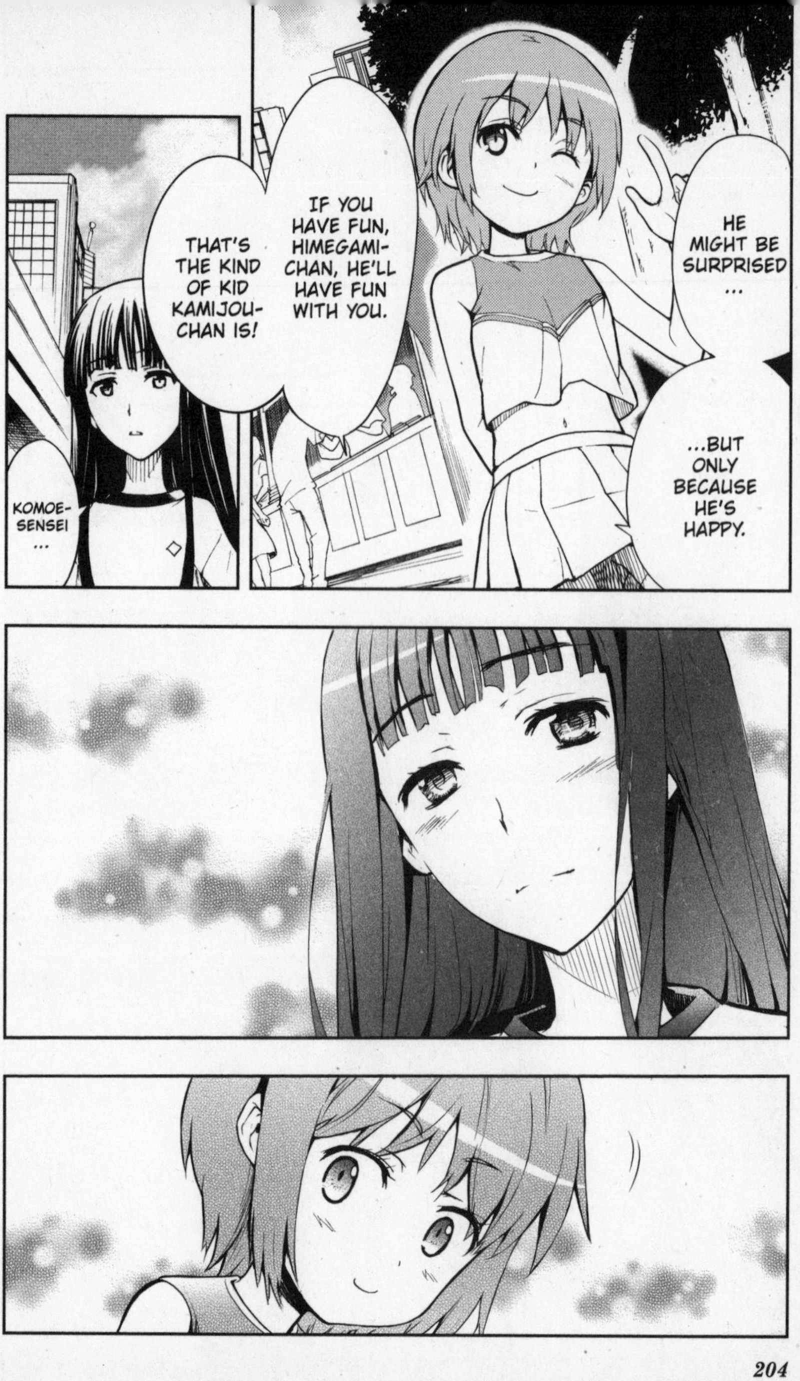
HE MIGHT BE SURPRISED ...
...BUT ONLY BECAUSE HE'S HAPPY.
IF YOU HAVE FUN, HIMEGAMI-CHAN, HE'LL HAVE FUN WITH YOU.
THAT'S THE KIND OF KID KAMIJOU-CHAN IS!
KOMOE-SENSEI ...

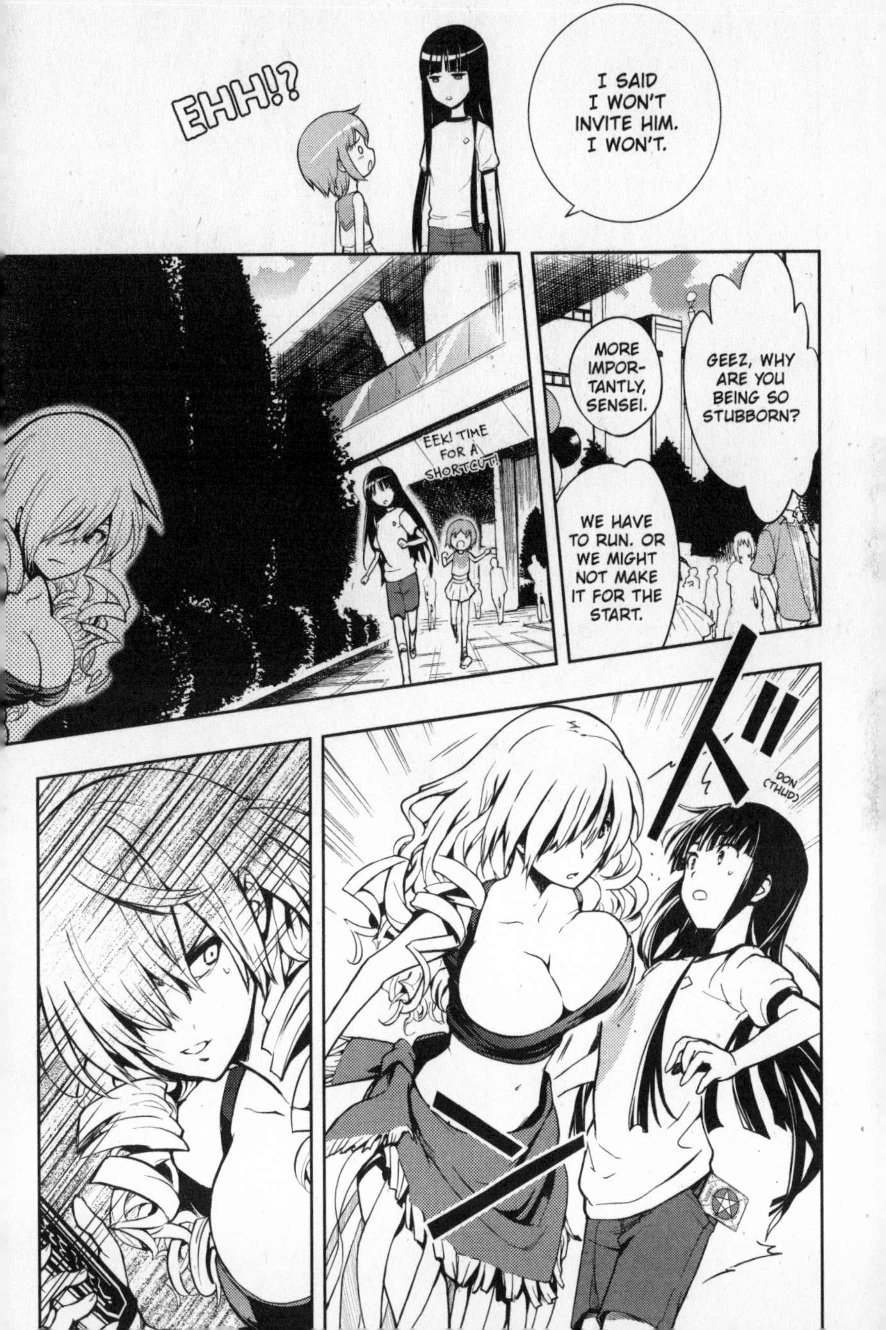
I SAID I WON'T INVITE HIM. I WON'T.
EHH!?
GEEZ, WHY ARE YOU BEING SO STUBBORN?
MORE IMPOR-TANTLY, SENSEI.
WE HAVE TO RUN. OR WE MIGHT NOT MAKE IT FOR THE START.
EEK! TIME FOR A SHORTCUT!
DON (THUD)

OH NO.

I GUESS I WENT AND DID IT AGAIN... AND—

I'M SORRY. RIGHT NOW. I'M IN A HURRY.

...LOOKS LIKE HE WASN'T BLUFFING ABOUT HAVING OTHER FRIENDS.

KA (GRIP)

HUH ...?

A RUNE CARD...

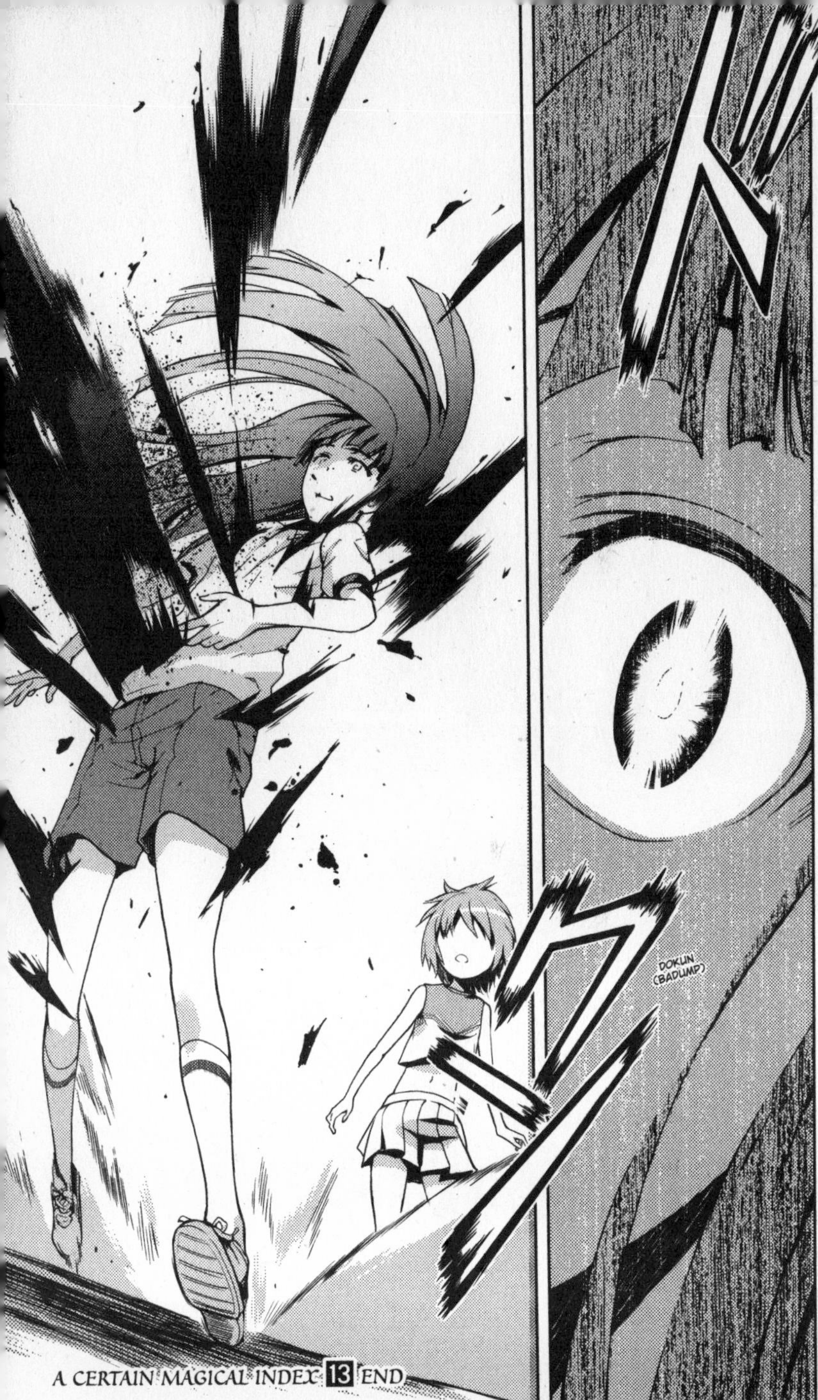
DOKUN
(BADUMP)

A CERTAIN MAGICAL INDEX 13 END

The Phantomhive family has a butler who's almost too good to be true...

...or maybe he's just too good to be human.

Black Butler

YANA TOBOSO

VOLUMES 1-25 IN STORES NOW!

A CERTAIN MAGICAL INDEX ⑬

Kazuma Kamachi
Kiyotaka Haimura
Chuya Kogino

Translation: Andrew Prowse

Lettering: Brndn Blakeslee

TOARU MAJYUTSU NO INDEX Vol. 13
© 2014 Kazuma Kamachi
© 2014 Chuya Kogino / SQUARE ENIX. CO. LTD.
Licensed by KADOKAWA CORPORATION ASCII MEDIA WORKS
First published in Japan in 2014 by SQUARE ENIX CO., LTD.
English translation rights arranged with SQUARE ENIX CO., LTD.
and Yen Press, LLC through Tuttle-Mori Agency, Inc.

English translation © 2018 by SQUARE ENIX CO., LTD.

Yen Press
1290 Avenue of the Americas
New York, NY 10104

Visit us at yenpress.com
facebook.com/yenpress
twitter.com/yenpress
yenpress.tumblr.com
instagram.com/yenpress

First Yen Press Edition: April 2018

Yen Press is an imprint of Yen Press, LLC.
The Yen Press name and logo are trademarks of Yen Press, LLC.

The publisher is not responsible for websites (or their content) that are not owned by the publisher.

Library of Congress Control Number: 2015373809

ISBN: 978-0-316-34609-2

10 9 8 7 6 5 4 3 2 1

WOR

Printed in the United States of America